EFFICIENCY IN EUROPEAN BANKING

EFFICIENCY IN EUROPEAN BANKING

Philip Molyneux, Yener Altunbas, and Edward Gardener

John Wiley & Sons
Chichester • New York • Brisbane • Toronto • Singapore

Published by John Wiley & Sons Ltd,
　　　　　Baffins Lane, Chichester,
　　　　　West Sussex PO19 1UD, England

　　　　　National 01243 779777
　　　　　International (+44) 1243 779777

e-mail (for orders and customer service enquiries):cs-books@wiley.co.uk
Visit our Home Page on http://www.wiley.co.uk
　　　　　on http://www.wiley.com

Other Wiley Editorial Offices

John Wiley & Sons, Inc., 605 Third Avenue,
New York, NY 10158-0012, USA

Jacaranda Wiley Ltd, 33 Park Road, Milton,
Queensland 4064, Australia

John Wiley & Sons (Canada) Ltd, 22 Worcester Road,
Rexdale, Ontario M9W 1L1, Canada

John Wiley & Sons (Asia) Pte Ltd, 2, Clementi Loop #02-01,
Jin Xing Distripark, Singapore 129809

Library of Congress Cataloging-in-Publication Data

Molyneux, Philip.
　Efficiency in European banking / by Philip Molyneux, Yener
Altunbas, and Edward Gardener.
　　　p.　cm.
　Includes bibliographical references and index.
　ISBN 0-471-96211-2
　　1. Banks and banking—Europe—Cost effectiveness.　I. Altunbas,
Yener.　II. Gardener, Edward P. M.　III. Title.
HG1616.C6M65　1996
332.1′094—dc20　　　　　　　　　　　　　96–3367
　　　　　　　　　　　　　　　　　　　　　CIP

British Library Cataloguing in Publication Data

A catalogue record for this book is available from the British Library

ISBN 0-471-96211-2

Typeset in 10/12pt Times by Laser Words, India
Printed and bound in Great Britain by Biddles Ltd, Guildford

Contents

Preface

Important elements that impact on the effects of the single European banking market relate to competition, efficiency and changes in market structure. Developments in the European financial services industry have been rapid and the level of competition has increased in recent years. New competitors have entered the industry as cross-border constraints have been abolished or decreased altogether and the demarcation lines between the various types of financial institutions (such as commercial banks, savings banks, finance companies and other non-bank intermediaries such as securities firms and insurance companies) have become increasingly blurred. Technological innovations have stimulated the deterioration of statutory and physical barriers between countries and sectors. The process of conglomeration (the merging of banks, securities firms and insurance companies into single institutions) has increased, posing new challenges, both for banks and regulatory authorities. To date, banking and other financial institutions in EU countries appear to operate under conditions of freer price than they did a few years ago. Product and territorial competition has also heightened. In the light of these developments it is important to investigate and evaluate the relationships between market structure and bank performance across European systems as well as to investigate cost economies and efficiency issues.

The first part of the text provides a detailed account of the structural characteristics of EU banking markets highlighting recent trends and developments and then leads on to investigate the relationship between market structure and bank performance. There are two important reasons for taking this approach. First, very little empirical work has so far been undertaken investigating the competitive behaviour of European banking systems and, therefore, undertaking such an investigation should yield insights that could be of interest to academics, bankers and policymakers. Secondly, the EU's 1988 Cecchini Study on the completion of the internal market drew attention to the fact that aspects of the structure–performance relationship could be used to evaluate the evidence of profitability in EU banking systems.

The second part of the text provides the most detailed account to date of cost economies and efficiency in European banking. We evaluate the following questions:

- Are there economies or diseconomies of scale and scope in European banking systems?
- Do the structural features of the banking markets explain the evidence on cost economies?
- Are there any cost synergies resulting from hypothetical domestic big-bank mergers?
- Are there cost synergies associated with potential cross-border bank mergers in the EU?
- Is there evidence to support the view that there will be significant cost advantages resulting from the completion of the single European market?
- Does bank efficiency differ across ownership types in European banking?
- Do managerial X-inefficiencies exceed scale and scope economies in European banking markets?

It is also hoped that the text will provide the most comprehensive analysis of the industrial structure of European banking markets to date.

We have benefited considerably from reading the works of others who have written at length on issues discussed in this text, in particular the works of: Allen N. Berger, David Humphrey, Loretta Mester, Neill Murphy, Stephen A. Rhoades, Jack Revell, Sigbjorn Berg, Leigh Drake, Timothy Hannan, James Kolari, Keith Brown and Nick Collier at Morgan Stanley, Sherrill Shaffer, Alfred Steinherr and Rudi Vander Vennet. Thanks must also go to delegates at various conferences who have provided useful comments on many aspects of this research including: the Association of European Banking and Finance Professors Annual Conference; European Economics Associations Annual Conference; European Finance Associations Annual Conference and the European Financial Management Conference. We are also grateful to all the bankers, regulators and academics who contributed material and answered many questions. Thanks go to John Williams (Research Officer in the Institute of European Finance) who helped in the compilation of many of the tables in Chapter 2. IBCA Banking Analysis (London) and EURA-CD were also very useful in providing advice and support relating to their respective bank databases, which is now provided under the name of Bankscope. Special thanks go to Emily Smith who typed and retyped the manuscript *ad nauseam* but still manages to raise a smile. Thanks also to Chris Owen, Linda Jeavons, Mairwen Owen and Jane O'Dochartaigh, who continue to run the IEF efficiently and provide the back-up support when necessary. Sheena Renner and Sarah Sadeghi also provided useful computer support for some of the technical estimation.

Finally, thanks to all our families and loved ones for their usual forbearance with projects of this kind.

Philip Molyneux
Yener Altunbas
Edward P.M. Gardener

Institute of European Finance,
School of Accounting, Banking and Economics
University of Wales
Bangor, Gwynedd
United Kingdom
LL57 2DG

1

Introduction

THE FORCES OF CHANGE IN EUROPEAN BANKING

Banking structures and strategies are now involved in a fundamental, far-reaching process of realignment and change. In many banking markets, for example, concentration has increased as banks have sought to protect and strengthen their domestic position. The strategic priority in banking has shifted away from growth and size alone towards a greater emphasis on profitability, performance and 'value creation' within the banking firm.

During recent years there has been a great deal of study and speculation on the forces of change in European banking: see Arthur Andersen (1993), Canals (1993), Gardener and Molyneux (1990), Gardener (1994) and Revell (1994a). A marked feature of banking and financial markets in the EU during the 1980s and 1990s has been the evolution towards more open, or contestable, markets; this has been a major aim of much of the deregulation of financial sectors throughout Europe. *Inter alia* this deregulatory process has intensified banking competition and helped to lessen the historical segmentation of different groupings of financial institutions and markets. Although this has been a Europe-wide phenomenon, the pace, extent and style of this deregulation have, of course, differed between countries.

Concomitant with widespread structural deregulation, there has been a marked reregulation of supervision (and investor protection and conduct of business) rules. While structural deregulation increases the competitive pressures on banks, supervisory reregulation may impose additional costs. Banking revenues and costs, therefore, may come under simultaneous pressure. From a macro perspective, of course, there is also a dilemma here: 'too much' or the 'wrong kinds' of supervisory reregulation may reduce the economic gains (like greater banking innovation and a 'better' response by banks to market demands) targeted through structural deregulation. Regulation and competitive developments, then, are among the most important forces of change in EU banking sectors.

Figure 1.1 summarises the main forces of change. The Arthur Andersen (1993) survey of senior bankers and others concerned with European banking and financial markets found that regulatory developments, competition and technology were generally felt to be the three most important forces of change likely to affect the structure of financial markets in most EU countries: Table 1.1 summarises these survey results.

The kind of scenario that emerges from recent survey evidence is that the following banking changes are expected to be especially important throughout the decade of the 1990s:

- Profitability and return on equity (ROE) will become more important and 'size for size's sake' will be de-emphasised as a banking strategy. Profitable growth will be emphasised.

- Capital standards will improve as banks become more orientated towards, and skilled in, managing their overall risks and returns.

- Technology investment in banking will increase efficiency, but is likely to mean more job losses.

- A growing proportion of bank income will come from trading activities.

- Securitisation will help to de-emphasise lending; there will be greater orientation towards credit intermediation through capital markets.

- Bank funding costs will remain high as banks fight to retain core deposits. Fee and commission income will become more emphasised.

- Savings products will drive retail banking business. The main source of loan growth will be mortgages, and pension products will be attractive areas of new business.

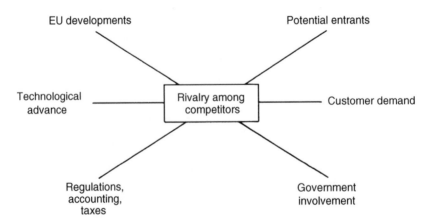

Figure 1.1 Forces of change in European banking (Source: Arthur Andersen, 1993, Figure 1.1, p. 1). ©The Economist Intelligence Unit Ltd and Arthur Andersen, 1996

Table 1.1 Forces for change in the financial markets

Survey question: What are the forces for change most likely to affect the structure of financial markets in your country? The columns below show the ranking (1 = survey respondents' most important factor; 14 is survey respondents' least important factor).

	Over-all	Aus-tria	Bel-gium	Central and Eastern Europe	Channel Islands	Den-mark	Fin-land	France	Ger-many	Greece	Ire-land	Italy	Luxem-bourg	Nether-lands	Nor-way	Por-tugal	Spain	Swe-den	UK
EC regulatory developments	1	1	1	5	1	1	2	2	1	1	2	1	1	1	6	1	2	1	1
Competition between banks and non-banks	2	4	3	6	5	10	6	4	4	7	1	7	5	2	1	6	13	12	2
Competition from foreign financial institutions	3	2	6	2	2	2	7	6	9	6	5	3	6	3	2	2	4	10	3
Domestic regulatory developments	4	3	3	1	2	6	4	1	11	2	7	4	3	9	14	10	7	3	9
Technological advance	5	4	7	10	8	9	12	11	3	5	3	6	8	5	3	5	3	9	4
Taxation changes	6	7	3	7	3	5	5	2	8	9	7	2	2	6	12	7	5	10	14
Competition from new entrants	7	4	9	3	5	10	10	5	2	3	6	11	7	10	4	3	1	6	11
Introduction of new products	8	10	9	4	13	8	11	7	7	4	7	5	9	8	8	9	8	7	5
Increase in influence of borrowers	9	8	8	12	11	13	9	9	6	8	10	9	12	7	8	4	10	5	7
Increase in influence of international investors	10	12	11	11	10	4	13	7	5	11	12	9	11	4	4	8	5	2	8
Increase in cost of funds	11	10	2	8	11	7	8	13	10	10	3	12	4	6	13	13	12	12	11
Depressed asset values	12	13	13	12	8	3	1	12	14	14	12	13	13	14	4	14	11	3	5
Credit crunch	13	13	14	9	14	10	2	10	12	12	11	7	14	13	13	11	8	8	10
Non-EC international regulatory developments	14	8	12	14	4	13	14	14	12	12	14	13	10	11	8	12	14	12	13

Source: Arthur Andersen (1993, Figure 1.2, p. 2). ©The Economist Intelligence Unit Ltd and Arthur Andersen, 1996.

This challenging and more hostile banking environment in Europe will help to stimulate consolidation and corporate restructuring within the EU banking industry. Improving productive efficiency is likely to be an increasingly important banking target and a key 'strategic driver' of banking structural change.

COST AND INCOME PRESSURES

Bankers throughout Europe have focused strongly on attempts to improve their cost/income ratios. The preceding environmental developments, asset quality problems (increased risks) and stagnating profits have all helped to focus bankers' attention on improving their cost management. Cost reduction and income (revenue) improvement are now major managerial challenges and targets. A recent and extensive study by Salomon Brothers (1993, p. 2) found that cost management was now a 'dominant strategic theme throughout the banking world'. This study also drew attention to the noticeably differentiated cost/income ratios of banks in different markets, which is partly a result of diverse approaches to cost management by banks in different countries and often within countries.

A sample of some comparative cost/income ratio data for European banks is shown in Table 1.2. Figure 1.2 summarises some individual bank cost/income ratio data across 10 countries from the Salomon (1993) study. The Salomon (1993) study found that there is an emerging consensus from many countries

Table 1.2   European bank cost/income ratios, 1988−93E (%)

	1988	1989	1990	1991	1992	1993E
Belgium	74.1	73.7	76.6	73.2	69.9	65.9
Denmark	53.2	69.8	70.6	62.5	76.6	49.5
Finland	67.0	70.5	73.1	92.3	84.8	75.4
France	69.0	68.5	72.9	70.8	69.0	67.5
Germany	67.2	66.6	68.1	67.2	64.9	61.3
Italy	69.1	65.4	63.6	65.8	65.3	65.0
Netherlands	67.5	66.6	69.2	67.7	67.1	66.3
Norway	65.9	60.7	73.0	85.2	63.7	53.7
Spain	51.9	52.7	56.9	60.0	60.1	61.8
Sweden	48.0	50.6	52.9	50.6	50.4	41.1
Switzerland	63.1	64.2	73.7	66.3	65.9	57.4
United Kingdom	65.2	64.7	65.9	65.7	60.2	58.8
Average	63.4	64.5	68.0	69.0	66.5	60.3
Core Europe	66.4	66.1	69.9	67.5	65.4	62.3
Scandinavia	58.5	62.9	67.4	72.6	68.9	54.9
Southern Europe	60.5	59.1	60.2	63.4	62.7	63.4

Note: The ratios for each country are the arithmetical average for selected banks. For 1993, forecasts have been used where data are not available.
Source: Company data, Morgan Stanley (1994a, Table 10, p. 8). E = Morgan Stanley Research Estimates. Reproduced by permission of Morgan Stanley (London).

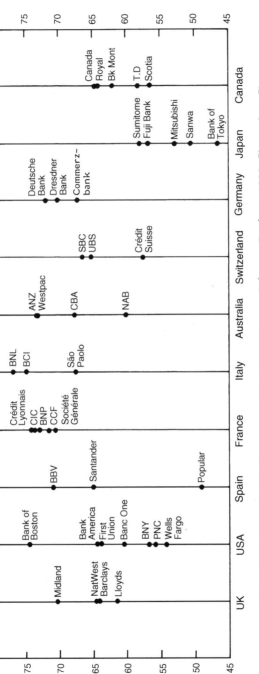

Figure 1.2 Individual bank expense ratios, 1992 (Source: Salomon Brothers, 1993, Figure 6, p. 7)

that a cost/income ratio of 50–55% is the minimum, realistic target for a full-service retail bank. Table 1.2 and Figure 1.2 show that many banks and banking systems still have a lot of potential for increased efficiency, reducing their cost/income ratios.

Two other interesting findings from the Salomon (1993) survey were:

- Few banks achieved consistent reductions in their cost/income ratios since around the mid-1980s (only in the UK, USA and Spain have total bank employees and branch numbers declined).

- Various banks have successfully pursued policies that have reduced their cost/income ratios.

Salomon (1993) found that low-cost banks followed a variety of policies, including a strong top management commitment to running a lean bank; developing a good database to measure performance; a continuous, relentless process (rather than once-and-for-all 'drives') of cost management; restructuring the retail function; and a good ability to manage successfully information technology (IT) projects. Other characteristics of low-cost banks were greater product standardisation, use of part-time staff, outsourcing non-strategic

Table 1.3 Branches and ATMs in the EU, 1987–92

(a) Branches[a] per country

	End 1987	End 1991	End 1992
Belgium	9 084	10 178	10 379
France	25 492	25 589	25 479
Germany	44 207	49 169	49 685
Italy	15 365	19 078	20 789
Netherlands	5 718	5 520	5 168
Sweden	3 498	3 064	2 910
Switzerland	4 005	4 190	4 111
UK	21 961	19 475	19 024

[a]Commercial, savings, cooperative and rural banks.

(b) ATMs per million people

	1988	1992
Belgium	85	109
France	206	305
Germany .	122	235
Italy	99	245
Netherlands	69	263
Sweden	206	254
Switzerland	262	387
UK	245	316

Source: Morgan Stanley (1994a, Tables 8 and 9, pp. 6 and 7).
Reproduced by permission of Morgan Stanley (London).

functions, use of customer input at the transactions level and branch restructuring and centralised processing. Business process re-engineering is being adopted relatively slowly in Europe compared with the USA. (The study found that US banks were often 'more productive' than their overseas peers.)

Rationalisation, restructuring and consolidation summarise much of the response activity by banks to the new banking environment in Europe. Table 1.3 shows one aspect of the current restructuring of the banking industry in the EU. Labour constraints have tended to slow down the rationalisation of the French, Italian and German banking industries compared with their EU counterparts. In the UK, Spain and the Nordic countries, on the other hand, there has been an improvement in efficiency with an attrition of staff numbers and branches. Table 1.3 (part b) also suggests a potential for the greater use of automation in countries like Belgium, Germany and Italy compared with the UK, Switzerland and France.

A sustained period of reconstruction appears now to characterise European banking. One crude (and partial) view of this process in many countries is that of a deregulation-induced cycle of enhanced competition, leading to lower margins and profits, stimulating more consolidation or specialisation in banking structures. Some of the broader strategic options open to banks appear to be growth through acquisitions or cooperation, be acquired, or become more specialised (and, perhaps, downsize); exit is, of course, another option. What is clear is that the majority of banks are unlikely to be able to survive profitably by being 'all things to all men'. Table 1.4 summarises the considerable differences that exist in overbanking (proxied crudely by asset per bank and capital per bank) throughout the EU. These data imply that the scope for rationalisation is greater in some countries (like Italy) compared with others.

Banks have followed many different strategies in responding to the new environment. *Bancassurance*, or *allfinanz*, has been an important European response, although the success of this kind of strategy has so far been 'mixed'. One interesting development in retail banking has been the emergence of the so-called 'virtual bank model' in contrast to the 'traditional bank model' (*Retail Banker International*, 1994). The latter 'model' is based on the branch, whereas the virtual bank model is characterised *inter alia* by the use of multi-channel delivery systems, is more willing to form strategic alliances with another bank or company in order to improve its competitive position, and is also more orientated towards coordinating inputs from various organisations into a final product rather than attempting to produce everything 'in house'.

THE IMPORTANCE OF PRODUCTIVE EFFICIENCY

The importance of cost and revenue efficiency in banking, then, has been heightened considerably in the current, developing European banking industry. It is important for bankers and policymakers to know whether and how banks are becoming 'more efficient'. Greater efficiency, for example, might be expected to

Table 1.4 Rationalisation of the European banking industry

Country	No. of banks in top 1000	Assets ($bn)	Asset per bank ($bn)	Capital ($bn)	Capital per bank ($m)	Capital as % of GDP
Austria	20	248	12.4	11.1	554	6.0
Belgium	10	444	44.4	12.3	1230	5.6
Denmark	11	155	14.1	7.4	671	5.2
Finland	7	110	15.7	5.4	778	5.0
France	24	2048	85.3	81.5	3395	6.2
Germany	85	2648	31.2	84.6	995	4.8
Ireland	2	53	26.5	2.6	1315	5.4
Italy	91	1464	16.1	79.9	877	6.5
Netherlands	13	653	50.2	30.5	2346	9.5
Norway	6	71	11.8	2.6	426	2.3
Spain	45	690	15.3	42.1	936	7.3
Sweden	9	283	31.4	10.6	1178	4.3
Switzerland	32	715	22.3	39.5	1234	16.4
United Kingdom	33	1217	36.9	56.0	1698	5.4

Source: Morgan Stanley (1994a, Table 15, p. 11). Reproduced by permission of Morgan Stanley (London).

lead to improved financial products and services, a higher volume of funds inter-mediated, greater and more appropriate innovations, a generally more responsive financial system, and improved risk-taking capabilities if efficiency profit gains are channelled into improved capital adequacy positions.

Banking efficiency questions have become more pressing as deregulation-induced changes, technology and wider market developments release new compet-itive pressures and accelerate the capacity and need for change. There is increasing pressure to use all of a bank's resources to maximum advantage. Under these kinds of circumstances, the penalties for incorrect decisions, faulty perceptions and flawed evaluations about banking efficiency are often more immediate and may be severe. The recent, dramatic developments in the central and eastern European financial sectors remind us again of the pressing need to understand the process and dynamics of improving bank efficiency. Although an extensive literature (mainly US) has been generated, Berger, Hunter and Timme (1993) in a recent, comprehensive review caution that 'the study of the efficiency of financial institutions has not kept pace with these changes'.

Although there has been a paucity of European empirical research on structure–performance relationships as well as bank efficiency, notions about competitive market structures and bank efficiency have continued to shape the thinking and actions of European policymakers, like the EC Commission, central bankers and banking supervisors. The Cecchini (Commission of the European Communities, 1988a, b) study, for example, suggested that the microeconomic consequences of opening up trade in financial services are to lower unit costs by facilitating more use of economies of scale, and (probably) lower the mark-up of prices over marginal costs to the extent that oligopoly is weakened. The impact of the completion of the internal market on overall banking productive efficiency was seen as positive through the erosion of economic rent (excess profit resulting from market protection), the reduction in X-inefficiencies and the benefit of economies (scale and scope) from restructuring. (The term X-inefficiency describes the differences between actual and minimum cost, reflecting differences in managerial ability to control costs (or maximise revenues). See Chapter 9 for more details.)

More recent studies, for example, Grilli (1989a, b), Neven (1990), Vives (1991), Molyneux (1993) and Gardener and Teppett (1995), have also suggested that unambiguous welfare gains may not necessarily result from the completion of the single European financial services market.

MARKET STRUCTURE, COST ECONOMIES AND EFFICIENCY IN EUROPEAN BANKING—WHY ARE THEY IMPORTANT?

Important elements that impact on the effects of the single financial market-place clearly relate to competition, cost efficiency and changes in market structure. Developments in the European financial services industry have been rapid and the level of competition has increased in recent years. New competitors have entered the industry as cross-border constraints have been abolished or decreased altogether and the demarcation lines between the various types of financial institutions (such as commercial banks, savings banks, finance companies and other non-bank intermediaries such as securities firms and insurance companies) have become increasingly blurred. Technological innovations have stimulated the deterioration of statutory and physical barriers between countries and sectors. The process of conglomeration (the merging of banks, securities firms and insurance companies into single institutions) has increased, posing new challenges, both for banks and regulatory authorities. To date, banking and other financial institutions in EU countries operate under conditions of freer price than they did a few years ago. Product and territorial competition has also heightened as EU countries' domestic markets have been opened up. In the light of the aforementioned developments it is important to investigate competitive conditions through structure–performance relationships and also to evaluate cost economies and efficiencies in European bank markets.

There are two important rationales for investigating the structure–performance relationship in European banking markets. First, very little empirical work has been undertaken investigating the competitive behaviour of European banking systems and such an empirical investigation may yield insights that could be of interest to academics, bankers and policymakers.

Secondly, the Price Waterhouse/Cecchini (1988) study on completion of an EC internal financial market drew attention to the fact that aspects of the structure–conduct–performance (SCP) framework could be used to evaluate the evidence of oligopoly profits in EC banking systems. If oligopoly profits are present in these banking systems then producer surplus losses may be substantial after integration. Or to put it another way, banking industry profitability (in the short term) would be eroded in these countries as a result of the increased competition resulting from the single market proposals. An analysis of the SCP relationship in European banking may help us to shed light on these issues.

The reasons for testing the SCP relationship in banking markets, as identified by Heggestad (1979, p. 450), are to address three main issues:

1. Does market structure matter in banking markets, or is the industry so highly regulated that market structure is not an important/relevant factor in determining market performance?

2. Which aspects of market structure are the most important, and, therefore, which type of regulations or regulatory reform have the greatest impact?

3. What aspects of bank performance are most sensitive to differences in market structure?

In general, analyses of the SCP relationship in banking can be used to help evaluate the main policy issue of which type of banking structure best serves the public in terms both of the cost and availability of banking services. This text aims to address the above issues by undertaking a thorough SCP analysis across European banking markets. Closely related to the aforementioned issues are the concepts of scale and scope economies as well as firm-level efficiency. Benston (1972) has indicated that to examine the impact of deregulation on the financial industry, it is necessary to know the cost structure of the industry. Optimal firm size and product mix can be determined once the structure is known. In addition, for policy purposes, it is important to know how different types of banks will be affected by the increased competitive pressures associated with banks' expanded powers and foreign entry. Interest in the subject of scale and scope economies has been stimulated by the recent outbreak of mergers and proposals for mergers between banks in Europe. The case made for these mergers often rests heavily upon the presence (or assumed presence) of scale and scope economies. One reviewer of the British Monopolies and Mergers Commission reported that the proposed Barclays–Lloyds–Martins Bank merger went so far that 'if economies of scale were the driving force then there would be a case for considering duopoly or even monopoly as a proper system of organisation' (Artis, 1968, p. 135). In addition, it is also necessary for industry to estimate its own costs as the detection of marginal and average cost for each service could help management decision-making.

Given the above factors and seeing that financial services market integration may lead to an increasingly competitive market outcome, with more cost efficient and larger banks, it is of interest to investigate cost economies and efficiency in European banking.

The main objectives of this book are to evaluate the following questions:

1. Are there any economies or diseconomies of scale and scope in various European banking systems?
2. Do the structural features of the banking markets under study explain the evidence of cost economies?
3. Are there any cost synergies resulting from hypothetical big-bank mergers within countries?
4. Are there any cost synergies resulting from hypothetical big-bank mergers cross-border within the EU?
5. Is there empirical evidence to support the view that there will be significant cost benefits resulting from the completion of the single European banking market?
6. Does bank efficiency differ across ownership types in European banking?
7. Do managerial X-inefficiencies exceed scale and scope economies in European banking markets?

It is also hoped that the text will provide the most comprehensive analysis of the industrial structure of European banking markets to date.

2

A single market for financial services in the EU

INTRODUCTION

This chapter examines the moves towards a single financial services market in the EU. The first part of the chapter briefly outlines the background to the single market in financial services and notes the main barriers to the cross-border provision of financial services which the EU legislation aims to abolish. This is followed by an outline of the EU single market programme for banking services, securities business and insurance, respectively. The main aim of this legislation is to establish a single market for financial services by providing banks and other financial firms with a 'single passport' to operate throughout the Union subject only, as a rule, to the supervision by the regulatory authority of their home member state. The chapter then considers European Monetary Union (EMU) and its implications for the single financial services market. The economic aspects of a single market in financial services are investigated with a particular focus on the Price Waterhouse (1988) study on EU financial sector integration after 1992. Given the differences in member country reserve requirements, tax treatments, cross-border payments systems and the flexibility to consolidate EU law into national legislation, the final sections of this chapter indicate the obstacles to achieving a perfect single market in financial services.

BACKGROUND TO THE SINGLE MARKET FOR FINANCIAL SERVICES

The original Treaty of Rome establishing the EU was signed in 1957. According to Article 2 of the Treaty:

> The Community shall have as its task, by establishing a common market and progressively approximating the economic policies of Member States, to promote throughout

the Community a harmonious development of economic activities, a continuous and balanced expansion, an increase in stability, an accelerated raising of the standard of living and closer relations between the States belonging to it.

Although the Treaty of Rome did not explicitly define the Common Market, its articles called for free internal trade, a common external tariff and free movement of services, people and goods within the European Economic Community. The signing of the Single European Act (SEA) in 1986 reaffirmed a solemn commitment to these original objectives of the Common Market by stating that an 'internal market' was to be created by 1 January 1993, which would be 'an area without frontiers in which the free circulation of goods, services and capital is ensured in accordance with the provisions of this Treaty' (Servais, 1988 from Article 8a of the Treaty). The amendments to the Treaty of Rome enacted in the SEA were aimed principally at improving decision-making procedures within the Community and confirming in the Community's basic charter the underlying ideas of the White Paper (Servais, 1988). The preamble to the SEA spoke of a general commitment to a complete 'European Union' (note that hereafter we will refer to the European Community as the European Union for ease of exposition and in line with the recent, late 1993, name change). However, the amendments to the Treaty of Rome brought in by the SEA permitted, rather than required, the member states to go further and establish a fuller economic and monetary union (see Holmes, 1992).

Over the last 30 years the EU has adopted banking legislation aimed at harmonising regulations and fostering competition. In this regard, Baltensperger and Dermine (1990) identify three distinct regulatory time periods: (i) deregulation of entry to domestic markets from 1957 to 1973; (ii) attempts towards harmonisation of banking regulations, 1973–83; and (iii) the recent European integration and 'internal market' proposal of freedom of cross-border services, single banking licence, home country control and mutual recognition.

Under the 1957 Treaty of Rome, the internal market was viewed as one which allowed 'free movement of goods, people and services', and the aim was to transform segmented national markets into a common single market. In July 1965, the Commission proposed a Directive on Abolition of Restrictions on Freedom of Establishment and Freedom to Provide Services in Respect of Self-employed Activities of Banks and other Financial Institutions. This Directive was adopted by the EU Council of Ministers in 1973 and aimed to ensure the equal treatment of national and other firms of member states with regard to entry into domestic markets and the conditions under which banks are allowed to operate. Subsidiaries of non-member state banks were to be regarded as EU undertakings in every way. As Clarotti (1984) and Molyneux, Lloyd-Williams and Thornton (1994a) noted, from 1973 onwards very little discrimination remained as to entry into member states although cross-border competition was still severely thwarted by capital restrictions. Moreover, there was no coordination of banking supervision,

so banks operating in different member states were subject to different prudential requirements. This resulted in the second period of attempts to harmonise
regulations.

Progress in harmonisations came in 1977 with the adoption of the First
Directive on the Coordination Laws, Regulations and Administrative Provisions
Relating to the Taking up and Pursuit of the Business of Credit Institutions.
This Directive established a definition of credit institutions and the principle
of home country control, whereby supervision of credit institutions operating
in several member states would now be the responsibility of the home country
of the parent bank. A Directive on the Supervision of Credit Institutions on a
Consolidated Basis was adopted in 1983, along with two other directives on
a Uniform Format for Bank Accounts and on Consumer Protection in 1986.
Baltensperger and Dermine (1990) indicate that, despite this legislation, European
financial markets were still far from full integration. A bank wishing to operate
in another member state still had to be authorised by the supervisors of the other
member state. It remained subject to supervision by the host country and its
range of activities may be constrained by host country laws. Moreover, most
countries' bank branches had to be provided with earmarked endowment capital
as if they were new banks. Finally, the supply of cross-border services was
severely impaired by the restrictions on capital flows.

The difficulty encountered by full harmonisation of national regulations
induced a new approach towards European integration. In 1983 a draft policy
paper on financial integration uttered clearly a renewed commitment to the Treaty
of Rome and in 1985 the EU Commission proposed, through a White Paper,
to establish guidelines for a single banking licence, home country control and
mutual recognition. These principles were incorporated in 1988 proposals for a
Second Banking Coordination Directive (89/646/EEC), which was adopted by
the EU Council of Ministers in 1989. It set out to eliminate the remaining intra-
EU barriers to freedom of establishment in the financial sector and provided for
full freedom of financial services across intra-EU borders. The main objective
of this legislation was to harmonise laws and rules for credit institutions so that
they could establish and operate freely across the Union, subject to adequate
supervision. In order to achieve this end the Directive provided for minimum
capital requirements, the monitoring and vetting of bodies that had substantial
bank shareholdings, controls over banks' long-term participation in non-financial
companies, and the establishment of a single banking licence to permit banking
activity anywhere within the Union.

The principle of the single banking licence was of especial importance. Once
a credit institution is authorised by its home supervisor it will have a licence to
undertake business throughout the Union as long as there is prior harmonisation of
essential supervisory rules (mutual recognition). A necessary reinforcing feature
of the Second Banking Directive is the associated supervisory arrangements. The
Own Funds Directive (1988) was formally passed by the EU Council of Ministers

in 1989, along with the Solvency Ratio Directive. Other directives harmonising regulations on accounting for foreign branches, reorganisation and winding-up procedures, and deposit insurance have also been adopted by the Commission. All the above legislation had been passed at EU level in time for the introduction of the single financial market from 1 January 1993. (One should note that there was a fundamental difference between the legislative approach set by the Treaty of Rome and that initiated by the 1985 White Paper. The former placed an emphasis on harmonisation of rules, etc. to achieve a single market. The reason why the SEA was passed was to change the way the single market was to be achieved. The emphasis was changed to mutual recognition in the formulation and implementation of directives.)

The completion of the European-wide frontier-free market on 1 January 1993 and the improvements in its operation envisaged by the strategic programme will according to the European Commission allow banks to benefit from economies of scale and scope, reduce their administrative and financial costs, have easier and more competitive access to private-sector and public-sector procurement, and cooperate more efficiently with one another (see Commission of the European Communities, 1993, p. 57).

BARRIERS TO INTEGRATION IN FINANCIAL MARKETS

The single financial market implies both freedom to trade and freedom of location for firms in EU member countries. There should appear to be no government regulations obstructing neutrality between buying financial products and services from domestic institutions, foreign institutions located in the consumer's country, or on a cross-border basis. However, in reality there have always been economic and market barriers that exist which may have a significant impact on the integration of EU financial markets. Llewellyn (1992) has identified five main elements to a single market in financial services:

1. the freedom to locate anywhere in the market area whether by branches or incorporated subsidiaries;
2. freedom to supply services anywhere in the market without the necessity of specific authorisation;
3. freedom of consumers to buy financial services from anywhere in the market and from any nationality of suppliers;
4. the absence of exchange controls limiting the free movement of capital;
5. a single securities market in that investors could issue and trade securities across national frontiers freely and without imposed hindrances.

Price Waterhouse (1988) have comprehensively investigated the barriers to cross-border provision of financial services in the EU prior to the implementation of the EU 1992 legislation. These findings are shown in Table 2.1 for banking, insurance and securities business respectively.

Table 2.1 Barriers to integration in financial markets

Barriers to establishment in banking

1. Restrictions on the legal form banks may adopt
2. Limitations on the number of branches that may be established
3. Restrictions on the takeover of domestic banks
4. Restrictions of equity or other control of domestic banks

Barriers to operating conditions in banking

1. The need to maintain separate capital funds
2. Differences in the definition of 'own capital' funds
3. The need to maintain certain capital−asset ratios
4. Exchange controls

Barriers to competing for business in banking

1. Limitations on services offered
2. Restrictions on local retail banking
3. Restrictions on acquisition of securities and other assets

Barriers to establishment in insurance

1. Lack of harmonisation of licensing procedures
2. Lack of harmonisation in the constitution of technical reserves

Barriers to operating conditions and competing for business in insurance

1. Direct insurance: restrictions on the placement of contracts with non-established insurers
2. Co-insurance: establishment of a permanent presence imposed on lead-insurers
3. Custom and practice in government procurement policies
4. Lack of harmonisation in the supervision of insurance concerns
5. Reinsurance: compulsory or voluntary cessation of a percentage of contracts to a central pool or prescribed establishment
6. Lack of harmonisation in the fiscal treatment of insurance contracts and premiums

Barriers to establishment in securities

1. Membership of some stock exchanges limited to national citizens
2. Constraints on the establishment of offices to solicit and carry out business in secondary markets
3. Restrictions on the takeover of or equity participation in domestic institutions
4. Limitations on the establishment of securities firms in a universal banking system

Barriers operating conditions in securities

1. Exchange controls and other equivalent measures which prevent or limit the purchase of foreign securities
2. Conflicting national prudential requirements for investors' protection
3. Discriminatory taxes on the purchase of foreign securities

Barriers to competing for business in securities

1. Limited access to primary markets in terms of lead management of domestic issues
2. Restricted access to secondary markets because of national stockbroker monopolies on some stock exchanges
3. Restrictions on dealing with investing public

Source: Price Waterhouse (1988, p. 62).

Barriers to the Cross-Border Provision of Banking Services

In reviewing the legal and regulatory barriers to a non-domestic bank establishing in an EU member state, the general picture was that there was little by way of overt discrimination against non-domestic entities in the Union. However, the First Banking Coordination Directive provided a right of entry and establishment within the EU to credit institutions which had their head office in a member state. Non-national entities basically had to go through the same sort of procedure as domestic entities in order to establish a banking operation. Moreover, obtaining authorisation for other than a representative office could be time-consuming and costly in administrative terms. The Price Waterhouse (1988) report found that:

- All banking establishments had to conform to the prescribed legal forms of the country in which business was set up. These could vary from state to state.

- With the temporary exception of Spain, the entry and establishment rules for foreign banks were essentially the same as for domestic institutions.

- There were few problems in establishing representative offices; prior authorisation was only required in some countries.

- There were licensing or prior authorisation requirements for all EU banking countries wishing to establish branches within other member states.

- With the exception of the UK, all branches had to maintain their own minimum endowment capital, the definition of which would vary from state to state. This seemed to provide possibly one of the major obstacles to trade.

- Some countries required 'comfort' letters. Such letters were essentially guarantees of support from the appropriate supervisory authority or parent institution and were not generally seen to be an onerous obligation. Yet, in Italy, a branch's operational activities were shortened if such a letter was not provided.

- There were no specific restrictions on the employment of foreign or EU nationals or special discriminatory rules in terms of professional qualifications or degrees of competence and management experience.

- Once certain conditions were met in relation to minimum capital requirements and the competence of personnel, there would appear to be no other obstacles to establishing subsidiaries other than in Spain and Italy.

- In Italy, France and Spain there were restrictions on foreign acquisitions or participation in indigenous banks; and in all EU states some prior authorisation was required from the appropriate supervisory authority.

- With the exception of Spain and Italy, it would seem there was little in the way of significant, openly discriminatory rules on the extent and range of services that could be provided. It appeared to be the custom, however, that domestic banks lead-manage domestic bond issues in most of these countries.

Overall, it appeared that the barriers to trade in banking services lay not so much in overt, discriminatory rules and regulations, but rather in national practices that applied equally to both domestic and foreign-controlled banks. Differences in licensing, minimum capital requirements and other territorial restrictions could just make some member states less attractive than others for foreign bankers.

Barriers to the Cross-Border Provision of Securities Services

The Price Waterhouse (1988) study also identified the barriers to establishment and operation by foreign entities in securities markets within the EU. Since banks tend to dominate these markets (especially in the universal banking countries), many of the obstacles of establishment were included in the former section on banking. However, some of the main conclusions were as follows:

- The vital obstacle to establishing a presence in a foreign securities market appeared to be regulations banning foreigners from being licensed as brokers.
- Difficulties were encountered by non-banking firms that wished to establish themselves in a universal banking environment — as exists, for instance, in Germany or Belgium — where a full banking licence would not be granted to an institution that did not offer a full range of banking services. Countries were, however, adapting and beginning to offer more limited licences for trading in securities only.
- There were restrictions on the establishment of offices either to solicit secondary market business from individual or institutional investors, or to disseminate information about possible investments. Moreover, barriers were placed in the way of dealing directly with the public executing such orders.
- Regarding primary operations, discriminatory restrictions on the lead management of domestic issues existed in some states.
- In addition to exchange controls, there were other measures which, while not directly prohibiting operations in foreign securities, were designed to prevent or limit their purchase. In Spain, for instance, banks, insurance companies and collective investment companies were limited in the amount of foreign securities that might be held in their portfolios.
- A small number of member states imposed discriminatory taxes on the purchases of foreign securities. While these taxes did not in most cases discriminate against foreign entities, the increased cost of undertaking business could act as a disincentive for trading securities in a particular market.
- National prudential requirements were deemed to be a problem in relation to collective investment. Hence, in Germany, many foreign applicants reported difficulty in meeting local requirements. This was not seen to be discriminatory, but lack of harmonisation of rules on collective investments could make some European markets less attractive than others.

Barriers to the Cross-Border Provision of Insurance Services

Insurance appeared to be similar to the banking sector in that established foreign and domestic insurers were treated in a homogeneous manner, with there being little in the way of open discrimination. Lack of harmonisation of national laws and regulations appeared to present the major barrier to free trade, as it tended to make some member states inherently less financially attractive than others in terms of open competition. In addition, an area of major concern appeared to be the lack of harmonisation in the financial treatment of insurance contracts and premiums. The European Court of Justice at the time also noted concern about the discrimination exercised by some member states against non-established direct and co-insurers.

THE INTERNAL MARKET PROGRAMME FOR BANKING SERVICES

The above gives us a broad indication of the barriers to the cross-border provision of financial services within the EU in the mid-1980s. The following aims to provide an overview of the EU legislation that has eliminated or lessened some of these obstacles and led to the introduction of the single financial market from 1 January 1993 onwards.

As we know, the legislation that forms the cornerstone of the EU's plan for the single banking market came into effect on 1 January 1993. A critical aim of this legislation was to create the largest and most open banking market in the world with institutions competing on a so-called 'level playing field'. This means that minimum regulatory standards would be implemented so as to confer no competitive advantage for any domestic banks over foreign competitors within the EU. The following sections investigate these issues in more detail.

The First Banking Directive

The idea of the establishment of the integrated European financial market was one of the main objectives of the Treaty of Rome. Article 67 of the Treaty called for the abolition of the restriction on the movement of capital as well as the abolition of any discrimination which depended upon the residence of the investor. However, despite the fact that the financial services industry is of substantial importance to the EU economy (accounting for 3% of the total employment and for 6.7% of its total GDP (see Cecchini, 1988) in 1985), the unified European financial market was delayed for almost 30 years.

Before the 1985 EU White Paper the legal progress towards integrated financial markets was very limited. The Freedom of Establishment Directive (73/183/EEC) permitted equal treatment of home country financial firms and subsidiaries of firms from other member states on the part of national authorities. Moreover, subsidiaries of firms set up in member states were to be considered in all respects as EU undertakings. The First Banking Coordination Directive was adopted by the Council in 1977 (77/80/EEC). The Directive established the ground rules for dealing with bank authorisation and supervision. It detailed the minimum legal requirements banks had to meet in order to be authorised in other member states: such as to have adequate capital (not specified in the Directive) and to be directed by at least two people of good repute and experience. If the bank met these requirements, the basic right to set up branches in other EU member states was established. Branches, however, also needed to be established in accordance with host country regulations. Dixon (1991) argued that the First Banking Coordination Directive was an important first step, but the basic right of establishment did not create a free internal market. Vesala (1993) pointed out that host country requirements for branch establishment after 1977 still translated into extra costs and time delays incurred by EU banks when they opened branches in other member states and thus sustained legal barriers to the free provision of banking services. These costs appeared to be burdensome if an institution operated in a number of EU countries. For instance, foreign branches had to satisfy the prevailing domestic capital requirements and be supported by so-called endowment capital rather than by the capital of the main institution in all countries except in the UK. Home countries' solvency requirements were placed on foreign branches, and the requirements varied markedly between the member states. Moreover, foreign bank branches were often limited, such as in Spain where the number of branches a foreign bank could open was three (see Canals, 1993; Bisigano, 1992). Furthermore, Baltensperger and Dermine (1990) also state that cross-border trade in banking services was substantially limited by restrictions on capital flows.

While setting up ground rules, the First Bank Coordination Directive left much detail open to interpretation, and a more precise directive was obviously required for the freeing up of the cross-border provision of banking services. Before EU legislation and the 1992 bandwagon started rolling there was one other EU directive which concerned banking business. This was the 1983 Directive on Consolidated Supervision, which dealt with the supervision of consolidated accounts and the harmonisation of rules relating to annual accounts of banks. The Directive extended the supervision of individual banks to banking groups, covering their domestic and foreign affiliates and their accumulated overall credit risk (European Documentation, 1989, p. 27). However, this was restricted to important principals, leaving the member states free to decide whether this extended system of banking supervision should also encompass minority holdings in banks and holdings in credit institutions of a special nature, such as mortgage banks.

The 1985 EU White Paper

By far the most important progress towards the reducing of barriers to the cross-border provision of banking services was the 1985 Commission White Paper on the Completion of the Internal Market, drawn up by Lord Cockfield at the request of the EU Council of Ministers. The White Paper contained a list of measures that had to be adopted before 1992 so that people, goods, capital and services could freely circulate in the EU. It attempted to identify the measures to be taken to remove all physical, technical and tax barriers among the member states by the end of 1992, complete with a detailed timetable for adopting them. It also put forward over 300 legislative proposals required for their removal (see Commission of the European Communities, 1985, White Paper, in Appendix of p. 5-35; European Documentation, 1989, p. 18).

Moreover, the White Paper also described what else remained to be undertaken in the field of capital movements and financial services in order to result in the single European financial market and called for new and stricter criteria for application of the EU Treaty's safeguard clauses and closer monitoring of exchange controls. The main proposals were classified into three broad groups: (i) the removal of physical barriers; (ii) the removal of technical barriers; and (iii) the removal of fiscal barriers.

In terms of financial services, such as the free movement of financial products, the Commission planned a new policy. The exchange of financial products such as insurance polices, home-ownership savings contracts and consumer credit was to be organised by three important principles, namely: the minimum coordination of individual national rules, mutual recognition and home country control. The Commission's approach was to produce legislation which guaranteed minimum standards in the areas of financial stability and prudential practice of financial institutions (see Palmer, 1989, Chapter 2, pp. 21–37). In addition, the White Paper stated that it would create a Union-wide market for investment, making finance available to business and industry from anywhere in the EU. The objective was to provide greater competition on the basis of minimum guarantees of protection, with the prospect for individuals or industry being free to seek finance and financial services from any country within the Union.

The 1985 White Paper was the impetus for a significant amount of legislation which followed up until the 1992 watershed. Even though Pelkmans (1992) noted that the original White Paper was not a good guide as many proposals have now been significantly altered, or more ambitious follow-up proposals have been made, it still provided the main force to the unity of new EU legislation which created a single market in banking services. It also lay at the core part of the project to give a new impetus to European integration.

The Second Banking Coordination Directive

The Second Banking Coordination Directive (89/646/EEC) is the cornerstone of the Commission programme for a single market in banking. It was issued on 13 January 1988, and approved by the EU Council of Ministers on 18 December 1989 and came into effect on 1 January 1993.

By far the most important aspect of the Second Banking Directive was the provision for a 'single passport' for banks and other financial firms to operate throughout the Union. This single passport allowed any banks which were authorised to act as such in a member state, to set up branches, or supply cross-border services, in other EU countries, without having to obtain further authorisation from the host country. The list of services banks could engage in is provided in the Appendix to the Second Banking Directive, which is shown in Table 2.2. This confirms the 'universal' banking model that the EU legislature had adopted. Llewellyn (1992) indicated that the list of activities shown in Table 2.2 was very broad, covering the realities of the financial markets and the gradual breaking down of the traditional demarcation lines between commercial and investment banking. He also noted that the most important thing was that the list included all forms of securities transactions. This would have an important impact on those member states (such as in Italy, Spain, Greece and Portugal) where various types of commercial banking and securities business were traditionally separated.

Secondly, the Directive aimed to remove barriers to banking throughout the EU by deregulating the requirement for branches to maintain a minimum level of endowment capital. This was a wide-range obstacle to the free establishment of branches in various EU countries (Price Waterhouse, 1988, p. 76).

Thirdly, in order to harmonise the financial system and increase competition, the Directive set out conditions for the free provision of banking services by adopting the White Paper's guidelines on mutual and home country control.

Table 2.2   The list of services credit institutions are allowed to offer under the Second Banking Directive

---

1. Deposit-taking and other forms of borrowing
2. Lending
3. Financial leasing
4. Money transmission services
5. Issuing and administering means of payments (credit cards, travellers' cheques and bankers' drafts)
6. Guarantees and commitments
7. Trading for own account or for account of customers in:
    (a)   money-market instruments
    (b)   foreign exchange
    (c)   financial futures and options
    (d)   exchange and interest rate instruments
    (e)   securities
8. Participation in share issues and the provision of services related to such issues
9. Money broking
10. Portfolio management and advice
11. Safekeeping of securities
12. Credit reference services
13. Safe custody services

Source: Second Banking Coordination Directive (see *Official Journal of the European Communities*, No. L 386/13, 30.12.89).

According to Article 19 of the Directive, a bank wishing to establish a branch and sell services within the Union only need obtain permission from the regulatory authorities of its home country if it wishes to establish in another member country. Branches no longer need to hold endowment capital for business authorised within the EU (Article 6 of Directive 89/646/EEC). Home country control implies that the EU member state that has granted the banking licence (to a certain institution) also supervises its activities in the EU, wherever the institution operates. Put simply, the Second Banking Coordination Directive (89/646/EEC) implemented more fully the principle of home country control and introduced the single European banking passport. This directive states that (see *Official Journal of the European Communities*, No. L 386/1 30.12.89):

> the approach that has been adopted is to achieve only the essential harmonisation necessary and sufficient to secure the mutual recognition of authorisation and of prudential supervision systems, making possible the granting of a single licence recognised throughout the Community and the application of the principle of home Member State prudential supervision

The banking authority of the home country will have responsibility for supervising the financial soundness of a bank and in particular its solvency including the application and monitoring of minimum standards of harmonisation, together with ensuring that there are good administrative, accounting and internal control mechanisms in place in foreign institutions' branches under their supervision. Overall, the Second Banking Directive provides for:

1. the harmonisation of minimum capital standards for the authorisation and continuation of banking business;
2. supervisory control of major shareholders and banks' participation in the non-banking sector;
3. proper accounting and control mechanisms;
4. standards on own funds, solvency ratios and deposit protection legislation.

Finally, the Directive also allows for reciprocal access to the single market for banks from non-EU countries. Subsidiaries of non-EU country banks set up in the EU are considered to be EU undertakings, and therefore benefit from the Directive's provision for freedom of establishment and cross-border activities. The following two sections describe the important supporting directives to the Second Banking Directive.

The Own Funds Directive

The Own Funds Directive (89/299/EEC) was issued by the Commission in September 1986 and was adopted on 17 April 1989 (effective 1 January 1993). This Directive defines what is meant by 'capital' for banks and is effectively the same as the Bank for International Settlements or 'Basle' requirements (Gardener, 1992).

The Directive includes various provisions outlining the items attributable to own funds, breaking own funds into two categories — original own funds and additional own funds of lesser status. Subject to a number of conditions put forward in the Directive, own funds comprise paid-up capital reserves, revaluation reserves, funds for general banking risks, value adjustments, the commitments of the members of credit cooperatives, cumulative preferential shares and subordinated loan capital. Additional own funds must not exceed the amount of original own funds (see Dixon, 1991). (Original own funds are analogous to Tier 1 capital and additional own funds are analogous to Tier 2 capital in the Basle regime.)

The Solvency Ratio Directive

The Directive on Solvency Ratios (89/647/EEC) constrains the own funds of a credit institution to at least 8% of its risk-weighted assets (European Documentation, 1989, p. 30). It is widely argued that the risk-adjusted approach to measuring banks' solvency is the most adequate and flexible one, since basic ratios do not distinguish between different degrees of risk. The capital adequacy requirements established by the Directive are in line with the Bank for International Settlements (BIS) proposals. For example, both regimes have similar categories of assets (four risk classifications) and identical weights associated with them: 0, 10, 20, 50 and 100% respectively (Dixon, 1991, p. 71). The BIS capital guidelines are, however, not legally enforceable as they are only recommendations for international banks. In contrast the EU's Second Banking Directive and attendant capital adequacy legislation is incorporated into EU and member country law and so is in fact legally enforceable.

Other Directives

This section briefly focuses on other Council directives which are important to the introduction of the single market for financial services sectors. These are listed under the headings below.

The Money Laundering Directive

Council Directive 91/308/EEC on the prevention of use of the financial system for the purpose of money laundering was adopted by the Council in June 1991 and came into force on 1 January 1993 (*Official Journal of the European Communities*, No. L 166/77, 28.6.91). The Directive was designed to prevent the Community financial area from being used for laundering the proceeds from criminal activities. Money laundering means the international handling of property knowing it to come from the commission of serious crime (in particular drug-related offences, organised crime and terrorism). The offence also extends to the concealment or aiding and abetting of money laundering (*Official Journal of the European Communities*, No. L 166/77, 28.6.91).

The directive covers both credit and financial institutions, including life assurance companies. In brief, EU banks and financial institutions will be obliged to provide for a series of measures, such as the identification of customers and beneficial owners, the retention of documentary evidence and records of transactions, the disclosure to the competent authorities of transactions suspected of involving money laundering and the obligation on the institutions concerned to introduce staff training programmes and internal control procedures (see *Bull. EC*, 1991). The Directive provides for a contact committee to be established. This committee would have the task of contributing to the harmonised implementation of the Directive through regular consultations between representatives of the member states and the Commission. It would also investigate the desirability of drawing up a list of professions and categories of enterprises whose activities could be used for money-laundering purposes (*Official Journal of the European Communities*, No. L 166/79, 28.6.91).

The Large Exposures Directive

Council Directive 92/121/EEC on monitoring and controlling large exposures of credit institutions was adopted by the Council on 21 December 1992 and came into force on 1 January 1994 (*Official Journal of the European Communities*, No. L 29/1, 5.2.93). The Directive is aimed at increasing the spread of risks incurred by banks in order to prevent default by one client from jeopardising the existence of such an institution (and having repercussions on the financial system in general). The directive provides in particular for the large exposures of banks to be limited to 40% of own funds during a transitional period and to 25% thereafter, for large exposures to be reported to authorities as soon as they reach 10% of own funds, and for the combined total of such exposures to be limited to 800% of own funds (see *Official Journal of the European Communities*, No. L 29/4, 5.2.93).

The Deposit-Guarantee Schemes

The harmonisation of the deposit-guarantee schemes within the EU was not fully in effect from 1 January 1993. The Commission at the end of 1986 noted that it would be appropriate for the credit institutions of all member states to participate in a deposit-guarantee scheme. Deposit-guarantee schemes are intended to protect the interest of mainly retail depositors of an insolvent financial institution which faces financial difficulties and thus aims to guarantee the stability of the banking system as a whole. Under these schemes, the depositors are guaranteed compensation or protection against losses. The draft directive on deposit-guarantee schemes stated that Portugal and Greece must establish a guarantee scheme, and Spain, Belgium, Luxembourg and Ireland increase the coverage up to the standard (ECU 20 000). France, the UK, Ireland and Belgium need to extend the protection to foreign exchange deposits. The organisation of deposit insurance schemes may differ among EU countries. For example, in Belgium, France, Germany and Italy deposit insurance schemes were privately organised by bankers' associations, while in the UK and Spain deposit insurance is administered by the central bank.

The Proposal for a Council Directive on Deposit-guarantee Schemes (93/C 178/14), adopted by the Commission on 7 June 1993, involves the fixing of the minimum guarantee amount at ECU 20 000 and the recognition of certain alternative guarantee schemes, such as those introduced by credit cooperatives and savings banks in some countries, as being equivalent to traditional deposit-guarantee schemes (see *Bull. EC*, 1993c).

THE SINGLE EUROPEAN MARKET PROGRAMME FOR SECURITIES AND INSURANCE SERVICES

Securities Legislation

A single European financial market without restrictions requires a single securities market where investors may issue and trade securities within the EU freely and without hindrance. Since 1979 the Commission has issued a series of important directives in order to achieve the operation of a single securities market. The first step was the adoption on 5 March 1979 of a Directive (79/279/EEC) coordinating the conditions for the admission of securities to official stock-exchange listings. The Directive established the conditions that must be met by issuers of securities, including the minimum issue price, the company's period of existence, free negotiability, sufficient distribution and the provision of appropriate information for investors. The Council adopted another Directive, which is closely connected to the former, on 17 March 1980 (80/390/EEC) coordinating the requirements for the drawing up, scrutiny and distribution of the listing particulars to be published for the admission of securities to official stock-exchange listings (European Documentation, 1989).

The third step in 1982 was the Council Resolution on the Directive (82/121/EEC) on information to be published on a regular basis by companies whose shares were admitted to official stock exchanges. According to this Directive companies listed on a stock exchange must publish half-yearly reports on their activities and profits and losses.

By far the most important Directive aimed at creating an integrated European securities market, however, was taken by the Council on 18 November 1985 when it passed the Directive on the free marketing of units issued by investment funds (undertakings for collective investment in transferable securities) (see Vesala, 1993 in section 1.2.4). This Directive introduced for the first time in the securities sector the 'new approach' (see European Documentation, 1989, p. 40) which was called for in the 1985 White Paper on completing the internal market. The principles of mutual recognition and home country control were incorporated in this EU legislation to the structure of investment funds and their investment policy. Furthermore, the Council set out a Directive of 22 June 1987 (87/345/EEC) amending Directive 80/390/EEC coordinating the requirements for the drawing up, scrutiny and distribution of the listing particulars to be published for the admission of securities to official stock exchanges. The goal of the Directive was to ensure that listing particulars complied with earlier directives and approved in one member state were automatically recognised on the stock exchanges of other EU members.

In this Directive an investment firm was described as 'any natural or legal person' whose business was related in one or more listed activities. These listed activities defined market-making, brokerage, underwriting, portfolio management, and providing investment advice, in connection with a range of financial instruments: transferable securities, money market instruments (including certificates of deposits and Eurocommercial paper), financial futures and options, and exchange and interest rate instruments.

The Commission took two further steps towards greater transparency and to complete the programme for the creation of a single European securities market. The first Directive (87/345/EEC) related to the information to be published when a major holding in a listed company was acquired or disposed of. The goal of the Directive was to ensure that investors and the public were informed of major shareholdings, changes in holdings above or below certain ranges and changes in voting rights for listed companies in the EU. The requirements applied when a holding reached 10, 20, 33, 50 and 66% respectively. The EU may apply a single threshold of 25% in place of the 20 and 33% thresholds, and 75% in place of the 66% threshold (European Documentation, 1989, p. 41). The second step was that the Community established a Directive on 17 April 1989 (89/298/EEC) coordinating the requirements for the drawing up, scrutiny and distribution of the prospectus to be published when transferable securities were marketed to the public. This Directive was an important supplement to the above 1982 and 1987 directives on transparency and investor protection in the securities markets.

The above directives aim to give an opportunity to investment companies to provide cross-border services on the same basis that the Second Banking Directive allows banks to operate in different EU countries. Barriers to the cross-border provision of investment services, however, have not been fully removed by the above directives, and the EU introduced two significant pieces of legislation — the EU's Investment Services Directive and its attendant Capital Adequacy Directive — at the beginning of 1996. This will create a single investment licence for EU investment firms and will, it is hoped, do for the investment industry what the Second Banking Directive has done for the EU's banking sector.

EU Investment Services Legislation

The Investment Services Directive (ISD) and its attendant Capital Adequacy Directive (CAD) came into effect on 1 January 1996 and it rests with the parliaments of EU member states to incorporate the directives into national laws by that date.

On 29 June 1992 both the ISD and CAD were agreed by the EU Council of Finance Ministers (*Bull. EC*, 1992, p. 37). The aim of this legislation is to help establish freedom to provide services for investment firms by creating a single licence (the 'European passport') on the basis of mutual recognition and home country control. After achieving the European passport, an investment firm could carry out its activities throughout the EU. Moreover, the aim of the CAD was to establish equivalent capital requirements for non-bank investment operators as those laid down in the Own Funds Directive for banks (89/299/EEC). Both the CAD and the ISD were scheduled to come into force by 1 January 1993, but this did not happen. Areas of disagreement on the ISD among member states related to three main issues:

1. *Concentration.* Member states comprising, France, Italy, Spain, Portugal, Greece and Belgium (the so-called Club-Med group) wished, on the grounds of investor protection, that trading in all forms of equities and bonds should be conducted on a regulated market, whenever a trade involves an investor who is a resident of that particular member state and relates to securities which are listed on a regulated market in that member state. If the concentration requirement were to be enforced by the Directive, this would have important implications for banks, since it is a non-regulated market on which many securities listed on the regulated markets of other member states are traded. Opposition to the concentration view came from the UK, Germany, Ireland, Luxembourg and the Netherlands (or 'Alliance' group) who argued that the concentration requirement was disproportionate to the stated goal of investor protection and would involve unacceptable limitations on the current flexible operations of unregulated (such as over-the-counter (OTC)) international securities markets (*Financial Industry Monitor*, 1993).

2. *Reporting and publication issue.* The Club-Med group also insisted that all trades, both on regulated and unregulated markets, should be the subject of extensive reporting requirements. They also insisted on 'immediate' publication of all trades (at least for the trades executed on the market). This latter requirement was vigorously opposed, especially by the UK authorities, who argued that it could restrict the proper functioning of markets.

3. *Direct bank access to stock exchanges.* Here the Club-Med group insisted the member states should be allowed to require banks to incorporate separate subsidiaries in order to access local stock markets.

At the Council of Ministers meeting on 29 June 1992, some of the above points which had delayed constructive discussion of the ISD were agreed upon. With regard to the concentration issue, various 'opt-out' clauses were made, which meant that if the ISD becomes law in 1995 there may be requirements for certain financial instruments to be traded on regulated markets, but that these requirements are not compulsory. The June agreement also called for transitional provisions which allowed member states to maintain their present regimes in relation to the direct access of banks to stock exchanges, at least until 1996 (Greece and Spain have derogations until 1999) (*Bull. EC*, 1992). In fact, by the beginning of 1996 virtually all EU stockmarkets had deregulated which allowed foreign bank acquisition of capital market firms.

Moreover, Council Directive 93/22/EEC on investment services in the securities field adopted by the Council on 10 May 1993 (*Bull. EC*, 1993b), complements that on the capital adequacy of investment firms and credit institutions, and authorises an investment firm in any member state to conduct its activities throughout the Community on the basis of a single authorisation ('European passport') issued by the home member state. The CAD (effective January 1996) applies risk-based capital requirements to (non-bank) investment firms and also introduces consolidated supervision for (non-bank) investment firms. Various banking directives will be modified so that banks have to carry capital on their 'trading book' calculated in the same manner as securities firms. (In other words, position and counter-party risk positions will need to be evaluated instead of the usual credit-based bank evaluations.) This Directive also brings in own funds requirements for securities firms similar to those for banks. In general the definitions of capital for banks and investment firms will be lined up with both types of firms being given the opportunity to gear up their regulatory capital to support trading positions. Combined with ISD this legislation harmonises the conditions governing authorisation and business activity and will establish uniform rules for prudential supervision by the authorities of the home member states in the investment services industry. Upon full implementation of the relevant banking and investment directives, both credit institutions and investment firms will be able to carry out the whole gamut of investment business in capital markets which mutually recognises listing particulars and prospectuses, and which has an all-encompassing set of minimum standard harmonising rules relating to the running and regulation of investment firms and markets. The main objective is ultimately for the free flow of capital throughout the EU which should eventually lead towards a single integrated European capital market, rather than back to the traditional fragmented collection of separate national markets. As a result, investors doing business within Europe should have fewer obstacles to trade and this should lead eventually to a more competitive and efficient investment industry.

Proposed UCITs Directive

On 9 February 1993 the European Commission submitted to the Council a proposal for a Directive to extend the scope of the 1985 Directive on Undertakings for Collective Investment in Transferable Securities (UCITs) to money market funds and funds of funds (*Bull. EC*, 1993a). The submission proposes that member states amend their legislation and bring in the laws, regulations and administrative provisions necessary to comply with this Directive by 1 July 1994 at the latest (see *Official Journal of the European Communities*, No. C 59/18, 2.3.93). The EFTA countries joining the EU must set up the necessary national legal basis for bringing the Directive on UCITs into force simultaneously with the EU Agreement (see Vesala, 1993, p. 42). This gave financial institutions the opportunity to provide new fund management products in this area from mid-1994 onwards out of any EU centre.

In addition to this major amendment to the 1985 UCITs Directive, other amendments include issues relating to: depositaries (relating to the establishment and management of unit and investment trusts), the use of derivatives, risk spreading and technical consequences of including money market instruments and funds of funds. The proposal relating to derivatives was of interest to financial institutions as it will enable them to create new investment products. The proposal states that UCITs will be allowed to invest in 'financial derivative instruments provided that the exposures relating to these instruments are covered in the sense that UCITs must hold assets which may reasonably be expected to fulfil actual or potential obligations which exist or may arise as a result of the derivatives themselves' (see *Official Journal of the European Communities*, No. C 59/16, 2.3.93).

A Note on the Liberalisation of Insurance Services

Like the banking industry, the Treaty of Rome has also made noticeable movements to achieve the freedom to provide services in the field of insurance. Increasing regulation of the sector during the 1960s and 1970s had made it more difficult for insurance companies to operate throughout the EU and the number of foreign insurance firms operating cross-border in Europe has decreased significantly over the past 25 years (see Quelch and Hibbard, 1991, Chapter 4).

However, there has been a significant delay in harmonising EU insurance legislation because the member states have widely differing arrangements for insurance operations, supervision and consumer protection rules. In this sector, the liberalisation really began when the European Court of Justice delivered a significant judgment on 4 December 1986 (see European Documentation, 1989, p. 33).

The European Court of Justice's judgment brought about a new momentum to the waning effort to achieve a free European insurance market. In response to the Commission's legal action against four member states (Denmark, France, Germany and Ireland), the judges stated that the restrictions placed by these member states on the authorisation of insurance companies from other EU countries were in part illegal but also in part justified (European Documentation, 1989, p. 35). This stimulated the way for further progress towards a deregulated insurance market.

The Council of Ministers issued the Second Council Directive (88/357/EEC) in June 1988 on the coordination of laws, regulations and administrative provisions relating to direct insurance other than life insurance (see *Official Journal of the European Communities*, No. L 228/1, 11.8.92). This Directive introduced a single licensing system under which an insurance company with its head office in a member state could establish branches across EU borders without being subject to authorisation procedures in those countries. Non-life insurance policy-holders would have access to the whole range of products on offer in the EU. According to the Directive (Article 57), the member states had to adopt the laws, regulations and administrative provisions necessary for their compliance with this Directive before 1 January 1994 and bring them into force no later than 1 July 1994 (see *Official Journal of the European Communities*, No. L 228/23, 11.8.92). The Directive also provides for the coordination of financial rules, i.e. in particular the rules governing the categories, diversification and localisation of assets used to cover technical provisions, required as a basis for the introduction of the single licensing system. There are also provisions relating to the law applicable to insurance contracts (see *Bull. EC*, 1992).

OVERVIEW OF EU FINANCIAL SERVICES LEGISLATION

The EU's critical date of 1 January 1993 has passed and various important banking directives have come into force. Banks and financial institutions within the EU can now begin to see the framework which is to be applied and can consider their strategies. In brief, we have seen that there are nine main directives which will have a significant impact on the banking industry:

1. *The Second Banking Coordination Directive* (effective 1 January 1993). This Directive, in conjunction with the Own Funds and Solvency Ratio directives, gives EU incorporated banks the right to branch into, or provide services into, any other EU country.

2. *The Own Funds Directive* (effective 1 January 1993). This defines what is meant by 'capital' for banks and is effectively the same as the BIS requirements.

3. *The Solvency Ratio Directive* (effective 1 January 1993). This establishes the amount of capital banks need to hold for regulatory purposes (related to their weighted risk assets similar to BIS methods).

4. *The Consolidated Supervision Directive* (effective 1 January 1993). This requires supervisors to look at banking groups on a consolidated basis, rather than only undertaking solo supervision.

5. *The Money Laundering Directive* (effective 1 January 1993). This imposes certain obligations on credit and financial institutions designed to prevent money laundering. (Money laundering means the international handling of property knowing it to come from the commission of serious crime, principally drug-related offences, organised crime and terrorism.)

6. *The Large Exposures Directive* (effective 1 January 1994). This places limits on the exposures to individual companies or groups which banks can take on (generally 25% of capital).

7. *The deposit-guarantee schemes* (effective 1 January 1993). This proposes a Council Directive on minimum standards for deposit-guarantee schemes which would protect depositors in the event of bank failure.

8. *The Investment Services Directive* (effective January 1996). This is intended to give the same passport to (EU incorporated) non-bank investment service firms as the Second Banking Directive. It will become operational in conjunction with its associated Capital Adequacy Directive.

9. *The Capital Adequacy Directive* (effective December 1995). This implies risk-based capital requirements to investment firms and also proposes consolidated supervision for investment firms. This Directive will also bring in own funds requirements for securities firms similar to those for banks.

At the heart of the above legislation is the EU's objective to create a single market for financial services by providing banks and other financial firms with a 'single passport' to operate throughout the Community subject only, as a rule, to the supervision of the competent (regulatory) authority of their home member state. Moves towards such a single market, however, are currently and will continue to be restricted by three main distortionary factors: firstly, the freedom national authorities have in opting out of EU legislation; secondly, tax obstacles; thirdly, the flexibility with which governments can incorporate EU law into national legislation and finally, different reserve requirements (these issues will be discussed in more detail later in this chapter).

So far we have discussed the EU's objective of creating a single market for financial services but this is just part of the EU's broader objective of achieving European Monetary Union.

EUROPEAN MONETARY UNION (EMU) AND ITS IMPLICATIONS FOR THE SINGLE FINANCIAL SERVICES MARKET

On 11 December 1991 at the Maastricht Summit, the member states of the EU adopted comprehensive amendments to the 1957 Treaty of Rome. When ratified by all the EU countries, the amendments would extend the domain of the Union in many directions. In particular, the European Council agreed that monetary union would be established no later than 1 January 1999. Subject to ratification by EU member states, the fundamental point was that the decision to introduce EMU in the Union and to introduce the Euro as the Union's single currency would be put into place at the latest by 1999 (see Italianer et al., 1992). By then, exchange rates between the participating EU member states would have been fixed and the European Central Bank (ECB) would be ready to operate (Bank of England, 1992, p. 64). The Maastricht Treaty also stated that EMU could be established before 1999 if a majority of member states have achieved a sufficient degree of economic convergence, as indicated by certain criteria. For purposes of business planning, the main issues of concern for financial institutions relate to (*De Pecunia*, 1992a, p. 17):

- the timing of the move to EMU;
- which countries will meet the economic convergence criteria;
- the date on which a single currency will be introduced.

Timetable and Procedure

Table 2.3 provides an overview of the three stages leading to EMU. The first stage of EMU began on 1 July 1990 with a view to promoting economic convergence. During this stage much greater attention was paid to multilateral surveillance of economic conditions in member states, to reinforce monetary policy coordination and to promote the role of the ECU (see Commission of the Economic Communities, 1991, p. 14). Thus, the European Council was required to examine on a yearly basis the prospects and policies in the Union as well as the effects the external economic environment had on the EU. The process of monetary policy coordination was also supposed to be strengthened in Stage 1 (see Spagnolo, 1993, p. 104).

Stage 2 of EMU began on 1 January 1994, when the European Monetary Institute (EMI) was established (see Commission of the European Communities, 1992a, Briefing Note p. 8). During this stage, there could be no 'monetary financing' or bail-outs of public entities, and a procedure to eliminate excessive budget deficits would start to operate (Bank of England, 1992, p. 67). The EMI should aim to strengthen cooperation among the central banks and the coordination of their monetary policies. This coordination would focus on price stability; include holding consultations on issues falling within the central bank's competence and affecting the stability of financial institutions and markets; involve monitoring the functioning of the European Monetary System (EMS) and, among other things, to promote the use of the ECU (see Commission of the European Communities, 1992a; p. 8). At the latest by 31 December 1996, the EMI should specify the regulatory, organisational and logistical framework necessary for the

Table 2.3 The three stages of EMU

Time period	Objectives
Stage 1 until 1 January 1994	Closer economic and monetary cooperation between member states within the existing institutional framework aimed at greater convergence of economic performance. It includes the completion of the single market and the strengthening of Union competition policy
Stage 2 January 1994 to no later than 1 January 1999	Will reinforce economic convergence beyond Stage 1, including the necessary institutional developments: setting up of the EMI, while still leaving ultimate responsibility for monetary policy with national authorities, will also involve technical preparation for Stage 3

(It was agreed by member states at Maastricht that full EMU — known as Stage 3 — should commence for those judged eligible to participate, no later than 1 January 1999. But if the heads of state of government decide, by qualified majority, they may set an earlier date for the start of Stage 3. Stage 3 could begin as early as 1997, or earlier if the necessary conditions are met.)

Stage 3 1 January 1999 at the latest	Full EMU includes:
	• irrevocable locking of exchange rates between participating currencies and a single monetary policy leading to the adoption of single currency in due course
	• the European Central Bank (ECB) and European System of Central Banks (ESCB) will be responsible for issuing and managing the single currency — the ECU (now the 'Euro') — that will replace national currencies
	• the primary objective of the ECB and the ESCB in undertaking monetary policy will be to maintain price stability — they will also be required to support the general economic policies in the European Union

Note: For a detailed exposition of the three stages, see the *Bank of England Quarterly Bulletin*, February 1992, pp. 66–68 and Bank of England Fact Sheet, May 1994, pp. 1–7.

European System of Central Banks (ESCB) to perform its tasks. Just before Stage 3 commences, the ECB will be established and the EMI liquidated (Bank of England, 1992, p. 67).

If, by qualified majority vote, the member states agree that a majority of them meet the necessary convergence conditions they may, not later than 31 December 1996, set a date for the start of EMU. If they have not set a date by the end of 1997, EMU will start automatically on 1 January 1999 among those member states which it has been determined (by qualified majority vote before 1 July 1998) meet the convergence criteria (see Spagnolo, 1993, p. 104).

Convergence Criteria

The Maastricht agreement stipulates that the countries which enter Stage 3 of EMU must meet certain criteria of economic convergence. Country compliance will be monitored by the EMI which has its headquarters in Frankfurt. The EMU can be introduced as early as 1997 if a majority of EU countries meet the following four main criteria (Bank of England, 1992, p. 66):

1. *High degree of price stability.* Each country must attain an average rate of inflation, observed over a period of one year prior to admission, that does not exceed the average inflation rate of the three best performing member countries by more than 1.5 percentage points.

2. *Sustainable government financial position.* The ratio of government deficit to gross domestic product (GDP) cannot exceed 3% and the ratio of government debt to GDP cannot exceed 60% (see Commission of the European Communities, 1992a, Briefing Note p. 10).

3. *Long-term interest rates.* In the year preceding EMU admission a country's average nominal long-term interest rate may not exceed the average of the three best performing member countries by more than two percentage points.

4. *Participation in the narrow bands of the Exchange Rate Mechanism (ERM).* In the two years preceding admission to EMU the currency of each member country must have remained within the normal bands of fluctuations in the ERM without experiencing severe tension.

The main objective of these criteria is to establish an economic environment of sustainable low inflation in all the member countries and thus in the EMU. The fiscal criteria are aimed to reduce a potential source of inflation in the EMU, the monetisation of public debt. Together with the interest rate criteria, the fiscal guidelines are meant to prevent increasingly indebted countries exerting upward pressures on interest rates in the entire EMU.

Given the state of various EU economies over recent years, however, the likelihood of all the EU countries achieving these convergence criteria is in some doubt. For example, the EU Commission's Annual Economic Report for 1993 (European Economy, 1993, p. 3) made sombre reading, both generally and in the context of the Maastricht Treaty objective of EMU by 1 January 1999, or even earlier. On the first page of the report the EU noted that 'the turmoil with the Exchange Rate Mechanism ... severely dented the credibility of the EMU timetable'. Ratification of the Maastricht Treaty had taken place in the majority of EU countries by the end of 1993, yet in an increasing number of these countries, the convergence momentum seems to have become impeded by a general economic slow-down. Uncertainties regarding political progress towards EMU, and the markets' continued awareness of the unsustainable nature of various ERM exchange rates, have been a major factor behind the problems faced by the EMS. Opponents of the Treaty viewed the turmoil in the EMS exchange rate markets as demonstration of the impossibility of establishing a common monetary policy — and therefore a single currency — which may well be the case for those countries whose economies are still not convergent and are each faced with their own structural problems (see European Economy, 1990; Bank of England, 1994).

This outlook is supported, at first sight, by recent drifts away from the Maastricht criteria on the part of those countries regarded as constituting the hard core of the EMS. The only country that claimed to satisfy the criteria for monetary union at the end of 1993 was Luxembourg (although Luxembourg has an economic union with Belgium which does not meet the EMU criteria) (European Economy, 1993). France and Denmark met the criteria in 1990, but have since moved away from them. In addition, the possibility that the most divergent economies might reduce their respective gaps to the point at which they could participate in the third phase of EMU seems to have been deferred.

The Single Currency

The move towards a single currency (which will be known as the 'Euro') will have the most immediate impact on the banking sector (see Praet, 1992). Stage 2 would be the preparatory period for implementing the single currency during which the newly established EMI (the forerunner of the ECB and ESCB) will be required:

- to facilitate the use of the ECU and oversee its development, including the smooth functioning of the ECU clearing systems;
- to promote the efficiency of EU cross-border payments;
- to 'consult' with central banks on issues affecting the stability of financial institutions and markets;
- to coordinate monetary policy between member states.

During this preparatory phase, banks will have to undertake many changes relating to the integration of the Euro which concern (see *De Pecunia*, 1992a, pp. 33–41):

- translation of accounting records and systems, monetary instruments, documentation of all kinds;
- drafting of legal rules in contracts;

- software conversion and adaptation;
- changes in hardware, to accept and distribute new Euro notes (ATMs and counting machines);
- training of bank staff;
- provision of information to customers.

These changes, as well as the cost of manufacturing, warehousing and distribution of Euro denominated notes and coins, will impose burdens on the banks and will undoubtedly cause confusion, given that there will be two legal tenders — the Euro and the national currency — in circulation at the same time (see Mayes, 1990). Management of notes and coins in Euro and national currency will cause problems if a dual circulation system develops; this is especially the case if the demand for Euro currency by bank customers is negligible. Customers will only shift to Euro's if the benefits of using this currency outweigh the costs of using national currencies. Other potential costs to banks include (see *De Pecunia*, 1992a, pp. 33–41):

- reduction in need for specialist currency teams to advise corporations on EU currency swap and forward transactions;
- the risk of having to undertake greater risk taking in order to make up for lost income (the adverse selection problems);
- increased competition — at present no single bank has more than a 2% share of the overall European foreign exchange market and no one financial centre currently enjoys a significant competitive advantage;
- diversion of capital flows from outside the EU to intra-Union transactions because of the lower risk and attractiveness of the larger single market;
- risks associated with financial instruments denominated in national currencies whose maturity dates exceed the conversion to single currency date;
- decline in business for banks who dominate the lead management and underwriting of issues denominated in their national currencies.

Many of the above factors will primarily affect the larger international banks, although it is these banks that are more likely to benefit from the increased scope of Euro lending and investment opportunities throughout member states brought about by greater intra-EU trade and investment. Larger banks would be more inclined to undertake business throughout the EU, especially given that they are more inclined to undertake business in different EU currency denominations or to incur risk on an open foreign exchange position. The benefits accruing to these banks would clearly be closely related to the scale of cross-border provisions of services.

Moves towards a single currency will also require that efficient arrangements for cross-border payments and settlement are in place (see *De Pecunia*, 1992b). A discussion paper published by the European Commission in September 1990 called 'Making payments in the internal market' noted that existing cross-border retail payments systems are deficient in transparency (consumers do not know which system is the best), speed, reliability and cost. In a paper presented to the Association for the Monetary Union of Europe by Sir John Quinton in May 1992, it was noted that, in the case of wholesale payments, the ECU Bankers' Association ECU clearing systems have been successful in facilitating the growth in the private use of the ECU, but with the increased volume of business envisaged in the run-up to EMU, and given the EMI's brief to develop clearing and settlement systems, it is uncertain as to whether new systems should be privately operated or run by the EMI or its successor the ECB. It might even be the case that two systems — one private and one public — evolve. It also needs to be considered as to who would have access and membership to such a system and who decides on these issues. Perhaps EU competition policy would have influence in determining some of these matters.

ECONOMIC ASPECTS OF A SINGLE MARKET IN FINANCIAL SERVICES

The Price Waterhouse/Cecchini Report and its Findings

The previous section outlined the expected impact of EMU on the financial services industry. This section of the text examines the economic aspects of a single market in financial services. The Cecchini study was the first and most important empirical work to analyse comparative competitive conditions across EU banking and financial systems. This research set out to examine the economic consequences of completing the EU internal market, on various economic sectors. The microeconomic study of the financial services sector was carried out for Cecchini by Price Waterhouse Management Consultants (Dublin), whose results were published in detail by Price Waterhouse (1988). The following section investigates the sources of the economic gains from EU integration and then focuses on the main features of the Price Waterhouse (1988) study.

Sources of the Economic Gains from Integration—Competition, Efficiency and Scale and Scope Economies

The Price Waterhouse (1988) study postulated that completion of the internal market would induce a series of integration effects which would promote the efficiency and competitiveness of EU firms through two channels — namely through increased market size and heightened levels of competition. The expected economic effects could be grouped primarily into the following categories (see European Economy, 1988, p. 104):

1. There would be lower costs resulting from economies of scale and learning, made possible by the associated larger volume of output and by restructuring processes.

2. The pressure of competition on prices should lead (mainly in the formerly protected sectors) to a reduction in price cost margins and to incentives for firms to increase their technical efficiency by minimising their costs (X-inefficiency) so as to maintain their margins.

3. Increased competition should also have non-price effects, firms being encouraged to improve their organisation, the quality and range of their products and, in particular, to engage in process and product innovation. Moreover, the combined effects of these changes would be to increase the GDP of the EU as presented in Figure 2.1.

The relationship between the single financial market and the possibility of utilising potential economies of scale and scope is often presented as a clear argument in favour of the internal market. The completion of the Community's financial integration was a uniquely important part of the internal market programme because of the extent of other effects on the economy, even if their magnitude could not easily be measured (see Price Waterhouse, 1988). The completion of the internal market would be expected to bring an expansion of market size and hence the size of business, and this in turn would enhance scale and scope economies resulting in considerable reductions in costs. The term 'scale and scope', used generally to explain the effects on size and product mix on costs, in fact covers a wide range of phenomena, from purely static economies of a technical nature to dynamic phenomena linked to experience. The exploitation of benefits from removing non-tariff barriers is crucially dependent upon fundamental reconstruction in many industries. This is largely based on achieving economies of scale,

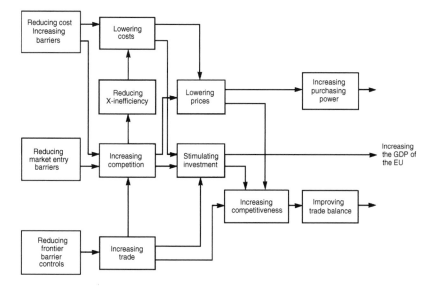

Figure 2.1   How the SEM increases GDP of the EU (Source: Penketh, 1992, p. 28)

and by firms integrating activities in fragmented markets. Substantial benefits accruing from economies of scale and scope also imply that many European firms are too small (see Penketh, 1992, p. 31).

True economies of scale are said to exist when average cost of production falls as output increases, all other things being constant. In financial services, the arguments are that there are large fixed costs to operating a network of branches or agents (Llewellyn, 1992). These may be scattered over many customers in large operations. Moreover, it is believed that another supposed economy derives from the benefits of scale in participating in capital markets. Unit transaction costs appear to be lower, the larger you are. Furthermore, consumer recognition is an advantage to the large firms who may expect to attract customers most easily. Finally, it has also been argued that a large diversified institution can afford to cross-subsidise price wars which occur spasmodically and given that entry and exit cost something, large firms can ensure that they are not forced out of any market (see Centre for Business Strategy, 1989).

Economics of scale and scope are important concepts for the financial services industry. In theory financial institutions doing business in all major European market-places may find it more cost efficient to serve clients than similar-sized institutions that are locally concentrated. In addition a large universal bank may be better placed to serve international clients, and would gain strategically valuable information about the range of markets from its dealings abroad (Steinherr, 1992; Bollenbacher, 1992).

According to Cecchini (1988), the elimination of (the remaining) cross-border barriers, such as frontier controls and different technical standards, should result in a reduction of costs, which can then be translated into either a widening of profit margins or a lowering of prices or a combination of both. The Cecchini study laid great emphasis on the scope for further economies of scale as learning economies. It referred to the minimum efficient technical scale (METS), and argued that in many sectors (including financial markets) the actual firm size is significantly smaller than the estimated METS (see European Economy, 1988, pp. 107–118). However, strong criticisms have been voiced about the benefits to be exploited from economies of scale and scope. The financial market is a multi-product industry segmented structurally, both from the demand and the supply sides. This may perhaps be one of the reasons why past researchers have found it difficult to find strong evidence of economies of scale and scope in the financial service sectors (see Centre for Business Strategy, 1989; Vives, 1991 and Chapter 5 later in this text which provides a detailed review of the scale and scope literature in banking markets).

Aims and Methodology of the Price Waterhouse/Cecchini Report

The main objective of the Price Waterhouse/Cecchini study was to estimate the economic impact of 1992 on the financial services sectors in eight EU countries (namely Belgium, France, Italy, Luxembourg, the Netherlands, Spain, UK and West Germany) under the assumption that the law of one price prevailed. In other words, the principal assumption was that after 1992 EU prices would settle at (or at least move towards) some uniform level for each financial product/service, thereby bringing about economic gains from EU integration.

The Price Waterhouse study, firstly, investigated in detail the economic dimensions of the three main financial service sectors — (i) banking and credit business, (ii) insurance business and (iii) brokerage and securities business — across the eight EU countries under study. The study then focused on comparative price differences (obtained mainly by field survey) of 16 financial products or services, spread over the banking and credit sectors, insurance and securities and brokerage sectors. This dataset was posited by Price Waterhouse to be broadly representative of three financial sectors and Table 2.4 illustrates the standard financial products and services they used in their analysis. From this 'standard' set of (16) financial products and services, prices were simulated to decrease to the average of the four lowest prices for each product/service. It is these hypothesised price falls that are the basis of the calculation of the economic gains from integration. These economic gains can be defined simply as the consumer surplus gains resulting from price falls generated by the hypothetical creation of a single market in financial services (see Table 2.5).

Results of the Price Waterhouse/Cecchini Report

The results of the economic analysis (published in detail in Price Waterhouse, 1988) show a broad indication of the kinds of competitive forces that may be released when the 1992 single market is completed. Table 2.6 presents the estimated price falls, hypothesised from completing the internal market, on the standard set of (16) financial products as reported by the Price Waterhouse study. The estimated gains from 1992 are shown in the corresponding differences between the prices in individual countries compared with the level at which overall prices are estimated to fall when the single market is completed. Although the data are not forecasts and have been estimated subject to strong assumptions, they represent a heroic attempt to suggest possible post-1992 developments.

The theoretical, potential price reductions presented in Table 2.6 show the different competitive conditions that exist in the three main financial service (banking, insurance and securities) sectors for eight countries. It can be seen that price falls for banking services are expected to be the largest in West Germany, Spain, France and the UK. Section 2 adjusts the theoretical potential price reduction to reflect more accurately expected price falls and indicates that price falls for financial services as a whole are expected to be the largest in Spain, Italy, France and Belgium. These estimated price falls appear to be the largest in countries that have historically been more heavily regulated and hence less competitive (see Molyneux, Lloyd-Williams and Thornton, 1994a).

Table 2.4 List of standard financial services or products surveyed

'Standard' service	Description of standard service
Banking services	
Commercial loans	Annual cost to a medium-size firm of a commercial loan of 250 000 ECUs. Measured as excess over inter-bank rates
Consumer credit	Annual cost of consumer loan of 500 ECUs. Excess interest rate over money-market rates
Credit cards	Annual cost assuming 500 ECU debit. Excess interest rate over money-market rates
Mortgage	Annual cost of home loan of 25 000 ECU. Excess interest rate over money-market rates
Commercial draft	Cost to a large commercial client of purchasing a commercial draft for 30 000 ECUs
Travellers' cheques	Cost for a private consumer of purchasing 100 ECUs worth of travellers' cheques
Current cheque account	Annual cost assuming 200 cheques p.a., 20 standing orders, 50 cash withdrawals, 20 credits
Letter of credit	Cost of letter of credit of 50 000 ECUs for three months
Insurance services	
Term insurance	Average annual cost of term insurance
Home insurance	Annual cost of fire and theft cover for house valued at 70 000 ECUs with 28 000 ECUs contents
Motor insurance	Annual cost of comprehensive insurance, 1.6 litre car, driver 10 years' experience, minimum no claims bonus
Commercial fire and theft	Annual cover for premises valued at 387 240 ECUs with stock and contents at 232 344 ECUs
Public liability cover	Annual premium for engineering company with 20 employees and annual turnover of 1.29 million ECUs. Includes employer liability cover
Brokerage services	
Private equity transactions	Commission costs of cash bargain of 1440 ECUs
Private gilts transactions	Commission costs of cash bargain of 14 000 ECUs
Institutional equity transactions	Commission costs of cash bargain of 288 000 ECUs
Institutions gilt transactions	Commission costs of cash bargain of 7.2m. ECUs

Source: Price Waterhouse (1988, Table 5.1, p. 15).

Table 2.5   Estimate of potential falls

	B	D	E	F	I	L	NL	UK
1. Theoretical, potential price reduction[a]								
Banking	15	33	34	25	18	16	10	18
Insurance	31	10	32	24	51	37	1	4
Securities	52	11	44	23	33	9	18	12
Total	23	25	34	24	29	17	9	13
2. Indicative price reduction[b]								
All financial services								
Range	6–16	5–15	16–26	7–17	9–19	3–13	0–9	2–12
Centre of range	11	10	21	12	14	8	4	7

[a]These data show the weighted averages of the theoretical potential falls of selected financial product prices.
[b]Indicative price falls are based upon a scaling down of the theoretical potential price reductions, taking into account roughly the extent to which perfectly competitive and integrated conditions will not be attained, plus other information for each financial services sub-sector, such as gross margins and administrative costs as a proportion of total costs.
B = Belgium, D = West Germany, E = Spain, F = France, I = Italy, L = Luxeinbourg, NL = Netherlands, UK = United Kingdom.
Source: European Economy (1988, Table 5.1.4, p. 91).

Table 2.6   Estimated gains resulting from the indicative price reductions for financial services (%)

	Average indicative price reduction (%)	Direct impact on value-added for financial services		Gain in consumer surplus as a result of average indicative price reduction[a]	
		million ECU	% of GDP	million ECU	% of GDP
B	11	656	0.6	685	0.7
D	10	4 442	0.5	4 619	0.6
E	21	2 925	1.4	3 189	1.5
F	12	3 513	0.5	3 683	0.5
I	14	3 780	0.7	3 996	0.7
L	8	43	1.2	44	1.2
NL	4	341	0.2	347	0.2
UK	7	4 917	0.8	5 051	0.8
EUR 8	10	20 617	0.7	21 614	0.7

[a]Based on the assumption that the elasticity of demand for financial services is 0.75.
B = Belgium, D = West Germany, E = Spain, F = France, I = Italy, L = Luxembourg, NL = Netherlands, UK = United Kingdom.
Source: European Economy (1988, Table 5.1.4, p. 91).

The price falls calculated by Price Waterhouse in Table 2.5 were then used to model the impact on value-added and the gains in consumer surplus that are hypothesised to result from the law of one price assumption. Table 2.6 indicates the results and shows that the largest gains in consumer surplus, as a proportion of GDP, accrue to Spain (1.5%), Luxembourg (1.2%) and the UK (0.8%). Overall, the gains in consumer surplus to the eight EC countries under study were estimated to amount, on average, to 0.7% of GDP.

Limitations of the Price Waterhouse/Cecchini Study

Various authors, such as Gardener and Teppett (1990, 1991), Neven (1990) and Vives (1991), have examined the Price Waterhouse findings and the impact of European integration on the competitive conditions in banking and financial markets. The estimated results of the Price Waterhouse study have been called both too low (Baldwin, 1989) and too high (Centre for Business Strategy, 1989). While it is agreed that there are different competitive conditions existing across EU banking systems and that the Price Waterhouse study was a useful exercise, there are reservations about the methodology and assumptions used in the overall analysis.

Pelkmans (1992) has pointed out that there are two main points which should be made. Firstly, the external dimension (the impact on the rest of the world economy) of 1992 was not discussed in the report. Secondly, whatever the biases that one may believe to find in the exercise, the report surely underestimates the gains by excluding certain aspects, such as the impact of integration on innovation (e.g. Geroski, 1988); the analysis of X-efficiencies in many services; and the incomplete coverage of the White Paper proposals concerning the removal of exchange controls and the proposals on property rights.

The microeconomic gains from completing the internal market are hypothesised to stimulate competition. They are also believed to incorporate cost reductions, increase efficiency in the financial sector industry, and promote a higher rate of financial innovation. These factors are then believed to have positive influences on important EU macroeconomic variables. This is an extremely positive picture of advantage for the single market programme. There is an important major scepticism, however, relating to the microeconomic methodology which is used to model these effects.

The microeconomic approach adapted to estimate the economic gains from the internal market was strongly influenced by the study of Venables and Smith (1986) which 'had the advantage, alongside their academic respectability, of producing comparatively high welfare gains' (Gardener and Teppett, 1991, p. 159). The marginal analysis adopted to evaluate the gains accruing to integration may be distorted, for instance, according to the relative speeds at which various countries adjust. For example, there is an implicit assumption in the analysis that price uniformity will be achieved by the establishment in high-price countries of institutions from low-price countries or by the delivery (offer) of cross-border services. This concept sounds straightforward and in full accord with economic theory, yet it begs many questions when one considers it as a practical process in the market.

Another criticism relating to the Price Waterhouse methodology focused on the role of economies of scale. The Centre for Business Strategy (1989) indicated that trade liberalisation of the type envisaged for 1992 had its primary effects on supply and not demand. This study cautioned that the scale economy argument was far from unambiguous, and they state (p. 104):

> It is puzzling that economies of scale are so widely touted as a source of competitive advantage when there is so little evidence of their significance.

They continue to argue:

> Successful operators in an integrated financial market will be those who correctly exploit the scale of scope economies that do exist without sacrificing the specialisation that can also be very important.

Moreover, the Centre for Business Strategy (1989) study was critical of Price Waterhouse for ignoring important factors such as consumer/customer behaviour, cultures, habits and strategic issues in their analysis. They also indicated that in the shorter term other major environmental factors (such as different legal, regulatory and fiscal systems) would thwart financial sector integration — especially in the retail and lower segments of the corporate banking market.

Focusing on the specific methodology, a major undesirable characteristic of the overall analysis relates to the strong 'upward bias' in the interpretation of economic gains. Gardener and Teppett (1991) imply the calculation of economic gains published in the report excludes the cases where prices of some financial products are hypothesised to rise. They argue that price rises for specific financial products suggest possible credit rationing and/or the existence of cross-subsidies. Under both of these scenarios, it is likely that price will rise under the law of one price assumption and 'ignoring these possible price rises, therefore, may be unrealistic unless a strong, rigorous case can be made for this approach' (p. 160). Llewellyn (1992) also noted that there are many factors other than lack of competition or financial regulation that might account for price differences. Price differentials may reflect the major differences in institutional structure rather than lack of competition, contestability or differences in basic efficiency. In this case, it could be misleading to associate differences in prices of individual products or services as evidence of the general lack of competition in certain markets, or to assume that competition would prove an equalisation of prices between EU member countries. Llewellyn (1992, p. 118) notes that:

> As there are also significant differences in prices for specific financial products within countries, it is unlikely the removal of regulatory and other imposed barriers would result in a single price throughout the EC.

The aforementioned author also argues that liberalisation does not necessarily increase competition enough to force price equalisation, and does not in itself guarantee that competitive conditions will be equalised between EU member states. Because of economic reasons such as entry cost and scale constraints, banking and financial markets could remain partially segmented (e.g. in the retail sector) without formal controls, regulation barriers, or imposed entry restrictions.

Gardener and Teppett (1991) also point out that the estimated economic gains are overstated because the findings downgrade estimates of the hypothesised losses in producers' surplus. A short-term fall in firms' profits could have more negative economic effects than were emphasised by the Price Waterhouse findings. For example, the calculation of economic gains may be strongly influenced by the issue of corresponding producer losses. While price decreases obviously increase consumer surplus gains, they have a corresponding negative impact on producer surpluses. The rationale for this, as indicated by Gardener and Teppett (1991, pp. 116–117), is that:

> ... producers may experience internal economies of scale leading both to inefficient small-scale production when the market is restricted within national boundaries, and to an oligopolistic market structure. Within a non-integrated Europe, therefore, average costs are unnecessarily high; the mark-up of prices over marginal costs is also higher than necessary to cover fixed costs. This economic perspective suggests the consequences of opening up trade are: (1) to lower unit costs by facilitating more use of the economies of scale, (2) and (probably) lower the mark-up of prices over marginal costs to the extent that oligopoly is weakened. Whilst the consumer will gain (increased consumer surplus); there will also be reductions in excess profits (reduced producer surplus).

McDonald (1992) summarises the criticisms of the Price Waterhouse analysis under three main headings: (i) the assumption that the legislative programme would not be completed before 1 January 1993; (ii) inadequacies in the legislative programme; (iii) the view that the non-tariff barriers are the main obstacles to free movement. The report has been also criticised because it ignored other certain key factors, such as the effects on member states and the effects resulting from the redistribution of income.

Despite the above limitations and the major data problems associated with such an analysis, the Price Waterhouse study was an heroic attempt to include both international trade theory with industrial organisations theory, in a static framework, to provide us with the first step towards attempting to evaluate the benefits and costs of financial sector integration.

THE PROBLEMS OF CREATING THE SINGLE MARKET

It has been recognised that it is important to view the single market programme as a dynamic process. It is also an incomplete process that requires constant surveillance and revision. In the evaluation of the single market the EU needs not only to fill in the gaps in the original programme but also to establish new rules where they are needed. Turner (1994, p. 9) has indicated that 'despite the deadline being reached, the Internal Market has yet to be fully implemented'.

The Commission of the European Community noted that there has been much intensified progress in the march towards a single market in Europe. Over 90% of the measures for eliminating borders have already been adopted by the Community institutions, and 75% have been transposed into national law of the EU member states. However, the expectation of the business community is that there is still important work to be done to capture the full potential of the single market. Vesala (1993) has noted that certain legal discrepancies remain within the single market area that potentially distort the establishment of financial institutions and emerging trade flows in banking services. The most important differences relate to the following areas:

- reserve requirements;
- taxation;
- freedom for member states to alter EU legislation when incorporated in national law or/and use the 'general good' opt-out to avoid implementation of EU laws.

Vesala (1993) has noted that different reserve requirements of various EU banks' systems has a distorting effect on banking competition within these countries. Reserve requirements may result in a 'regulatory gap' due to an existence of reserve-exempt offshore markets, for example Eurocurrency markets in wholesale banking. Distortions in reserve requirements across countries can also act as a tax on high reserve requirement banking systems and they will also create competitive anomalies within the EU.

Taxation is another important area where the lack of harmonisation distorts competition within the EU. Molyneux (1993) has pointed out that there are two main types of tax obstacles which have traditionally stood in the way of the cross-border provision of financial services and which are unaffected by the EU single market directives:

1. Tax provisions which directly affect 'foreign' EU financial firms providing cross-border services in another EU country. A clear example is the withholding tax. Withholding tax applied to interest paid to the domestic lender will be fully set off against the corporation tax paid by the domestic lender on its profit margin (and any excess withholding tax refunded). In the case of the foreign lender, withholding tax is a final, non-refundable tax.
2. Tax measures which are not specifically imposed on foreign EU financial institutions but make it more costly for domestic customers to do business with foreign EU firms.

Dassesse (1993) indicated some important examples which are as follows:

- non-availability of tax relief or interest subsidy on mortgage capital on interest repayments, if the lender is based outside the jurisdiction;

- provisions whereby interest paid by local corporate borrowers to a foreign bank will not be treated as tax-deductible expenses if it exceeds a certain ceiling, whereas no such ceiling is applicable when the interest is paid to a local branch;

- non-deductibility for income tax (or as the case may be, corporation tax) purposes of life insurance or group insurance contributions if paid to a firm established outside the member state of the individual or company concerned;

- provisions whereby personal pension plans benefit from tax rebates on the condition that the plans are invested, at least for a minimum proportion, in local bonds and shares. This would exclude, for example, shares in mutual funds licensed in other member states under the 1985 UCITs Directive.

The above, by no means exhaustive, list indicates the tax disadvantages that EU financial firms may come up against by undertaking business cross-border. The situation is unlikely to alter enormously in the future given that member states jealously guard their rights on tax policy and any attempts to achieve wider coordination of EU tax laws would be highly problematic (Commission of the European Communities, 1991). The EU Court appears to be sensitive to this risk and generally has been unwilling to find that it contravenes EU law for a tax system to discriminate against financial products supplied by foreign firms. Two recent rulings, however, have clouded the picture regarding the EU Court's stance on national autonomy in taxation matters. (The first was the European Court of Justice ruling on *Bachmann* v. *Belgium Tax Authorities*, Case 209/90, 28 January 1992. The second was the European Court of Justice ruling on *Commerzbank* v. *UK Inland Revenue*, Case 330/91, 13 July 1993.)

There is also significant freedom for national governments to act in derogation of the EU single market by using the concept of the 'general good' opt-out allowed to member states. The European Court of Justice has resolved conflicts between EU and national laws intended to protect consumers of goods with the help of provisions in the Treaty of Rome which make exceptions to the principle of free movement of goods for reasons of public morality, public policy, public security or protection of health. In cases regarding the freedom to provide services the Court has used the related concept of the 'general good'. The European Court's rulings in such cases have been studied in detail by Katz (1992) who shows that host state 'general good' exceptions to the freedom to provide services have been justified when they are:

- not related to areas of law already harmonised by the EU;

- not duplicative of laws already applied by home states;

- applicable without discrimination to all persons and undertakings in the host country;

- necessary to protect the interest at stake and proportional to the protection of that interest.

Molyneux (1993) notes that the above suggests that EU member states have been left an easy protectionist tool to assert national law over EU legislation in order to protect the so-called 'general good'. In addition, the aforementioned study also finds that as well as differences in tax treatment of financial firms and products across EU member countries and the opportunity to opt out of EU legislation there is also the potential for different national implementation of EU directives. This may also provide state authorities with an additional degree of autonomy. Given differences in reserve requirements, tax treatments, cross-border payments systems and the flexibility to incorporate EU law into national legislation, it is unlikely that we will ever achieve a perfect single market in financial services. The internal market programme, however, has gone a long way towards harmonising market regulations and implementing minimum standards which should help to provide a more competitive environment and efficient banking and financial system across the EU.

CONCLUSION

The single market programme has substantially changed the regulatory environment for financial institutions operating within the EU. The major features of change relate to the liberalisation of cross-border trade of banking and financial services and the right to establishment of EU financial institutions in other EU member states. The level of harmonisation of rules has advanced substantially since the 1985 White Paper although there are still some areas which require further legislation. The completion of the European-wide frontier-free market on 1 January 1993 and the improvements in its operation are envisaged to allow banks to benefit from economies of scale and scope. The analysis of the Price Waterhouse report has illustrated that different competitive conditions exist across European banking and financial markets and that consumer surplus gains resulting from the 1992 integration process would be substantial, although more recent studies have shown that these economic gains may be overstated. The cost implications resulting from the completion of the single European market are important to the efficiency outcomes generated by the breakdown in cross-border barriers in EU financial sectors. This clearly provides us with an important justification as to why it is useful to analyse economies of scale and scope across European banking markets.

It should be noted, however, that there are still major obstacles to the provision of a single banking market throughout the EU. Overall, it appears that some of the important barriers to trade in banking services lie not so much in overt, discriminatory rules and regulations, but rather in national practices that are not applied equally to both domestic and foreign-controlled banks.

3

Recent changes and structural developments in European banking systems

INTRODUCTION

For the past decade or more, EU governments (and indeed many others outside the EU area) have sought to continue economic reforms based on the proposition that open and efficient markets for goods and services, exposed to domestic and international competition, provide the crucial underpinnings for dynamic, high income economies. The agenda for reform of financial systems that emerges from this proposition is a many faceted one, ranging over such areas as: freeing up international trade in goods and services as well as capital flows; introducing competition into previously segmented and regulated sectors — not least those dominated directly by governments; liberalising financial markets both domestically and internationally; reducing distortions to saving and investment, and improving the overall efficiency of financial systems. The political and economic agenda throughout Europe in recent years has been marked by many of the above forces. The aim of this chapter is to outline the major forces of change and to show how they have impacted on European banking markets.

AN OVERVIEW OF THE GENERAL MACROECONOMIC ENVIRONMENT IN THE EU

In 1993, the output in the EU declined by about a quarter of a percentage point in real terms, only the second time in the 35-year history of the EU that a real decline in GDP (see Table 3.1) was generated (see European Economy, 1994, p. 7). Moreover, employment declined by a record amount — 2.4 million jobs lost in the course of the year — and unemployment rose at a fast pace,

Table 3.1 Growth of real GDP (percentage changes from previous period)

	1988	1989	1990	1991	1992	1993	1994[a]	1995[a]
United States	3.9	2.5	1.2	−0.7	2.6	3.0	4.0	3.0
Japan	6.2	4.7	4.8	4.3	1.1	0.1	0.8	2.7
Germany	3.7	3.6	5.7	4.5	2.1	−1.3	1.8	2.6
France	4.5	4.3	2.5	0.8	1.2	−0.9	1.8	2.9
Italy	4.1	2.9	2.1	1.2	0.7	−0.7	1.5	2.6
United Kingdom	5.0	2.2	0.4	−2.2	−0.6	1.9	2.8	3.2
Canada	5.0	2.4	−0.2	−1.7	0.7	2.4	3.7	4.3
Spain	5.2	4.7	3.6	2.2	0.8	−1.0	1.2	2.7
Total OECD	4.4	3.3	2.5	0.8	1.7	1.2	2.6	2.9
OECD Europe	4.1	3.5	3.2	1.3	1.1	−0.2	1.9	2.8
EU	4.2	3.5	3.0	1.5	1.0	−0.4	1.9	2.8

[a]Projections.
Source: Adapted from OECD (1994, p. A4).

reaching a level of 10.9% of the civilian labour force. However, most member countries showed a stagnating or falling GDP with the exception of the UK, which started to emerge from a very severe recession, as well as Ireland, Luxembourg and the Netherlands (although not shown in Table 3.1). The most significant declines resulted in the western part of Germany (−1.3%). In addition, substantial falls in output (about 1%) also occurred in France and Spain, while in Italy the contraction was about a quarter to half a percentage point. Positive rates of growth (about 2%) were registered in the UK, where the recovery took hold firmly (see European Economy, 1994, p. 8).

Unemployment has been a particularly severe problem in the EU countries (Table 3.2). This is due both to the severity of the decrease in economic activity and to the fact that employment trends have become more responsive to the economic cycle (see European Economy, 1994, p. 10). In contrast to the early 1980s unemployment is now increasingly dominated by prime age (25- to 45-year-old) male workers (see BIS, 1994, p. 17), while female workers have generally found it easier to obtain jobs in the services sector, although in many cases as involuntary part-time workers.

Against the backdrop of economic recession and record levels of unemployment, public finances in many EU countries have significantly worsened in recent years. In particular the gross public debt/GDP ratio has increased in the main economies during recent years as shown in Table 3.3. The table also illustrates the large level of outstanding government debt in Italy compared with Germany, France and Spain. This has implications for the financial sector because in Italy the government has traditionally relied heavily on the banking sector to finance its deficits by holding government bonds. With increasingly liberalised and deregulated markets, banks find it less attractive to hold substantial government bonds, thus the financing of fiscal deficits becomes more problematic. This is one reason

Table 3.2 Unemployment rates (% of total labour force)

	1988	1989	1990	1991	1992	1993
United States	5.5	5.3	5.5	6.7	7.4	6.8
Japan	2.5	2.3	2.1	2.1	2.2	2.5
Germany	7.6	6.9	6.2	6.7	7.7	8.9
France	10.0	9.4	8.9	9.5	10.4	11.7
Italy	12.1	12.1	11.5	11.0	11.6	10.4
United Kingdom	8.2	6.2	5.9	8.3	10.0	10.3
Canada	7.8	7.5	8.1	10.3	11.3	11.2
Spain	19.5	17.3	16.3	16.3	18.4	22.7
Total OECD	6.9	6.4	6.3	7.0	7.8	8.2
OECD Europe	9.3	8.6	8.1	8.6	9.6	10.7
EU	10.3	9.3	8.7	9.2	10.3	11.3
(Millions)						
North America	7.7	7.5	8.0	9.9	10.9	10.3
OECD Europe	16.8	15.5	14.8	16.5	18.5	20.4
EU	14.8	13.5	12.8	14.3	16.0	17.4
Total OECD	26.7	25.1	14.8	28.7	31.9	33.5

Source: Adapted from OECD (1994, p. A23).

Table 3.3 Gross public debt[a] (as % of nominal GDP)

	1988	1989	1990	1991	1992	1993
United States	52.7	53.2	55.4	58.9	62.0	63.9
Japan	70.6	70.6	69.8	67.7	71.1	74.7
Germany	43.2	43.2	44.0	41.7	44.4	48.5
France	40.6	40.6	40.2	41.2	45.5	52.5
Italy	97.9	97.9	100.5	103.8	108.3	113.9
United Kingdom	36.7	36.7	34.6	35.4	40.6	46.5
Canada	69.8	69.8	72.5	80.0	87.5	92.3
Spain	47.4	48.4	48.7	50.0	53.2	59.1
Total OECD	58.1	57.6	58.4	60.1	63.7	67.4
Europe	57.9	57.1	57.2	58.0	62.0	67.4

[a]Refers to general government debt. It should be noted that the definition of debt applied under the Maastricht Treaty differs from the national accounts definitions used by the OECD.

why the Italian and other governments have resorted to widespread privatisation programmes in the financial and non-financial sectors to help reduce pressures on public finances (see IMI, 1994). The rapid growth in government debt combined with the substantial future pressure on government expenditure due to ageing populations has also dominated the debate about the appropriate fiscal policy stance of European governments. The BIS (1994) noted that the effectiveness of fiscal policy as an instrument to stabilise the economy has been in serious doubt since attempts at fiscal stimulus in the 1970s and early 1980s helped fuel inflation and generated rising debt/GDP ratios. It is also pointed out that high government debt has been associated with a fall in worldwide saving, increasing real interest rates, the crowding-out of interest-sensitive private investment projects and a slowing growth.

Dornbush (1991) has noted that the debt issue has resulted in two major reform policies. Firstly, increased government indebtness has reduced the exchange-risk premia that there were in real interest rates, and secondly it has forced governments to reduce budget deficits. These two policies, Dornbush argues, are strongly complementary. Recent evidence illustrates the pressure on public indebtedness. For example, in 1993, none of the EU member countries could significantly reduce their budget deficits (general government net borrowing, national accounts definition which includes central government, regional and local authorities and social security) as a percentage of GDP, due to the widespread heavy recession. Germany, Spain and France (as well as Denmark, Greece, Portugal and the UK) recorded considerable rises in their deficits (see Table 3.4). In Italy the deficit was contained by rigorous fiscal measures, whereas some member states, for example France (and the UK and Denmark), took discretionary action to support demand (see European Economy, 1994, p. 20).

As European governments have borrowed so have their households. For example, during the 1970s and 1980s, while household savings rates decreased or remained relatively stable, the real stock of consumer credit increased rapidly and the ratio of consumer debt to income rose in most major industrial countries. For

Table 3.4 General government primary balance/general government net borrowing

	General government primary balance (excluding interest payments)			General government net borrowing		
	1991	1992	1993	1991	1992	1993
Belgium	3.9	4.3	3.7	−6.8[a]	−7.1[a]	−7.0[a]
Denmark	5.1	4.2	3.1	−2.2	−2.6	−4.4
Germany	−0.5	0.7	0.1	−3.2	−2.6	−3.3[a]
Greece	−3.5	0.4	−0.5	−16.3	−13.2	−15.5
Spain	−1.2	−0.4	−2.2	−5.2	−4.6	−7.2
France	1.0	−0.5	−2.2	−2.1	−3.8[a]	−5.5[a]
Ireland	5.6	4.9	4.2	−2.0	−2.3[a]	−2.3[a]
Italy	0.0	1.9	2.0	−10.2	−9.5	−9.4[a]
Luxembourg	−0.4	−1.9	−1.7	−1.0	−2.5	−2.5
Netherlands	3.6	2.7	2.3	−2.5	−3.5	−4.0
Portugal	1.7	4.3	−0.4	−6.6[a]	−3.3[a]	−7.1[a]
United Kingdom	0.3	−3.0	−4.5	−2.7	−6.3[a]	−7.6[a]
EU	0.4	0.4	−0.9	−4.6	−5.0	−6.0[a]

[a]European Commission estimates of November 1993 except for the figures marked where more recent information has been included.
Source: European Economy (1994, p. 22).

instance, between 1980 and 1989 'total consumer credit in the United Kingdom increased from 4.75 per cent of GDP to 9 per cent, while in France loans to households by financial institutions, excluding real estate lending, rose from 2.25 per cent of GNP to 6 per cent' (IMF, 1991, p. 109). In the 1990s, although household sectors were generally net creditors to other sectors, financial stress has emerged in various cases where parts of the household sector have significantly increased their debt-to-income ratios (see OECD, 1993, p. 26). By the early 1990s household debt ratios remained well above their early 1980s levels. The increased indebtedness of consumers could be partially explained by the fact that household financial assets were growing faster than liabilities in the major European economies (during the early 1980s at least) and this trend, together with the increasingly more sophisticated demands of the retail bank customer and the change in individuals' attitudes towards debt, have been important forces creating change in retail banking markets throughout Europe.

Closely related to the increased build-up of debt have been the substantial changes in national savings and investment rates. National savings and investment rates in most European countries were generally lower in the 1980s than in the 1970s although inter-country differences have remained large (Dean et al., 1990). Table 3.5 illustrates that a fall in net national saving between 1970–79 and 1980–89 is evident in all the major industrial countries, with the largest fall in France (8.1 percentage points). The average decrease for the seven countries as a whole was 3.75 percentage points (see Hutchison, 1992, p. 9). It is clear from this table that there was a continually wide variation of the level of national saving across countries. Out of the European countries shown in Table 3.5, savings levels are substantially higher in Italy, France and Germany than in the UK. This is not only apparent in net national saving but also in household savings rates. Various studies have examined the reasons for cross-country differences in savings rates (see Hayashi, Ito and Slemrad, 1988; Kaufman, 1991; Arrelli and Micossi, 1992). In the case of Italy, Rossi and Visco (1992) argue that it has been the relatively underdeveloped nature of its capital market and financial system which has encouraged high levels of savings although household savings rates have fallen substantially between 1985 and 1993. A recent report by the Deutsche Bundesbank (1993) argues that the high level of German household savings is mainly attributable to the country's strong economic performance. The same article also notes that savings in the new eastern Germany, despite the much lower levels of disposable income (around 45% of western German disposable income in 1993) are surprisingly similar to those in the western part of the country. A high savings level, with substantial investment income resulting, helps boost the level of financial assets available for intermediation and/or other forms of investment in the economy. Having said this, recent studies have shown that despite the broad array of investment opportunities available to European investors, the bulk of household financial assets are still intermediated through the banking system, although insurance companies, pension funds and unit trusts

Table 3.5 National savings rates in major industrial countries

Countries and periods	Gross national savings[a]	Net national saving	of which				Memo: general govern- ment net lending[a]
			Public[b]	Private			
				Total	House- holds	Business enterprises[c]	
			as a percentage of national income				
USA							
1970−79	19.4	9.1	−1.2	10.3	7.6	2.6	−1.2
1980−89	16.3	4.0	−3.8	7.8	6.0	1.9	−3.4
Japan							
1970−79	35.3	25.6	5.0	20.6	16.5	4.1	−1.7
1980−89	31.6	20.9	5.1	15.7	13.1	2.6	−1.4
Germany							
1970−79	24.3	15.2	3.7	11.5	9.7	1.7	−1.7
1980−89	22.5	11.6	1.5	10.1	8.9	1.2	−2.0
France[d]							
1970−79	25.8	17.0	2.7	14.4	11.9	2.5	−0.4
1980−89	20.4	8.9	−0.4	9.3	7.9	1.4	−2.1
UK							
1970−79	17.9	8.3	1.4	6.8	4.3	2.5	−2.6
1980−89	16.6	5.5	−0.8	6.3	3.7	2.6	−2.4
Italy							
1970−79	25.9	16.2	−5.2	21.4	21.3	0.1	−7.0
1980−89	21.9	11.0	−7.7	18.7	15.9	2.8	−11.1
Canada							
1970−79	22.9	13.1	1.4	11.7	6.0	5.6	−0.9
1980−89	20.7	9.9	−3.4	13.3	9.2	4.2	−4.8
Average[e]							
1970−79	23.4	13.6	0.8	12.8	10.1	2.7	1.7
1980−89	21.5	10.0	−0.9	10.9	8.8	2.1	3.2

[a] As a percentage of GNP.
[b] General government.
[c] Includes public enterprises.
[d] Based on the old system of national accounts.
[e] Calculated using GDP weights and exchange rates in 1975 for the 1970−79 period and in 1988 for the 1980−89 period.
Source: Adapted from Hutchison (1992, p. 9).

are playing an increasingly important role especially in the 1990s (for example Revell, 1994b). This trend is shown in Table 3.6 which illustrates the propensity of households to intermediate through institutional investments has grown in all the major economies, although the importance of institutional investments is markedly less in Italy compared with the other countries.

Gardener and Molyneux (1990), among others, have indicated that the macroeconomic climate experienced by European banks throughout the 1970s

Table 3.6 The growth of institutional investors

| | Financial assets as percentages of household financial assets | | | | | | | | |
| | Pension funds and life insurance | | | Collective investment institutions | | | Total | | |
	1980	1985	1990	1980	1985	1990	1980	1985	1990
France	8.0	11.2	14.7	2.7	12.4	21.7	10.6	23.6	36.3
Germany	19.4	24.2	27.1	3.2	4.8	8.1	22.6	29.0	35.1
Italy	1.6	0.9	3.2	na	2.1	2.9	na	2.9	6.1
United Kingdom	39.9	49.9	53.7	1.6	3.1	4.9	41.5	53.1	58.6
United States	17.8	21.1	23.5	2.2	5.0	7.7	20.0	26.0	31.2
Japan	13.8	16.6	20.8	1.8	3.6	5.6	15.6	20.2	26.4
Canada	19.4	23.3	26.7	1.0	1.6	3.0	20.4	24.9	29.7

Notes:
1. Figures for Italy (book value) and UK refer to total assets.
2. 1989 figures are used in 1990 column for UK and Italy.
Source: Bank for International Settlements, *Annual Report 1991/92*, p. 194.

and 1980s has been of a much more volatile nature than that characterised by the economic environment of the 1950s and 1960s. The increased variability of all macroeconomic variables such as interest rates, exchange rates, budget deficits and surpluses has resulted in a much more uncertain environment. The degree of uncertainty and inability of the banks to plan for cyclical downturns has been reflected in the performance of European banks in recent years during recessionary periods.

After interest rates increased in late 1988 and early 1989, Europe went into recession, and the cost to the banking sector became apparent through extensive bad debts. The main impact of this recessionary period on the banking system, argue Morgan Stanley (1994a), has been that European banking systems have become driven more by profitability than by size. (This shift from a preoccupation with size to one of profitability has been observed by various commentators since the early 1990s, although a notable exception includes the French state-owned bank, Crédit Lyonnais, which adopted an (unsuccessful) expansionary programme over this period.) By early 1994 European banks were operating under a favourable environment with low interest and inflation rates. Morgan Stanley (1994a, p. 1) argue that this new operating environment has been characterised by the following:

- A de-emphasis on lending and banks have competed aggressively to retain core deposits. The overall impact has been that fee and commission income has become increasingly important for banks' earning capacities.

- The retail market has become driven increasingly by savings products, with mortgages the principal source of loan growth.

- An increasing proportion of income has and will continue to be obtained from trading activities.

- The financial services sector as a whole has become more efficient resulting from investment in technology, but this has generated substantial job losses (they forecast that up to 250 000 jobs will be lost in the European banking industry up to the year 2000).

- Since the early 1990s managements have become more focused on cost and profitability than purely on size and market share.

- Capital standards have improved, resulting from the changed (and changing) nature of business.

- The role of the state has fallen and will continue to diminish, particularly in the ownership of the banking industry.

In addition to the above trends it is also important to note that demarcation lines between particular markets, intermediaries and lines of business have also been rapidly eroding. The blurring of distinctions between bank credit and securities, domestic and international paper, cash and derivatives products has helped to foster the integration of cross-border investment. The implication of the EU Second Banking Directive in domestic banking legislation has also had the effect of establishing universal banking practice for credit institutions within EU countries, rendering the old distinctions between different types of credit institutions obsolete.

A SHORT HISTORY OF BANKING IN EUROPE

History shapes where we are today and as such it is important to provide a brief history of European banking to illustrate how various systems have developed. The historical development of European countries' banking and financial systems has been moulded by a wide range of diverse socio-economic, political and geographical factors. Nevertheless, it is possible to identify various broad banking trends that have been experienced in many of the industrialised European countries since the seventeenth century.

During the seventeenth and eighteenth centuries all European banking systems were unit-based. Banks were predominantly small private institutions that specialised in serving the needs of local markets. A small proportion of these banks were engaged in financing international trade and these tended to be based in the main financial centres. Revell (1987, pp. 17–18) identified that by the first half of the nineteenth century banking systems were characterised by two main banking groups; those based in large towns financing both domestic and international trade and those groups dispersed throughout the country financing local industry, which was predominantly agricultural. Kindleberger (1984, p. 73) argues that, even by this stage, in many cases banking business was no more than an additional activity undertaken by goldsmiths, merchants, notaries, industrialists and tax farmers.

As the Industrial Revolution gained momentum it encouraged the establishment of new, large, joint-stock banks based in metropolitan areas. These banks competed with the unit banks which were country-based as well as with a whole range of (mainly) newly established mutual bodies such as savings banks, building societies, cooperatives, agricultural credit associations and the like. The private country banks gradually declined in numbers, partially because the larger metropolitan joint-stock banks acquired them, and also as a result of the desire of the larger banks to establish substantial branch networks. As industry began to spread to new areas and also became more concentrated, banks increased their geographical coverage through branching and also grew in size so as to provide the funds required by their large industrial customers. In the last quarter of the nineteenth century nationwide branch networks were created by the large banks in most European countries.

Kindleberger (1984) identified the nineteenth century as also witnessing the rise of 'single financial centres', such as London and Paris, which tended to dominate national finance. The same process was at work in countries like Germany and Italy where 'political unification came later'. It was in these centres that groups of dominant or 'core banks' were based:

> Between about 1880 and 1920 there appeared in all countries a recognisable group of dominant or 'core' banks, recognised both by the authorities and by the general public. They were referred to popularly as the Big Three, the Big Five, or whatever the number may have been (Revell, 1987, p. 21).

As the branch networks of the larger banks became dominant at the turn of the century, there were two main factors that restricted their growth. Firstly, there had been a trend in various Continental European countries, like France, for the local and regional banks to create groups that could compete effectively with the larger national banks in their own region. Secondly, political factors in various countries sought to encourage (protect) competition between regional and national banks. In those countries with Federal governments, like Germany and Switzerland, regional institutions will play a more important role. It is still the case that, until recently, in countries such as France, Italy and Spain banks registered at a local, regional and national level. In addition, branching restrictions that remained in many European countries until the 1960s also helped to preserve the status of various regional and local institutions.

Throughout the nineteenth and early twentieth centuries the relationship between banking and commerce differed substantially from country to country. In the UK banks mainly financed trade, and most industrial finance came via the capital markets or from internal funding. Occasionally UK banks undertook industrial lending but only on a short-term basis. In contrast, Continental banks fostered much closer relations with industry. Kindleberger (1984) notes that industrial banking began in Belgium in the second quarter of the nineteenth century. Banks in Germany, Austria, Sweden and, until the 1930s, in Italy formed the closest links with industry. The twentieth century has witnessed the polarisation of many of these trends. Banking markets have become more concentrated, sectoral ownership has continued to change and universal-type banking is becoming the 'norm' rather than the exception.

STRUCTURAL DIFFERENCES BETWEEN EUROPEAN BANKING SYSTEMS

The study of structural development in European banking markets involves an examination of the changes in the size, numbers and comparative significance of banks and other financial institutions within a financial system as well as embracing those institutional changes which alter the ways in which financial services are demanded, used, developed and delivered. Although every European banking system has its distinguishing features, there are various characteristics that help to distinguish Continental banking systems from those based on the

British model. Revell (1987) identified five common elements of Continental banking systems:

1. the presence of various special credit institutions which are usually publicly owned and provide funds for various sectors such as industry, agriculture and property;

2. the increased importance of savings banks, cooperative (popular) banks and cooperative credit associations, together with their central institutions;

3. a long history of commercial banks' participation in the ownership and management of industrial enterprises, 'relics of which still linger on';

4. the importance in many European countries of banks and other institutions which are organised on a local or regional basis, 'usually reflecting the prevalence of small enterprises in both industry and agriculture';

5. a degree of similarity between the new banking laws that were enacted in many countries following the crisis during the early 1930s.

Sometimes a distinction is made between the role that commercial banks in different countries play in financing industry. Some commentators (Frazer and Vittas, 1984; Rybczynski, 1984, 1988) distinguish between bank-based systems, such as those found in Germany, France, the Netherlands and Sweden, and market-based systems such as those found in the UK (and the United States). In the former group of countries, commercial banks have traditionally been strongly orientated towards the corporate sector, and this has provided opportunities for public sector and mutual institutions to adopt a more significant role within the banking system, through concentrating their business on the retail customer and small to medium corporate clients.

Frazer and Vittas (1984) explain that commercial banks in Germany, the Netherlands and Sweden made a concerted effort to improve their standing in the retail banking market from the late 1950s onwards. They also found that during the 1960s similar developments took place in northern and central European banking systems. This they have termed as the 'start of the retail banking revolution'. Changes in the competitive environment for retail banking took longer to emerge in southern Europe (because of regulatory constraints and low standards of living) and in the UK (where there was less incentive for the clearing banks to move into retail banking business).

An indication of the divergent sectoral ownership characteristics in European banking can be seen from Table 3.7(a). This table illustrates the relative importance of private, public, mutual and foreign banks in various banking systems. The table is now somewhat dated and one would probably expect to see a decline in the relative importance of state banking at the expense of the private sector. (Note, however, that the opposite is the case for all Scandinavian markets, apart from Denmark, where large chunks of the system have been nationalised because of a systemic crisis and bank failure in the early 1990s.)

Table 3.7(a) Summary of sector ownership of European banking institutions, 1988 (% of aggregate total assets)

Country	Private	Public (central and local government)	Mutual	Foreign
Austria	0.4	43.8	55.8	—
Belgium	37.0	16.8	11.0	35.2
Denmark[a]	69.5	1.3	29.2	—
Finland	44.5	10.5	44.2	0.8
France	24.2	42.2	20.2	13.5
Germany	32.0	49.5	16.7	1.8[b]
Greece[c]	11.0	83.7	—	5.3
Ireland	61.7	4.0	12.9	21.4
Italy	12.3	67.9	16.8	3.0
Netherlands	61.2	8.1	17.7	13.0
Norway	41.2	19.9	38.9	—
Portugal	6.8	87.1	1.9	4.2
Spain	49.0	2.3	37.7	11.0
Sweden	52.9	19.3	24.9	2.9
Switzerland	53.4	19.6	15.8	11.2
United Kingdom	31.8	1.0	14.0	53.3

[a]Figures for percentage of total deposits.
[b]Branches of foreign banks.
[c]Figures for percentage of total credit.
Source: Gardener and Molyneux (1990).

STRUCTURAL DEVELOPMENTS

The trends of the 1980s, notably liberalisation, deregulation, innovation, internationalisation, institutional change and technological development, have left their marks on the financial services sectors in the EU. The structure of the EU banking industry has altered during the 1980s mostly as a reaction to domestic deregulation processes and in anticipation of EU-wide regulatory changes as illustrated in Chapter 2. Gual and Neven (1993) have pointed out that both structural and conduct deregulation have had a significant impact on the structure of the industry:

1. Structural deregulation has stimulated changes by reducing entry barriers (both for domestic and foreign competitors). In addition, structural changes have generated the reduction of functional separation and the elimination of the compulsory specialisation of banking institutions. These developments have stimulated entry by many institutions on lines of business in which they could not previously compete.

2. Conduct deregulation and the prospect of increased competition has had an indirect effect on market structure, to the extent that these changes have led to increased rivalry and lower profitability. That is, through the link of conduct, the performance of institutions in a particular market is tied to the structure of that market.

(The above distinction between structural and conduct deregulation, however, may be problematic because it is often difficult to separate the way a market is organised from the behaviour of firms within the market. For example, if there are only a few firms in a market they may be able to persuade the authorities that self-regulation is optimal, which in turn, will influence future conduct and organisation.)

Gardener and Molyneux (1990, p. 32) have shown that every banking market in Europe has a group of dominant or 'core banks' which are recognised by both the authorities and the general public. In most European banking markets, there has been a trend, however, for local and regional based banks to form groups that could effectively compete against the national 'core' banks. Those countries with a large number of mutual and cooperative banks, for instance France, Germany, Italy and Spain, tended to have a stronger regional focus than countries which have a small number of relatively large private banks. The strength of the mutual banks within the EU can be identified if we consider the various changes in structural characteristics shown in Table 3.7(b). In most countries it can be seen that the total number of banks declined between 1987 and 1992. The sharp decline in France was a result of the halving of the number of savings banks from 364 to 186 (between 1987 and 1990), reflecting the strong consolidation movement in this sector at that time (see Banque de France, 1992, p. 49). There was a more modest decline in the number of banks in Italy over the period, mainly resulting from the fall in the number of state commercial banks and cooperative and rural banks through merger. Again the decline in the number of banks in Spain was most notable in the cooperative bank sector, as well as for savings banks. Clearly in most banking systems there has been a fall in the number of mutual banks in each system apart from in Germany.

Despite a fall in the number of banks in almost all European systems between 1987 and 1992 the number of bank branches appeared to increase during the period apart from in the UK. In Germany, between 1987 and 1990 the number of branches increased by a staggering 16 000 or so, by nearly 3000 in Italy and over 2000 in Spain. In France, the expansion of branch numbers was not so impressive compared with other banking markets. The main motive for the expansion of branch networks in Germany and Spain perhaps was to enable banks to compete for market share (a form of non-price competition). In Italy, branching restrictions had been removed in 1989 and this subsequently led to an increase in branch networks as market forces took over. This is particularly noticeable for the commercial banks which witnessed a doubling of branches between 1990 and 1992.

Finally, Table 3.7(b) reveals some interesting features about deposit market share during the late 1980s. Commercial banks' share of non-bank deposits fell in all the countries under study apart from in Germany where the share of this sector grew by 3.7% to 39.7% by 1990. German commercial banks increased their market share of households' deposits at the expense of the cooperative

Table 3.7(b) Institutional, framework in banking markets of selected EU countries 1987, 1990 and 1992

Country	No. of banks			No. of branches			Market share (as % of deposits by the non-bank public)	
	1987	1990	1992	1987	1990	1992	1987	1990
Belgium								
Commercial banks	86	87	93	3 631	3 592	3 515	67.54	64.30
Savings banks	32	28	28	19 804	14 797	12 890	6.58	8.10
Public credit institutions	3	6	6	—	—	—	15.00	17.30
Post Office	1	1	1	—	—	—	10.88	10.30
Total	122	122	128	23 435	18 389	16 405	100.0	100.0
Denmark[a]								
Commercial banks	84	89	113	2 114	2 884	2 467	na	92.20
Savings banks	143	na		1 327	na	na	na	na
Cooperative banks	36	33		93	na	na	na	0.40
Post Office	1	1		1 293	1 317	na	na	7.40
Total	264	223		4 827	4 201	na	na	100.0
France								
Commercial banks	377	419	448	9 939	10 212	12 197	na	53.60
Savings banks	364	186	180	4 378	4 307	4 205	na	3.40
Cooperative and rural banks[b]	190	194	na	11 175	11 125	na	na	30.10
Post Office	1	1	1	17 089	16 967	na	na	12.90
Total	932	800	629	42 581	42 611	na	na	100.0
Germany								
Commercial banks[c]	331	415	416	6 643	7 186	7 696	36.00	39.70
Savings banks	598	781	691	18 136	20 128	20 201	36.70	36.10
Cooperative and rural banks	3 482	3 384	2 776	19 428	20 819	20 375	21.80	19.60
Postal Giro Offices	13	14	13	17 515	29 193	na	5.50	4.60
Total	4 424	4 594	3 896	61 722	77 326	53 156	100.0	100.0
Italy								
Commercial banks	164	153	120	7 019	7 940	15 950	57.30	56.40
Savings banks	86	86	100	4 169	4 697	3 896	25.30	26.60
Cooperative and rural banks	859	825	671	4 177	5 084	2 226	14.00	14.90
Post Office	1	1	1	13 958	14 441	na	3.40	2.10
Total	1 110	1 065	892	29 323	32 162	22 133	100.0	100.0

continued overleaf

Table 3.7(b)   *(continued)*

Country	No. of banks			No. of branches			Market share (as % of deposits by the non-bank public)	
	1987	1990	1992	1987	1990	1992	1987	1990
The Netherlands								
Commercial banks	83	97	na	2 338	2 275	na	47.20	47.80
Savings banks	58	54	na	1 035	1 027	na	4.30	3.60
Cooperative and rural banks	926	1	na	2 345	2 144	na	23.50	25.50
Post Office	1	1	na	2 705	2 715	na	25.00	23.10
Total	1 068	153	177	8 423	8 161	7 518	100.00	100.0
Spain								
Commercial banks	138	154	164	16 554	16 835	18 180	58.56	52.60
Savings banks	79	65	54	13 482	15 476	14 145	37.74	43.40
Cooperative banks	129	107	101	3 113	2 919	2 989	3.70	4.00
Total	346	326	319	33 049	35 230	35 314	100.0	100.0
United Kingdom								
Authorised banks	567	537	486	14 994	14 509	11 878	45.40	56.70
Building societies	137	99	87	6 967	6 051	6 024	53.60	42.70
Post Office[d]	1	1	1	21 211	20 871	20 018	1.00	0.60
Total	705	637	574	43 172	41 431	37 920	100.0	100.0

[a]Since 1989 commercial and savings banks are not reported separately, post giro has been transformed into a bank (Girobank) and it uses the branches of the Post Office.
[b]Includes 21 'Caisse de Crédit Municipal' that have 76 branches.
[c]Commercial banks include mortgage banks, instalment sales financing institutions, banks with special functions and loan associations.
[d]National savings bank facilities are available at post offices on agency basis.
Includes all banks listed in *Bundesbank Monthly Report*, excluding post offices and own updates.
Source: Vesala (1993, pp. 185–186) and own updates.

and rural banks and postal giro offices. Savings banks in Germany (which are governed by a public law and can be regarded as public banks) held 36.1% of non-bank deposits in 1990. In France, Italy and Spain the commercial banks all controlled more than 50% of this market although in these markets they all lost market share to the mutual banks between 1987 and 1990. We are uncertain as to how this trend has continued into the 1990s but we do know that all types of banks have lost market share to collective investment funds in terms of the holdings of household financial assets since the turn of the decade.

Market Size, Branching and Concentration

The previous section identified that in recent years the market for credit intermediation has resulted in a progressive homogenisation in the activities of credit institutions and to a narrowing of the operational differences between commercial banks and other types of banking firm (i.e. savings banks, cooperative banks and public credit institutions) (see Masera, 1992, p. 343).

Table 3.8 illustrates various size characteristics of European banking markets for 1987 and 1992. The table shows that the German, French, Italian, and Spanish and UK banking systems are by far the largest banking sectors in the EU. As illustrated in Table 3.8, the Italian banking system is relatively unsaturated. Many of the new branches set up after the abandonment of branching restrictions have also been 'high-tech' or 'light' branches selling only a few products and being staffed by only three or four employees, and the incremental cost of the expansion in Italian banks in the early 1990s has been relatively modest (European Economy, 1993). Between 1987 and 1990 in Germany, Italy and Spain, the number of inhabitants per branch gradually declined and the lowest figure was recorded by Spain (1110 inhabitants per branch in 1990). For France, however, the figure increased slightly from 2184 in 1987 to 2207 but it is still lower than for Italy compared with other EU countries.

Table 3.8 also illustrates the number of ATMs per million inhabitants: France and the UK surprisingly appear to have the highest density of ATMs especially compared with Belgium which stands out by having the lowest ATM concentration at 108 per million inhabitants. Figures not reported in the table indicated that in Italy, the number of inhabitants per ATM decreased by almost threefold, over 7000, by nearly 3000 in Germany and around 1000 in France. This perhaps indicated that the aforementioned banking systems have invested in new technological development to improve their network systems. It also appears that the smallest average branch size in terms of both total assets and non-bank deposits (ECU millions) was in Spain, followed by France and then Belgium.

Perhaps better indicators of market size are relative measures, such as the importance of banks' capital in relation to GDP. Table 3.9 illustrates that the concentration of banking power and the number of banks which were listed in *The Banker*'s (1994) top 1000, together with their assets size in 1993. The last column of Table 3.9 indicates capital as a percentage of GDP. It is interesting to note the strong capital position in Spain, Italy and the Netherlands, whereas Germany has the lowest level of capital as a percentage of GDP, resulting from the hidden value of investments and property not included in published capital (Morgan Stanley, 1993a).

In the majority of industrialised countries a large level of market concentration appears to be evident, such that a small core number of banks represent a large proportion of banking sector assets.

Table 3.8 The size of the banking systems of the EU (at the end of 1993)

	Number of banks			Number of branches			Total assets size (ECU m.)	No. of ATMs per 1 million inhabitants	No. of transactions per inhabitant	No. of inhabitants per branch	Total assets per branch (ECU m.)		
	1987	1990	1993	1987	1990	1993	(1993)	(1992)	(1992)	(1992)	1987	1990	1993
B	121	121	121	9 084	10 244	16 405	379 833	109	8.8	804	45.05	46.84	35.34
DK	263	222	113	3 534	2 884	2 467	na	na	na	na	31.00	49.34	na
F	931	799	610	25 492	25 569	na	1 500 174	305	11.0	1 214	43.82	57.51	28.22
D	4 411	4 580	4 038	44 207	48 133	53 156	3 473 104	235	na	1 127	36.82	43.15	65.31
I	1 109	1 064	1 637	15 365	17 721	22 133	1 676 000	245	3.6	1 612	42.62	48.87	75.72
NL	1 067	152	177	5 718	5 446	7 518	560 925	263	32.0	2 019	46.63	78.38	74.61
E	346	326	319	33 049	35 230	na	1 383 869	na	na	na	10.47	15.13	na
UK	704	636	574	21 961	20 560	11 878	1 929 456	316	19.8	1 475	58.21	86.12	162.44
SWE	–	–	109	na	na	3 540	154 951	254	25.1	1 843	na	na	43.77
SWI	–	–	435	na	na	4 262	953 225	287	7.4	872	na	na	223.66

Note: Post Office was not included.

B = Belgium, DK = Denmark, D = West Germany, E = Spain, F = France, I = Italy, L = Luxembourg, NL = Netherlands, UK = United Kingdom, SWE = Sweden, SWI = Switzerland.

Sources: BIS (1994), *Deutsche Bundesbank Monthly Report*, December 1994, De Nederlandsche Bank (1993) *Annual Report, Annual Abstract of Banking Statistics* (1994), British Bankers Association (11 May), Switzerland in Figures (1994), UBS Economic Trends in Switzerland 1993/94 and Vesala (1993, pp. 188–189).

Table 3.9 The number of banks in the top 1000 and their capital and asset size for selected EU countries in 1993

	No. of banks in top 1000	Assets ($bn)	Average assets per bank ($bn)	Capital ($bn)	Average assets per bank ($ m.)	Capital as % of GDP (1992)
Belgium	11	466	42.4	13.4	1218	6.4
Denmark	10	159	15.9	7.0	701	8.6
France	27	2019	74.8	77.7	2878	7.7
Germany	97	2917	30.1	86.1	888	4.7
Ireland	3	56	18.7	3.0	1015	6.8
Italy	101	1296	12.8	71.1	704	10.4
Netherlands	13	586	45.1	26.3	2024	10.0
Spain	41	654	16.0	37.1	905	11.5
United Kingdom	35	1369	39.1	61.0	1743	7.2

Source: Adapted from Morgan Stanley (1993a, p. 7) and updated from *The Banker* (1994) September.

Table 3.10 Market concentration in the EU banking systems (market share of the five largest banks, % of total assets)

	1987	1988	1989	1990	1993
Belgium	58.2	57.5	57.9	54.9	59.3
Denmark	—	74.3	77.1	—	73.5
France	42.8	42.8	42.8	45.0	41.2
Germany	24.6	25.7	26.3	27.4	27.2
Greece	63.7	62.3	63.4	—	77.6
Italy	39.1	41.1	44.5	43.0	35.6
Luxembourg	25.4	26.8	25.9	24.7	29.9
Netherlands	86.8	90.4	83.7	84.1	84.4
Portugal	—	—	56.4	—	55.8
Spain	33.2	38.7	38.8	41.8	45.0
United Kingdom	—	29.0	29.1	27.8	38.1

Source: Gual and Neven (1993, p. 166) and own updates.

As can be seen from the five-firm concentration ratios in Table 3.10, the EU banking industry appears to be characterised by a few large institutions and a substantial number of smaller, local and more specialised banks. Following Buigues and Jacquemin's (1988) categorisation of structural environments, it could be argued that the European banking industry has characteristics common to both an environment where volume is the main feature and where specialism is also important. For instance, in the supply of traditional services, such as retail banking, size could be more important to compete efficiently. Alternatively, many of the functions of investment banking have some specialised aspects, which make the services non-homogeneous and the relation between lender and customer specific, in particular when the customer is a local small or medium-sized institution.

Competition and Competitors

The opening of the EU banking markets has provided domestic banks and other financial services firms with an opportunity to expand their activities abroad but has also forced them to face increased foreign competition in their domestic market-place. The important element in the process of financial deregulation has been the opening-up of the European banking system to domestic and foreign competition. This move has been important in shaping the current state of the European financial market-place. For example, foreign banks in Spain were instrumental in introducing new financial services. They fostered the development of the inter-bank market, established investment banking and introduced new technology in banking services (see Pastor, 1993, p. 20). During the last decade or so, competition has increased rapidly in financial services markets, between banks as well as between banks and other financial institutions (see Revell, 1989). This intense competitive environment has motivated banks and financial institutions of all kinds to broaden and improve the quality of their services and hence their customer bases (Gardener and Molyneux, 1990).

In order to gain sufficient mass to compete in more open markets banks have either merged or been acquired. Rationalisation and modernisation have especially affected savings banks. Arthur Andersen (1993) noted that savings banks were traditionally associated with retail banking and characterised by small size, limited geographical areas of operation, traditional products, weak management and management interference by local authorities. However, they have now become more profitable and one of the fastest growing segments across European banking markets.

Regulation has clearly heightened the level of competition in banking markets. In Italy, for instance, the 1989 Amato law allowed banks to operate in other sectors of the financial markets through subsidiaries owned by a central group holding company and provided banks with financial incentives to restructure in this way. Moreover, Italian banks were no longer restricted to operating in either the short-term or the medium to long-term borrowing and lending business, provided that the Bank of Italy's capital and risk ratios were maintained. Guiso, Jappelli and Terlizzese (1992) have also noted that during the 1980s the easing of regulation in certain sectors, particularly in the insurance industry and the progress of the EU's single financial services market programme, has resulted in the increased competitive climate in banking markets. They argue that these changes have sharpened competition among lenders and insurance and credit firms.

The Banque de France (1992) has noted that the concentration moves were the result of a systematic drive to reduce costs and optimise the size of institutions. Competition has been strengthened in France in recent years, and would become even keener with the effective completion of the single financial services market. As a result, the Banque de France reported that the banking industry has been pressured to adapt their business and organisation so as to increase productivity and hence the level of competitiveness. Liberalisation has also heightened the degree of competition in the Spanish banking market; the Banco de Espana (1993) reported that the years 1989–92 were the culmination of the opening-up and liberalisation of the Spanish banking system. The legal reserve and investment requirements have been eliminated, the only remnant being the Banco de Espana certificates which have begun to be redeemed in 1993; capital movements have been liberalised; new markets and alternative instruments to traditional banking ones have taken root. The overall outcome has been an increase in competition in the Spanish banking industry.

Schneider-Lenne (1993) has noted that most German banks have been universal banks that offer all possible types of banking services under one roof. The high degree of competition in the German banking market was reflected in the total number of banks in Germany, where over 4000 banks registered with the Bundesbank with more than 45 000 branches. In addition, there is increasing competition from non-banks and near-banks such as credit card companies or insurance groups which offer an ever larger range of financial products without being subject to the same regulation.

The large hike in the UK's five-firm concentration ratio is mainly brought about by including the Hong Kong Shanghai Bank Corporation's consolidated figures in the calculations. Despite this exaggeration, recent moves by Lloyds Bank to buy Cheltenham and Gloucester Building Society, the merger between the Halifax and Leeds Permanent Building Societies and the increasing pressures to restructure and consolidate will further promote concentration in the UK market.

Most recently, Molyneux, Lloyd-Williams and Thornton (1994b) have examined the competitive conditions in European banking between 1986 and 1989 and suggested that, other things being equal, competitive conditions in European banking have increased. The authors indicated that banks in Germany, France and Spain earned revenues as if under conditions of monopolistic competition in the period. In the case of Italy, they were consistent with banks having earned revenues as if under monopoly or conjectural variations short-run oligopoly conditions.

Overall, there has been a process of increased competition in European banking sectors, the main driving forces of which have been the need for banks to maintain and expand market shares, and profitability levels in a deregulating environment. This has been accompanied by increased concentration in certain cases and perhaps gives some credence to the view that banking markets are contestable.

UNIVERSAL VERSUS SPECIALISED BANKING IN EUROPE

Another important feature of the financial scene over the last two decades or so has been a marked trend towards the universalisation of banking business. The EU's Second Banking Directive has helped promote this trend because it legislates for a universal banking market. This, of course, does not mean that all banks in Europe will have to be universal. Revell (1991), however, has noted that universal banks have been around for a long time, starting in the latter half of the nineteenth century in Germany. Universal banking does not have a clear definition, but it is most commonly accepted to describe a large commercial bank that undertakes corporate, wholesale and retail banking, investment banking and securities business (Steinherr and Huveneers, 1992). Recently, large banks have also set up close links with insurance companies or even merged, and so nowadays the definition of universal banking could be expanded to contain also insurance business (see Revell, 1992).

The main factors why banks have diversified are numerous and have been widely analysed (see Gardener, 1990; Abraham and Lierman, 1991; Cesarini, 1992; Canals, 1993). In general the main reasons appear to be:

1. to utilise efficiently the existing network of branches, and to spread costs over a wider range of business areas so as to enhance profitability;

2. because of the increased capital standards to enter certain business areas;

3. to reduce the variability of revenues;

4. to reduce interest rate, credit and liquidity risks attached to banking activity;

5. to benefit from substantial scope economies that are believed to be present in the provision of financial services.

While universal banks may benefit from both economies of scale and scope (see Steinherr and Huveneers, 1992), the concept of the universal bank has come under fire in recent years. Lohneysen, Baptista and Walton (1990), for example, have argued for the dismantling of universal banks and their transformation into 'federal' (or 'federated') banks. The aforementioned study pointed out that the history of banks that form the core of universal banks has left them with a reliance on branches as the principal channel of distribution and thus with a generally low level of skill among their staff. Increased competition, especially in the form of ever higher interest rates on deposits, together with the relative stagnation of retail markets in recent years, it is argued, have indicated that this type of organisation is no longer the most efficient form of banking organisation.

Revell (1992) points to the fact that the 'new' competitors in European banking were mainly specialists operating in one of the separate areas of production, distribution or processing. (Mester (1990) has also indicated a related point showing that there are scope diseconomies for the traditional bank functions of originating and monitoring loans but not for the non-traditional ones of loan selling and buying.)

Lohneysen, Baptista and Walton (1990) grouped the broad classes of specialised banking institutions, including also UCITs and money-market funds, into three subclasses: (i) product, (ii) distribution and (iii) processing specialists. Product specialists utilised product differentiation opportunities, for instance in the mortgage and consumer loans areas. Other forms include substitutes for time and demand deposits, such as mutual funds and other forms of managed investment. Distribution specialists offer services to specified customers. Finally, processing specialists capitalise on scale economies in certain service areas such as credit card processing. In addition, it is argued that these specialised institutions can utilise further cost advantages by adopting more advanced technology and labour skills than universal banks.

Commentators such as Forestieri and Onado (1989), Gardener (1990), Metais (1990), Shaw (1990), Abraham and Lierman (1991) and Revell (1992) have also emphasised the disadvantages of the universal banking model but, nevertheless, this is the model most large European banks are adopting in the light of EU legislation. (It is also the banking model which is gradually evolving in the USA; see, for example, Saunders and Walter (1994).) Another major factor encouraging banks to adopt the universal banking model relates to the cross-selling opportunities and the supposed scope economies relating to such activity. In fact, scale and scope economies, incorporating cost management, have been of primary importance in justifying the rationale for the universal banking concept in European banking.

A NOTE ON TECHNOLOGICAL LEVELS IN EUROPEAN BANKING SYSTEMS

Over recent years, banking activities have been strongly affected by the implementation of advanced electronic information technology (IT), both as regards the production of financial services and their distribution. OECD (1992a) has noted that there has been a rapidly increasing awareness that many activities in the markets for financial services meet in an almost ideal way the conditions for a successful introduction and application of IT:

- Financial services activities involve increasingly standardised operations or processes which lead to automation.

- An important volume of traditional paperwork and paper storage could be replaced by computerised data entry and storage.

- There are many processes that are considerably complex with regard to the number of successive operations or variables involved, which could justify the use of computers.

- In most banking activities the use of computers leads to significant time savings as compared with manual or mechanical machine procedures.

- The use of IT improves the required standards and criteria of cost/benefit analyses because of the resulting time-saving effects and the decrease in the number of processing errors.

In the financial services sector IT could be used significantly in the following major areas (see OECD, 1992a, p. 122):

- general management of financial institutions;
- payments services;
- money market and foreign exchange market transactions;
- securities market operations;
- operations in new financial instruments;
- asset and liability management including portfolio management;
- financial market information services.

The application of new technology to the financial services sectors, especially in the payments field, has advanced considerably in all European countries. The use of ATMs, cash dispensers and bank cards, and the effecting of automatic transfer payment and retrieval of basic account information by individuals have also become substantially common in these countries. In addition, EFTPOS (Electronic Funds Transfers at the Point of Sale) terminals and home banking developments have become important for retail banking. Meanwhile, these changes together with advanced computer technology and telecommunications have, some argue, resulted in economies of scale and scope in the financial services sector.

A number of developments have progressed in the area of electronic payments systems and fund transfers. The European Commission and Council of Ministers have been involved in such matters as the standardisation of electronic payments systems in Europe, the efficient use of resources and the protection of consumers with regard to electronic funds transfers (EFT) and the privacy of electronically held data. The Commission has been concerned with the standardisation of electronic payments systems within Europe and has also encouraged agreement on common standards for the European payments industry.

Technological innovations during the 1980s have already had a significant impact on the activity of the financial services markets. New technology has been reducing cost in what traditionally has been a labour-intensive high-cost business.

Table 3.11 EFTPOS network and transactions in selected European countries, 1988 and 1992

Country	No. of terminals per million inhabitants		No. of transactions per inhabitant		Average value of transaction ($US)	
	1988	1992	1988	1992	1988	1992
Belgium	1925	4034	5.3	12.0	34.8	57.7
France	2154	5594	7.5	22.7	81.6	62.5
Germany	141	640	0.01	0.35	94.8	43.5
Italy	76	1094	0.02	0.28	102.1	161.6
Netherlands	102	758	—	3.1	—	45.9
Sweden	83	1647	0.2	4.7	163.1	100.7
Switzerland	211	1640	0.4	2.8	25.3	51.8
UK	426	3806	—	—	—	—

Source: BIS (1993).

The networking of computer systems has transformed the speed, accuracy and economies of both retail and wholesale payments and delivery systems. The rapid expansion of the ATM networks and EFTPOS in all European countries implies an apparent rise in technological levels. ATM network instalments increased sharply in most European countries between 1987 and 1992; however, there were still significant differences in ATM usage across countries. Table 3.11 reports the size of EFTPOS networks and transactions in various European countries for 1988 and 1992. The table reveals that the growth in EFTPOS terminals was substantial over these years although the German, Dutch and Italian banking systems still tend to be relatively underdeveloped compared with their other European neighbours.

OPERATING EFFICIENCY IN THE EUROPEAN BANKING MARKETS

Salomon Brothers (1993, p. 2) recently argued that cost management has become the most important strategic theme throughout the banking world: 'European banks, hampered with asset quality problems, slim loan demand and the difficulty of building reliable noninterest income streams, have globally turned to cost reduction as one of the principal drivers of earning growth.'

Operating efficiency in the production of the banking system can be defined as employed inputs per unit of output, which corresponds closely to the concept of productivity. While most banks depend heavily on internal productivity measures such as relating output to staff time, these figures are not usually available to the outside analyst, and even if available Salomon Brothers (1993) have noted that these indices would not necessarily be comparable between banks across borders. Most comparisons of cost efficiency usually use aggregate ratios relating cost to revenues or assets. These measures suffer from the limitation that they do not account for business mix or the risk profile of a bank's business. They also do not take into account the quality of service. Nevertheless, it is these measures which are most frequently drawn up to use cross-country comparison of bank efficiency. For example, Table 3.12 illustrates these efficiency measures of various European banking systems.

It can be seen that the figures in Table 3.12 reveal large efficiency differences across European countries. Vesala (1993) argues that it is the low price competition in countries (such as Italy, France and Spain) where regulations persisted which has generated low levels of efficiency. When we compare the average figures for the periods 1983–86 and 1987–90 there seems to be an overall improvement in the labour usage efficiencies with respect to total deposits and this is especially marked if we compared those with the 1993 data. Non-staff operating costs to non-bank deposits, however, appear to have escalated in recent years and this perhaps reflects the shift of labour to capital-intensive operations. In fact, Vesala (1993) concludes that production in banking has become more capital intensive resulting from the adoption of new banking technologies, given that the share of non-staff operating costs has in most systems increased.

Table 3.12 Banks' aggregate operating efficiency in selected European countries, 1983–90 (%)

	(Staff costs/non-bank deposits) × 100				(Non-staff operating costs/non-bank deposits) × 100			
	Average 1983–86	Average 1987–90	Average 1983–90	1993	Average 1983–86	Average 1987–90	Average 1983–90	1993
Belgium	3.22	2.66	2.88	2.46	1.60	1.47	1.53	1.50
Denmark	2.76	2.69	2.72	2.20	1.56	1.61	1.59	2.55
France	3.75	3.03	3.32	2.00	2.03	1.94	1.99	4.66
Germany	2.10	2.04	2.06	1.97	1.14	1.14	1.14	4.61
Italy	3.74	3.76	3.75	3.35	1.45	1.54	1.49	2.32
Netherlands	2.45	2.30	2.36	1.52	1.36	1.61	1.49	1.60
Spain	2.98	3.01	3.00	2.5	1.45	1.46	1.45	2.76
United Kingdom	na	na	na	2.28	na	na	na	3.22

Notes: Staff costs include salaries and other employee benefits plus transfers to pension reserves. Non-staff operating expenses covers all non-interest expenses related to regular banking business including expenses for property and equipment and related depreciation expenses.
Source: Vesala (1993, p. 196) and own updates for 1993.

Table 3.13 presents operating costs for the French, German, Italian, Spanish and UK banking markets during the 1980s and early 1990s. Operating costs as a percentage of total assets fell constantly in France until the 1990–91 period and then appeared to accelerate in 1993. Cost falls for Italy and Spain appeared greater between 1982–83 and 1986–87 than in the later period 1990–91. These systems appeared to handle their costs marginally better with no substantial growth in 1993. The operation activity increased in Germany in 1986–87 but fell back in 1990–91. In 1990–91 the cost ratios calculated by Conti and Maccarinelli (1993) all fell to around 60% and they still appear to remain in that area apart from in the UK where senior management appear to have been more successful in reducing costs as partially indicated by the low cost/income ratio (the UK figure was calculated including all commercial banks and building societies).

Salomon Brothers (1993) noted that within the cost categories, European banks predominantly focused on staff expenses, which have begun to decline in all the major banks (see Table 3.14). Italian and to a lesser extent Spanish banks

Table 3.13 Operating costs for the French, German, Italian, Spanish and UK banking systems (%)

	Operating expenses as a percentage of total assets				Operating expenses as a percentage of gross income			
	1982–83	1986–87	1990–91	1993	1982–83	1986–87	1990–91	1993
France	2.18	1.91	1.58	2.60	67.5	67.5	66.9	66.7
Germany	2.13	2.28	2.05	2.66	61.4	65.6	64.9	63.3
Italy	3.89	3.04	2.99	2.99	65.5	66.3	63.3	57.6
Spain	3.18	3.02	2.99	2.93	66.1	63.2	57.6	62.1
United Kingdom	na	na	na	2.54	na	na	na	49.8

Source: Adapted from Conti and Maccarinelli (1993, pp. 8, 10) and own updates for 1993.

Table 3.14 Staff costs for the French, German, Italian, Spanish and UK banking systems (%)

	Staff expenses as a percentage of total assets				Staff expenses as a percentage of operating costs			
	1982–83	1986–87	1990–91	1993	1982–83	1986–87	1990–91	1993
France	1.45	1.20	0.95	0.78	66.7	62.8	60.0	52.8
Germany	1.47	1.49	1.29	0.80	68.8	65.1	63.1	42.7
Italy	2.07	2.17	2.11	1.77	71.6	71.5	70.4	93.15
Spain	2.15	2.11	1.91	1.23	67.6	69.9	63.8	72.3
United Kingdom	na	na	na	0.98	na	na	na	70.6

Source: Adapted from Conti and Maccarinelli (1993, pp. 8, 10) and own updates for 1993.

appear to have relatively high staff cost ratios. Despite the increase in staff numbers, competitive pressures have been forcing the Italian banks to reduce their costs, especially public banks. Italian banks have, until recently, placed a low management priority on cost management, focusing more on building national branch networks to get cheap customer deposits needed to sustain profitable asset growth. Once the preoccupation with building nationwide branches has been completed it is believed that all the main banks will increasingly focus on cost reduction (Salomon Brothers, 1993). In addition, the Banco de Espana (1993) has noted that in Spain the large banking institutions have launched market strategies to raise funds in the savings-account segment; as a result there has been a further heightening of competition for deposits. This has made the typical financing of these institutions more sensitive to changes in short-term market rates and resulted in a reduction in operating margins by increasing the proportion of higher-yield liabilities (see Banco de Espana, 1993, p. 48).

Table 3.15 shows banks' cost/income ratios for selected EU countries between 1988 and 1993. This ratio was calculated including the principal mainstream banks but excluding specialist institutions (see Morgan Stanley, 1994a, p. 7). The table demonstrates that there was potential to improve efficiency in a number of countries. In the five years to 1992, the most significant improvements appeared to be in Germany and the UK compared with France, Italy and Spain.

Overall, the information available on cost and efficiency levels suggests that European banking markets have become more efficient and cost effective in recent years, with falls in cost/income ratios and other cost-related measures in most markets. Non-staff costs appear, however, to be decreasing relatively less slowly than staff costs. The aforementioned tables also indicate that in France and Italy, banking markets which have traditionally had high levels of public ownership, cost levels do appear to be higher compared with in the UK, Germany and Spain.

Table 3.15   Cost/income ratios for selected EU countries, 1988−93 (%)

	1988	1989	1990	1991	1992	1993[a]
Belgium	74.1	73.7	76.6	73.2	69.9	65.9
Denmark	53.2	69.8	70.6	62.5	76.6	49.5
France	69.0	68.5	72.9	70.8	69.0	67.5
Germany	67.2	66.6	68.1	67.2	64.9	61.3
Italy	69.1	65.4	63.6	65.8	65.3	65.0
Netherlands	67.5	66.6	69.2	67.7	67.1	66.3
Spain	51.9	52.7	56.9	60.9	60.1	61.8
United Kingdom	65.2	64.7	65.9	65.7	60.2	58.8

Note: The ratios for each country are the arithmetical average for selected banks.
[a]Morgan Stanley research estimates.
Source: Adapted from Morgan Stanley (1994a, p. 8).

PERFORMANCE COMPARISONS

A comparative analysis of banks' performance suffers from two methodological problems. The first relates to the choice of the appropriate measure of profitability. The second is concerned with the standardisation of data from different countries and, more generally, the need for an accurate reference point from which to compare the results obtained. Gilbert (1984), Molyneux and Thornton (1992) and Canals (1993) (among others) have noted that the two indicators, return on equity (ROE) and return on assets (ROA), are widely recommended for the comparison of profitability between different banks and banking systems. Despite the range and complexity of a bank's activities, its business may be classified broadly into two categories: income and expenses. These simple revenue and cost categories enable bank profitability and performance to be traced and allow meaningful operating comparisons between banks, both domestically and internationally.

In recent years as market conditions have become tougher and more competitive the focus of profitability management has tended to shift away from interest earnings towards fees and other income generated from sales of insurance, travel and other investments (see Shaw and Whitley, 1994). The OECD (1992a) has also identified these trends by stating that the process of deregulation has influenced the profitability of banks, in particular by putting considerable pressure on their interest margins and forcing them to concentrate on fee income and cost reduction. The main reasons for increasing pressure on interest margins are:

- the removal of administrative constraints when fixing interest rates on customer deposits which has caused negative repercussions on the cost of funding in many countries;
- the elimination of the remaining protectionist barriers in place with regard to foreign market participants and the liberalisation of capital movements which have prompted growth in competition, specifically in lending to large corporations;
- the move of banks towards disintermediation resulting from the greater opportunities for large corporations to access capital markets directly;
- the removal of the still existing limitations on the opening of new branches which has brought about an erosion of monopolistic earnings which various small and medium-sized credit institutions had enjoyed in local markets.

Table 3.16 shows trends in net interest margins between 1987 and 1993 for the world's main banking systems. Between 1986/87 and 1992 margins fell in all systems apart from in Finland, Norway and the USA. Margins appear to be high in Italy and Spain, which may be a possible reflection of the highly regulated nature of both systems. In fact, Spain has tended to be a high-margin banking system; even though the country had its worst recession between 1991

Table 3.16   Interest margins (%)

| | Interest margin as % of total assets | | | | | | |
	1982–83	1986–87	1990–91	1993	D1	D2	D3
France	2.69	2.41	1.82	1.50	−0.28	−0.59	−0.87
Germany	2.58	2.44	2.10	1.58	−0.14	−0.34	−0.48
Italy	3.17	3.21	3.48	2.81	0.04	0.27	0.31
Spain	3.93	3.83	3.99	2.70	−0.10	0.16	0.06
UK	3.18	3.18	2.96	1.96	0.00	−0.22	−0.22
Belgium	1.66	1.56	1.35	1.48	−0.10	−0.21	−0.31
Netherlands	2.33	2.37	1.94	1.74	0.04	−0.43	−0.39
Switzerland	1.30	1.30	1.38	1.25	0.00	0.008	0.08
Finland	1.88	1.42	1.60	1.69	−0.46	0.18	−0.28
Norway	3.41	2.81	2.63	3.20	−0.60	−0.18	−0.78
Sweden	2.13	2.55	2.08	1.82	0.42	−0.47	−0.05
Japan	1.53	1.24	1.01	1.14	−0.29	−0.23	−0.52
USA	3.15	3.35	3.51	3.43	0.21	0.16	0.37

Notes:
D1 = Absolute change between 1986/87 and 1982/83.
D2 = Absolute change between 1990/91 and 1986/87.
D3 = Absolute change between 1990/91 and 1982/83.
Source: Conti and Maccarinelli (1993, p. 5) and own updates for 1993.

and 1993, margins at levels of around 4% were still being achieved (Morgan Stanley, 1994a). (The high margins recorded for the Norwegian market are a reflection of the revival of Scandinavian banks' post-systemic crisis of the early 1990s. High margins are now being generated mainly as a result of substantial government restructuring of the market and other market-based reforms. One can also see that the US system, despite trouble in the late 1980s and early 1990s, still appears to generate relatively high interest margins.)

At the end of the 1980s, Arthur Andersen (1993) noted that the performance of the French banking industry compared favourably with that of other EU countries. More recently, however, French banks have suffered from the effects of Europe's deteriorating economy. In addition, interest margins have been under severe pressure resulting from increased competition and disintermediation, including the increasing preference of French investors for higher-yielding money-market funds over bank deposits. This is a trend nowadays common in most banking markets.

Table 3.17 illustrates the decline in importance of interest income as proportion of total income in banks' business across Europe. The only EU banking system that experienced an increase in the relative percentage of interest income between 1986/87 and 1990/91 was in Italy. In the other EU banking systems there was clearly a move to generate increased fee and commission income as a proportion of total income over this period, a trend which in fact is continuing to the present (Arthur Andersen, 1993, pp. 53–58).

Table 3.17 Interest income as a percentage of gross income

	1982−83	1986−87	1990−91	D1	D2	D3
France	83.4	85.2	77.3	1.8	−7.9	−6.1
Germany	74.2	70.2	66.7	−4.0	−3.5	−7.5
Italy	71.8	70.1	73.6	−1.7	3.6	1.9
Spain	81.6	80.1	77.0	−1.5	−3.2	−4.6
UK	66.9	63.2	60.2	−3.7	−3.1	−6.7
Belgium	77.2	73.7	76.0	−3.5	2.3	−1.2
Netherlands	76.6	75.1	71.0	−1.5	−4.1	−5.6
Switzerland	52.3	49.4	48.7	−2.9	−0.8	−3.6
Finland	48.6	41.4	48.9	−7.2	7.5	0.3
Norway	72.9	70.3	74.1	−2.6	3.8	1.2
Sweden	70.2	68.0	73.8	−2.2	5.8	3.6
Japan	85.7	77.7	83.1	−8.0	5.4	−2.6
USA	74.3	69.9	66.4	−4.4	−3.6	−8.0

Notes:
D1 = Absolute change between 1986/87 and 1982/83.
D2 = Absolute change between 1990/91 and 1986/87.
D3 = Absolute change between 1990/91 and 1982/83.
Source: Conti and Maccarinelli (1993, p. 7).

Finally, Table 3.18 reports the pre-tax ROA and ROE for selected European countries between 1982 and 1993. Over the years the variability in profitability performance is marked, although one can see that 1993 was a relatively poor year for all banking systems. Viewing the ROA figures up to 1990 and 1991 for the largest European banking markets, one can see that over the period the largest improvements in profits were experienced by banks operating in the Spanish and Italian markets. Returns to German banks appear to be relatively stable over the period. A fall in overall profitability levels during the period was recorded by banks operating in the UK and French markets. In 1993, however, the systems that performed weakly during the 1980s (the UK and Belgium) seemed to be performing much better in 1993. Many French banks reported losses in this year and substantial domestic loan-loss provisioning costs hit the Spanish and Italians. Although it is difficult to point out precise conclusions from these figures, one may tentatively suggest that the marked difference in variability of performance of banks across countries may result from one or more of the following factors: markedly different operating conditions; varying competitive environments and profit activities in some banking systems. The size and number of foreign banks may also add to the variability of foreign bank performance of banking system returns.

Table 3.18 also reports the ROE figures across large European banking markets between 1982 and 1993. It can be seen that the highest figures for ROE, on average, were for Italian banks, with 1990/91 and 1993 values over 10%, while the lowest ratios were for the French banking system, below 6%. This is a general reflection of the reasonable profitability yet low levels of capital held

Table 3.18   Pre-tax return on assets and return on equity for selected European countries

	1982–83	1986–87	1990–91	1993	D1	D2	D3
Return on assets							
France	0.36	0.35	0.27	0.04	−0.01	−0.08	−0.09
Germany	0.57	0.71	0.61	0.53	0.14	−0.10	0.04
Italy	0.80	1.01	1.21	0.73	0.21	0.20	0.40
Spain	0.62	0.91	1.55	0.33	0.29	0.64	0.93
UK	0.82	0.74	0.56	0.72	−0.09	−0.17	−0.26
Belgium	0.34	0.41	0.32	0.47	0.07	−0.09	−0.02
Return on equity							
France	7.94	8.84	5.90	0.84	0.89	−2.93	−2.04
Germany	5.58	7.17	6.31	12.80	1.89	−0.86	0.73
Italy	8.72	8.57	10.56	12.59	−0.15	1.88	1.73
Spain	5.69	7.78	10.36	5.36	2.09	2.58	4.67
UK	12.68	7.75	6.72	12.72	−4.93	−1.03	−5.95
Belgium	7.96	8.45	6.88	17.26	0.49	−1.57	−1.08

Notes:
D1 = Absolute change between 1986/87 and 1982/83.
D2 = Absolute change between 1990/91 and 1986/87.
D3 = Absolute change between 1990/91 and 1982/83.
Source: Adapted from Conti and Maccarinelli (1993, p. 15) and own updates for 1993.

by the state French banks during this period. For Germany, ROE rose rapidly in the first half of the 1980s, then decreased and overall improved slightly until a dramatic increase for 1993. In the case of UK banks, ROEs appear to have systematically fallen throughout the 1980s and early 1990s until the collapse in loan-loss provisioning in 1993 led to a substantial turnaround in the banks' profitability.

A major factor impacting on bank profitability is asset quality. As can be seen from Table 3.19, bank asset quality has varied among the regulatory environments. The table shows loan quality figures for the major EU banking countries and the United States. The ratios in the table focus on two kinds of measures of asset quality. The first group, which was most readily available, depends on the loan-loss provisions banks make. The classes are: 'loan loss provision' and 'loan loss reserves/gross loans'. The second group included actual losses or past due loans. The major difference between these two kinds of measures is that the provisions data are based on the banks' estimates of potential loan losses, while the other figures rely on actual data. It can be seen from Table 3.19 that the 'loan loss provision' figures ranged from 0.29% of loans for France to 1.63% in the USA for 1990. Moreover, when we examine actual reserves, by 'loan loss reserve/gross loans' the 1990 figures appeared to be similar for the UK, USA, Spain and Italy. France experienced the lowest loan-loss provisions of 0.41%.

Table 3.19   Loan quality figures by country for the period 1987–90

Country	1987	1988	1989	1990
France				
Write-off/average loans	0.01%	0.03%	0.01%	0.01%
Loan-loss provision	0.54%	0.38%	0.42%	0.29%
Past due loans/gross loans	0.32%	0.87%	0.72%	0.76%
Loan-loss reserve/gross loans	0.83%	0.70%	0.52%	0.41%
Loans to customer	2 799 339	3 588 542	4 879 021	5 447 563
Loan growth rate	na	28.16%	35.96%	11.65%
Germany				
Write-off/average loans	na	na	na	na
Loan-loss provision	0.51%	0.35%	0.53%	0.63%
Past due loans/gross loans	0.00%	0.00%	na	na
Loan-loss reserve/gross loans	na	na	na	na
Total loans	2 135 827	2 355 401	2 560 387	2 818 538
Loan growth rate	na	10.28%	8.70%	10.08%
Italy				
Write-off/average loans	0.00%	0.00%	0.00%	0.00%
Loan-loss provision	0.72%	0.81%	0.96%	0.91%
Past due loans/gross loans	0.70%	0.69%	0.62%	0.72%
Loan-loss reserve/gross loans	2.99%	2.59%	2.50%	2.56%
Total loans	400 134	508 026	610 784	691 912
Loan growth rate	na	26.96%	20.23%	13.28%
Spain				
Write-off/average loans	0.97%	1.10%	0.74%	0.52%
Loan-loss provision	1.65%	1.27%	1.01%	1.12%
Past due loans/gross loans	2.90%	3.29%	3.46%	3.17%
Loan-loss reserve/gross loans	3.32%	3.15%	2.95%	3.02%
Bills and loans, net	23 696 995	31 576 476	36 150 118	45 110 086
Loan growth rate	na	33.25%	14.48%	24.79%
United Kingdom				
Write-off/average loans	0.30%	0.65%	0.83%	0.93%
Loan-loss provision	0.45%	1.04%	0.70%	0.88%
Past due loans/gross loans	0.59%	0.49%	0.26%	0.41%
Loan-loss reserve/gross loans	2.72%	3.38%	2.93%	3.10%
Total loans net	493 104	608 169	738 562	749 428
Loan growth rate	na	23.33%	21.44%	1.47%
United States				
Write-off/average loans	1.15%	1.22%	1.47%	1.83%
Loan-loss provision	2.44%	0.84%	1.70%	1.63%
Past due loans/gross loans	3.69%	3.32%	3.34%	4.01%
Loan-loss reserve/gross loans	3.07%	2.67%	2.90%	2.84%
Total loans	1 160 721	1 349 789	1 596 309	1 539 177
Loan growth rate	na	16.29%	8.14%	5.45%

Source: Adapted from Bollenbacher (1992, pp. 90–92). Reproduced by permission of Irwin Professional Publishing.

OWNERSHIP AND PERFORMANCE IN EUROPEAN BANKING

Recently, there has been concern about the effect of ownership on the efficiency of banks. Generally, there has been worry about the incentives for managers to efficiently allocate resources under different ownership arrangements. In other words, if owners do not have the incentive or capability to monitor the activity of management, then agency problems and subsequent costs are thought to increase.

In Europe, this concern covers the effect of mutual and government ownership on banks' efficiency. There are questions about how the benefits of competition are going to be passed on to consumers if substantial segments of the banking sector do not have incentives to be efficient nor do they fear the possibility of a takeover. This is the environment in the EU where the 'single passport' gives banks the apparent ability to do business in any country, but growth through acquisition across countries may be severely limited because of the large size of the mutual sector and the public ownership of large segments of various banking systems (most noticeably in Italy and France). Thus, an important method of entry and stimulation of competition by outside institutions is effectively thwarted.

In an analysis of the ownership and performance characteristics of top banks in the EU between 1985 and 1987, Molyneux (1989) notes that an important feature distinguishing Continental European banking systems from British-based systems was that publicly controlled banks (whether by central or local government) were much more important in EU countries. Table 3.20 illustrates that out of the 162 EU banks listed in the 1987 *Banker* 'top 500', 69 were privately owned and 67 publicly owned. The mean performance figures for the public banks appeared marginally worse than those for private banks, however both sectors displayed remarkably similar characteristics, apart from the average number of employees. The average public bank employed half as many staff as the private banks. Molyneux (1989) noted that the reasons for this were not clear, but it could be the case that central management costs and staffing levels of some public banks were hidden in government accounts.

In the aforementioned analysis, credit cooperatives were found, on average, to be larger than their public and private bank counterparts, and this was because they represented central institutions that did business on behalf of very large groups of smaller institutions. The mutual institutions (savings banks) tended to be smaller in size, although their ROA and ROC (return on capital) figures were comparable with those of private and public banks. Molyneux (1989) also noted that of the top 162 banks in the EU, 93 were not operated for a commercial profit or to satisfy the requirements of private shareholders. These institutions may not be acquired through hostile takeover. Since Molyneux's (1989) study, however, various countries have established legislation enabling mutual and public banks to convert to corporate status and achieve stock-exchange listings.

A more recent empirical study by Molyneux and Thornton (1992) has investigated the relationship between bank performance and state ownership in European banking. The study found a statistically significant positive relationship between

Table 3.20   Statistical summary of the ownership characteristics of top banks in the EU, 1987 (arithmetic means and standard deviations)

No. of EU banks in *Banker's* top 500		Assets ($m.)	PTP	PTP/ assets	PTP/ CAP (%)	CAP/ assets	NINT/ assets	Emplo- yees
Private	69	37 601	207.2	0.77	16.36	4.81	3.01	15 948
		(1.15)	(1.61)	(0.89)	(0.80)	(0.48)	(0.59)	(1.36)
Public (central and local government)	67	31 133	158.9	0.61	14.30	3.70	2.14	7 261
		(1.09)	(1.43)	(1.10)	(0.66)	(0.54)	(0.60)	(1.48)
Cooperative	14	41 402	242.8	0.892	17.31	5.16	0.06	12 124
		(1.36)	(0.95)	(0.60)	(0.40)	(1.36)	(0.62)	(1.69)
Mutuals	12	10 421	77.5	0.81	14.78	6.14	3.99	4 419
		(0.50)	(0.64)	(0.46)	(0.52)	(0.39)	(0.29)	(0.56)

Notes:
1. Classification after Revell (1987). Large German savings banks are controlled by local government organisations and therefore are classified as public rather than mutual organisations.
2. Figures in parentheses are standard deviations/means.
3. PTP = pre-tax profits, CAP = capital, NINT = net interest income.
Source: Gardener and Molyneux (1990, p. 35).

state ownership and bank profitability, suggesting that state-owned banks generated higher returns on capital than their private-sector competitors. The authors argued that the results may not be so surprising because state-owned banks generally maintain lower capital ratios (because the government implicitly underwrites their operations) than their private-sector counterparts.

MERGERS, ACQUISITIONS AND COOPERATION AGREEMENTS IN THE 1990s

Since the early 1980s, EU member countries have experienced a continued expansion of operations by foreign banks in their markets. This development can be illustrated by various factors. Firstly, EU member countries continued to deregulate their financial markets and foreign exchange controls over this period (especially after the 1985 EU White Paper), which broadened the area of activities for internationally operating banks. Secondly, in general, member countries have accepted or reverted to a policy of adopting a more favourable attitude towards the new entry of foreign financial institutions. Thirdly, banks have been expanding their operations abroad by cross-border mergers and acquisitions.

The financial integration of Europe has been generating a powerful boost to the opening-up of banking systems. This has been seen in the increase in banking activity carried out on international markets and in the creation of a broad network of connections among financial institutions in various European countries. Meanwhile, technological improvements have had an important impact on the way in which financial services are provided. New technologies have enabled institutions to operate or compete in new markets, by reducing the cost of entry. These rapid developments coupled with the powerful forces outlined in the introduction of this book have generated substantial merger and acquisition business in Europe in the run-up to 1993. Table 3.21 shows that within the EU there was a significant increase in both the number of domestic bank mergers and acquisitions of minority holdings during the late 1980s and early 1990s. After the peak for 1990, the number of acquisitions of majority holdings including mergers and of cross-border operations in particular decreased noticeably. Since both Union and international operations were exceptionally numerous in 1990, it could be that in many cases acquiring firms acted in anticipation of various EU Merger Control Regulations implemented in the early 1990s. It can be seen from the table that the banking and insurance industry were far less open towards foreign takeovers and domestic acquisitions were the most important. Over this period, the insurance sector appeared to be relatively more open towards cross-border deals as compared with the banking industry.

The Commission of the European Communities (1992b, p. 426) has noted that large-scale takeovers by EU firms were strongly concentrated in the banking sector, while more limited operations occurred in other sectors (see Table 3.22). The aforementioned study also indicated that in the banking sector, acquisitions were mainly concentrated in France, Germany and Italy. In terms of the number of deals, domestic takeovers were predominantly in Germany and Italy, with 34 out of 51 takeovers, concerning largely savings banks and cooperative banks. Takeovers by foreign banks, and in particular EU banks, occurred above all in France. Table 3.21 also reveals that cross-border operations are generally dominated by acquisition of minority holdings in financial services firms. In the banking industry, minority acquisitions were mainly concentrated in France, Spain and Italy, with very few operations in other EU countries (see Commission of European Communities, 1992c, pp. 415–428).

In the process of the single market programme, the Cecchini Report (1988) pointed out that regulation in domestic retail markets was largely responsible for preventing price competition, the economic cost of which was passed on to consumers. By removing restrictive regulations, the report predicted that the single market would be created for banks to compete in foreign markets that were previously closed to them. This was expected to have the effect that when a bank became a target of an unfriendly takeover from a foreign bank it may be encouraged to combine with other domestic banks as a defence against the external large predator institution (see Revell, 1991).

Market forces, especially those fostered by the single market programme, have been encouraging banks to compete for retail business on an EU basis. Various forms of cross-border banking activity have spread rapidly throughout the EU (Molyneux, 1991; Bank of England, 1993). However, it is important to identify that the restructuring in domestic banking markets and the consequent degree

Table 3.21 Bank acquisitions of majority holdings (including mergers) and minority holdings in the European Union

	Banking	Insurance	Total
Acquisition of majority holdings			
Domestic			
1987–88	53	14	67
1988–89	51	15	66
1989–90	65	16	81
1990–91	51	15	66
Union			
1987–88	12	14	26
1988–89	16	8	24
1989–90	23	18	41
1990–91	13	7	20
International			
1987–88	13	12	25
1988–89	16	10	26
1989–90	25	12	37
1990–91	11	6	17
Total			
1987–88	78	40	118
1988–89	83	33	116
1989–90	113	46	159
1990–91	75	28	103
Acquisition of minority holdings			
Domestic			
1987–88	38	8	46
1988–89	32	9	41
1989–90	40	13	53
1990–91	28	4	32
Union			
1987–88	15	4	19
1988–89	19	13	32
1989–90	33	24	57
1990–91	21	12	33
International			
1987–88	28	7	35
1988–89	11	7	18
1989–90	23	7	30
1990–91	8	8	16
Total			
1987–88	81	19	100
1988–89	62	29	91
1989–90	96	44	140
1990–91	57	30	87

Source: Adapted from Commission of European Communities (1992b, pp. 426–427).

of concentration could stimulate further cross-border activity. In other words, markets which are concentrated offer relatively limited opportunities either to new entrants or to existing organisations. *Ceteris paribus*, banks in such markets would possibly focus on merger or acquisition abroad. For example, the banking markets which appear to be less concentrated (and have relatively small banks compared with the top institutions from France, Germany and the UK) were those of Italy and Spain. In Italy this seemed to make little difference, however, to the number of domestic and cross-border merger and acquisition deals which were broadly equal, while in Spain there were more domestic merger activities than cross-border.

The most noticeable characteristic of cross-border activity in European banking has been the lack of any sizeable bank merger. Salomon Brothers (1990) have identified that cross-border acquisitions so far have involved large banks acquiring much smaller banks. There have, of course, been various large domestic bank mergers. As a result, it could be argued that the deregulation of the internal market has resulted in greater concentration and less competition in domestic markets since domestic banking firms have merged in order to improve their competitive position relative to potential EU foreign competitors. Countries such as Spain and Italy have seen a number of mergers of major domestic banks: in Germany, the small cooperative and savings banks have been restructuring through mergers, in response to domestic competition.

Molyneux (1991) and the Bank of England (1993) have analysed and documented the type of corporate restructuring taking place across banking markets. Molyneux (1991) examined the type of cross-border activity being undertaken by the world's top 150 banks between January 1989 and April 1991. Molyneux pointed out that the majority of cross-border activities was taking place in Europe and that banks tended to build up majority holdings in markets in which they had past experience. The Bank of England (1993) conducted a similar study which extended Molyneux's (1991) work by using a sample of 247 cross-border alliances in banking and financial services in the EU single market between 1987 and 1993. The study suggested that French banks have been by far the most active, initiating 74 transactions out of 247 instances identified, and UK, German and Spanish banks initiated 36, 35 and 33 alliances, respectively. This study, however, said nothing about the impact of bank mergers within a European context.

Gual and Neven (1993) examined extensively the type and scale of private acquisition (which included mergers, acquisition with controlling interest and minority holdings) activity between banks, insurance companies and other financial intermediaries in both intra- and extra-EU for the period from 1984 to June 1991. Table 3.22 summarises their findings. The study revealed the following:

• There was little restructuring activity in Greece, Portugal, Ireland and Luxembourg.

Table 3.22 The number of deals of intra- and extra-EU private acquisitions for the period 1984 to June 1991

Target country	B	DK	D	GR	E	F	IRL	I	L	NL	P	UK	Non-EU	NA	Total	% domestic
B	14	0	1	0	4	7	0	1	0	3	0	1	1	0	32	44
DK	0	24	1	0	0	0	0	0	0	1	0	1	9	0	36	67
D	0	1	67	0	1	5	0	5	0	5	0	3	12	0	99	67
GR	0	0	0	1	1	0	0	0	0	1	0	1	0	0	4	25
E	0	0	1	0	19	19	0	6	0	5	2	4	8	0	64	42
F	6	0	2	0	3	72	1	14	1	1	1	8	8	1	118	61
IRL	0	0	0	0	0	1	3	0	0	0	0	4	1	0	9	33
I	0	0	3	0	1	14	0	140	0	1	0	5	17	5	186	75
L	4	0	0	0	0	2	0	1	0	1	0	1	3	0	12	
NL	4	0	1	0	0	3	1	0	0	38	0	2	3	0	53	72
P	0	0	0	0	1	2	0	0	0	0	0	1	0	0	4	
UK	0	0	2	0	1	2	0	1	0	1	0	185	10	0	202	92
Non-EU	0	1	7	0	0	9	0	1	0	2	0	4	252	1	277	
NA	2	2	5	0	1	6	3	7	2	5	0	5	17	0	55	
Total	30	18	90	1	32	142	8	176	4	64	3	225	341	7	1151	
% domestic	47	86	74		59	51	38	80		59		82				

Source: Gual and Neven (1993, p. 167).

- The majority of private acquisitions were of a domestic nature (70% of the deals in the data), there was no apparent decline over time in the relative importance of domestic deals.

- In Belgium and Spain around 40–45% of the acquisitions of domestic firms involved domestic institutions. Moreover, this proportion increased to about 70% for the rest of the large banking systems. As for the acquisitions undertaken by domestic institutions, they were mostly domestic in Italy, the UK and Germany, but much less so in France and Spain.

- In terms of absolute numbers, France, the UK and Italy were the main bidding markets in cross-border deals. The main target markets for cross-border activity were France, Italy and Spain, and to a lesser extent Germany. This was in accordance with predictions at least for Spain and France where deregulation has been undertaken on a relatively large scale.

Overall, Gual and Neven (1993) found that most of the cross-border merger and acquisition activity has been undertaken in southern Europe (in Italy and Spain) and the acquirers have generally been firms from the northern EU countries (including France). Finally, a comprehensive study recently undertaken by Vennet (1995) empirically investigates the performance effects of acquisitions and mergers between EC credit institutions over the period 1988 to 1993. The results indicate that domestic mergers among equal-sized partners significantly increase the performance of the merged banks. Improvement of cost efficiency is also found in cross-border acquisitions. Domestic majority and integral acquisitions are found to be predominantly influenced by defensive and managerial motives such as size maximisation.

Furthermore, the single market process is still in its infancy and will not cover securities institutions until 1996 (Turner, 1994). The process of reviewing and then implementing strategies to respond to the opportunities of the single market by financial institutions is thus an ongoing process. The approach of the single market has been an important factor which banks have considered in their strategies; however, it is still very difficult to measure the extent to which cross-border activity has been stimulated by the approach of the single market. On the other hand, the strategic decisions of banks have been influenced by a number of other important factors, for instance market deregulation, increased competition, new technology and the economic environment. Also, a number of future developments such as the implementation of further single market measures (the Capital Adequacy Directive, the Investment Services Directive and the Insurance directives), further deregulation in national markets (e.g. the privatisation of state-owned financial services firms), progress towards the integration of European economies and EMU will affect banks' strategic policies. It could still be argued that the expected benefits of the single market programme (e.g. lower costs to consumers through more open markets and increased competition as indicated in the Cecchini (1988) Report) have yet to be fully achieved. Nevertheless, financial services firms are continuing to engage in substantial domestic and cross-border restructuring.

PRIVATISATION AND RESTRUCTURING

The motivation for privatising banks varies by country, from the fiscal needs of deficit-burdened governments to growing political discomfort with anything affiliated to market socialism. It is said that whatever the motivation, however, the transfer of ownership to private hands will increase the competitiveness of the banking sector and will subsequently enhance its efficiency. Essentially the general arguments for the privatisation of state activities are concerned with raising efficiency, both static and dynamic. Static efficiency gains relate to producing any given output at a lower cost. Costs can be above their feasible minimum because inputs are being used in the wrong proportions, given their marginal productivity and prices; and/or too little output is being produced from a given set of inputs. Dynamic efficiency gains are more focused on longer-term benefits in terms of product innovation and improvements in the process by which services are produced (Parker, 1994). The argument goes that privatisation could eliminate or reduce the distortions which occur where the public and private sectors coexist in a number of European countries, such as in Italy and France. The degree of a state's influence on its own banks varies throughout the EU; however, there is evidence of cases where banks have received and provided finance that would not be justified on normal commercial banking criteria (see Morgan Stanley, 1994b).

Table 3.23 shows a list of financial institutions that have been privatised or are earmarked as potential privatisation candidates over the next few years. The motivation for the rapid privatisation of the Italian financial system is strongly driven by the parlous state of budget finances (see Morgan Stanley, 1994c). Proceeds of sell-off are channelled into reducing public indebtedness, helping to prevent an increase in the deficit and interest payments.

The Banco di Napoli was the first public sector bank to have a stock-market flotation. In November 1991, it issued 100 million new ordinary shares, corresponding to around 20% of its capital. The Banca San Paolo was the next candidate. On 16 March 1992 it floated 125 million ordinary shares to a value of about L1525 billion, 20% of its stock.

In Italy, the Amato law aimed to restructure the Italian banking market. The Amato law allowed the major public law banks such as San Paolo di Torino and Monte dei Paschi di Siena, and savings institutions such as Cariplo, to transform themselves from foundations into limited companies with share capital and subsequently to obtain stock-exchange quotations (see Morgan Stanley, 1992, p. 31). The shareholder base of the former public law banks that have been transformed into limited companies continued to broaden in 1993. Of the 77 savings banks,

Table 3.23 Selected recent bank privatisation in the French, Italian and Spanish banking markets

Country/bank	Comment
France Crédit Local de France (June 1993) BNP (Oct. 1993) Crédit Lyonnais (early 1997)	The privatisation process in France has begun. Early candidates included the two largest banks in domestic market as well as in Europe
Italy Banca di Napoli (Nov. 1991) San Paolo di Torino (Jan. 1993) Credito Italiano (Dec. 1993) BCI (Feb. 1994) IMI (Feb. 1994)	The motivation for the rapid privatisation of the Italian financial system is strongly driven by the parlous state of budget finances. Privatisation also helps rationalisation of the financial sector
Spain Argentaria (late 1994)	The state aims to reduce its involvement in the banking industry through the privatisation of its only state-owned bank, Argentaria, and to adopt an unprecedented process of competition and change

Source: *Financial Times* various; Morgan Stanley (1994a, p. 10).

all of them now limited companies, only 23 are still wholly owned by their respective foundations (see Bank of Italy, 1994, p. 142).

Investors' interest in the Italian banking industry was fully evident on the occasion of the privatisation of three large banks. The public offers for the sale of Credito Italiano, IMI and Banca Commerciale Italiana drew applications for 8.8 billion shares, compared with the 1.6 billion offered. The proceeds aggregated to L6.87 trillion, equivalent to roughly one-third of total net share issues in 1993 (Bank of Italy, 1994).

The Instituto Mobiliare Italiano (IMI), the treasury-controlled financial services group, was privatised in February 1994 (Morgan Stanley, 1994c). A third of IMI's capital was offered which involved selling 200 million shares. As a result, the combined public-sector stake in the bank fell to about 25% from more than 60% previously. At the time of issue it was announced that the state's remaining shares in IMI would be sold in the next two years.

The privatisations of Credito Italiano and Banca Commerciale Italiana hailed as very successful at the time have since become the centre of a political controversy (see *European Banker*, 1994). Objections have been raised about the composition of their board which appeared to be heavily weighted in favour of the influential investment bank, Mediobanca. Criticism was fiercest in political circles, especially from the new government who felt that Mediobanca had been too influential in the privatisation process. It is further suggested that anger had been roused because the Italian privatisation programme has been dominated by one investment bank (see *European Banker*, 1994 p. 1). Possible future prospects for privatisation include Banca Nazionale de Lavora and Cassa di Risparmio Verona. It is expected that, market conditions permitting, there will be continued consolidation within, and share issues from, the savings banks sector (Bank of Italy, 1994).

In Spain, the state has gradually reduced its involvement in the banking industry through the privatisation of state-owned institutions, the main example of which had been the privatisation of part of the government's stake in Argentaria announced on 21 January 1993. *Retail Banker International* (1993) noted that the privatisation was a landmark event among the large Spanish banks, prompting an influx of private shareholders whose total investment reached Pta450 billion ($3.3 billion). The banking sector has undergone an unprecedented process of competition and change in recent years. The major banks have become increasingly differentiated in areas that were critical to their future development, such as the weight of international business, investment banking and capital market strategies, mutual funds management, strategy *vis-à-vis* industrial holdings and policies of strategic alliances. Morgan Stanley (1993a, 1994a) has stated that Argentaria has gradually been rationalised so that it will be ready for full privatisation when the government deems the timing appropriate.

As with other Continental European banking markets, the privatisation programme is well under way in the French system. The Banque Nationale de Paris (BNP) privatised in October 1993 (see *European Banker*, 1994, p. 8) and the following institutions have all been cited by government as potential targets: Banque Harvet, Marseillaise de Crédit and insurers Assurances Générales de France (AGF), Groupe Assurances Nationale (GAN) (and its affiliate, Crédit Industriel et Commercial — CIC, is to be privatised separately), Union des Assurances de Paris (UAP), Caisse Centrale de Réassurance and Caisse Nationale de Prévoyance. After Crédit Lyonnais recorded losses of Fr6.9 billion ($1.28 billion) for 1993, however, the privatisation process was halted and according to recent Morgan Stanley (1994b, p. 10) reports, it is unrealistic to expect further privatisation before 1997.

In Germany, the public banks (mainly savings banks) have traditionally played a more important role both at the Federal government and regional levels. Arthur Andersen (1993), however, has noted that the concept of privatisation has not been discussed so intensively as, for example, in France or Italy. The German Savings Banks Association has stated that the privatisation of savings banks would disturb the balance between the public and private sector in the banking industry, leading to distortion of competition, but pressures for privatisation of savings banks is growing, because the government has estimated that it could raise funds of DM150 billion ($93.7 billion) (see *European Banker*, 1993, no: 95, p. 4) which would help in funding the restructuring of eastern Germany. The most likely candidate for privatisation in the short term appears to be Postbank, the Bonn-based postal bank which operates via the post office network. Although the Postbank management was strongly in favour of privatisation, the government appears to be reluctant to proceed with the plan because of the large number of staff cuts which would inevitably follow (see *European Banker*, 1993, no: 92).

The overall privatisation programme may be good business for European banks. They can be active in the distribution of shares and also have advisory and corporate finance roles. Increased bank privatisation may also raise liquidity in bank securities which could help trading. Moreover, the privatised institutions would have greater managerial freedom to manage their businesses which should lead to increased efficiency. Table 3.23 provides a snapshot of recent bank privatisation in the French, Italian and Spanish banking markets.

CONCLUSIONS

This chapter has examined the forces generating change and structural developments in the European banking market-place. The implementation of the EU Second Banking Directive in domestic banking legislation has had the effect of establishing universal banking practice for credit institutions within EU countries, rendering the old distinctions between different types of credit institutions obsolete. The blurring of distinctions between bank credit and securities, domestic and international paper, cash and derivatives and so on, has helped foster cross-border investment. These forces continue to shape European banking business and increase the competitive threat between banks and non-banks alike. The financial integration of Europe is generating a powerful boost to the opening-up of banking systems. In recent years as market conditions have become more competitive the focus of profitability management has tended to alter. Macroeconomic recession coupled with the ongoing process of deregulation has influenced the profitability of banks, in particular, by putting considerable pressure on their interest margins and forcing them to concentrate on areas such as fee income and cost reduction.

This chapter also indicates that, despite various obstacles, there has been substantial restructuring of the industry reflected by the significant amount of cross-border merger and acquisition activity in European financial markets in recent years. In addition, privatisation programmes in various countries, coupled with the political will to liberalise banking systems in line with EU legislation, continue to reshape the structural characteristics of European banking markets. Given these developments, and considering that there is a trend towards larger bank size, it is important that the structure–performance and cost characteristics of banking systems are investigated so as to evaluate the potential efficiency implications and opportunities arising from some of these changes.

4

The structure-performance relationship in US and European banking

INTRODUCTION

This chapter provides an overview of how the structure–conduct–performance (SCP) relationship has been investigated in US and European banking markets. The rationale for testing the SCP relationship in banking markets is first discussed and there then follows a brief description of how the structure–performance debate emerged in US banking at the end of the 1950s to early 1960s. An overview of the general form of the structure–performance model is provided together with an analysis of the model variables. The remainder of this chapter investigates the empirical evidence on the concentration–performance relationship and finally we conclude with a note on the limitations of bank SCP modelling.

THE RATIONALE FOR TESTING THE SCP RELATIONSHIP IN BANKING

The SCP model is a general statement on the determinants of market performance. Simply stated, the conduct or rivalry in a market is determined by market structure conditions, especially the number and size distribution of firms and the condition of entry. This rivalry leads to unique levels of prices, advertising, profits and other aspects of market performance. Through the link of conduct, the performance of firms in a market is tied to the general structure of the market.

Analysis of the SCP relationship in banking is used to help evaluate the main policy issue of which type of banking structure best serves the public in terms both of the cost and the availability of banking services. In general two main objectives have been sought; firstly, the attainment of an 'efficient' banking system which in some way, secondly, minimises the likelihood of bank failure.

We have seen from Chapter 3 that 'efficiency' is associated with competition. Under perfect competition firms price equal to marginal cost, maximise their profit, and achieve levels of output which bring about an optimum allocation of resources. The other extreme is monopoly which leads to a suboptimal allocation of resources. In general, the more competitive a market, the more 'efficient' it is.

Other factors, however, make it difficult to choose between the objectives of 'efficiency' and 'soundness' in banking markets. Under a competitive environment 'inefficient' firms are forced to leave the market because they cannot maintain prices high enough to cover costs. On the other hand, under monopolistic conditions high-cost firms are to a certain extent immune from the forces of competition which allows them to operate in an efficient manner and yet still survive. As such, a monopolistic industry is more compatible with the policy objective of maintaining a failure-proof banking system, while competition is more consistent with the goal of 'efficiency'.

The existence of substantial economies of scale makes the choice between the two market regimes even more difficult as Edwards (1965, p. 2) notes:

> Since economies of scale occur as bank size increases, there is usually a reduction in the number of competitors. Thus, another dimension is added to efficiency, one that cannot be equated with competition in the narrow sense of number of competitors. As long as economies of scale exist, a judgement has to be made about the extent to which diminished competition is offset by the benefits of lower costs.

In general there are a range of views concerning the application of the above to the problem of competition in banking markets. Those who believe that failure of a bank should be avoided at all cost due to the serious repercussions on the financial system and economy at large would probably be willing to sacrifice 'efficiency' for 'soundness'. In other words, the gains from increased competition (efficiency) would be small in relation to the costs associated with bank failure. At the polar extreme there would be those who believe that the cost of bank failures is small (given that deposit insurance arrangements and flexible monetary policy arrangements could be capable of preventing panics induced by failures) and these observers would be willing to sacrifice 'soundness' for greater competition and therefore efficiency.

Another viewpoint originally espoused by Phillips (1964) and Holland (1964), among others, is that because (the US) banking markets are inherently oligopolistic, conventional anti-trust or regulatory policy aimed at changing market structure would be unable to increase competition or the quality of bank performance. As Phillips (1964, p. 43) states:

> It would be possible and, within limits, it probably is desirable to improve the performance of commercial banking markets. It appears, however, that the rule of conventional antitrust policy — the prevention of mergers and combinations in restraint of trade — in achieving this result is an extremely limited one, because of the continuing necessity for some public regulation and supervision and also because of the

impossibility of altering substantially the oligopolistic structure of the typical banking market.

In short, if bank performance is not affected by changes in the structure of banking markets then regulatory authorities need not be concerned about bank mergers. If evidence from the SCP literature found this to be the case then it would suggest that it is the organisation, rather than market structure, of the industry which is the major determinant of bank performance. It would then follow that the main means of altering performance was through changing the organisation (for example by altering bank participation in organisations such as clearing houses and trade associations), especially that part which emanates from bank regulation.

There are two important rationales for testing the SCP hypothesis in European banking markets. First, very little empirical work has been undertaken investigating the competitive behaviour of European banking systems and as such an empirical investigation may yield insights that could be of interest to academics, bankers and policymakers. Secondly, the Price Waterhouse/Cecchini study on completion of an EC internal financial market drew attention to the fact that aspects of the SCP framework could be used to evaluate the evidence of oligopoly profits in EC banking systems. If oligopoly profits are significant in those banking systems, then producer surplus losses would be substantial post-integration. An analysis of the SCP relationship in European banking may help us to shed light on these issues.

THE EMERGENCE OF THE SCP DEBATE IN THE US BANKING MARKET

The emergence of the SCP debate in the United States is based on the view that the performance of the banking system — that is, its effectiveness in serving the deposit and credit needs of the country — is in some way related to its structure and organisation.

Prior to 1950 there were only two studies which examined the competitive situation in banking — Chandler (1938) and Berle (1949). Chandler (1938, p. 1) applied Chamberlin's (1933) theory of oligopoly and monopolistic competition to the structure and behaviour of banking markets and noted that:

> ... important elements of monopoly exist in the commercial banking system, even in the absence of collusive agreements, and that it is the theory of monopolistic competition, rather than the theory of pure competition, that is the more useful in explaining the rates of interest on bank loans to customers, the rates of interest paid to bank customers on time and savings deposits, and the prices paid by customers for other banking services.

In particular Chandler focused on the case that banks are sellers of differentiated products. Customers deal with one bank rather than another for a variety of different reasons which include: age of the bank and its record of honesty, fair dealing and safety; location, size and architecture of the bank building; personalities of the bank staff and so on. Because of customer preferences arising out of the variations in these factors, the demand for bank services will not be perfectly elastic, 'and each bank has some degree of freedom in determining the prices and rates which it will pay or charge' (Chandler, 1938, p. 3). In general Chandler concluded that the lack of pure competition in the US banking market helped to explain many 'phenomena' in the field of commercial banking.

Berle (1949) examined the application of competition laws to banking and he concluded that competition (or anti-trust) policy was thought to have very limited applicability to banking because of its regulated character. This widely held view set the scene for the lack of research into banking structure during the 1950s (with the exception of Alhadeff, 1954) as identified by Smith (1964, p. 489):

> The previous indifference of economists, even those in the industrial organisation field, to research into banking structure stemmed principally from the view that banking was a regulated industry and that its major problem was one of overbanking and excessive competition rather than one of monopolistic markets and imperfect competition. In the atmosphere of the 1930s the safety and liquidity of the banking system became an overriding concern and bank mergers were welcomed as a means of shoring up weak situations in an overcrowded industry. After the sharp reduction in a number of banking offices during the depression years, concern with overbanking largely subsided and was replaced by emphasis on the need to maintain vigorous competition in banking markets.

According to Philips (1964) the average annual number of bank mergers and holding company formations in the 1940s was 81, during the 1950s it was 150 and in the three years after 1960 it was around 160 a year. Gradual public concern in the United States over decreasing competition resulting from a 'wave' of bank mergers and holding company formations in the 1950s led to the Bank Holding Company Act of 1956 and the Bank Merger Act of 1960. The aforementioned laws required policymakers to focus their attentions on the economic issues in bank holding company and merger cases, and the Federal bank supervisory agencies had to consider the competitive implications as well as 'public interest' matters.

By the early 1960s competition in banking had emerged as an ostensibly relevant public policy consideration and this 'stimulated academic interest in the problems of banking structure' (Smith, 1964, p. 489). Further academic interest was generated by the landmark US Supreme Court decision in the *United States* v. *Philadelphia National Bank* case in 1963 when it was found that commercial banking was to be treated as any other industry under the basic anti-trust laws. In short, the ruling emphasised the need to preserve and promote competition in banking within the boundaries established by Federal and state regulation. As Rose (1987, p. 59) notes:

The result ... was a veritable explosion of bank market structure and competition studies mirroring earlier industrial studies. Overwhelmingly, these studies have concentrated on the relationships among bank market structure, the key prices in banking — the rate of interest on loans and the promised rate of return on deposits, and bank profitability as barometers of how well or how poorly the public is being serviced by American banks.

THE SCP MODEL APPLIED TO THE BANKING INDUSTRY

Heggestad (1979, p. 467) states that in general, a model of the structure–performance relationship in banking would make the equilibrium price of any product a function of the following:

1. the level and elasticity of market and firm demand;
2. the firm's cost function;
3. the prices and quantities of related financial products, and their interactions with the firm's demand and cost functions;
4. the objective function of firms in the market;
5. the interaction among firms in the market.

Every firm would simultaneously or 'iteratively' obtain the equilibrium price, and market structure influences this process by its effect on the interaction among firms. As a way of modelling this process, the US structure–performance studies have mainly used multiple regression analysis as a means of relating structure to performance in banking markets. The general form of the structure–performance model (see Rhoades, 1977; Heggestad, 1979; Gilbert, 1984) is as follows:

$$P = f(CR, S, D, C, X) \tag{1}$$

where P is a performance measure, CR is a measure of market structure (usually a concentration measure), S is a measure of the size of the market or other market structure variables, such as proxies for barriers to entry, D a set of variables to reflect market demand conditions, C a set of variables to reflect differences in costs across firms and X a variety of control variables related to a specific product's characteristics.

Measurement of Bank Performance

There are various approaches to measuring the performance of a banking firm. Traditionally there have been two main types of measure of bank performance. The first type of measure generally relates to the price of a particular product or service; the second type of performance measure are profitability measures. Table 4.1 provides a classification of performance measures used in 73 US SCP studies between 1964 and 1991, the details of which are set out in Appendix I.

Table 4.1   Performance measures used in the US SCP literature[a]

Performance measures	Number of times the respective performance measures have been used in the SCP literature	Number finding the performance measure to be unambiguously significantly related to market structure[b]
Loan interest rates		
Interest and fees on loans/total loans	19	7
Interest rate on business loans	6	3
Interest rate on new car loans	3	2
Interest rate on residential mortgages	2	2
Total	30	14
Deposit interest rates		
Interest payment on time and savings deposits/total time and savings deposits	16	5
Interest rates on money-market deposit accounts	2	2
3, 6, 12 and 30-month CD rates	2	1
Interest rate on Super-NOW accounts	1	1
Interest payment on time deposits /total time deposits	1	1
Interest rate on time deposits	1	0
Interest rate on passbook savings	1	0
Interest rate on $1000 CD	1	0
Total	25	10
Service charges		
Revenue from service charges on demand deposits/total demand deposits	14	3
Revenue from service charges on demand deposits	5	2
Monthly service charge on demand deposits	1	1
Charges for returned cheques	1	0
Service charges on a standardised account	1	0
Total	22	6

Table 4.1 (*continued*)

Performance measures	Number of times the respective performance measures have been used in the SCP literature	Number finding the performance measure to be unambiguously significantly related to market structure[b]
Profitability measures		
Return on assets	24	12
Return on capital	14	8
Total	38	20
Other measures		
Lerner index	2	0
Elasticity of loan demand	2	1
Number of bank employees	1	0
Standard deviation of return on equity	2	2
Concentration measures	1	0
Market share stability indices	2	2
Portfolio selection	2	2
Senatorial votes	1	0
Service quality measures	1	1
Labour expenses	2	2
Other expenses	2	2
Total	133	62

[a]These performance measures were found to be used in a review of 73 US SCP studies.
[b]Many studies use a variety of performance and market structure measures covering different time periods. Figures included in this column relate to those studies that find regression coefficients on measures of market structure with t-statistics greater than 1.95 and which unambiguously report a significant result.
Source: See Appendix I.

It can be seen from the table that the most common type of price measures are as follows:

- average interest rate on loans, calculated as interest and fees on loans during the year divided by the volume of outstanding loans at a given point in time;
- average interest rate paid on deposits, estimated as the total amount of interest paid over the year divided by the volume of deposits at the end of the year;
- average service charges on demand deposits, which is calculated as the annual service charge revenue over the volume of demand deposits at a specified point in time.

Several commentators (see e.g. Gilbert, 1984; Smirlock, 1985; Evanoff and Fortier, 1988) have criticised the use of average deposit and loan rate ratios as measures of bank performance for the following reasons. Firstly, average measures combine flow variables (i.e. interest on loans over a one-year period) with stock variables (i.e. loans outstanding at the end of the year). It is unclear as to whether prices should be defined using average or year-end values; depending on the criteria chosen the value of the ratios will be different.

Secondly, some studies have used average interest paid on deposits as a performance measure when Regulation Q, which imposed ceilings on interest payable on deposits in US banking, was in existence. Given this restriction, average interest rate paid on deposits 'is more likely to be a function of the maturity distribution of a bank's deposits and their denomination than a function of market structure' (Gilbert, 1984, p. 632). Finally, average service charges on deposit accounts do not take into account the fact that service charges vary according to such things as account activity, minimum balance requirements and so on.

These measurement problems can be avoided by using survey data to obtain information on interest rates and service cost for particular categories of loans and deposits as illustrated in Table 4.1. A much simpler and more widely adopted approach, however, has been to use profitability measures. As Gilbert (1984, p. 632) observes:

> The only measures of bank performance derived from the report of income and report of condition that do not have major measurement problems are bank profit rates. If banks in areas with higher market concentration charge higher interest rates on loans, set higher service charges on deposits and pay lower interest rates on deposits, these effects will be reflected in the pattern of bank profit rates.

Brown (1985), Rhoades (1985d) and Evanoff and Fortier (1988), to name a few, provide support for the use of a profitability measure to account for the performance of the firm. The two major advantages of such a measure are its simplicity and the fact that it consolidates information about a multi-product firm into one single figure. The major disadvantage of profitability measures is that they combine flow variables (i.e. profits) with stock variables (i.e. assets or capital). The most commonly used profitability measures as shown in Table 4.1 are net income divided by total assets (return on assets) and net income divided by capital (return on capital). Studies that have used profitability measures have also been more successful in finding a significant relationship between market structure and industry performance.

Definition of a Market and Measurements of Market Structure

Because banking is a multi-product industry, a simple all-inclusive market area is difficult to delineate and no single measure of structure precisely reflects the degree of monopoly, nor does economic theory help choose which measure is most important. Measures of market structure suffer from deficiencies which may lead to erroneous conclusions. Vernon (1971, p. 623) points out that because banking markets are mainly categorised into the 'modestly' concentrated regions:

> There are no monopolies and no highly competitive market forms. This being the case, concentration ratios relating to the local banking markets may be rather insensitive indicators of monopoly performance. ... The connection between structure and performance is tenuous even where a wide range of structures is present.

In addition, without a control group of banks existing in a perfectly competitive environment, there is not an absolute standard for comparing the influence of alternative bank structures.

To account for the multi-product nature of banking markets the majority of US research studies on bank structure and competition 'usually choose between studying the market for one banking service or viewing banks as offering a bundle of services within the boundaries of a single market area' (Rose, 1987, p. 52). Banking markets have been approximated in most studies by the standard metropolitan statistical area (SMSA) for urban banks and counties for other banks. Gilbert (1984, p. 634) notes that:

> There is empirical support for such market area designations. Surveys of where bank customers obtain banking services indicate that the relevant market area for banking services are substantially smaller than states or nations. ... These surveys indicate that the geographic areas over which customers shop for banking services are different for various banking services.

This definition of banking markets, however, may not be entirely appropriate because as Tolley (1977, p. 5) identified, bank regulatory agencies frequently employ SMSAs and counties as 'approximations' for banking markets, mainly because deposit data are readily obtainable for these geographic areas.

Most US banking markets — as identified in studies undertaken by Heggestad and Mingo (1977), Savage (1982) and Rhoades (1985a, b) — have historically been highly concentrated. For example, Rhoades (1985b) shows that in 1983 the 25 states that permitted statewide branching had, on average, five-bank deposit concentration ratios of 72%. In local (SMSA) markets, Savage (1982) reports five-bank deposit concentration ratios ranging from 76.7% (for SMSAs in unit banking states) to 83.7% (in limited branching states). As Rose (1987, p. 177) notes:

> ... across the United States as a whole the top three banks in each of the nation's urban centres (SMSAs) appear to control about 70 per cent of local deposits.

As typified by the above, concentration has been most widely used as a measure of market structure in the SCP literature. Table 4.2 provides a summary of market structure measures used in this literature.

Heggestad (1979, p. 469) identifies three major problems of measuring monopoly in banking markets: 'choosing the appropriate general index of monopoly power, choosing the appropriate economic variable with which

Table 4.2 Market structure measures used in the US SCP literature

Measures of market structure	Number of times the respective market structure measures have been used in the SCP literature
Concentration ratios	
5-Firm deposits	2
3-Firm deposits	37
2-Firm deposits	3
1-Firm deposits	9
Herfindahl index (*H*) deposits	17
Numbers equivalent (1/*H*)	2
Number of firms in the market	16
Gini coefficient	2
Entropy	2
Hall–Tideman index	2
Dummy variable for markets with relatively high 1-firm or 3-firm concentration ratios	1
Herfindahl index (*H*) multiplied by a dummy variable for markets with relatively low *H*	1
Change in *H*	1

Note: These market structure measures were found to be used in a review of 73 SCP studies; see Appendix I for further information.
Source: See Appendix I.

to measure differences in bank size, and accounting for differences in institutional competition (or for competition between banks and nonbank financial institutions)'. In virtually all the cases referred to in Table 4.2, the measure of market structure is based on total bank deposits. This may well be relevant when studying general bank performance, but may be less appropriate when evaluating the SCP relationship in say the consumer loan market where measurement of monopoly power should ideally be related to the distribution of consumer loans among banks. This may seem to be a serious error in many studies, but Heggestad goes on to suggest that because various measures of monopoly in banking are likely to be highly correlated and because all measures are only approximations for monopoly, using a commonly available deposits-based measure can be viewed as satisfactory.

Choosing the appropriate measure of market structure is also important. Most US studies have used a simple concentration ratio, but this type of measure does not take account of the dispersion of bank size in the market and also does not reflect the number of competing firms. The Herfindahl index is responsive to the number and dispersion of firms in the market and is therefore generally viewed as a superior measure. It has been suggested, however, that these measures are actually so highly correlated (see Rose and Fraser, 1976) that the choice of market structure measure is 'not of critical importance for testing structure–performance hypotheses' (Heggestad, 1979, p. 470).

Other Market Structure Variables

Entry Barriers

Economic theory implies, *ceteris paribus*, that the entry of new firms into a given market will necessarily increase rivalry. This is because the entry of such firms has long been regarded as a stimulus to competition. If the number of firms in a market increases, it will become more competitive and less concentrated (see Bain, 1956; Scherer, 1980). Rhoades (1980, p. 424) points out:

> In addition, particularly in the short run, new entry will tend to increase uncertainty among the firms in a market with respect to their views of the actions and reactions of their rivals as well as to their views of the action of new entrants.

In US banking markets, many decisions that affect the number of competitors in various markets are made by Federal and state regulatory agencies. These authorities have the power to approve or deny applications for new bank charters or branches, and therefore they can determine the number of competitors in banking markets. Public policy of this nature seeks to protect the public interest by avoiding excessive competition. This role of the authorities is based on the view that unrestricted competition would not safeguard the public interest: consequently, competition should be restricted as Phillips (1964, p. 41) observed, in order to 'preserve the liquidity of the payments mechanism, and to provide safety for depositors'.

In contrast to this view, there are other commentators who believe that entry barriers into banking markets should be relaxed in order to foster competition. King (1979) notes that in order to evaluate the costs and benefits of Federal and state entry barriers (e.g. branching versus unit banking states, liberal bank holding company (LBHC) legislation versus restricted BHC regulations) one must evaluate whether decisions that loom so important in theory have any influence in practice. In other words, entry conditions are included in the SCP model in order to evaluate the impact they have on bank performance as well as to see how they relate to concentration levels.

The majority of US studies that account for entry barriers do so by assuming that lower entry barriers — the ability to undertake branching — enter the performance equation only as a shift parameter (see Rhoades, 1980, 1981, 1982a; Rhoades and Rutz, 1982; Berger and Hannan, 1989, to name but a few). The findings of these studies, though not conclusive, suggest that higher entry barriers result in greater profits. In other words, in unit banking states it should be easier for banks to exert market power than in areas where there is always the threat of potential entry: these areas are termed liberal branching states. Evanoff and Fortier (1988) suggest that the use of a binary variable to take account of entry barriers may distort the influence of other explanatory variables, given that determinants of market performance may be quite different across the two types of banking markets. As a result, they suggest that it is better to estimate separate equations for unit banking and liberal branching states — they do, however, use a binary variable to account for whether 'liberal' holding company expansion is allowed or not.

We have discussed the regulatory barriers to entry. There are also, of course, non-regulatory barriers to entry, such as the relative-minimal-efficient size of firm, and SCP studies usually account for this by including a variable for the size of the market, since most studies in US banking assume the minimum efficient size of firm is the same in all markets. In addition, product differentiation may be achieved through a proliferation of branches (see Stolz, 1976; White, 1976) or high levels of advertising expenditure (see Edwards, 1973). Only a few studies, however, control for product differentiation.

Other Market Structure Variables

Other market structure variables included in the SCP models are used to control for other structural factors that are believed to impact on bank performance. For example, number of bank branches; market share of banks; binary variables to account for competition between bank and non-bank financial intermediaries; binary variables to capture differences in bank behaviour attributable to holding company affiliation; binary variables indicating banks located in metropolitan statistical areas; and so on.

Market Demand Conditions

All the SCP studies use some variables to proxy for market demand conditions, the most popular being measures of market size and market growth. Market size, either total bank deposits or assets in respective markets, is used as a proxy for market potential on the basis that the larger the market the greater the likelihood of new entry and potential for increased competition (see e.g. Evanoff and Fortier, 1988; Hannan, 1991a). Growth in market deposits is also often used as a proxy to account for change in local demand conditions. Other variables that are used to control for market demand conditions include: per capita income or wage levels in the relevant markets (see Rhoades, 1981; Berger and Hannan, 1989); coefficient of variation of per capita income in the market (to capture variation in the demand for bank services); population density to control for demographic differences across markets; and the rate of in-migration into specific markets to account for changes in demand.

Cost Differences

The most common variable used in the SCP literature to account for cost differences across banks is a measure of individual bank size, namely total assets. This is included in virtually every model that has been tested and is included to account for size-induced differences between banks, such as scale economies. Other measures, such as local banking wage rates (a proxy for the cost of labour: see Calem and Carlino, 1989) and interest paid on deposits (a proxy for the cost of funds: see Berger and Hannan, 1989), are also used to account for cost differences across banks. Many studies also use the ratio of demand deposits to total deposits as a crude proxy for the relative cost of funds on the grounds that demand deposits are a relatively inexpensive source of funds.

Other Control Variables

SCP studies that adopt loan and deposit rates as a measure of bank performance use a variety of other variables to account for their characteristics such as the type, size and maturity of these items. In addition, all the studies also utilise a variety of variables to control for different risk characteristics associated with individual banks. For example, the loans-to-assets ratio is sometimes used as a rough proxy of portfolio risk based on the view that loans tend to be risky relative to other assets typically held in a commercial bank's portfolios. Studies, particularly in the 1980s, tended also to incorporate a capital-to-assets (or equity-to-assets) ratio to account for differing risk levels between banks — lower ratios implying a more risky position. Clark (1986b) introduces loan-loss reserves to total loans as an indicator of default risk.

CONCENTRATION AND PERFORMANCE — THE EMPIRICAL EVIDENCE FROM THE UNITED STATES

Details of all the studies cited in the following section are provided in Appendix I. This appendix provides information on: sample used; measure of bank performance; R^2 or adjusted R^2 ($\bar{R}^2$), measures of market structure and shows whether the coefficients on the measures of market structure are statistically significant. It covers US SCP studies from 1960 to 1991.

Concentration and Loan Rates

In the earliest SCP study of banking markets, Schweiger and McGee (1961) came to the conclusion that the smaller the number of banks in a region, the higher the level of automobile and instalment loan rates. The sample was taken from 11 large cities for 1960, but unfortunately the study did not provide adequate statistical tests to determine whether differences detected were other than random.

Edwards (1964) in his study of 49 SMSAs found that for data provided by the Federal Reserve Survey on business loan rates these were found to be significantly related to concentration levels in 1955 but not for 1957 (these conflicting results, it was suggested, may be due to different monetary policies pursued by the central authorities in those years). The positive relationship between individual business loan rates, obtained through survey data, and concentration has been substantiated by the majority of subsequent studies (see e.g. Phillips, 1967; Jacobs, 1971; Hannan, 1991a).

Fleschig (1965), however, used a similar dataset to Edwards (1964) in order to undertake two tests of the SCP relationship and found that concentration had no effect on those rates in 1957 and only a marginal impact for 1955 data. He concluded (p. 310):

> Although concentration in metropolitan areas in some instances appears to be directly associated with bank rates on these loans it is not significantly related to loan rates when adequate account is taken of the differences in loan characteristics and in the supply and demand conditions in local and regional markets.

The studies mentioned above all used individual loan rates as a measure of performance. The data were usually obtained from Federal Reserve Surveys of business loan rates or individual researchers' surveys. Average loan rates, calculated by dividing interest and fees on loans by total loans, however, have been the most widely used measure in the US SCP literature. This is because data on average loan rates are much easier to obtain. The difficulty arising from using this measure is that 'average' loan rates make no allowance for major differences in risk and types of loans held by banks. This problem, however, has not restricted the amount of studies using this specific performance indicator as illustrated in Table 4.3.

The results from those studies have been very mixed. Ware (1972), so as to avoid problems associated with variations in regulations across states, restricted his study to markets within the state of Ohio (see Fraser and Rose, 1971 and Kaufman, 1966 for examples of other studies). Ware concludes that concentration has no significant effect on any of his measures of performance, average loan rates included. Conversely, Beighley and McCall (1975, p. 466) found that concentration had an important effect on average loan rates:

> The results clearly provide a firm basis for the conclusion that competitive market structure is statistically significant in explaining variations in the market power of individual banks in large and medium-sized local instalment loan markets.

Studies by Edwards (1965), Kaufman (1966), Fraser and Rose (1971), Whitehead (1978), Savage and Rhoades (1979), Rhoades and Rutz (1979), Rhoades (1979), Rose and Scott (1979), Rhoades (1981) and Hanweck and Rhoades (1984) all substantiate the case that concentration does have a significant effect on average loan rates. However, the remaining studies do not find any significant link between the level of concentration and average loan rates.

Table 4.3   Concentration and loan rates

	Study	Individual loan rates	Average loan rates	Coefficient on the measure of market structure are statistically significant[a]
1.	Schweiger and McGee (1967)	Automobile loan rates	—	Higher rates with fewer banks
		Instalment loan rates	—	
2.	Edwards (1964)	Business loan rates	—	Yes 1955 No 1957
3.	Edwards (1965)	—	IL–TL	Yes
4.	Fleschig (1965)	Business loan rates	—	Yes 1955 No 1957
5.	Kaufman (1966)	—	IL–TL	Yes
6.	Phillips (1967)	Rates on short-term business loans	—	Yes
7.	Taylor (1968)	—	IL–TL	No
8.	Aspinwall (1970)	Rates on residential mortgages	—	Yes
9.	Fraser and Rose (1971)	—	IL–TL	No 1966 Yes 1967
10.	Jacobs (1971)	Business loan rates	—	Yes
11.	Fraser and Rose (1972)	—	IL–TL	No
12.	Ware (1972)	—	IL–TL	No
13.	Yeats (1974)	—	IL–TL	No
14.	Fraser and Alvis (1975)	—	IL–TL	No
15.	Beighley and McCall (1975)	—	IL –TL	Yes
16.	Heggestad and Mingo (1976)	Interest rate on new car loans	—	Yes
17.	Whitehead (1977)	—	IL –TL	No
18.	Whitehead (1978)	—	IL –TL	Yes
19.	Graddy and Kyle (1979)	—	IL–TL	No
20.	Harvey (1979)	—	IL–TL	Ambiguous
21.	Savage and Rhoades (1979)	—	IL–TL	Yes
22.	Rhoades (1979)	—	IL–TL	Yes
23.	Rhoades and Rutz (1979)	—	IL–TL	Yes
24.	Rose and Scott (1979)	—	IL–TL	Yes
25.	McCall and Peterson (1980)		IL–TL	Yes

continued overleaf

Table 4.3   (*continued*)

Study	Individual loan rates	Average loan rates	Coefficient on the measure of market structure are statistically significant[a]
26. Rhoades (1981)	—	IL−TL	Yes (in 5 out of 7 years)
27. Marlow (1982)	Rates on residential mortgage loans	—	Yes
28. Hanweck and Rhoades (1984)		IL−TL	Yes
29. Hannan (1991a)	Commercial loan rates	—	Yes in only 1 out of 8 cases for 1984 Yes in 5 out of 8 cases in 1986

[a]Where *t*-statistics on the market structure coefficient are greater than 1.95.
IL = interest and fees on loans.
TL = total loans.
Source: See Appendix I.

A study by McCall and Peterson (1980), focusing on 155 SMSAs and counties in 14 unit banking and limited branching states, is of particular interest
because it uses the Lerner index (i.e. the spread between average loan and deposit
rates) as the main bank performance indicator, and tests for non-linearity in the
structure–performance relationship. Using a switching regression technique, the
authors find evidence of a critical level of concentration in business loan markets.
This finding of a critical level of market concentration above which the market
power of leading firms exerts a significant effect on performance supports similar
findings by Rose (1976), Rhoades (1980) and Daskin and Wolken (1989).

Hanweck and Rhoades (1984) and Rhoades (1985a) evaluate whether market
share has an effect on bank prices, loan rates included. Hanweck and Rhoades
(1984) examine 147 SMSAs and 112 country-wide banking markets and Rhoades
(1985a) analyses 6500 banks both during the 1970s:

> The underlying hypothesis of their studies is that some banks, may be so large relative
> to their competitors, possessing markedly superior resources and diversification, that
> they are able to intimidate smaller banks into adopting the larger institutions pricing
> schemes (Rose, 1987, p. 196).

This predatory pricing thesis is generally supported in both studies, especially
for loan interest rates (as well as service charges on deposits and non-interest
operating expenses).

In general we can make two main conclusions about the concentration/loan
rate relationship. Firstly, as Gilbert (1984, p. 631) has observed, average loan

rates are poor measures of bank performance and studies that use individual loan data obtained through survey avoid measurement problems and yield satisfactory results. As we have noted, virtually all of these suggest that the traditional structure–performance relationship holds. Secondly, even when the relationship between concentration and loan rates is found to be significant, there is a quantitatively small impact. The range of estimates of effects of a 10% increase in market concentration on loan rates (individual or average) varies between 18 basis points (Edwards, 1964) and 0.1 basis points (Rhoades, 1981). In addition, the R^2 for the equations in most of the market structure studies on bank loan rates vary between 0.15 and 0.60, suggesting that there are important omitted variables in these equations. The estimated effects of concentration on loan rates may therefore be biased if the measure of market concentration is correlated with the omitted variables.

Concentration and Deposit Rates

Interest on time and savings deposits has also been used as a performance indicator in the structure–performance studies. As in the case for loan rates, the majority of studies have used average deposit rates (mostly interest payments on time and savings deposits divided by time and savings deposits) as a performance measure. This measure is subject to the same criticisms as average loan rates because the numerator is an annual expense flow (income flow in the case of loans), but the denominator is a balance sheet item recorded at a point in time, which may be different from the average deposit balance (or loan) over the year.

Despite these problems, it can be seen from Table 4.4 that all but 5 of the 23 studies that use deposit rates as a performance measure employ average rates. Most studies that use average deposit rates find that there is no significant relationship between market structure and these rates. The earliest work using individual deposit rates (Klein and Murphy, 1971; Heggestad and Mingo, 1976) also find no significant relationship. One should note, however, that US pre-1980 studies using deposit rates as a performance measure give a biased picture of performance, because in most periods studied Regulation Q was in force. It is, therefore, more sensible to consider briefly the literature that uses sample data from outside this period.

Berger and Hannan (1989) examine 470 banks in 195 local banking markets observed quarterly over the period between September 1983 and December 1985. They use as performance measures, interest paid on money-market deposit accounts (MMDAs), Super-NOW (negotiable order of withdrawal) accounts, and 3, 6, 12 and 30-month CDs. These price data were obtained from the Federal Reserve's Monthly Survey of Selected Deposits and Other Accounts. Their findings are strongly consistent with the implications of the structure–performance hypothesis (Berger and Hannan, pp. 298–299):

Table 4.4   Concentration and deposit rates

Study	Individual deposit rates	Average deposit rates	Coefficient on the measure of market structure are statistically significant[a]
1. Edwards (1965)	—	IT–TS	Yes
2. Kaufmann (1966)	—	IT–TS	Yes
3. Fraser and Rose (1971)	—	IT–TS	No for 1966 Yes for 1967
4. Klein and Murphy (1971)	Interest rate on time deposits	—	No
5. Fraser and Rose (1972)	—	ITD–TD	No
6. Ware (1972)	—	IT–TS	No
7. Fraser and Alvis (1975)	—	IT–TS	No
8. Yeats (1974)	—	IT–TS	No
9. Heggestad and Mingo (1976)	Interest rate on passbook savings Interest rate on 1 year $1000 CD	—	No
10. Fraser and Rose (1976)	—	IT–TS	No
11. Rose and Fraser (1976)	—	IT–TS	No
12. Stolz (1976)		IT–TS	No
13. Whitehead (1977)	—	IT–TS	Yes
14. Whitehead (1978)	—	IT–TS	No
15. Graddy and Kyle (1979)	—	IT–TS	No
16. Harvey (1979)	—	Interest payments on TD–TD	Yes
17. Savage and Rhoades (1979)	—	IT–TS	Yes
18. Rhoades (1979)	—	IT–TS	No
19. Rose and Scott (1979)	—	IT–TS	No
20. Rhoades (1981)	—	IT–TD	Yes in 4 out of 7 cases
21. Hannan (1984)	Passbook savings rate	—	Yes (from Tobit maximum likelihood estimates)
22. Hanweck and Rhoades (1984)		IT–TD	Yes

Table 4.4   (*continued*)

Study	Individual deposit rates	Average deposit rates	Coefficient on the measure of market structure are statistically significant[a]
23. Berger and Hannan (1989)	Money-market deposit account rate 3, 6, 12 and 30-month CD rate	—	Yes in 8 out of 10 equations
24. Calem and Carlino (1989)	Money-market deposit account rate 3 and 6-month CD rates	—	MMDA's Yes 6-month CD Yes 3-month CD No

[a]Where *t*-statistics on the market structure coefficient are greater than 1.95.
IT = interest payment on time and savings deposits.
TS = time and savings deposits.
ITD = interest payments or time deposits.
TD = time deposits.
Source: See Appendix I.

... banks in the most concentrated local markets in the sample are found to pay MMDA rates that range from 25 to 100 basis points less than those paid in the least concentrated markets, depending on the time period examined. Similar results are found for Super-NOWs and shorter-term CDs.

These results are also unusual because their equations have much higher R^2 than other studies — ranging between 0.33 and 0.88.

Calem and Carlino (1989) use a sample of 466 commercial banks and Federal savings banks insured by the Federal Deposit Insurance Corporation (FDIC) in 1985 covering 145 SMSAs. Using MMDAs and 3- and 6-month CD rates as performance measures, they find that a 10% increase in concentration creates a fall in MMDA rates by 5.9 basis points and for 6-month CDs a fall of 3–4 basis points — the relationship was not significant for 3-month CDs. One should also mention that despite individual deposit rates being a better measure of performance, the explanatory power of these models (R^2 ranging for most between 0.01 and 0.25) is lower than those that use average rates (R^2 ranging between 0.2 and 0.5 in most cases).

To conclude, individual deposit rates are a better measure of bank performance than average deposit rates, although the majority of studies provide biased results because of the impact of Regulation Q in the 1960s and 1970s. The most recent studies, using individual deposit rates, find strong evidence of the traditional structure–performance hypothesis.

Profitability and Concentration

Most bank concentration studies have examined the relationship between bank market structure and profitability ratios, either using ROA (net income divided by total assets) or ROC (net income divided by total equity capital). Table 4.5 provides the findings of those studies that examine the profitability–concentration relationship, and it illustrates that ROA is the most popular profitability measure. Edwards (1965), Kaufman (1966), Fraser and Rose (1976), Heggestad (1977), Rhoades (1979), Glassman and Rhoades (1980), Rhoades (1982a), Kwast and Rose (1982) and Rhoades and Rutz (1982) all find a statistically significant relationship, suggesting that ROA for banks operating in more concentrated markets is higher. Studies undertaken by Yeats (1974) and Rhoades and Rutz (1979), however, find no such relationship. Early studies using ROC as a measure of performance also tended to find no such relationship, although later studies (such as Clark, 1986b) provide a little more evidence that the traditional structure–performance relationship holds.

Conventional economic theory links concentration to individual firm profitability, but it can be seen from the above results that there is no clear agreement on the concentration–profitability connection. Wall (1985) in a study of independent SMSA banks finds that neither market concentration nor bank size has a major impact on profits, and he suggests that bank profits are dominated by asset and funds management strategies and by management's ability to reduce non-interest expenses, not by market structure or regulation.

Other negative results for banking concentration were reported by Smirlock (1985) and Evanoff and Fortier (1988) who both argue that the major linkage is between market share and profitability, which are positively related. In testing Demsetz's (1973) efficiency hypothesis they both find that once the market share of individual banks is controlled for, concentration provides no additional explanatory power in influencing variations in bank profits. A study undertaken by Hanweck and Rhoades (1984), which examined 259 metropolitan and country-wide banking markets, contradicts the above findings when applied to the market share of the major banks in each market. They find that the presence of 'dominating' banks affects service prices but not profitability. Rhoades (1985c), in a study of 3777 commercial banks in 372 markets across the United States for 1976 to 1980, finds that profits tend to be higher where there were relatively few fringe banks (those ranked 4, 5 and 6 in market share). As Rose (1987, p. 198) has identified:

> This finding clashes with the conventional argument that mergers among fringe banks should be encouraged in order to create new market leaders to challenge the dominant banks.

Finally, although Gilbert (1984, p. 632) has stated that bank profit rate is an appropriate measure of bank performance, it is these studies that have the lowest explanatory power with R^2 or adjusted R^2 ($\bar{R}^2$) typically ranging between 0.01 and 0.15.

Table 4.5 Concentration and profitability

	Study	Profitability measure	Coefficient on the measure of market structure one statistically significant[a]
1.	Edwards (1965)	NI–TA	Yes
2.	Kaufman (1966)	NI–TA	Yes
3.	Fraser and Rose (1971)	NI–C	No
4.	Vernon (1971)	NI–C	Yes
5.	Emery (1971)	Deviations from the capital market line	No
6.	Fraser and Rose (1972)	NI–TA	No
7.	Ware (1972)	NI–C	No
8.	Edwards (1973)	NI–C	No
9.	Yeats (1974)	NI–TA	No
10.	Fraser and Alvis (1975)	NI–TA	No
11.	Fraser and Rose (1976)	NI–TA	Yes
12.	Mingo (1976)	NI–TA	No
13.	Heggestad (1977)	NI–TA	Yes
14.	Whitehead (1977)	NI–C	No
15.	Whitehead (1978)	NI–C	No
16.	Harvey (1979)	NI–C	Yes
17.	Savage and Rhoades (1979)	NI–C	Yes
18.	Rhoades (1979)	NI–TA	Yes
19.	Rhoades and Rutz (1979)	NI–TA	No
20.	Glassman and Rhoades (1980)	NI–TA	Yes
21.	Rhoades (1981)	NI–TA	No
22.	Rhoades (1982a)	NI–TA	Yes
23.	Kwast and Rose (1982)	NI–TA	Yes
24.	Rhoades and Rutz (1982)	NI–TA	Yes
25.	Smirlock (1985)	NI–E NI–C NI–TA	Yes when market share not included as an explanatory variable. (No when included)

continued overleaf

Table 4.5 (*continued*)

Study	Profitability measure	Coefficient on the measure of market structure one statistically significant[a]
26. Wall (1985)	NI−TA	No
	NI−C	No
27. Clark (1986a)	NI−E	No
28. Clark (1986b)	NI−E	Yes
29. Evanoff and Fortier (1988)	NI−TA	Yes (but only in two equations when market share is not included as an explanatory variable). No otherwise

[a]Where *t*-statistics on the market structure coefficient are greater than 1.95.
NI = net income.
TA = total assets.
C = capital.
E = equity.
Source: See Appendix I.

Service Charges and Concentration

Demand deposit service charges have also been used as a performance indicator for assessing the effects of concentration. Heggestad and Mingo (1976) find that these charges increase with concentration in a non-linear fashion. Stolz (1976), in a study noted for its good survey data, analysed the effect concentration had on demand deposit service charges in 333 banking offices in 75 rural countries. Using a novel 'area of convenience' approximation to banking markets, Stolz found that these service charges were not influenced by concentration.

Weiss (1969), in his study of 25 SMSAs, noted that higher concentration is related to the absence of 'free checking'. Not only does the study identify this finding, but it also mentions the need to observe mutual interdependence on the part of major competitors in the market (Weiss, 1969, p. 105):

> When this condition exists, a decision-maker in the market explicitly considers the reactions of his competitors to any market action he may take. ... If this situation goes undisturbed, unilateral price reduction is not likely to occur.

Average service charges have been the most commonly used measures of performance. Table 4.6 illustrates this point. The problems associated with this choice of performance indicator are similar to those associated with the average loan and deposit rate indicators, as mentioned earlier. In general, however, studies that use individual service charge measures tend to be no more conclusive in their findings than those that use average measures.

Table 4.6 Service charges and concentration

Study	Service charge measure	Coefficient on the measure of market structure one statistically significant[a]
1. Bell and Murphy (1969)	Estimated service charge on demand deposits	Yes
2. Weiss (1969)	Offering of no service charge on demand deposit accounts	Concentration related to the absence of free chequeing a/c
3. Fraser and Rose (1971)	SC–DD	No
4. Klein and Murphy (1971)	Service charge revenue divided by:	
	1. No. of DD accounts	No
	2. No. of debits to DD accounts	No
5. Fraser and Rose (1972)	SC–DD	No
6. Ware (1972)	SC–DD	No
7. Fraser and Alvis (1975)	SC–DD	No
8. Heggestad and Mingo (1976)	Service charge on standardised account	No
	Charge for returned cheque	No
9. Fraser and Rose (1976)	SC–DD	No
10. Rose and Fraser (1976)	SC–DD	Yes
11. Stolz (1976)	SC–DD	No
12. Heggestad and Mingo (1977)	Monthly service charge on demand deposits (based on a survey)	Yes
13. Graddy and Kyle (1979)	SC–DD	No
14. Savage and Rhoades (1979)	SC–DD	Yes
15. Rhoades (1979)	SC–DD	Yes
16. Rhoades and Rutz (1979)	SC–DD	Yes
17. Osborne and Wendel (1981)	SC–DD	Yes
	SC–Number of DD accounts	No
	Explicit SC for 20 cheques	Yes (opposite sign to the SCP paradigm)
	Price per number of cheques written (6, 20, 42 or 84)	No in all four cases
18. Rhoades (1981)	SC–DD	Yes (in 5 out of 7 years tested)
19. Hanweck and Rhoades (1984)	SC–DD	Yes

[a]Where *t*-statistics on the market structure coefficient are greater than 1.95.
SC = revenue from service charges on demand deposits.
DD = demand deposits.
Source: See Appendix I.

Extra-market Structure and Communication

Extra-market factors are those 'structural considerations outside the market that influence behaviour in the market' (Heggestad, 1979, p. 483). Only a handful of studies have been centred on these peripheral effects. Rose (1976), using 90 senatorial votes as his sample and the vote on the Helm's Amendment to the Financial Institutions Act of 1975 as the performance measure, attempted to see whether large banking organisations could influence the passing of legislation. The study concluded that concentration had no effect on the legislation passed by government.

As mentioned previously, other effects of an inter-institutional kind have been identified in various studies. Heggestad and Rhoades (1978) attempted to evaluate empirically the performance of 'links between the dominant banks' in markets throughout a state. They concluded that collusion between banks was apparent, and that multi-market meetings between dominant banks do adversely affect the degree of rivalry within markets.

Edwards (1965) also identified this interaction and noted that, if firms have close contact with each other in many markets, they may develop interdependence, thus forming a type of oligopoly within the banking system (see Stolz, 1976).

Non-price Competition and Concentration

Edwards (1973) studied the effects of concentration on advertising intensity, using 36 of the largest American banks in 23 SMSAs as his sample. He found that concentration had no effect on his performance measure.

From previous, major reviews of the SCP literature (see Heggestad, 1979; Gilbert, 1984), it is generally accepted that the strongest non-price competition results are obtained by Stolz (1976), White (1976) and Heggestad and Mingo (1977). White (1976) assesses the linkage between concentration and service quality; he measures quality of service by the number of branch offices in each of 40 SMSAs in statewide branching states based on the view that more branches imply greater convenience to customers. The expected negative relationship between concentration and number of branches is found to be statistically significant and quantitatively important — a 0.1 decrease in the Herfindahl index is associated with a 14.4% average rise in the number of bank offices in each SMSA.

Behavioural Models of Banking Structure

Expense-preference Behaviour

Behavioural models of banking structure aim to observe the managerial objectives of banks. Edwards (1977, p. 147) in his study on expense-preference behaviour in banking suggests 'that managers of regulated firms may be utility maximisers rather than profit maximisers'. His findings, using a sample of banks based in

44 SMSAs for 1962, 1964 and 1966, indicate that expense-preference behaviour better explains the performance of regulated firms than does a profit-maximising framework. Edwards's model found that wage and salary expenditures in banking increase with monopoly power.

Hannan's (1979a) study, using 367 banks based in 49 local banking markets in the state of Pennsylvania, finds that banks' wage and salary expenditures and the number of bank employees are significantly related to the market structure measure, leading him to support strongly evidence of expense-preference behaviour in local banking markets. In a similar study of banks operating in Pennsylvania in 1970 Hannan and Mavinga (1980, p. 680) also find strong evidence of expense-preference behaviour:

> Consistent with the implications of expense preference behaviour (and inconsistent with those of profit maximisation), manager-controlled banks operating in non-competitive markets are found to spend more on inputs likely to be preferred by managers than do owner-controlled banks in the same situation.

Of all the studies that test the structure–performance relationship those which find evidence of expense-preference behaviour have (by far) the highest explanatory power. Other studies, however, reject the expense-preference hypothesis: for example, Rhoades (1980) finds bank expenses to be lower in more concentrated than in less concentrated markets. Smirlock and Marshall (1983) argue that if the market share of individual banks is included in the type of equations used by Edwards (1977) and Hannan and Mavinga (1980) to control for bank size, there is no evidence of a relation between market concentration and expense-preference behaviour by managers.

Market Power and Risk Reduction—the Quiet Life Hypothesis

A few studies during the 1970s and 1980 have tested the relationship between market power and risk reduction, otherwise known as the quiet life hypothesis. This hypothesis was developed by Hicks (1935, p. 8) who suggested that 'the best of all monopoly profits is a quiet life'. This hypothesis suggests that a bank with greater market power will be more risk-averse, and thus will be able to achieve some combination of both higher return and lower risk than firms possessing lesser power in the market.

Edwards and Heggestad (1973), in their study of 'uncertainty avoidance' within the banking system, found evidence that profit maximisation may not necessarily be the objective of some banks. The study indicated that 'uncertainty avoidance' increased with high concentration, implying that banks become more risk-averse the fewer competitors they have. Edwards and Heggestad measure risk as the coefficient of variation in bank profit rates. Using this as the dependent variable, the significant independent variables are market concentration (negative sign) and bank size (negative sign). Their equations explain about 12–17% of the variability of profit rates. Heggestad (1977), using a similar measure of risk, also found that banks (from a sample of 238 in SMSAs between 1960 and 1970) became risk-averse the higher the level of concentration.

Rhoades and Rutz (1982) use a sample of 6500 unit banks operating between 1969 and 1978 to test the Hicksian quiet life hypothesis. They use four performance measures to account for risk: coefficient of variation of ROA (overall risk measure), equity to assets ratio (balance sheet risk measure), loans to assets ratio, and the net-loan-losses to total loans ratio. The measures are regressed against the three-bank concentration ratio along with variables to control for bank size, market size, growth and deposit volatility. For all performance measures (apart from net-loan-losses to total loans) they find a statistically significant relationship with the concentration variable, which suggests that risk is associated with higher levels of concentration. These findings, however, have to be qualified as the R^2 for all five equations range between 0.003 and 0.06, and as such one could alternatively state that no meaningful relationship between concentration and risk-aversion was found in this study.

Clark (1986a, b) uses two approaches to test for the concentration–risk relationship in banking markets. Both studies use the same dataset, 1857 banks located in 152 SMSAs in unit or limited branching states operating between 1973 and 1982. Clark (1986a) uses ordinary least squares regression procedures and the standard deviation of return on equity as the risk measure and finds that, even when controlling for bank size, there is no statistically significant relationship between concentration and risk. The explanatory power of this model is also weak with an R^2 of 0.05. In his second paper Clark (1986b) shows how simultaneous estimation using a two-stage least squares (2SLS) procedure generates more satisfactory results. He finds evidence supporting the traditional structure–performance hypothesis on profitability and risk, and also rejects the efficiency hypothesis.

Gilbert (1984, p. 633) notes that influences other than risk affect the variance of bank profits: for example, capital gains and losses on securities and the incidence of loan-losses. He suggests that more 'direct' indicators of risks undertaken by banks can be obtained by examining the composition of assets held by banks. Mingo (1976) tests the hypothesis that banks in areas with higher concentration hold less risky assets. He finds no significant relation between market concentration and the percentage of bank assets invested in US government securities, but does find that banks in areas with relatively high market concentration hold relatively high percentages of their assets in commercial loans.

These results obviously contradict the hypothesis that banks hold less risky assets in more concentrated markets.

Other Studies

Various studies focus on inter-institutional competition in banking markets, and there is evidence to suggest that this factor may be important in explaining performance. Heggestad and Mingo (1977) find that service charges on demand deposits are cheaper ($1.52 per month) in markets where savings and loan (S&L) institutions are allowed to offer NOW (notice of withdrawal) accounts. White (1976) shows that the presence of S&Ls increases the number of commercial bank branches within SMSAs. Curry and Rose (1984) test for the relationship between bank holding company presence and banking market performance: the results suggest that outside banking holding company presence leads to increased bank lending, particularly in the real estate and consumer loan market. Berger and Hannan (1989) note that the presence of S&Ls has no significant effect on deposit rates charged in concentrated commercial banking markets.

CONCENTRATION AND PERFORMANCE — EMPIRICAL EVIDENCE FROM INDIVIDUAL EUROPEAN COUNTRIES

As far as we are aware there have only been a limited number of SCP studies on individual European banking markets; Mooslechner and Schnitzer (1992), Molyneux and Teppett (1993), Molyneux (1993), Vennet (1993a), Lloyd-Williams, Molyneux and Thornton (1994), Goldberg and Rai (1994) and Lucey (1995a). The reason for the scarcity of European SCP studies relates to the lack of publicly available regional banking market data. As a result it is much more difficult to define banking markets in Europe. The US studies, on the other hand, are able to obtain data on a large number of banks which operate in statistically identified local and regional markets according to metropolitan statistical areas and non-metropolitan statistical area county boundaries. Concentration ratios and market share values are calculated on the basis of these local markets. This is the standard approach adopted in the US studies. This poses problems for the researcher who wishes to study the SCP paradigm for individual European countries, because it is very difficult to define and obtain data on local banking markets: publicly available data generally only allow the researcher to calculate national concentration ratios.

Various studies (which will be discussed later) such as those undertaken by Bourke (1989) and Molyneux and Thornton (1992), have examined the relationship between bank profitability and concentration across different countries which has enabled them to avoid this problem. These studies, however, tell us little about the SCP relationship in individual countries. To counter this problem, Molyneux and Teppett (1993) pool their data over the period 1986–88 so that they can include both concentration ratios and market share variables to test two competing hypotheses — the SCP paradigm and the efficiency hypothesis. Their results for five EFTA banking markets (Sweden, Norway, Finland, Austria and Switzerland) tend to support the traditional SCP hypothesis while rejecting the competing efficiency hypothesis.

A more detailed study undertaken by Mooslechner and Schnitzer (1992) on the Austrian banking system examines the SCP and efficiency hypothesis over the years 1988 and 1989. As Mooslechner and Schnitzer (1992, p. 14) note:

> One of the major problems of the structure–performance literature is how to measure market structure. Market structure is usually approximated by market-share and concentration. But it is extremely difficult to define a meaningful (relevant) market area and a reasonable measure of concentration under universal banking and nationwide banking conditions because banks are operating in many different product and geographical markets.

To deal with this problem Mooslechner and Schnitzer (1992) categorise the Austrian banking market into various districts; each bank has a relevant market of its own, ranging from at least one district for a local bank to nationwide banks which serve many districts. They classify the number of districts relevant to an individual bank according to the geographical distribution of each bank's branch network. They point out that: 'Because there are in general no balance sheet data for bank branches, market structure is measured empirically within the relevant market of each bank separately, including the balance sheet totals of all banks headquartered in one of the districts of the relevant markets' (p. 15).

Using cross-sectional estimates on a sample of 956 banks for 1988 and 1989 they find almost no significant influence of market share and market concentration variables on indicators of profitability. On the other hand, pooled time-series calculations for 13 large banks produce significant impacts for both variables. These findings lead them to conclude that (Mooslechner and Schnitzer, 1992, p. 24):

> those results point to the fact that it is rather difficult to apply the standard US-approach of structure–performance to European universal and nationwide banking conditions. Very poor data availability and severe problems in geographical market delineation limit the empirical possibilities.

Molyneux (1993) examined the SCP hypothesis for a range of 19 European countries and finds that the traditional SCP hypothesis holds for banks located in Portugal, Spain, Sweden, the UK and Turkey. Lloyd-Williams, Molyneux and Thornton (1994) also find support for the traditional hypothesis for Spanish banks for the period 1986–88. Vennet (1993a) uses efficiency scores calculated from stochastic estimates in his tests of the competing SCP and efficiency hypotheses — his results indicate that in some European countries, Belgium, Ireland, Portugal and Spain, collusion appears to be predominant.

The recent study undertaken by Goldberg and Rai (1994) uses the stochastic frontier model to calculate measures of X-inefficiency and scale-inefficiency. These measures of inefficiencies are then directly used in the SCP and efficiency hypothesis tests as proposed by Berger and Hannan (1993). Goldberg and Rai (1994) do not find a positive and significant relationship between concentration and profitability for a sample of banks across 11 European countries over a four-year period, 1988–91. They do, however, find evidence of the X-efficiency version of the efficient-structure hypothesis for banks located in countries with low concentration levels. (Here the efficiency measure is broken up into two components — X-efficiency and scale-efficiency. The former states that firms with superior management or production processes operate at lower costs and subsequently reap higher profits. The scale-efficiency component states that firms with similar production and management technology operate at different levels of economies of scale.) The policy implications of the Goldberg and Rai (1994) findings suggest that strict limitations on cross-border acquisitions and growth which might increase domestic concentration are not warranted.

Finally, Lucey (1995a) undertakes a similar study to Goldberg and Rai (1994) and investigates the competing SCP and efficiency hypotheses for the Irish banking market. Using data envelopment analysis (DEA) to calculate efficiency scores for banks, and Berger's (1993) distribution free efficiency approach to estimate firm-level society efficiencies, the author tests for the standard SCP approach, the efficiency hypothesis and the quiet life hypothesis. The results indicate that the SCP paradigm does not hold in either the banking or the building society market.

CONCENTRATION AND PERFORMANCE — EMPIRICAL EVIDENCE FROM INTERNATIONAL STUDIES

Concentration in International Banking

In general there are two types of study that compare concentration in international banking. Firstly, there are those that focus on changes in concentration levels between the world's largest banks, such as Aliber (1975), Tschoegl (1982), Rhoades (1983) and Thornton (1991a). Secondly, other studies have examined the relationship between the relative size of banks and industrial firms across countries (Rhoades, 1982b; Thornton, 1991b).

Aliber (1975) found that concentration in international banking had altered little between 1964 and 1974. The measure of concentration used was the percentage of total deposits of the world's largest 100 banks accounted for by the largest (top 10, 20, etc.) banks. Tschoegl (1982) presents evidence that concentration in international banking decreased over the period 1969–79 and suggested that it would continue to decrease. The study used both static and dynamic measures applied to asset data for the world's 100 largest banks and the top 20 medium-term Euroloan syndicators (1977–79). Both the static and dynamic measures of concentration indicate that for the 100 largest banks concentration fell between 1969 and 1973 but remained relatively stable up to 1979. Results for the top 20 syndicators of Euroloans suggest 'dramatic' falls in the level of concentration between 1977 and 1979.

In accordance with previous findings, Rhoades (1983) found that concentration in international banking markets had decreased steadily since 1956. The study used deposit data for the world's 100 largest banks between 1956 and 1980 and found (Rhoades, 1983, p. 431):

> The five largest banks in the world have steadily lost their share of the deposits
> controlled by the top 100. It declined from 22.6% to 13.3% between 1956 and 1979.
> It is worth noting that since 1975, the decline in share of the five largest was much
> smaller than in the previous period — while the banks ranked 1–5 lost share, banks
> ranked 6–10 and 26–50 held their own. The greatest gains within the 100 largest banks
> were made by banks ranked 26–50 as their share of the top 100 deposits rose from
> 20% in 1956 to 25.9% in 1979.

This study also revealed that the importance of US banks within the world's largest banks had declined dramatically since 1956. It was argued that this trend was the result of readjustment to 'The distortions of World War II, the rise of the commercial paper market in the United States, and the large number of US banks compared to other countries' (Rhoades, 1983, p. 427).

Thornton (1991a), using asset data on the world's 100 largest banks obtained from *The Banker*, replicated Rhoades's (1983) study for the period 1979–89. He found that the percentage of banking assets accounted for by the world's 100 largest banks had generally declined since 1979, but the five largest banks experienced a marked increase in their share of world bank assets. Thornton also noted that banks within the top 100 have become less equal in size, a finding which conflicts with those of Rhoades (1983) who reported an increase in the share of world assets controlled by the top 100 banks and a tendency for the banks to become more equal in size. The results also reveal that Japanese banks have become more dominant within the world's largest banks, mainly at the expense of US and German banks. Thornton (1991a, p. 271) suggests that the pre-eminence of Japanese banks in the top 100 'could not be accounted for by greater bank asset concentration in Japan than in other countries, since Japan has a large number of relatively large banks'. He suggests that advantages due to the lower cost of capital in Japan may be the reason for the noticeable growth of Japanese banks during the 1980s.

Rhoades (1982b) examines the relative size of banks and industrial firms in the United States and other major industrialised countries for 1978. Using deposits as a measure of bank size and total sales as a measure of the size of large corporations, he shows that US large banks are small in relation to large industrial corporations in comparison with other countries. For example, the deposits to sales ratio for the five largest banks to five largest corporations is estimated to be 1.09 for US organisations in 1978 which compares with 5.15 in France, 4.27 in Germany and 4.58 in Japan. A study using similar methodology (Thornton, 1991b) examines the size relationship between large banks and corporations in Japan, United States, France, Germany, the UK and Italy for 1989. The results indicate that, with the exception of the five largest French banks, banks in Japan are much larger in relation to industrial corporations than in other countries. The difference is especially notable with respect to the United States which has by far the lowest assets-to-sales ratios, for example; the five largest banks' assets to five largest corporations' sales ratio is 1.40, compared with 8.49 in Japan, 8.62 in France, 4.29 in Germany, 4.85 in Italy and 4.15 in the UK. Even when one considers the '20 largest bank to 20 largest corporate ratio' the Japanese figure of 9.44 compares extremely well with the 1.75 for the United States. Thornton suggests that the largest Japanese banks have such a significant size advantage over their major competitors, that US and EC banks may find it difficult to compete against them in the international market-place.

Bank Concentration Across Countries

There have been a variety of studies which examine concentration across different banking markets, IBRO (1976), Honohan and Kinsella (1982), Smith and Quinn (1983) and Baer and Mote (1985), but by far the most detailed and authoritative has been that undertaken by Revell (1987). Revell undertakes an extensive country-by-country study examining concentration levels (3, 5 and 10 firm deposits and assets) on an unconsolidated and consolidated groups basis in 14 countries for 1983. A summary of his findings is shown in Table 4.7.

Table 4.7 illustrates some of the difficulties in calculating concentration ratios for banking systems. In the table it can be seen that ratios are reported for three groups. Those based on unconsolidated figures are for individual banks registered in the country, including in the case of Spain and France business of their branches situated outside the country, '... it is the nearest that we can get to a measure of concentration within a domestic banking system, although much international business is conducted from domestic offices' (Revell, 1987, p. 26). At the other extreme, the consolidated group figures cover the worldwide business of the institutions. The table clearly illustrates the different concentration ratios that can be arrived at depending on whether one uses consolidated or unconsolidated data; this of course can also be strongly influenced by data availability.

Revell (1987) also identifies various statistical problems in interpreting concentration measures across countries:

1. When considering concentration within a population of commercial banks there is the problem of the different definition of a commercial bank in each country.

2. Problems arise when one includes public and mutual banks within the population because they may not compete in 'strictly' the same market.

3. Definition of all banking institutions (i.e. the market) depends ultimately on subjective judgements.

4. The paucity of ratios on fully consolidated accounts is unfortunate because there are considerable differences between countries and between individual banks in the proportion of the activity of the banking group conducted through subsidiaries, both at home and abroad. 'For all these reasons like is rarely being compared exactly with like' (Revell, 1987, p. 26).

Table 4.7   Summary of 1983 concentration ratios

Country	Coverage	Percentages of total assets of category					
		Commercial banks			All banking institutions		
		3	5	10	3	5	10
Unconsolidated							
Germany	A	43.0	60.7	69.4	16.6	24.0	38.2
Italy	A	28.0	40.8	61.3	17.5	25.5	40.4
Spain	A + B	28.3	42.6	57.9	17.6	26.3	35.7
Japan	A	22.6	36.3	58.1	22.9	29.6	41.5
Australia	A	66.9	92.3	99.1	30.4	46.4	65.5
France	A + B	48.5	57.4	—	33.1	47.3	60.9
Belgium	A	51.6	75.0	97.5	35.8	52.1	67.7
Ireland	A	48.0	—	—	40.0	—	—
Switzerland	A	70.6	74.7	79.8	44.8	51.5	59.3
Sweden	A	76.4	88.8	97.4	52.0	60.4	67.5
Partly consolidated or combined							
UK	A + C	18.9	25.2	—	16.3	21.7	—
Australia	A + C	65.1	87.2	98.2	46.3	62.0	69.8
Ireland	A + B + C	76.0	—	—	66.9	—	—
Consolidated groups							
Germany	E/H	44.5	60.3	68.8	15.0	22.0	35.0
UK	H	24.4	34.0	38.8	21.3	29.7	37.1
Spain	H	38.4	59.7	77.9	23.8	37.2	58.2
Italy	E	—	—	45.4	—	—	41.3
France	H	51.8	68.7	—	35.1	53.6	70.5
Netherlands	H	69.3	83.9	89.0	58.7	72.9	81.5

Notes:
1. Belgium 1982; Spain 1985.
2. Commercial banks include foreign banks (branches and subsidiaries).
A = parent bank offices in home country.
B = branches in other countries.
C = bank subsidiaries in home country.
D = bank subsidiaries in other countries.
E = consolidated banking group.
F = non-bank subsidiaries in home country.
G = non-bank subsidiaries in other countries.
H = consolidated group.
Source: Revell (1987, p. 27, Table 2.2).

Revell (1987, p. 256) identifies that every banking system appears to have a group of dominant or 'core banks' recognised by both the authorities and by the general public:

> The main significance of the core group (or the group of a few large banks if there is a divergence in membership between the two groups) is that they are highly visible. We have already seen that they attract special attention from the central bank, but they

also act as the focus of attention to the general public. In all countries there is a latent populist feeling arising out of a largely unconscious fear of finance and banks. This feeling has been behind anti-Semitism in some countries, behind persecution of Asians in African countries, and behind the dislike of the financial power of the Eastern states of the United States felt by those further to the West. In its less lucid moments the general public finds it difficult to distinguish between bankers and moneylenders. In most countries the populist feeling takes the form of an expressed fear of banking monopoly, which means that an alleged monopoly of banks is pursued with far more vigour than the alleged monopoly of industrial empires.

There are two consequences for banks as soon as it is recognised that a group of 'core' banks has emerged. Firstly, when large banks in the group wish to become even larger by merging among themselves, they need to provide public plausible reasons for doing so. Secondly, mergers between core banks become a public policy issue, and the approval of the authorities is nearly always required.

Mention should also be made of the Honohan and Kinsella (1982) study which provides a critique of cross-country comparisons of traditional measures of concentration (although this study will also be discussed in the following section). This study notes that when one compares concentration across countries one must take into account the effects of market size on the 'minimum practicable degree of concentration having regard to the desirability of an efficient scale of production' (p. 262). They develop, with the help of a theoretical model, a measure which takes account of market size — essentially Herfindahl indices scaled up by an amount proportionate to the level, or the square root of GDP. Their study, using data obtained from Short (1979) for 1973, shows that if their measures are used, Japan which had the least concentrated market as measured by the Herfindahl index would have almost the highest degree of concentration of any country if either of their measures were chosen. Belgium and Sweden which appeared among the most concentrated according to the Herfindahl index would seem to have the 'minimum feasible level' of concentration across countries if the Herfindahl multiplied by GDP measure was used.

Other European Evidence of the SCP Relationship

A handful of studies has appeared in recent years testing the relationship between concentration and bank performance across individual countries. The earliest was a paper by Short (1979) that links profit rates of 60 banks in Canada, western Europe and Japan to concentration in their national banking systems over a three-year period (1972–74). Bank profitability is measured by the ratio of after-tax profits to shareholders' equity. Because of the lack of information on system-wide profitability or capital scarcity measures, Short chooses the central bank discount rate and the yield on long-term government securities to represent these features of each national economy. Individual bank profitability is regressed against variables measuring bank leverage (assets to equity ratio), bank size, asset growth, whether each bank is privately or state owned, and concentration measured by the Herfindahl index, numbers equivalent and one-, two- and three-bank concentration ratios. Short finds that state ownership, market concentration and capital scarcity dominate the regression equations. Concentration, however, is the least important of these variables and its effect is quantitatively small: for example, one equation indicates that nearly a 30% reduction in the three-bank concentration ratio is necessary to reduce individual bank profit rates by about 1%. Short (1979, p. 214) concludes:

> Nevertheless, even very small reductions in banks' lending rates or increases in their borrowing rates may in aggregate result in substantial redistribution of income to bank customers.

A recent study by Bourke (1989) on the determinants of international bank profitability replicated and extended the earlier work undertaken by Short (1979) and found support for the view that concentration was positively and moderately related to profitability. The data used in Bourke's study were based on the financial statements of 116 banks each year from 1972 to 1981 in 15 countries or territories (Australia, New Zealand, California, Massachusetts, New York, Canada, Ireland, Scotland, England and Wales, France, Belgium, the Netherlands, Denmark, Norway and Spain). The banks included in the sample were every bank in these countries which fell within the top 500 banks in the world in June 1980, ranked by total assets. Bourke used a pooled time-series approach to estimate a linear equation, regressing performance measures (ROA, ROC — before and after tax) against a variety of internal (staff expenses, capital ratios, liquidity ratios) and external (concentration ratios (three-bank), government ownership, interest rates, market growth and inflation) determinants of bank profitability. His results find support for the view that concentration was positively and moderately related to profitability. The results also provide some evidence for the Edwards–Heggestad–Mingo hypothesis (Edwards and Heggestad, 1973; Heggestad and Mingo, 1976) of risk avoidance by banks with a high degree of market power.

Molyneux and Thornton (1992) replicate Bourke's methodology in order to evaluate the determinants of European bank profitability. A sample of European banks, 671 for 1986, 1063 for 1987, 1371 for 1988 and 1108 for 1989, are taken across 18 countries. Standardised accounting data for the banks were obtained from International Bank Credit Analysis Ltd (IBCA), a London-based bank credit-rating agency and the variables used were as follows.

Dependent Variables

(NPBT = net profit before tax; NPAT = net profit after tax)
BTCR   NPBT as percentage of capital and reserves
ATCR   NPAT as percentage of capital and reserves

BTCRTB   NPBT as percentage of capital and reserves and total
          borrowings
BTTA   NPBT as percentage of total assets
BTSETA   NPBT + staff expenses as percentage of total assets
BTSEPLTA NPAT + staff expenses + provision for loan losses as
          percentage of total assets

Independent Variables

GOVT   a binary variable representing government ownership, one
          when a bank is owned by a government, national or
          provincial, zero otherwise
CONC   ten-bank asset concentration ratio
INT   the long-term bond rate for each country for each year (IMF)
MON   growth in money supply for each country for each year (IMF)
CRTA   capital and reserves as percentage of total assets
CBINVTA   cash and bank deposits + investment securities as percentage
          of total assets
CPI   percentage increase in consumer price index for each country
          for each year (IMF)
SE   staff expenses as percentage of total assets

As with previous studies, Molyneux and Thornton (1992) estimate a simple linear equation using a pooled sample of European banks between 1986 and 1989. Results are shown in Tables 4.8 and 4.9.

Table 4.8 estimates the relations between ROC and various independent variables and these are more or less similar to the equations estimated by Short (1979). As with Bourke, Molyneux and Thornton (1992) find an 'almost total lack of correspondence' (p. 75) between their ROC results and those of Short. For European banks they find a statistically significant positive relationship between ROC and concentration and a positive relationship for nominal interest rates (which is used as a capital scarcity proxy variable). Unlike Short and Bourke, however, who both find a statistically significant inverse relationship between ROC and government ownership, Molyneux and Thornton find a statistically significant positive relationship, suggesting that state-owned banks generate higher ROC than their private-sector competitors. In one way this result is surprising because it conflicts with earlier findings, but it is not unexpected because state-owned banks generally maintain lower capital ratios (because the government implicitly underwrites their operations) than their private-sector counterparts. A simple explanation for their findings could be that, because their sample comprises a much larger proportion of state-owned banks (for example, over 200 in 1988), these results are more representative than the two aforementioned authors who only included the largest government-owned banks

Table 4.8 Estimates of the relation between return on capital and selected independent variables for 1986–1989

	Intercept	GOVT	CONC	INT	MON	R^2	F
1. BTCR	90.0629 (−0.74)	0.0007 (0.02)	0.0007[a] (3.44)	0.0019[a] (24.42)	−0.0007[a] (−3.93)	27.6	246.25
2. BTCR	−0.2830[a] (−3.10)	0.0070 (0.14)	0.0092[a] (5.99)	—	—	1.1	18.59
3. BTCR	−0.1630 (−1.76)	−0.0297 (−0.64)	0.0071[a] (4.80)	—	0.0025[a] (16.53)	10.8	105.29
4. ATCR	−0.3090[a] (−4.49)	0.0905[a] (2.38)	0.0075[a] (6.47)	0.0010[a] (17.56)	—	10.9	125.60
5. BTCRTB	−0.8150[a] (−5.41)	0.4050[a] (5.34)	0.0168[a] (7.01)	—	0.0003 (1.19)	2.2	20.32
6. BTCRTB	−0.6620[a] (−5.47)	0.2990[a] (4.54)	0.0156[a] (7.77)	0.0003[a] (2.61)	—	2.4	26.45

[a]Significant at the 5% level.
t-statistics in parentheses.
Source: Molyneux and Thornton (1992, p. 1175).

Table 4.9 Estimates of the relation between return on assets and selected independent variables for 1986–89

	Intercept	CRTA	CBINVTA	GOVT	CONC	INT	MON	CPI	SE	R^2(adj)	F
1. BTTA	-0.0146[a] (-6.18)	0.1200[a] (14.23)	-0.0122[a] (-4.66)	0.0056[a] (5.05)	0.0004[a] (12.07)	0.00002[a] (10.41)	—	—	—	13.6	97.39
2. BTTA	-0.0153[a] (-6.44)	0.1150[a] (13.35)	-0.0113[a] (-4.25)	0.0050[a] (4.47)	0.0004[a] (11.90)	—	—	0.0003[a] (3.32)	—	10.8	75.46
3. BTTA	-0.0153[a] (-6.43)	0.1190[a] (13.92)	-0.0125[a] (-4.70)	0.0052[a] (4.63)	0.0004[a] (12.92)	—	—	—	—	10.5	91.27
4. BTTA	0.0064[a] (4.22)	0.1200[a] (13.67)	-0.0107[a] (-3.93)	0.0021 (1.89)	—	—	—	—	0.00002[a] (12.14)	9.9	84.27
5. BTTA	0.0051[a] (6.35)	0.1120[a] (12.69)	—	—	—	—	—	—	—	4.9	160.99
6. BTSETA	0.0664[a] (2.96)	0.0930 (0.70)	-0.0353 (-0.85)	-0.0333 (-1.94)	—	—	—	—	—	0.1	1.65
7. BTSETA	-0.1570[a] (-3.25)	0.1390 (0.88)	-0.0420 (-0.81)	0.0051 (0.23)	0.0039[a] (5.56)	—	0.00004 (0.53)	—	—	1.2	7.34
8. BTSETA	-0.0739 (-1.37)	0.2150[a] (2.36)	-0.0615 (-1.18)	-0.0236 (-1.00)	0.0036[a] (5.12)	—	0.00003 (0.38)	-0.0128[a] (-3.42)	—	1.7	8.09
9. BTSETA	-0.1160 (-3.10)	0.1250[a] (2.94)	-0.0344 (-0.83)	-0.0060 (-0.34)	0.00319[a] (5.94)	0.00006[a] (2.30)	—	—	—	1.4	9.70
10. BTSEPLTA	-0.1890[a] (-3.74)	0.0540[a] (2.32)	-0.1630[a] (-2.73)	0.0686[a] (2.41)	0.0059[a] (8.47)	—	—	—	—	3.4	20.86
11. BTSEPLTA	-0.2710[a] (-4.12)	0.1120[a] (2.55)	-0.1870[a] (-2.32)	0.1200[a] (3.49)	0.0068[a] (7.23)	—	0.00001 (0.10)	—	—	3.0	12.06
12. BTSEPLTA	-0.3410[a] (-3.98)	0.1090[a] (0.54)	-0.1750[a] (-2.16)	0.1200[a] (3.50)	0.0073 (7.21)	—	0.00001 (0.17)	0.0076 (1.27)	—	3.0	10.33
13. BTSEPLTA	-0.1860[a] (-3.68)	0.0520 (0.31)	-0.1620[a] (-2.70)	0.0695[a] (2.44)	0.00583[a] (8.30)	0.00005 (2.17)	—	—	—	3.4	16.96

[a]Significant at the 5% level.
t-statistics in parentheses.
Source: Molyneux and Thornton (1992, p. 1176).

in their much smaller samples (e.g. Bourke, 1989 used 200 banks over 10 years, of which there were only 30 or so government-owned institutions).

The results shown in Table 4.9 use asset-based returns and, in general, show that capital ratios and nominal interest rates are positively related to profitability. These findings are to be expected and are confirmed in the Bourke (1989) study. Government ownership also appears to have a positive impact on bank profitability. In the case of liquidity ratios, Molyneux and Thornton find a weak inverse relationship with profitability which is also to be expected as liquidity holdings (particularly those imposed by the authorities) represent a cost to the bank. Molyneux and Thornton find that concentration shows a positive, statistically significant correlation with pre-tax ROA, which is consistent with the SCP paradigm. When the value-added measure is used to test for the expense-preference theory, one would expect the sign on the CONC variable to be positive and strengthen. This is because the measure of value-added largely removes the possibility of either managerially induced expenditure or labour union-negotiated wage demands appropriating excessive proportions of net income. Their results appear to find evidence of expense-preference behaviour in European banking. Another value-added measure (BTSEPLTA) is used to test for the Edwards–Heggestad–Mingo risk aversion effect: using this as a dependent variable one would expect the sign on the CONC variable to be negative and the relationship to strengthen, which illustrates that higher levels of concentration are associated with lower loan costs. Molyneux and Thornton (1992) find no evidence of the risk aversion effect.

In general, Molyneux and Thornton's analysis of the determinants of European bank profitability conflict with the earlier findings of Short (1979), yet the main results on asset-based returns confirm Bourke's (1989) findings, apart from the relationship between government ownership and profitability. The results are in agreement with the traditional concentration and bank profitability (SCP) studies for the US market, and they find no support for the Edwards–Heggestad–Mingo hypothesis. Support, however, is found for the expense-preference expenditure theories in European banking.

Ruthenberg (1991) employs a transcendental logarithmic function (translog) to estimate the structure–performance relationship using 1984 to 1988 data on the EC and several non-EC banking markets (Israel, Finland, Norway, Sweden, Australia, Canada, Switzerland, Japan and the United States). The dataset employed was obtained by questionnaires responded to by the central bankers in the countries listed above. The data, therefore, relate to aggregate commercial banking markets. In order to test the relationship between structure and performance, Ruthenberg uses the general form of the performance equation:

$$\pi_{ij} = (H_{ij}, PC_{ij}, NNI_{ij}, R_{ij}, V_{ij}) \tag{2}$$

where π_{ij} are performance measures, the Lerner index (the differences between price (interest rate on loans) and marginal cost (rate paid on deposits) divided by price) and net interest margin; H_{ij} is the Herfindahl index; PC_{ij} is proxy for potential competition. The two measures used are (1) population per number of branches and (2) population per number of banks; NNI_{ij} is non-interest income (overhead expenses less fees and commissions); R_{ij} are risk measures which include: (1) loans to assets ratio, (2) equity to total loans ratio, (3) loan-loss reserves to total loans, (4) standard deviation of the return on equity; V_{ij} is the vector of control variables to account for banking market and/or economy specific characteristics.

Two types of binary variable were also included (i) to account for the time trend effect between 1984 and 1988 and (ii) to account for inter-country differences in size (zero if GNP per capita is less than \$10 000 and 1 otherwise). The performance function estimated was as follows:

$$\ln \pi = \alpha_0 + \alpha_1 \ln H + \alpha_2 \ln NNI + \alpha_3 \ln PC + \alpha_4 \ln R$$
$$+ \alpha_5 \ln V + \tfrac{1}{2}[\beta_1(\ln H)^2 + \beta_2(\ln NNI)^2 + \beta_3(\ln PC)^2$$
$$+ \beta_4(\ln R)^2 + \beta_5(\ln V)^2] + T_1 \ln H \ln NNI$$
$$+ \ldots + T_4 \ln H \ln V + \ldots T_{10} \ln R \ln V \qquad (3)$$

α_0; α_i, $i = 1, \ldots 5$; β_i, $i = 1, \ldots 5$; T_i, $i = 1, \ldots 10$ are the parameters to be estimated.

Despite reservations about the nature of the data obtained, and aggregate data for each country that yield only 54 observations for SCP estimates for EC countries between 1984 and 1988, the study has some interesting findings.

Ruthenberg finds that (at the sample means) there is a statistically significant relationship between the concentration measure (the Herfindahl index) and one of the performance measures (Lerner index) when the European Community is considered, but not when the larger sample of countries is used. When they deviate from the sample means of the Herfindahl index, empirical results suggest the existence of a 'critical level' of concentration (consistent with earlier US findings by McCall and Peterson, 1980). In the EC, the banking markets which consistently fall above the 'critical level' of the Herfindahl index are Ireland, Greece, Netherlands and Portugal.

Ruthenberg (1991, pp. 21–22) concludes:

In sum, it appears that only relatively small (probably with the exception of Canada), concentrated banking markets: with an H greater than 0.13, that are characterised with relatively few competitors, and high entry barriers can offer banking organisations that expand their activities across borders a potential for decreased profits. We arrive at this conclusion because in that group of countries the positive effect of structure on performance is most profound.

Recent studies on the US market undertaken by Jackson (1992), Berger and Hannan (1992) and in Europe by Goldberg and Rai (1994) also find evidence of the non-linear price-profits–concentration relationship.

Molyneux (1993) uses a single-equation methodology to test for inter-firm behaviour between leading banks across European banking markets. The results indicate that a large leading bank appears on average to promote cooperation with other leaders and this increases banking industry profitability. A large second bank, however, seems to induce rivalry with leaders rather than cooperation. The impact of more distant rivals does not seem to affect profitability of banks in the industry. In general, the analysis presented in the Molyneux (1993) paper illustrates that uniform levels of industry-wide cooperative behaviour as suggested by market concentration measures are misleading as more complex inter-firm behaviour seems to be apparent. The paper concludes (Molyneux, 1993, p. 14):

> when we test for evidence of the two competing hypotheses — the traditional SCP paradigm and efficiency hypothesis — across European banking markets we find strong evidence that the former holds. In other words, it appears that the degree of concentration in European banking markets lowers the cost of collusion between firms and increases average industry profitability. Confronted with this evidence regulators might feel compelled to prohibit large bank mergers so as to reduce, or at least restrict, the build-up of monopoly power across European banking systems. Our later empirical findings suggest that this view would be misguided. A large leading bank does appear, on average, to promote cooperation with other market leaders and this seems to increase banking industry profitability. However, the appearance of a large second bank, seems, on average, to induce rivalry with leaders rather than cooperation. The impact of more distant rivals does not seem to affect the profitability of banks in the industry. Larger second banks induce rivalrous conjectures which reduce, on average, industry profitability, but this reduction is not large enough to bring about a negative relationship between industry profitability and the market concentration variable. In other words, our empirical evidence on rivalrous and cooperative behaviour in European banking markets suggests that policymakers should be concerned if the largest bank in the system is substantially bigger than its nearest competitors. In the interests of competition it may well be justified to encourage mergers between large banks so they can act as strong rivals to the leading institution. Our evidence also finds that the third, fourth and fifth sized banks do not seem to affect average industry profitability, suggesting that they neither cooperate nor compete with the largest bank, thus operating independently. From our results we tentatively suggest that mergers between these banks may be justified on competitive grounds if the combined market shares of the merged bank is similar to the largest bank. If a merger creates an institution which is substantially larger than the present largest bank then this may well result in explicit or implicit collusion. As national authorities generally use merger policies in the financial sector in a flexible manner so as to improve the efficiency of the banking system it may well be in their interests to consider these policy prescriptions.

Using an approach similar to Clark (1986b), Altunbas and Molyneux (1994a) estimate the concentration–profits relationship in European banking using a system of structural equations which allows them to investigate both the nature of the structural parameters as well as the reduced-form coefficients derived from the structural model. Using the three-stage least squares estimator they find that the structural parameters suggest that the traditional concentration–profits paradigm and efficiency hypothesis both hold in European banking markets. In contrast with these findings, the OLS (Ordinary Least Squares) reduced-form parameter estimates, derived from the structural model, strongly suggest that only the traditional concentration–profits paradigm holds. (These latter findings are also clearly shown in Molyneux and Forbes, 1995.) These conflicting results draw attention to the ambiguities which may arise when estimating reduced-form equations which only indirectly test the concentration–profits relationship. Overall the Altunbas and Molyneux (1994a) results indicate how the use of a single-equation reduced-form methodology can, at best, lead to biased and inconsistent estimates of the underlying structural parameters.

LIMITATIONS OF BANK SCP MODELLING

A positive relationship between concentration and performance has been found in some, but far from all, of the empirical studies investigating bank market structure and performance. The lack of consistent results have led some researchers to argue that the literature contains too many inconsistencies and contradictions to establish a satisfactory SCP relationship in banking. In addition, despite there being numerous empirical studies, these have not been based on an explicit model of the banking firm (see Hannan, 1991b).

The defects of trying to quantify empirically the relationship between commercial bank performance and market structure are numerous and (some might say) obvious. We have already mentioned that because banking is a multi-product industry, a simple all-inclusive market area is difficult to delineate and no single measure of structure precisely reflects the degree of monopoly, nor does economic theory help choose which measure is most important.

Adequate standards of performance measurement have also not been developed, as can be seen from the variations noted previously. In many past studies it is difficult to argue that output was a homogeneous measure, i.e. all banks do not offer the same services (see Bell and Murphy, 1969), and while banks are multi-product firms, the majority of studies have been limited to analysing the prices of a single product, thus underestimating the total impact of monopoly power on performance.

To illustrate this argument Klein and Murphy (1971) developed a model to test whether an individual bank faces different markets for different activities. They state: 'the possibility that local market structure may have a differential impact on bank performance in different activities, seems to have escaped systematic investigations' (p. 747). This study points to the limitations of other 'non-differentiated' investigations. In addition few studies have empirically considered the possibility that banking competition is best reflected in non-price dimensions. These factors could be of paramount importance in determining performance.

The functional form of the structure–performance model will now be briefly reiterated. It is quite possible that the relationship will be non-linear, so that changes in concentration would have different impacts on performance at different levels of concentration. Heggestad and Mingo (1976, p. 108) point out:

> Specifically, a given increase in concentration will have a greater impact on prices (services), the less concentrated is the market initially.

Studies undertaken by McCall and Peterson (1980) and Daskin and Wolken (1989), Jackson (1992), Berger and Hannan (1992) and Goldberg and Rai (1994) have been used to examine this issue. Hannan and Liang (1993) also find that localised competition effects and spatial factors are important in determining bank performance. In addition, the one-way causality assumption of the SCP relationship has also been clearly questioned by many authors (see e.g. Bresnahan, 1989; Britton, Clark and Bell, 1992) but has rarely been empirically addressed (see Clark, 1986b).

The statistical results obtained from a large number of the SCP studies cannot confirm the hypotheses of central relationships which they aim to show. Taylor (1968, p. 803) notes that: 'No regression ever produces definitive answers about cause or effect', and that 'This study reinforces the scholar's conclusion that, no matter how sophisticated the techniques that are applied to poor data, the results are likely to be poor.'

Another important factor (see Phillips, 1967) is the weighting problem involved in aggregating within and among banks. Previous studies on banking have also been criticised for assuming that banks behave as profit maximisers under condition of complete certainty. As Edwards and Heggestad (1973, p. 148) noted:

> Implicit in this argument is the assumption that the managements of large firms are insulated from the kind of stockholder pressure that would prevent them from pursuing objectives other than the maximisation of the value of the firm.

They argue that if managerial objectives vary systematically with firm size and market power, the findings of past studies may be biased and therefore fail to disclose the true structure–performance relationship.

Furthermore, these studies, by isolating one sector from the rest of the economy, fail to examine interactions between sectors (any distortion away from a perfectly competitive order may be necessary to maintain a 'second-best' position).

Rhoades (1982a) claims that many of the equations are misspecified, thus biasing the estimated coefficients on the concentration measure. For example, if one does not take account of bank management risk–return preferences operating in different concentrated markets then one is ignoring the possibility of trading off potential profits for lower risk. Thus it is important to account for differences in risk-taking across the observations. Clark (1986b) goes further and suggests that risk and profitability should be determined simultaneously.

Others suggest that many of the studies have ignored the existence of potential competitors to the relevant markets. This omission was justified on the grounds of technological conditions, and the existence of strict regulation either on the type and variety of services offered and/or the ability to expand geographically. Therefore, even if concentration is high in a particular market, the threat of competition (potential entry) can lead to lower profits than otherwise. Evanoff and Fortier (1988) have shown that accounting for differences in entry barriers across markets adds significantly to the impact of structure on profits.

Demsetz (1973), Brozen (1982) and others have argued that an industry's structure may exist as a result of a superior efficiency in production by some firms which enables them to increase market share thus increasing market concentration. This efficiency hypothesis suggests that it is not collusion which leads to higher than normal profits but rather economies of scale and scope. Smirlock (1985), Evanoff and Fortier (1988) and Jackson (1992) find that once firm-specific efficiency is accounted for in banking markets, market concentration adds nothing in explaining performance. Conversely, Clark (1986a, b) and Berger and Hannan (1989) find no evidence to support the efficiency hypothesis.

In a recent study Berger (1995) substantially refines the SCP debate by empirically investigating different market power and efficient-structure hypotheses. He identifies two relative market power hypotheses — the traditional SCP hypothesis and the relative market power (RMP) hypothesis. The latter asserts that only firms with large market shares and well-differentiated products are able to exercise market power in pricing these products and earn supernormal profits. He also identifies two efficiency explanations of the positive profit–structure relationship — the X-efficiency version which suggests that firms with superior management or production technologies have lower costs and therefore higher profits. These firms are also assumed to gain large market shares which may result in higher levels of concentration. (This is the same as the efficiency hypothesis discussed above.) Berger (1995) also identifies a scale-efficiency version of the efficient-structure hypothesis; some firms just produce at more efficient scales than others, resulting in lower unit costs and higher profits. Using an extensive US dataset he attempts to distinguish among all four hypotheses using various measures of both market structure and efficiency. In brief, the results provide partial support for the X-efficiency version of the efficient-structure hypothesis and some support for the RMP hypothesis. In conclusion he states, 'Despite the limited support for two of the hypotheses, it does not appear that any of the efficient structure or market-power hypotheses are of great importance in explaining bank profits' (Berger, 1995, p. 249).

Gilbert (1984) notes that one of the major criticisms of this type of methodology for investigating banking markets is that it neglects the role of regulation. There may be strong interactive effects between regulation and other variables which have a significant impact on market concentration and performance. Heggestad (1984, p. 648), however, notes that the importance of this problem is overstated and he argues that 'Regulation does still permit market forces to work but may change the intensity of their effect. For example, liability rate ceilings may make collusion less difficult, as may high entry barriers. Consequently, markets with low concentration may exhibit collusive behaviour. On the other hand, competition may be enhanced by regulatory oversight.' In general, rates of return are not directly regulated and firms treat regulation as an operational constraint. They maximise some objective function within the environment in which they do business. Different regulatory regimes may lead to different relationships between structure and performance, but as Heggestad (1984, p. 648) states, '. . . it is highly likely that structure will have an impact on performance'. The empirical biases resulting from regulation may also be overstated because most bank SCP studies are cross-sectional and in general they control for important cross-sectional changes in regulation.

CONCLUSIONS

This chapter has examined the empirical literature on SCP modelling in banking markets. The bulk of these studies investigate the structure–performance relationship in US banking markets, although there have been recent attempts to investigate the relationship across European countries. In general one can conclude that statistical studies of structure and performance reveal the existence of important relationships, whose presence stands out more sharply the better the quality of the data and methodology employed. The limited evidence to date seems to suggest that when one uses the single-equation standard SCP methodology then the traditional paradigm appears to hold. More technical empirical evaluations, using systems estimators and/or different measures of firm efficiency, seem to yield alternative results. There still seems to be no consensus as to which hypothesis holds across European markets.

Clearly there is still a need for researchers to continue to undertake more research in the bank concentration and market power area, especially in European banking. Berger's (1995) paper, in particular, provides an excellent role model for the direction of future research. With the advent of the single European banking market after 1992, it is of interest to know how strongly or weakly these relationships hold in established markets so one can evaluate how the industry will change in the new, broader markets and in markets linked by common competitors and especially, in the run-up to EMU by 1999.

5

Scale, scope and cost efficiency in banking markets: a theoretical perspective

INTRODUCTION

This chapter examines the theory behind economies of scale and scope studies for financial institutions. The first section focuses on the definition of economies of scale and scope and analyses the effects of technology on bank costs. Following on the chapter discusses the importance of the shape of average costs to firms' decision-making and also explains the sources of scale and scope effects and their implications for the banking firm. We discuss the relationship between production and cost functions and then provide an overview of the functional forms of various cost functions used in the cost literature. The final section outlines recent approaches to estimating efficiency in banking markets.

DEFINITION OF ECONOMIES OF SCALE AND ECONOMIES OF SCOPE

Economies of Scale

The concept of scale economies, or returns to scale, refers to the rate at which output changes as all factor quantities are varied. Scale economies are based on the shape of the average cost curve, which illustrates average costs at each level of output. Figure 5.1 displays the long-run average cost (LAC) curve and the long-run marginal cost (LMC) curve with a series of short-run average cost (SAC) and short-run marginal cost (SMC) curves. The average cost curve shows

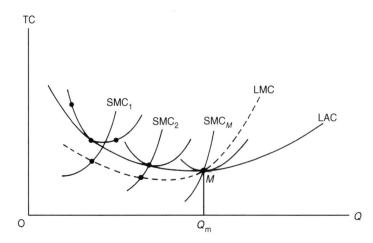

Figure 5.1 Economies of scale and the average and marginal cost curve shapes (Source: adapted from Koutsoyiannis, 1979)

the average cost per unit of output at different levels of output, and the marginal cost, the additional cost incurred when producing a very small increment of output, which is similar to the rate of change in average cost. The long-run curves allow for simultaneous changes in all inputs of production whereas the short-run cost curves also represent cost changes as output increases but not all inputs are changeable. The LAC is declining at outputs up to Q_m, beyond which point the LAC begins to rise. At the minimum point Q_m the LMC intersects the LAC. Economies of scale (or increasing returns to scale) are illustrated up to the output level Q_m, where the LMC curve lies below the LAC curve, and diseconomies of scale (decreasing returns to scale) thereafter, where the LMC lies above the LAC curve. Figure 5.1 shows the conventional U-shaped cost curve, which is used for ease of exposition, although the above exposition would still hold if the curve were flat-bottomed, with constant returns to scale, over a large range of output. In this case the LMC would be equal to the average cost since average cost per unit of output is not changing.

The existence of scale economies means that the average cost of producing a product, in the long run, *ceteris paribus*, decreases as more of the output is produced. Thus, economies of scale are measured by the ratio of the percentage change in output. Since a firm expands its scale of operations, economies of scale arise if it reduces the average cost of output, holding all other factors constant. Hence economies of scale can be defined either in terms of the firm's production function or its corresponding cost function, since scale economies are the inverse of increasing returns to scale. As a result, it is said that there are constant costs, when the production function presents constant returns to scale, scale economies when the production function presents increasing returns to scale and diseconomies of scale when the production function presents decreasing returns to scale. In other words, if the scale economies ratio is smaller than one, economies of scale arise, as average long-run cost is declining. If the ratio is equal to one, no scale economies are present, as average cost is constant and when the ratio exceeds one, diseconomies of scale exist, as average cost is increasing. Figure 5.1 shows these three alternative relationships between average cost and output.

The concept of scale economies in the single product firm applies to the behaviour of total costs as output increases, and economies of scale exist if total cost increases less proportionately than output. Given the following total cost function, $TC = f(Q)$ where Q is an output then average cost can be derived as $ATC = f(Q)/Q$ and marginal cost can be shown as $\partial TC/\partial Q$. As average cost will decline as long as marginal cost lies under average cost, so scale economies are simply as follows:

$$SE = \frac{ATC}{MC} = \frac{f(Q)}{Q(\partial TC/\partial Q)} \tag{1}$$

which is simply the elasticity of cost with respect to output. Therefore, when $SE \geqslant 1$, $SE = 1$ and $SE \leqslant 1$, we experience increasing, constant or decreasing returns to scale, as the derivative of average cost with respect to output is negative, zero or positive, respectively.

Minimum Efficient Scale

The shape of LAC curves is important not only because of their implications for scale decisions, but also because of their effects on the potential level of competition in the market-place. Although U-shaped cost relations are quite commonly reported in the industrial economics literature, they may not always apply universally. It may be the case that firms in manufacturing encounter first increasing, then constant returns to scale (Scherer, 1980). In such instances, an L-shaped LAC curve emerges, and very large organisations are at no relative cost disadvantage compared with smaller institutions. Typically, the number of competitors and ease of entry will be greater in industries with U-shaped LAC curves than those with L-shaped or continuously downward-sloping LAC (see Geroski, 1991). Minimum efficient scale is explained as the output level at which LACs are first minimised (Sawyer, 1985). Therefore, minimum efficient scale will be found at the minimum point on a U-shaped LAC curve (output Q_m in Figure 5.1) and at the corner of an L-shaped LAC curve. Firms are not usually at an output level below MES (minimum efficient scale), because that increases their costs and squeezes their profits (Shepherd, 1985).

In general, the number of competitors will be large and competition will tend to be most intense within industries in which the minimum efficient size is small relative to total industry demand because of correspondingly small barriers to entry, namely those relating to capital investment and very specialised labour requirements (see Scherer, 1980). Competition can be less intense when minimum efficient size is large relative to total industry output, because barriers to entry tend to be correspondingly substantial, limiting the number of potential competitors (Hay and Morris, 1991). Overall, Shepherd (1985) states that the barrier-to-entry effects of minimum efficient scale depend on the size of the minimum efficient scale institution relative to total industry demand as well as the slope of the LAC curve at points of less than minimum efficient scale-size operations.

The exposition above has primarily focused on the costs associated with a single product firm. For the multi-product firm, the concept of average cost is more complicated. Here the approach is to focus on the concept of ray average cost developed by Baumol (1977). According to this approach, output quantities are varied proportionally but input quantities follow the least cost expansion path.

Ray Average Cost (RAC)

Following Baumol, Panzar and Willig (1988), *RAC* is an extension of the concept of single product scale economies and implies the behaviour of cost as the production levels of a given output bundle change proportionately. This relationship is referred to as ray average cost. Ray average costs are a natural generalisation of single product average cost and are defined as follows:

$$RAC(Q) = \frac{TC(Q)}{\sum Q_i} = \frac{TC(tq^0)}{t} \tag{2}$$

where q^0 is the unit bundle for a particular mixture of outputs — the arbitrary bundle assigned the value 1 — and t is the number of units in the bundle $tq^0 = Q$ (Baumol, Panzar and Willig, 1988). This is the average cost of the composite commodity whose unit is the vector q^0 and whose scale output is given by the scalar t.

The ray average cost of producing the output vector $Q \neq 0$, indicated $RAC(Q)$, is defined to be as

$$\frac{TC(Q)}{\sum_{i=1}^{m} Q_i} \tag{3}$$

Ray average cost is said to be increasing (decreasing) at Q if $RAC(Tq)$ is an increasing (decreasing) function of scalar t, at $t = 1$. Moreover, ray average cost is said to be minimised at Q if $RAC(Q) < RAC(Tq)$, for all positive $t = 1$. This is illustrated in Figure 5.2, which also shows the behaviour of TC along that ray, OR. It can be seen that RAC and TC have the usual relationships. Hence, they intersect at the unit level of output, q^0, and RAC reaches its minimum at the output $Q = Q^0$ at which the ray OT is tangent to the TC surface in the hyperplane erected on OR.

Figure 5.2 shows the concept of RAC for a multi-product firm as a three-dimensional diagram. The lower part of the diagram is the output space for total loans and total securities, which are produced in the proportion given by the vector or ray called OR. The term 'ray' illustrates why the production cost is

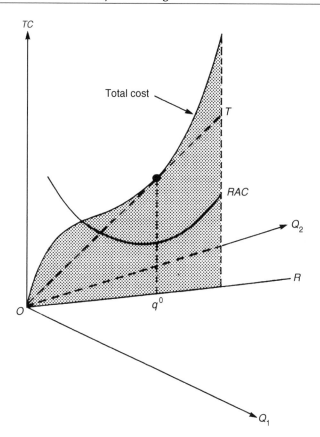

Figure 5.2 Economies of scale for multi-product firms: the concept of ray average cost (Source: adapted from Baumol, Panzar and Willig, 1988, p. 50)

called ray average cost. In terms of Figure 5.2, the output vector moves along the ray OR. The point of minimum RAC, the output bundle q^0, corresponds to the most efficient scale (size) for the firm producing loans and securities in the proportion specified by the ray QR. Thus, the degree of scale economies at q^0 is defined as the elasticity output with respect to cost which is equal to $1/(1 - e)$, where e is the elasticity of relevant average cost curve. This variable (the degree of scale economies) is greater than, less than or equal to one as returns to scale are locally increasing, decreasing or constant and as the RAC curve's slope (derivative) is negative, positive or zero, respectively.

Product-specific Economies of Scale

The concept of multi-product economies of scale explains the behaviour of costs as output increases or reduces along a given ray, but it may not explain the full behaviour of costs as output bundles change. Panzar and Willig (1977a) show how total costs change as the output of one commodity changes, which is called product-specific economies of scale. As was shown in the previous section, the concepts of RAC and multi-product scale economies refer to proportional changes in the quantities in the entire product set. However, another important way in which the magnitude of a firm's operations could change is through variation in the output of one product, holding the quantities of other products constant. To analyse the cost of such output variation it is useful to define the incremental cost of product i as the addition to the firm's total cost caused by the given output of product i. That is, it is the firm's total cost with a given vector of outputs, minus what that total cost would be if production of output i were abandoned, all other output remaining unchanged.

In order to calculate the measure of product-specific economies of scale, it is necessary to define the average cost concept: the average incremental cost (AIC) that is defined as the extra cost of adding the production of that given product at a specific level of output as compared with not producing it at all, divided by the output of that product (Willig, 1979).

The incremental cost of the product i elements m at Q is shown as (Baumol, Panzar and Willig, 1988):

$$IC_i(Q) = TC(Q) - TC(Q_{m-i}) \qquad (4)$$

where Q_{m-i} is a vector with a zero component in place of Q_i and components equal to those of Q for the remaining products. Hence, we can show the average incremental cost of output i as follows:

$$AIC_i(Q) \equiv \frac{IC_i(Q)}{Q_i} \qquad (5)$$

Thus, for instance, the AIC curve of a particular output (such as total loans or total securities) can be expressed as

$$AIC(Q_1) = \frac{TC(Q_1, Q_2) - TC(0, Q_2)}{Q_2} \qquad (6)$$

Then, the degree of product-specific returns to scale i at output vector Q is measured by

$$PSES_i(Q) = \frac{IC_i(Q)}{Q_i TC_i} = \frac{AIC_i}{\partial TC / \partial Q_i} \qquad (7)$$

Thus, the AIC and marginal cost curves are interrelated in the same way as are single product average and marginal costs (Willig, 1979). Thus, $PSES \geqslant 1$, $PSES = 1$ and $PSES \leqslant 1$ show decreasing, constant or increasing returns to scale with respect to output i.

'Although measures of product-specific scale economies partially reflect the effect of the output mix upon costs, they necessarily do so only in a partial manner since they measure the effect on cost of a *ceteris paribus* change in one output type. Thus, to capture fully the effect of changes in the composition of output on cost, more global measures are needed' (Bailey and Friedlaender, 1982, p. 1031). Further the theoretical discussion and proofs on this issue can be seen in the study undertaken by Baumol, Panzar and Willig (1988).

Economies of Scope

Economies of scope generate cost savings from delivering multiple goods and services jointly through the same organisation rather than through specialised providers. These potential cost savings are to be differentiated from economies of scale, which refer to lower costs per unit of a single good or service as total output of that good or service rises.

Two groups of potential economies of scope should be characterised. Firms can realise internal scope economies through joint production and marketing, while consumers can realise external scope economies through joint consumption. On the production side, scope economies seem to be available where facilities devoted to one objective or to serving a single market are not fully utilised and are capable of being deployed simultaneously to serve other targets and other markets. On the consumption side, however, scope economies exist where providing multiple products or services at a single location or through a single firm saves consumers the time and expense of searching for and purchasing these items through specialised providers.

Willig (1979) states that there are two fundamental reasons to study multi-product firms. Firstly, casual empiricism indicates that there are virtually no single product firms. Secondly, the technological characteristic which is termed 'economies of scope' may force firms' industry equilibrium to produce more than one good.

Panzar and Willig (1975, 1981) suggested that economies of scope are said to exist if the cost of producing outputs jointly is less than the total cost of producing the same outputs separately. That is, considering two outputs, Q_1 and Q_2, and their separate cost function, $TC(Q_1)$ and $TC(Q_2)$. If the joint cost of producing the two outputs is expressed by $TC(Q_1, Q_2)$ then economies of scope are present if

$$TC(Q_1, Q_2) < TC(Q_1) + TC(Q_2) \tag{8}$$

There are said to be diseconomies of scope if the inequality is reversed.

The concept of scope economies can be explained geometrically in Figure 5.3. The figure illustrates that the scale economies concept involves a comparison of $TC(Q_1^*, 0) + TC(0, Q_2^*)$, the sum of the heights of the cost surface over the corresponding points on the axes, with $TC(Q_1^*, Q_2^*)$, the height of the cost surface at point (Q_1^*, Q_2^*) which is the vector sum of $(Q_1^*, 0)$ and $(0, Q_2^*)$. If $TC(Q_1^*, Q_2^*)$ lies below the hyperplane OAB which goes through the origin and

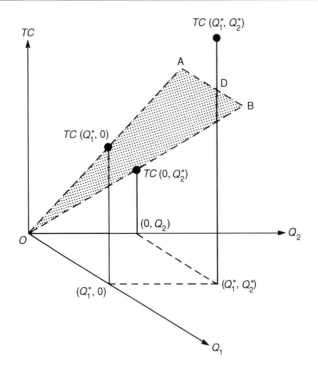

Figure 5.3 The concept of scope economies (Source: adapted from Baumol, Panzar and Willig, 1988, p. 72)

points $TC(Q_1^*, 0)$ and $TC(0, Q_2^*)$, then the condition for scope economies is achieved. Thus, in Figure 5.3 the height of D, the point on plane OAB above (Q_1^*, Q_2^*), must equal $TC(Q_1^*, 0) + TC(0, Q_2^*)$ since the hyperplane is defined by $TC = aQ_1 + bQ_2$ for some constants a, b. Hence $TC(Q_1^*, 0) = aQ_1^*$ and $TC(0, Q_2^*) = bQ_2^*$, and $TC(Q_1^*, Q_2^*)$ must be less than $aQ_1 + bQ_2$ for scope economies to hold (Baumol, Panzar and Willig, 1988).

According to Panzar and Willig (1975, p. 3) 'it is clear that the presence of economies of scope will give rise to multiproduct firms' and also 'with economies of scope, joint production of two goods by one enterprise is less costly than the combined costs of production of two specialty firms' (Willig, 1979, p. 346). The degree of economies of scope can be measured as follows:

$$SC = \frac{TC(Q_1) + TC(Q_2) - TC(Q_1, Q_2)}{TC(Q_1, Q_2)} \tag{9}$$

Baumol, Panzar and Willig (1988) indicated that when the firm produces many products, even where *RAC* decline everywhere, the absence of economies of scope may prevent natural monopoly. For example, if there are no economies of scope, a multi-product institution can be split up into several specialised firms without any increase in cost. Economies of scope, and the concepts related to it, play an important role in the analysis of the banking firm given its multi-product industry structure.

Technical Change and Economies of Scale and Scope

Firms (or banks) have production functions which embody the present state of technology. The bank usually has some scope for choice — among the inputs, and the level of output. In addition, the optimal choice depends upon the prices of the inputs and the outputs. The underlying technology of the production function, however, determines the way in which services are produced.

Technology determines two levels of operation, plant level and firm level. Economies of scale may be gained at either the plant or multi-plant level or both (Humphrey, 1985). Both production and cost functions are estimated under the assumption of constant technology. In other words, the cost curve assumes no changes in technology. Technical changes deal with the processes and consequences of shifts in the production function because of the adoption of new advanced techniques: 'Technical change is said to result when the maximum of efficient output that can be produced from any given set of inputs increases over time due to such factors as experience, increased knowledge, new innovations, and better production techniques' (Hunter and Timme, 1986, p. 153). That is, technical change arises when a given set of inputs is capable of producing a larger maximum output.

Revell (1983) has argued that technical change in banking has mainly occurred on two fronts: (i) the development of electronic funds transfer systems and (ii) advances in back-room computer operations. He argues that the early computer technologies were highly involved record-keepers of customer accounts. However, the effect of technological changes, i.e. the cheapening of computers and the development of new information networks, has led to a sharp reduction in the average cost of electronic information processing. Advances in new technologies have also reduced the entry barriers to the financial market-place.

In addition, Revell (1983) also suggested that technological advances could bring about greater scope economies as well. Small financial institutions could offer the same range of products and services to customers as larger banks, by sharing or using new technology.

The effects of greater technological advances on bank average costs should be visible. For instance, the U-shaped average curve should become flatter because of technological effects reducing the average cost. Overall, technological changes generally reduce the ratio of inputs to outputs, thereby achieving a genuine increase in economic efficiency and a reduction in costs.

THE IMPORTANCE OF THE SHAPE OF AVERAGE COSTS IN DECISION-MAKING

Knowledge of cost functions is important for optimal decision-making by firms and by regulatory bodies. It is also said that an understanding of short-run costs is important for pricing and output decisions, while long-run costs provide useful information for planning growth and investment policies of firms.

Cost curves have been widely studied by various authors, such as Bresnahan and Reiss (1990), Farrell and Shapiro (1990), Gilbert (1989), Baumol, Panzar and Willig (1988), Tirole (1988), Demsetz (1982), Rowley (1973) and Williamson (1968); these studies observe the following important reasons why cost functions deserve empirical investigation.

Cost and price–output decisions   Costs are one of the main determinants of price in all market structures and in all models relating to the explanation of the behaviour of the firm (see Scherer, 1980; Koutsoyiannis, 1979). Costs are one of the determinants of price and output, both in the short and the long run, since the profit-maximising objective of the firm is defined by the marginalistic approach (that is, marginal cost equals marginal revenue) (see Varian, 1984).

Costs and barriers to entry   Costs, either in the form of absolute cost advantages or in the form of the minimum efficient scale of output, have been stated as being the most important determinants of barriers to entry in many industries (see Scherer, 1980; Demsetz, 1982; Office of Fair Trading, 1994). The way that scale economies could be a barrier to entry when fixed costs are sunk. In other words, scale economies, together with some sunk costs, may establish a barrier to entry that allows long-run extra profits which are not based on superior efficiency (see Baumol, Panzar and Willig, 1988).

Costs and market structure   Costs determine, to a large extent, the market structure. It is said that given the size of the market, the greater economies of scale, the smaller the number of optimal firms in the market. Hence, industry which exhibits substantial scale economies may result in an oligopolistic market structure in the long run. If scale economies are not important it seems that there may be a large number of firms in the market (see Scherer, 1980).

Costs and growth policy of the firm   The growth of firms results mainly from cost considerations, given market size. Moreover, if firms are faced with U-shaped average cost curves and the market is stagnant, firms will probably diversify their business by merging into other markets (see Scherer, 1980). In addition, if scope economies are present, firms may expand their activities by adding new products in established markets (Litan, 1987). Merger and acquisition may be based mainly on cost considerations (Rhoades, 1985d). If cost advantages are predicted from say vertical integration of the production process, this would create a strong incentive for firms to adopt such policies.

Cost and the regulation of markets Knowledge of costs is important for the regulation of markets by the government. Regulatory authorities require detailed information on the cost of bank mergers in consideration of anti-trust matters. If regulators believe that there are too many small banks in an industry (in which scale economies are substantial), then the government may issue a policy aimed at increasing the size of firms (see Revell, 1987, 1991). If economies of scale are not important and the market is highly concentrated, however, the government may discourage mergers on anti-competitive grounds.

Cost functions have been the subject of a significant amount of investigation in the financial industry and the reasons specified by Benston (1972) are as follows:

1. *Regulation.* Entry, merger, branching and some prices in the finance industry are regulated, requiring regulators to estimate the cost consequences of their decisions.

2. *Importance to the finance industry.* If firms understand their costs better, they may be more efficiently managed and make decisions more rationally.

3. *Economic understanding.* Knowledge of the relationship between cost and output is basic to microeconomics and industrial economics. Study of the finance industry should provide empirical estimates that are relevant to theory.

SOURCES OF ECONOMIES OF SCALE AND SCOPE

Various authors (such as Scherer, 1980; Pratten, 1971; Robinson, 1958; Benston, 1965a; Bell and Murphy, 1968) have argued that there are many sources of cost reductions brought about through the expansion of output. Firstly, economies of scale are the effect of a more efficient use of some or all inputs with an increasing volume of output. Firms may have excess capacity of some inputs so that an increase in output cannot require a proportionate increase in all inputs over the entire production period. Specifically, some inputs might be as a whole or partly indivisible by output. The existence of indivisibility may help reduce costs per unit of output as the output level is increased.

Secondly, increased size could allow a more efficient organisation of resources. For instance, in small banks, where volume cannot permit specialisation, the same machines and workers must often be employed for a variety of tasks, say, tellers may also be assigned to sorting cheques and auditing accounts part-time. Large banks, however, may divide tasks so that employees and machines can be used in one facet of their operation. Thus, the productivity between both capital and labour arises with the scale of operations. Specialisation could also result in a more economical use of materials purchased by the bank.

Thirdly, some types of technological innovations, such as computers, may be economically more feasible for large banks. Thus, according to asset size, banks could employ different compositions of inputs with varying efficiencies.

Fourthly, Kolari and Zardkoohi (1987) state that the law of large numbers accounts for certain scale economies. Large banks do not need to hold cash balances in the same proportion as smaller banks. Since holding cash balances is costly, larger banks should have lower costs for holding cash balances than their smaller counterparts, to the extent that the law of large numbers smooths transaction demands. Moreover, larger banks are seemingly better able to diversify their assets and reduce risk as well as to offer various services to customers.

Benston (1972) indicated that the sources of economies of scale are characteristic of the use of lower skilled labour, use of fewer processing and administrative officers, and shifts in new technology available to larger-scale operations. Bell and Murphy (1968) examined the sources of economies of scale in the US banking industry, and suggested that for the processing of chequeing accounts economies of scale arise partly from the use of different kinds of equipment and partly from the specialisation of labour and machines.

Cost savings can also be achieved through scope economies, that is, cost savings resulting from the simultaneous production of several different outputs in a single firm. Possible sources of scope have been indicated by Baumol, Panzar and Willig (1988, pp. 75–79), Bailey and Friedlaender (1982, pp. 1026–1028), Berger, Hanweck and Humphrey (1987, pp. 503–504) and Mester (1987a, pp. 17–18). Adar, Agmon and Orgler (1975) and Panzar and Willig (1977b) also illustrate that interdependence results in the joint use of the inputs by many products. In banks, jointness in production is evident in the joint use of information by different divisions, for example in evaluating a loan application of a depositor. For the banking firm, costs can be saved or revenues improved by supplying joint products which result in:

1. *Spreading fixed costs.* If banks possess excess capacity, fixed or quasi-fixed brick-and-mortar branch costs, data processing costs, or loan officer and teller expenses could be spread over an expanded product mix (Berger, Hanweck and Humphrey, 1987).

2. *Information economies.* Arrow (1971) and Williamson (1975) showed that there are high costs to obtaining new information in the first place as well as organisational and strategic impediments to market transfer of information. In the case of the banking firm, information generated from servicing a customer's deposits and loans can be used as a costless input in dealing with an instalment or mortgage loan for the depositor at the same bank. Larger financial firms, for example, can develop standardised procedures as skills increase such as credit assessment, market information, documentation and

collection methods. Thus, it may be less expensive for the depositors' bank to provide them with loans than for other banks to provide the same type of service.

3. *Risk reduction.* Asset diversification across different asset groups may reduce portfolio and interest rate risks. Regulators often impose concentration limitations, such as loan limits to a single borrower or less formal restrictions, for example discouraging loan concentrations to certain industries and/or in loan categories that seem excessive.

4. *Customer cost economies.* Customers may reduce their transaction costs by doing business in a wide range of products and services at the same branch. Therefore, bank profits may be maximised by attempting to minimise both the sum of bank-incurred and customer-incurred costs, through large balances, or increased market share (Berger, Hanweck and Humphrey, 1987).

BANK COST FUNCTION TECHNOLOGY

The Nature of Production Costs

The cost function is derived from the production function, which describes the available efficient methods of production in one time period. Diewert (1992) indicates that the use of the cost function has the advantage over production functions in that statistical estimation of the unknown parameters is simpler. In addition, the cost function parameters, which characterise production technology, can be estimated much more accurately using various cost function techniques. Simply, total cost is a multivariable function which is determined by many explanatory factors. Where total cost is determined as the sum of expenditures on all inputs, however, the value of cost can be specified as a function of the level of output and the prices of all inputs. We refer to this function as the cost function. In other words, we can show that the bank's total cost which is the sum of quantities of inputs employed, $X = (x_1, x_2, \ldots, x_n)$, multiplied by their factor prices, $P = (p_1, p_2, \ldots, p_n)$. Specifically, the total cost, say TC, of producing output is simply as follows:

$$TC = p_1 L + p_2 K \qquad (10)$$

where p_1 and p_2 are the input prices for labour and capital. Consequently, we can derive the average total cost (ATC) from total cost (TC) by simply dividing by output (Q). Thus ATC can be shown as

$$ATC = \frac{TC}{Q} \qquad (11)$$

Then TC can be expressed in terms of the following formula:

$$TC = ATC \times Q = \frac{p_1 L + p_2 K}{Q} f(L, K) \qquad (12)$$

The equation implies that total costs are a function of inputs, L and K, input prices, p_1 and p_2 and the quantities of outputs produced, Q. If we hold the input price constant, the properties of the production function will be exhibited by the cost function.

The cost function, TC, can be derived from the production function $f(.)$ under certain conditions outlined in the following paragraph. It also provides an alternative and equivalent description of the technology of the production process (see Shephard, 1953, 1970).

Following Jorgenson (1986), the theory of production yields certain properties for the cost function:

1. *Positivity*. The cost function has to be positive for positive input prices and a positive level of production.

2. *Homogeneity*. The cost function is homogeneous of degree one in input prices.

3. *Monotonicity*. The cost function is increasing in the input prices and in the level of output.

4. *Concavity*. The cost function is concave.

Given differentiability of the cost function, we can define the cost shares of all inputs as elasticities of the cost function with respect to the input prices:

$$S_i = \frac{p_i x_i}{TC} = \frac{\partial \ln TC}{\partial \ln P_i} \quad 1 \leqslant i \leqslant n \tag{13}$$

Moreover, the returns to scale can be defined as the elasticity of the cost function with respect to the level of output:

$$v_{Q_i} = \frac{\partial \ln TC}{\partial \ln Q_i} \quad 1 \leqslant i \leqslant m \tag{14}$$

Using the notion of Jorgenson (1986), we can refer to this elasticity as the 'cost flexibility'. Furthermore, since the cost function TC is homogeneous of degree one in input prices, the cost shares must sum to unity.

Diewert (1974) has shown through the application of duality theory that given certain regularity conditions, cost and production functions are dual to each other. Therefore, the structure of production can be analysed empirically taking either a production function or a cost function. 'Direct estimation of the production function is attractive when the level of output is endogenous. Estimation of the cost function is more attractive, however, if the level of output is exogenous' (Christensen and Greene, 1976, p. 658).

Binswanger (1974) argued that there are several advantages in the use of a cost function rather than a production function. He said that first, it is not necessary to impose homogeneity of degree one on the production function to evaluate the estimation equations. Cost functions are homogeneous in prices regardless of the homogeneity properties of the production function, since a doubling of all prices will double the cost but will not change factor ratios. Second, the estimation equations have prices as explanatory variables rather than input quantities. Managers make decisions on input use according to exogenous prices, that makes the input levels endogenous decision variables. Finally, high multicollinearity in the production function estimations between the input variables brings about econometric problems. As there is usually little multicollinearity between input prices, this problem may not arise in cost function estimations.

ANALYSING SCALE AND SCOPE ECONOMIES IN BANKING MARKETS

A fundamental difficulty with analysing banking technology and its characteristics (i.e. economies of scale and scope) is the specification of an appropriate measure of output. No general consensus exists as to the precise definition of what a bank produces or how one can measure this product. Financial firms, however, provide services rather than readily identifiable physical products, and it is not clear how to measure service outputs. The definition and measurement of bank output and costs in the empirical analyses vary between studies. In addition, there are also problems associated with analysing scale economies at the branch or firm level, the source of data used as well as the exogeneity of bank output.

Bank Output Measures—The Production and Intermediation Approaches

Researchers have considerable difficulties in the definition and measurement of the concept of bank output. This section seeks to identify conceptual difficulties regarding bank output and how it can be measured. Unlike the outputs of manufacturing firms, service firms' outputs cannot be measured by physical quantities. In addition, banks provide a wide array of services. They provide customers with low-risk assets, credit and payments services, and play an important role as intermediaries in channelling funds from savers to borrowers as well as arranging non-monetary services such as the protection of valuables, accounting services and the running of investment portfolios. Not all services are charged for directly. Baltensperger (1980) and Kinsella (1980) have stated that banks are multi-product institutions; many of their services are joint or independent (i.e. economies of scope) and banking is subject to government regulations that may affect costs, prices or levels of output.

Studies that examine the cost structure of banking markets usually take one of two approaches, either the 'production' or the 'intermediation' approach (see later in this chapter, also Clark, 1988; OECD, 1992b). In the 'production approach', banks are treated as firms which employ capital and labour to produce different types of deposit and loan accounts. Outputs are measured by the number of deposit and loan accounts or number of transactions performed on each type of product, while total costs are the operating costs used to produce these products. The production approach, which mainly characterised the literature up to the early 1980s, views a bank as defined as a producer of two types of services: an acquirer of funds and user of funds (Humphrey, 1985). Under this approach, the appropriate measurement of output is the number of accounts of each type of service provided. Based on the production approach, operating costs are taken into account excluding interest expenses in the empirical analysis.

In the alternative 'intermediation approach', banks are viewed as intermediators of financial services rather than producers of loan and deposit account services. The values of loans and investments are taken as output measures; labour, capital and deposits are generally inputs to this process, thus operating costs and financial expenses (interest cost) are the relevant items indicated in total cost measures. The intermediation approach considers the intermediation role of banks. That is, banks produce intermediation services through the collection of deposits and other liabilities and the transfer of these funds to interest-earning assets, namely loans, securities and other investments (Colwell and Davis, 1992). In this approach, deposits are included as a third input along with capital and labour. As a result, operating costs, as well as interest cost, are taken into account in the production process. More recent studies such as Pulley and Humphrey (1993) have also included deposits as an output measure. This is because it is recognised nowadays that the taking of deposits contributes a substantial proportion of most banks' total costs (see Berger and Humphrey, 1992a for more detail).

Consequences of Bank Output Measures

The problem relating to the definition of a financial firm's output is concerned with the measurement unit employed. In banking, the question of economies of scale has been evaluated primarily by analysing banks' cost functions. The cost function implies that the minimum cost of producing bank output in a given time period is a function of the quantity of bank output produced during that period. This begs the question as to what is the appropriate measurement of bank outputs: the number and/or the value of accounts? Again, the lack of consensus on the definition of output leads to a diversity of measures of output employed in the economies of scale literature.

Studies that consider the relevant output measure as the number of deposit accounts serviced, focus on the following arguments. Firstly, depositors receive benefits (e.g. security and liquidity) from deposit accounts. Secondly, by providing these services to depositors, banks incur expenses. Bell and Murphy (1967, p. 2) pointed out, 'The servicing of demand deposits accounts is a distinct production line operation. Associated with this function are the receiving and processing of cheques, involving sorting, tabulating and many other detailed operations. Many kinds of equipment are employed to process or "produce" a demand deposits account.' The primary problem with this definition is that although this approach alleviates the problem of the homogeneity of bank output, it ignores the multi-product nature of commercial bank output and also the jointness of production of various bank activities. On the first point, the criticism has been that just because depositors receive benefits does not make them buyers; this is a voluntary transaction and both sides may expect and receive benefits. For the second point, it has been argued that both deposit and non-deposit funds are utilised to make loans and to acquire other assets. They are substitutes. This measure, also, ignores any relationship which might exist between account size and cost. It is argued that although the value of an account may to some extent affect the cost of processing it, the operating costs are determined by the number of accounts outstanding during an operating period or by the total number of transactions which occur in that period.

Sealey and Lindley (1977) suggested that using deposits as an output was incorrect, and they argued that the major confusion originated through the failure to distinguish between technical and economic aspects of production in financial institutions. The technical process of production deals with the transformation of inputs into other goods or services as output. The output of financial firms in a technical sense is the financial services provided to depositors and creditors. Economic production creates a product which has higher value than the original inputs and then this value must be measured at market prices. Hence, all of the technical outputs are not necessarily economic outputs such as the services received by depositors of financial firms. That is, these services reflect partial payment for the use of funds from depositors. Indeed, deposits do not create value until they are transformed into earning assets. Therefore, deposits are treated as inputs along with capital and labour to produce the final outputs of the bank that are the earning assets in the bank portfolio. As a result, earning assets are the primary source of revenue and they may therefore represent bank output. Pulley and Humphrey (1993) disagree with this view and believe that because deposits business accounts for a substantial proportion of most banks' costs it should be included as outputs.

Shaffer and David (1986) argue that deposits should be treated as an input in the production process of financial firms. They pointed out that there are two main reasons why this should be the case: first, deposits generate positive cost and do not produce revenue until they are intermediated into loans and other assets. Second, deposits are substitutes for other sources of funds in the production of loans and other assets.

Since returns to scale are a property of the production function, the most obvious way to gauge economies or diseconomies of scale in financial firms lies in studying the production process. Therefore, the definition of output can make a difference when one examines economies of scale using cost functions. Berger, Hanweck and Humphrey (1987) indicated that while all deposits such as demand deposits, saving deposits and time deposits are employed as inputs, economies of scale may be higher than when they are included in output, as loans expand more than proportionately with deposits. Consequently, output tends to grow rapidly when deposits are excluded from output and used as inputs. The aforementioned study also indicated that purchased funds grow faster than loans when financial firms became larger, and thus, the inclusion of purchased funds in output results in higher estimates of scale economies. In contrast, investment securities increase more slowly than loans so that their inclusion in output produces lower scale economies.

Kolari and Zardkoohi (1987) use the dollar value of accounts to measure bank output for three reasons: firstly, banks compete to increase their market share regarding dollar amounts, as opposed to the number of accounts. Secondly, the use of the number of accounts as the measure of output is correct unless all accounts have the same cost. For instance, an active demand deposits account might be more costly than a time deposits account. Furthermore, large accounts may be more costly than small accounts since they tend to be more active. Applying the dollar value of accounts alleviates this problem, as in a competitive environment, competition among banks, to attract more dollars in the form of low-cost accounts, raises their relative costs. That is, in equilibrium, the marginal cost per dollar of accounts across all deposits accounts is the same. Lastly, as long as the banks produce many services, dollar measurement is the only common denominator, i.e. securities and investments cannot be measured in number of accounts.

Studies employing the production approach assume that the main function of a bank is intermediation, that is, bringing together deficit and surplus units. Benston (1965a, p. 287) argues, 'The operations costs incurred are a function of the services. Since these services are related primarily to the number of deposits accounts and loans processed rather than the dollars loaned, economies of scale should be measured against this concept of output.' That is, two accounts, one of $10 000 and another of $1 million, should have the same operating cost. Benston, Hanweck and Humphrey (1982a, p. 10) stated that 'banks do not incur operating costs directly as a function of the number of dollars of deposits or loans they process ... the key cost causing output variable is the number and types of pieces of paper and electronic signals processed'. This flow concept eliminates some of the problems of the intermediation approach by removing the inflation bias. It also permits numbers of accounts and average size of accounts to have differential effects on costs. The number of studies based on the production approach have included the average size of accounts as an output measure, because the dollar value of accounts may play some role in affecting operating cost. However, using average size of accounts results in various econometric problems, such as multicollinearity among the explanatory variables (e.g. between the number and size of accounts). Since the number and size of accounts may be correlated, then their joint use may result in inefficient estimates of the cost function parameters.

This approach also suffers from the lack of a method of weighting the contribution of each service to total output.

The above argument suggests that what matters for a bank is not the number of accounts but the dollar value of accounts. The market evaluates a bank in terms of dollar value and no longer by the number of accounts managed by that bank. Mester (1987a, p. 19) indicated that 'The intermediation approach has an advantage over the production approach in that it includes the total costs of banking and doesn't make a distinction between a bank's purchasing deposits from other institutions or producing its own deposits.' However, Humphrey (1985, p. 756) indicated, 'But this conflict becomes a moot point if it can be shown that regardless of the definition used, the same general scale economy conclusions apply.' Moreover, Berger, Hanweck and Humphrey (1987, p. 511) stated that

> The appropriate choice between the production and intermediation approaches to banking depends upon the question being asked. ... However, for questions related to the economic viability of banks, the intermediation approach is preferred because it is more inclusive of the total costs of banking. ... From the view point of an optimising banker, interest and operating costs are functionally equivalent.

Banks with different ratios of assets and liabilities, however, could exhibit different degrees of scale economies (Revell, 1987). Large banks, for example, have higher ratios of purchased funds than small banks. Therefore, they should exhibit greater scale economies as long as purchased funds are included in the output measure. If purchased funds, however, are employed as inputs, then the studies should estimate lower scale economies (see e.g. Kolari and Zardkoohi, 1987; Noulas, Ray and Miller, 1990).

Colwell and Davis (1992) have also commented that none of the bank output measurements take into account risk factors. Risk is an additional feature of bank loans; a bank may be able to boost output in terms of the balance sheet by increasing risk. They suggested that it may perhaps be more appropriate to use some ex-post revenue measure, covering losses over the cycle, with provisions as negative output. Charnes et al. (1990) alternatively suggested that provisions and actual loan-losses could be counted as inputs. Colwell and Davis (1992) have indicated that the various measures do not allow for intertemporal relationships that are crucial in banking.

There have been various output measures which have been widely used in the economies of scale literature such as total assets, total deposits, demand deposits, the number of loan and deposits accounts, gross operating income, and divisia indeces. Indeed, one of the major problems in the theory of the financial firm is the specification of appropriate measures of outputs and inputs. The problem is compounded when financial firms, especially commercial banks, are treated as multi-product firms. It is then not only necessary to devise the measurement of output but also to consider the multi-product characteristics of the financial firm. In general, the earliest cost studies of banking used very simple models which resembled ratio-based analysis. However, each study applied a different indicator of banking output. This problem of output definition has persisted since the earliest studies and has continued to present problems to researchers as the banking literature developed over the last three decades.

Operating Versus Total Bank Cost

This section is concerned with the definition of cost that has been applied in the empirical studies of economies of scale and scope. There is also no consensus as to what cost figures (i.e. only operating cost or both operating and interest cost) should be used for the empirical analysis of the cost structure of banks. It is assumed that a bank could utilise all inputs appropriately to minimise its cost or maximise its profits. In general, according to two alternative definitions of bank output (the production approach and intermediation approach), there are two corresponding definitions of bank average costs: cost per accounts and cost per value of accounts, which have been used to analyse economies of scale and scope.

The views of the production approach advocates suggest that one should define average cost as only operating costs per account while the intermediation approach generates operating plus interest costs per value in the account. As a result, the intermediation approach always adds purchased funds when costs are shown per dollar value in the accounts (see Humphrey, 1985; Kolari and Zardkoohi, 1987). Operating cost can be specified to include wages, material costs, fringe benefits, expenses for physical capital, occupancy, along with management fees and data processing expenses paid to the holding company and other entities. Many studies use only operating cost, on the grounds that they are interested in the production process, for instance Benston, Hanweck and Humphrey (1982b), Gilligan, Smirlock and Marshall (1984) and Hunter and Timme (1986). Benston, Hanweck and Humphrey (1982a, p. 9) indicated that 'while interest is an important outlay to the bank, it is determined by market forces that reflect alternative investments available to depositors. Thus, interest is not an operating expense for purposes of measuring banks' efficiency.' As far as operating cost is concerned, there are two main arguments for not including interest expenses in the measurement of bank cost. Firstly, the inclusion of interest cost moves the focus from the ability of banks to produce output using internal resources and management to that of producing with purchased funds. Secondly, other impediments against using interest cost is that the price used is an average not a marginal cost of funds. As far as marginal cost differs from average cost, the estimation of the cost function parameters will be biased. However, the average interest rates could be a good proxy for marginal costs in a deregulated environment.

More recent studies have employed total cost to investigate economies of scale and scope in banking markets. Total costs are calculated by adding interest expenses on purchased funds and core deposits to operating costs. 'The interest expenses are large and exceed operating costs since they comprise around 35 and 40 per cent, respectively of total cost' (Humphrey, 1990, p. 39). Applying only operating cost can lead to biased estimation since, when banks get larger, the proportion of assets funded with non-deposit accounts increases (for example purchased funds). As mentioned earlier, the operating cost of non-deposit accounts is small, while their interest expense is higher. Since both demand deposit and non-deposit accounts are substitutes, using operating cost is biased towards finding greater scale economies for larger banks when scale economies might not be present (Humphrey, 1985). Moreover, operating cost per dollar of assets is seen to fall more rapidly than total costs per dollar of assets. Thus if only operating costs are used in a statistical analysis of bank costs, as some researchers have done, economies of scale will be overestimated (Humphrey, 1990).

Scale Economies at the Branch (Plant) Versus the Firm Level

The cost function of an individual branch may be considerably different from the cost function for the bank as a whole. This is generally referred to as the difference between plant (branch)-level economies and firm-level economies. Since optimal plant and firm sizes will be identical only when multi-plant economies are negligible, the magnitude of such influences should be carefully considered in evaluating the effect of scale economies. Both branch-level and firm-level economies can have an important effect on the minimum efficient firm size.

Cost studies in banking markets have used various approaches to analyse the effects of branching on the cost structure of banking institutions. When analysing the scale and scope economies for banks with branch networks it is important to separate two issues, the size of branches and the number of branches. There could be scale and scope economies in larger branches from which smaller branches may not benefit, and this could become more evident as bank services are extended. Put simply, there may be cost savings which could be generated by increasing the output of established branches (plant-level economies) but not by adding new branches (firm-level economies).

Different results have been reported according to the way branch variables are used in the cost function. Early studies examined cost differences between unit bank and branch banks in the USA separately (i.e. Alhadeff, 1954; Horvitz, 1963). These studies did not distinguish between scale economies at the single branch office or plant level from those (for all the branch network) at the firm level. However, some of the early studies did use dummy variables to distinguish between branch and unit banking (i.e. Benston, 1965b; Bell and Murphy, 1968). In order to measure scale economies at the branch and the firm level, later studies included branch variables in the cost function. Branch-level scale economies were calculated by holding the number of branches constant during the estimation. To estimate scale economies at the firm level, both the number of branches and outputs are allowed to vary. Since economies of scale, in general, show how average costs are affected as output expands, for unit banks output can only be increased by producing more of various banking services at a single branch. In the case of US unit banks, this single branch also represents the entire unit banking institution, and economies of scale at the firm or the plant level are the same. However, for branch banks, economies of scale at the branch level could be different from those for the entire institution (at the firm-level scale economies).

Banks can expand their operations or output by either: (i) increasing services to existing branch networks in given markets; or (ii) adding new branches, which attract new accounts and deposits, in new market areas. Early studies focused on the first method of output expansion which could be appropriate only for unit banks and banks with very few branches. In the case of banks with a large branch network, it seems that the second method of output expansion may be more important. Scale economies at the plant or branch level are calculated assuming that expansion of output occurs with no increase in the number of branches, while scale economies at the firm level are calculated assuming that output expansion is accompanied by branch expansion.

The Source of Data in US Banking Studies

Most of the US studies dealing with economies of scale and scope have generally used data from two main sources: the Functional Cost Analysis (FCA) programme of the Federal Reserve System and banks' own Call and Income Reports. The Federal Reserve's FCA programme is a voluntary one conducted by the 12 US Federal Reserve banks for commercial banks and savings banks in their districts (see Humphrey, 1985). The data have the advantage of providing standardised format and detailed information, notably the number of accounts for each service. However, there are some drawbacks to using the FCA data source. The major one is the size distribution of banks in the sample (Humphrey, 1985). The FCA data exclude large banks with deposits above $1 billion, which therefore limits the usefulness of the analysis because it is difficult to extrapolate the results of the analysis beyond the size distribution of banks found in the sample. In other words, forecasting about the cost structure of large banks on the basis of such samples is a critical extrapolation.

Heggestad and Mingo (1977) investigate the FCA programme, finding that banks in it have lower expense ratios, and that the influence of banks' size on cost is different for FCA banks. Furthermore, from a policy point of view, it is of no great matter whether economies of scale are exhausted for very small unit banks, in the sense that a merger between two small banks does not raise serious regulatory questions, since no danger of monopoly power could be suspected. The important interest concerns the cost of the large banks because mergers among the latter could have a significant impact on market shares and the competitive environment. Another problem that arises with the FCA data is that the sample is not random since the programme is voluntary (Noulas, Ray and Miller, 1990). Moreover, the FCA data made available to the public has some information masked to protect the confidentiality of the participating institutions (Gropper, 1991).

Recently, various US studies have used data from the Call and Income Reports of individual banks. These data cover both balance sheet and income statement items that are used in cost function estimation. The problem with these data is that they do not provide detailed service-based cost information (Gropper, 1991). It is impossible, for example, to identify the individual cost and levels of cross-substitution between different product lines and services.

The source of data is also questionable for European studies which generally use various balance sheet and income statements data from publicly available accounts. This limits the analysis of scale and scope economies to bank-level evaluations rather than more micro-level product line cost studies.

The Exogeneity of Bank Outputs

The modelling of cost functions requires the exogeneity of the explanatory variables which means that they are autonomous, or predetermined. That is, regression analysis requires that the relationship between dependent variables and explanatory variables be one-way, or unidirectional. However, many studies in the banking literature are plagued by the fact that the independent variables are endogenous. For example, Benston, Hanweck and Humphrey (1982b) reported that larger banks produce more deposit services as well as payroll, cash management and various funds transfer services per deposit account than smaller banks. This may lead to some bank outputs being endogenous since they simultaneously affect bank operating costs. The earlier studies undertaken by Benston (1965a) and Bell and Murphy (1967) argued that, given the US banking institutions, the exogeneity of the output could be an acceptable assumption. Their argument is that since the regulatory authority imposed geographical limits on banking activities, the banks (e.g. unit banks) were in a situation of local monopoly, and that their output was mainly determined by the local demand, thus exogenous to the bank. However, this argument becomes unclear when the authorities deregulate the market. The solution, which Benston, Hanweck and Humphrey (1982a) introduced, is to include an explanatory variable measuring average account size to adjust the number of accounts for bank size. Kolari and Zardkoohi (1987), however, have argued that the inclusion of account size in the model does not necessarily resolve the problem of endogeneity since the number of accounts and average size of accounts are highly correlated.

Kim (1985) provides a theoretical solution for the endogeneity of some outputs, which showed that the joint estimation of an equation system consisting of a translog cost function, a cost-share equation and a revenue-share equation along with the proper parameter restrictions (to ensure linear homogeneity in factor prices of one and symmetry), is the solution for obtaining consistent estimates with endogenous outputs.

Kolari and Zardkoohi (1987) indicated that Kim's procedure may not be totally necessary. They argue that firstly, the endogeneity problem for estimating the cost function parameters in banking is no more or less serious than cost estimations in other industries. Secondly, Kim's (1985) approach takes into account only the supply side of the market, without covering the demand side.

Given the above problems associated with studying scale and scope economies in banking markets the following section examines the nature of multi-product cost functions which are used to estimate scale and scope economies in the banking markets.

FUNCTIONAL FORMS FOR THE MULTI-PRODUCT COST FUNCTION

The total cost of production for a firm can be shown as $TC(Q, P)$, where Q is an m-dimensional vector of output quantities and P is an n-dimensional vector of input prices. Provided that TC satisfies regularity conditions (that is, non-negative, real valued, non-decreasing, strictly positive for non-zero Q, and linearly homogeneous and concave in P for each Q) it is said to be dual to the transformation function that can be written as $f(Q, X)$, where X is an n-dimensional vector of input quantities. The duality between cost function and transformation function ensures that they incorporate the same information about production properties. Thus, there is a duality between cost and production functions in the sense that either of these functions can be used to describe the technology of the firm equally well in certain circumstances.

The Cobb–Douglas Cost Function

Cobb–Douglas cost and production functions are linear in logarithms and both can serve as first-order approximations to arbitrary production or cost function in logarithms in the absence of uncertainty. It is necessary for the Cobb–Douglas production functions to be linearly homogeneous and strictly quasi-concave and the elasticity of substitution in inputs to be one. In addition, costs are positive for any non-negative produced output and input prices are given parametrical to any firm, with conditions of cost minimising and a competitive input market (Diewert, 1992).

Under the restriction that there exists a dual relationship between the production function and cost function, the total cost of production is defined for the two inputs case as (see Nerlove, 1963; Heathfield and Wibe, 1987; Kolari and Zardkoohi, 1987):

$$TC = p_1 L + p_2 K \tag{15}$$

where p_1 and p_2 are the prices of labour and capital.

The first widely used production function that allows substitution is the Cobb–Douglas (1928) production function which for a bank looks like the following:

$$Q = AL^{\alpha_1} K^{\alpha_2} \tag{16}$$

where Q is output per period, A represents fixed inputs, including the effect of technology, L is labour input, K is capital input and α_i are elasticity of Q with respect to inputs.

The conditions of cost minimising for banks indicates the marginal productivity conditions and these can be formulated as follows:

$$\frac{P_1 L}{\alpha_1} = \frac{P_2 K}{\alpha_2} \tag{17}$$

Using equations (15)–(17), the Cobb–Douglas cost function can be simplified as

$$TC = \gamma Q^{1/r} P_1^{\alpha_1/r} P_2^{\alpha_2/r} \tag{18}$$

where $\gamma = r(A\alpha_1^{\alpha_1}\alpha_2^{\alpha_2})^{-1/r}$; $r = \alpha_1 + \alpha_2$. The parameter r, which is equal to the sum of output elasticities with respect to inputs (i.e. K, L), shows the degree of returns to scale.

The cost function equation can be transformed into the logarithmic form to achieve the linear relationship as

$$\ln TC = \ln \gamma + \left(\frac{1}{r}\right)\ln Q + \left(\frac{\alpha_1}{r}\right)\ln P_1 + \left(\frac{\alpha_2}{r}\right)\ln P_2 \tag{19}$$

The duality condition requires that factor prices be homogeneous of degree one, that is, the exponents of P_1 and P_2 must sum to unity. In other words, $\alpha_1/r + \alpha_2/r = 1$. This means that doubling prices will always exactly double costs. Thus the Cobb–Douglas cost function must be homogeneous of degree one in input prices. Under this restriction, equation (19) can be rewritten as

$$\ln TC - \ln P_2 = \ln \gamma + \left(\frac{1}{r}\right)\ln Q + \left(\frac{\alpha_1}{r}\right)(\ln P_1 - \ln P_2) \tag{20}$$

Finally, economies of scale can be computed deriving equation (20). However, the Cobb–Douglas cost function allows us only to estimate increasing, decreasing or constant cost curves which does not allow U-shaped cost curves. Although this functional form defined by equation (19) is used a great deal in applied economics literature, unfortunately its use is not recommended because it imposes serious restrictions on the a priori admissible pattern of substitution between inputs and outputs. Moreover, the Cobb–Douglas function constrains the elasticity of substitution between inputs to equal unity.

The CES Cost Function

The next advance in functional forms for production functions came when Arrow et al. (1961) developed the constant elasticity of substitution (CES) function. The CES function is more general than the Cobb–Douglas function and it permits any degree of substitutability among inputs. That is, the CES production function also constrains the value of substitution to be constant, but not necessarily equal to one. The CES production function is shown:

$$Q = A[\beta L^{-\gamma} + (1 - \beta)K^{-\gamma}]^{-z/\gamma} \qquad (21)$$

where L and K are two inputs and z is the degree of homogeneity which can also represent measure of scale economies. Thus, the measure of elasticity of substitutions between inputs for the CES is $\sigma = 1/(1 + \gamma)$, which is constant but not necessarily equal to one. When $\gamma = 1$, the CES production function reduces to the Cobb–Douglas functional forms. The cost function that is the dual of the production function and shows total costs in terms of output and input prices can be defined as

$$TC = Q^{1/z}A^{-1/z}[\beta^{1/(1+\gamma)}P_1^{\gamma/(1+\gamma)} + (1 - \beta)^{1/(1+\gamma)}P_2^{\gamma/(1+\gamma)}]^{(1+\gamma)/\gamma} \qquad (22)$$

Arrow et al. (1961) indicated that the CES production function provides better results for analysis of production with one output and two inputs of production. The CES functional form is more general than the Cobb–Douglas one and is perfectly adequate in the two-input case; however, its generalisation to the three or more input case imposes unreasonably severe constraints on the substitution possibilities. Uzawa (1962) has demonstrated that constancy of elasticities of substitutions and transformation is highly restrictive for more than one output or more than two inputs. Overall, as its name requires, the production function permits the elasticity of substitution between pairs of inputs to differ from unity; however, it has been shown that the CES function does force the elasticities between each pair of inputs to be the same. The CES function is a step in the right direction but still seems too restrictive.

Consequently, these constraints resulted in the growth of the so-called 'flexible' functional forms, such as the generalised Leontief functional form introduced by Diewert (1971) and the transcendental logarithmic functional form introduced by Christensen, Jorgenson and Lau (1973). These functional forms share the common characteristics of linearity in parameters and the ability to provide second-order approximations to any arbitrary functions (Lau, 1986). Moreover, these functional forms also include linear, quadratic and interaction terms in the independent variables.

The Translog Cost Function

One of the most widely used flexible functional forms for a cost function is the transcendental logarithmic functional form which was developed for a single output technology by Christensen, Jorgenson and Lau (1971, 1973); the multiple output case was defined by Burgess (1974) and Diewert (1974). The translog production function is a second-order approximation in logarithms for arbitrary deterministic functions and more flexible functional forms (Diewert, 1974; Lau, 1974) which required that the own and cross-price derivatives (or equivalently the elasticities) of demand for inputs or commodities be free to attain any set of theoretically consistent values (i.e. the restrictive constraints a priori such as homotheticity, constancy of the elasticity of substitution, additivity). The functional form is also easily adaptable to include multiple outputs and multiple inputs. The general form of the translog production function can be expressed as

$$\ln Q = \alpha_0 + \sum_{i=1}^{n} \alpha_i \ln X_i + \frac{1}{2} \sum_{i=1}^{n} \sum_{j=1}^{n} \alpha_{ij} \ln X_i \ln X_j \qquad (23)$$

where $\alpha_{ij} = \alpha_{ji}$ for all i, j and X_i are n the quantities of inputs.

Following from the duality principle that cost functions can be obtained directly from production functions (for a formal proof of duality principles, see Diewert, 1974, 1982; Fuss and McFadden, 1980; Nadiri, 1982) the following translog cost functional form can be derived:

$$\ln TC = \alpha_0 + \sum_{i=1}^{m} \alpha_i \ln Q_i + \sum_{i=1}^{n} \beta_i \ln P_i$$

$$+ \frac{1}{2} \left[\sum_{i=1}^{m} \sum_{j=1}^{m} \delta_{ij} \ln Q_i \ln Q_j + \sum_{i=1}^{n} \sum_{j=1}^{n} \gamma_{ij} \ln P_i \ln P_j \right]$$

$$+ \sum_{i=1}^{n} \sum_{j=1}^{m} \rho_{ij} \ln P_i \ln Q_j \qquad (24)$$

where TC is total cost, Q_i is the level of output, P_i the price of inputs. There are $m+1$ independent α_i parameters, n independent β_i, $m(m+1)/2$ dependent δ_{ij} parameters since it is assumed that $\delta_{ij} = \delta_{ji}$ for $1 < i$, $j < m$, $n(n+1)/2$ independent γ_{ij} parameters since it is assumed that $\gamma_{ij} = \gamma_{ji}$ for $1 < i$, $j < n$, and mn independent ρ_{ij} parameters in the translog cost function defined by equation (24). However, if the constraint of the homogeneity of degree one in the input prices on the cost function TC defined by equation (24) is imposed, we will require that the following restrictions on the parameters hold:

$$\sum_{i=1}^{n} \beta_i = 1 \qquad \sum_{i=1}^{n} \gamma_{ij} = 0 \quad 1 < j < n$$

$$\sum_{i=1}^{n} \rho_{ij} = 0 \quad 1 < j < m \qquad (25)$$

In general, the translog cost function defined by equation (24) will not satisfy the appropriate regularity conditions globally (see Diewert, 1982, p. 554). Lau (1974), however, shows that the translog cost function may provide a good local approximation to an arbitrary twice differentiable cost function, linearly homogeneous in input prices. This gives the translog function a flexible functional form.

However, the derived demand for an input or cost share of input, X_i, is calculated by partially differentiating the cost function with respect to the input prices, P_i (see Shephard, 1953, 1970; Christensen, Jorgenson and Lau, 1973). Given differentiability of the cost function, we can show the cost shares of the inputs as elasticities of the cost function with respect to the input prices:

$$S_i = \frac{\partial \ln TC}{\partial \ln P_i} = \frac{\partial TC}{\partial P_i} \frac{P_i}{TC} = \frac{P_i X_i}{TC} \quad 1 < i < n \qquad (26)$$

where S_i are the share of the ith inputs in the total costs. Thus, for the translog functional form defined by equation (24) the cost share equations defined by equation (26) can be rewritten following the duality theory and referred to as Shephard's lemma (Christensen, Jorgenson and Lau, 1973):

$$\frac{P_i X_i}{TC} = \beta_i + \sum_{j=1}^{n} \gamma_{ij} \ln P_j + \sum_{j=1}^{m} \rho_{ij} \ln Q_j \qquad (27)$$

Note that since the sum of the cost shares is equal to unity, however, only $n - 1$ of the n equations defined by equation (26) can be statistically independent.

Overall, the translog cost function shown in equation (24) must have the following properties if production and cost function theories are to be fully integrated. Jorgenson (1986) notes that the function must have:

1. *Homogeneity*. The cost function TC defined by equation (24) is homogeneous of degree one in the input prices.

2. *Cost exhaustion*. The sum of cost shares is equal to unity. Cost exhaustion requires that the value of the i inputs is equal to total cost.

3. *Symmetry*. A necessary and sufficient condition for symmetry is that the second-order outputs and inputs parameters must be symmetric, that is, for instance, in the cost function defined in equation (24), $\delta_{ij} = \delta_{ji}$ for $1 < i$, $j < m$, and $\gamma_{ij} = \gamma_{ji}$ for $1 < i$, $j < n$, respectively.

4. *Non-negativity*. The cost shares and the cost elasticities must be non-negative. Since the translog cost function is quadratic in the logarithms of input prices and the output levels, we cannot impose restrictions on the parameters that indicate non-negativity of the cost shares and the cost elasticities.

5. *Monotonicity*. The cost function is increasing in the input prices and in the level of output.

The Hybrid Translog Cost Function

A major criticism of the conventional translog cost methodology is that it does not allow us to evaluate scope economies and product-specific economies of scale when one of the outputs becomes zero. To avoid the problem of zero output, the hybrid translog cost function developed by Caves, Christensen and Tretheway (1980) and Fuss and Waverman (1981) can be used as a generalisation of the translog cost function, that is the logarithm of the output $(\ln Q_i)$ is replaced by a Box–Cox (1964) transformation:

$$Q_i^* = \frac{(Q_i^\lambda - 1)}{\lambda} \quad \lambda \neq 0$$

$$= \ln Q_i \quad \lambda = 0 \tag{28}$$

When λ approaches zero, the hybrid cost function approaches the translog cost function. When λ equals one, the cost function becomes semilog. The hybrid cost function can be shown, using the Box–Cox transformation as follows:

$$\ln TC = \alpha_0 + \sum_{i=1}^{m} \alpha_i Q_i^* + \sum_{i=1}^{n} \beta_i \ln P_i$$

$$+ \frac{1}{2} \left[\sum_{i=1}^{m} \sum_{j=1}^{m} \delta_{ij} Q_i^* Q_j^* + \sum_{i=1}^{n} \sum_{j=1}^{n} \gamma_{ij} \ln P_i \ln P_j \right]$$

$$+ \sum_{i=1}^{n} \sum_{j=1}^{m} \rho_{ij} \ln P_i Q_j^* \tag{29}$$

where $\delta_{ij} = \delta_{ji}$ and $\gamma_{ij} = \gamma_{ji}$. In this cost function, it is clear that costs will not be zero even if some output is zero.

Like the translog cost function, since the duality theorem requires that the cost function must be linearly homogeneous in input prices, the following conditions must be restricted on the input price parameters:

$$\sum_{i=1}^{n} \beta_i = 1 \quad \sum_{i=1}^{n} \gamma_{ij} = 0 \quad 1 < j < n$$

$$\sum_{i=1}^{n} \rho_{ij} = 0 \quad 1 < j < m \tag{30}$$

In practice, these kind of restrictions are in general imposed explicitly in the process of estimation. Baumol, Panzar and Willig (1988) showed that the hybrid translog is substantively flexible at least to some degree. For instance, if $\gamma > 0$, then RAC becomes U-shaped; if $\gamma < 0$, then RAC cost curves have inverted U-shapes. They also indicated that the functional form can exhibit economies or

diseconomies of scope, product-specific economies of scale, and cost complementarities (or their opposite) as well as other properties of the cost function.

Baumol, Panzar and Willig (1988) also note that like the translog forms,
the property of the hybrid translog which makes them especially convenient for
estimation is the statistically tractable set of equations which can be obtained with
the aid of Shephard's lemma for the shares of total cost efficiently expended on
the inputs. These equations can be expressed as

$$\frac{P_i X_i}{TC} = \beta_i + \sum_{j=1}^{n} \gamma_{ij} \ln P_j + \sum_{j=1}^{m} \rho_{ij} Q_j^* \tag{31}$$

where X_i is the quantity of their ith input. In fact, the cost parameter values are
estimated by fitting the system of equations simultaneously to the relevant data,
while imposing the relevant restrictions on the equations.

Limitations of the Translog Functional Form

The translog cost function was developed as a local approximation to some
unknown 'true' underlying cost function. Interest in the approximation was motivated by the fact that it does not require restrictions on elasticities at the point
of approximation. In practice, the translog functional form usually gives poor
approximations to the true underlying cost function as one moves away from
the point of approximation (Barnett and Lee, 1985). In other words, the statistical methodology which depends on extrapolating a local approximation to fit
globally may behave poorly when the global behaviour of the function differs
from its local behaviour. Thus, in its application, the translog functional form
is potentially subject to misspecification (McAllister and McManus, 1993; Lau,
1986). Lau (1986) states that when global theoretical consistency fails, however,
there is still a set of prices of inputs over which theoretical consistency holds,
and this set may be large enough for all practical purposes.

A major problem involving the ordinary translog cost functional form arises
when one computes measures of product-specific economies of scale and global
economies of scope. One of the desirable characteristics of a multi-product cost
function is that it allows for one or more outputs to be zero (Caves, Christensen
and Tretheway, 1980). In the ordinary translog functional form, however, all of
the outputs enter in logarithmic form; thus the function has no finite representation
if any output has a zero value. Baumol, Panzar and Willig (1988) note that the
cost functional form should yield a reasonable cost figure for output vectors that
involve zero outputs of some products. To remedy this drawback the ordinary
translog functional form can be modified in order to redefine zero outputs. Simply,
the logarithm of the output is replaced by using Box–Cox's (1964) transformation
in the translog cost function. The resulting functional form, the hybrid translog
cost function, was suggested by Caves, Christensen and Tretheway (1980) and

Fuss and Waverman (1981) as a generalisation of the translog function. However, λ is usually estimated to be close to zero, which again yields properties similar to the ordinary translog cost functional form (see Pulley and Humphrey, 1993).

The translog functional form also has a large number of parameters (Diewert, 1992) which may result in multicollinearity between explanatory variables. Moreover, Guilkey and Lovell (1980) criticise the translog form by showing, with a Monte Carlo simulation, that the translog cost function slightly overstates economies of scale and that the simultaneous estimation (SUR) of the translog cost function, together with input share equations, does not achieve better results relative to a single equation estimation.

Although there are possible limitations, the translog functional form still remains attractive to other functional forms.

Desirable Features of Multi-Product Cost Functions

What properties should a multi-product cost function possess? What is the desirable form of a multi-product cost function? Or what are some of the criteria that could be used to help the ex-ante selection of an algebraic functional form for a multi-product cost function? Over the years, a number of criteria have evolved and developed. These can be broadly grouped into five categories (see Lau, 1986):

1. *Theoretical consistency*. This means that the algebraic functional form chosen must be capable of possessing the theoretical properties required of the cost function of a cost-minimising firm. It must be homogeneous of degree one, non-decreasing and concave in the prices of inputs and non-decreasing in the quantity of output (Jorgenson, 1986). Thus, any multi-product functional form selected to represent a cost function must be capable of possessing these properties for an appropriate choice of the parameters at least in a neighbourhood of the prices of inputs and quantity of output of interest. Fortunately, many functional forms will satisfy the test of theoretical consistency, at least locally.

2. *Domain of applicability*. This refers to the set of values of the independent variables over which the algebraic functional satisfies all the conditions for theoretical consistency (Lau, 1986). For example, Lau (1986) shows that under the necessary and sufficient restrictions for global theoretical consistency on their parameters both the generalised Leontief cost function and the translog cost function lose their flexibility. Both functional forms can be globally valid only under relatively stringent restrictions on the parameters; however, they can be locally valid under relatively less stringent restrictions. Lau (1986) also concludes that both the generalised Leontief and the translog cost functions cannot be globally theoretically consistent for all choices of parameters. However, even when global theoretical consistency fails, there

is still a set of input prices over which theoretical consistency holds and this set may be large enough for all practical purposes.

3. *Flexibility*. The concept of flexibility, first introduced by Diewert (1973, 1974), refers to the ability of the functional form to approximate arbitrary but theoretically consistent behaviour through an appropriate choice of the parameters. In other words, the cost function should be a flexible functional form, that is a form that requires no restrictions on the values of the first and second partial derivatives (Baumol, Panzar and Willig, 1988). Lau (1986) notes that flexibility of a functional form is desirable because it allows the data the opportunity to provide information about parameters. Lau (1986) shows that the translog cost function is flexible.

4. *Computational facility*. The computational facility of a functional form requires the following properties. First, unknown parameters of cost functions are straightforward to estimate from the data; this is known as 'linearity-in-parameters' (Diewert, 1992). Secondly, the functional form should be represented in explicit closed form (Lau, 1986). Thirdly, the number of parameters in the functional form should be the minimum possible number. In other words, the cost function should not imply estimation of the values of an excessive number of parameters. In most cases, the number of observations is relatively small and conservation of the degrees of freedom is an important consideration (Diewert, 1992).

5. *Factual conformity*. This implies consistency of the functional form with known empirical facts.

For the analysis of a multi-product industry, the cost function should generate reasonable cost estimates for output vectors when there are zero outputs of some products. The majority of functional forms, such as the Cobb–Douglas function, the CES function and the translog cost function, violate this property.

Overall, as shown by Baumol, Panzar and Willig (1988), the hybrid translog cost function satisfies our desiderata fairly well and it has already been employed in empirical studies of bank costs.

RECENT APPROACHES TO ESTIMATING EFFICIENCY IN BANKING MARKETS

Most studies of bank cost structures have concentrated on the cost advantages resulting from the scale and scope of production. There are, however, other aspects of efficiency which researchers have just begun to examine such as technical and allocative efficiency. Productive efficiency implies optimising behaviour with respect to output and inputs. The economic theory of the firm assumes that production takes place in an environment where managers attempt to maximise profits by operating in the most efficient manner possible (Fare, Grosskopf and Lovell, 1985). The competitive model also implies that firms which fail to do so will be driven from the market by more efficient ones. However, when natural entry barriers or regulation reduce the degree of competition, inefficient firms could continue to prosper (Evanoff and Israilevich, 1991).

The cost function approach has been widely used to model the technology of a firm operating in regulated environments, such as the banking industry. Outputs of banking firms are assumed to be exogenous. Since input prices are also deemed to be exogenous under the competitive factor market assumptions, we can obtain consistent parameter estimates by using cost function estimates. However, a problem associated with estimating cost functions is that it is assumed that banks are operating in an efficient manner. In other words, the only error in this type of methodology is noise and possible model misspecification (Beckers and Hammond, 1987).

Parametric Approach: Stochastic Cost Frontiers

In recent years there has been a substantial growing interest in the estimation of efficiency in production. Although the basic idea of measuring efficiency goes back to Farrell (1957), econometric estimation of stochastic frontier models was developed by Aigner, Lovell and Schmidt (1977) and Meeusen and van den Broeck (1977). In the frontier methodology, efficiency of an individual production unit is measured by comparing its performance to a standard, that is, either the cost, profit or the production frontier. Forsund, Lovell and Schmidt (1980) specified the cost frontier as the minimum cost function for a given level of output and input prices. Similarly, the profit frontier is the maximum profit function given input and output prices. Moreover, the production frontier is the locus of maximum output levels given the level of inputs. The notion of these frontiers is consistent with the optimising behaviour of producers where concepts of maximality (i.e. in the production function and profit function) and minimality (in the cost function) are emphasised (Kumbhakar, 1991).

The traditional cost function is specified to the extent that a cost-minimising firm cannot produce a given level of output with given input prices at a minimum cost if technical and allocative inefficiencies exist. Thus, sources of errors in the estimated cost or production functions can be defined as: (i) technical inefficiency, which relates to the failure to produce the maximum possible output, given inputs of production, (ii) allocative inefficiency, resulting from the suboptimal choice of input proportions, given input prices, and (iii) statistical standard noise (random errors), representing exogenous shocks, such as 'luck factors'. The last component, which is randomly distributed about the relationship, can also cover approximation error. As a result, the residuals in the cost function must represent these three types of errors. These result in the following definition of the cost function using the translog functional form:

$$\ln TC = \ln TC^* + \varepsilon \tag{32}$$

where $\ln TC$ is log of total cost, $\ln TC^*$ is log of minimum cost which reflects the cost frontier including the statistical standard noise, and ε equals $\ln C_\tau + \ln C_\alpha + \ln C_v$, where $\ln C_\tau$ and $\ln C_\alpha$ refer to the increase in log cost resulting from technical and allocative inefficiencies respectively. $\ln C_v$ is the statistical standard noise which could increase or decrease costs. Both $\ln C_\tau$ and $\ln C_\alpha$ should be non-negative since technical and allocative inefficiencies increase costs.

The stochastic frontier approach modifies a standard cost function and allows for inefficiencies to be included in the error term. The predicted value of a standard cost function is assumed to define the frontier, while any inefficiencies enter through the error component, which is by construction orthogonal to the predicted frontier. This assumption forces any measured inefficiencies to be uncorrelated with the explanatory variables or the scale or product mix economies derived linearly from these variables (Ferrier and Lovell, 1990). It also assumes that the inefficiencies are drawn from an asymmetric half-normal, exponential, truncated-normal or gamma distribution and the statistical standard noise is drawn from a symmetric normal distribution (Jondrow et al., 1982). Greene (1990) and Stevenson (1980) have indicated that the half-normal distribution is rather inflexible and it embodies an implicit assumption that most of the observations are clustered near full efficiency, with higher degrees of inefficiency being decreasingly likely. Berger and Humphrey (1991) and Caves and Barton (1990) also suggest that the half-normal assumption for inefficiencies is violated for many US banks and manufacturing industries.

Non-Parametric Approach: Data Envelope Analysis (DEA)

DEA methodology, first introduced by Charnes, Cooper and Rhodes (1978), has been used to measure the empirically derived relative efficiency (e.g technical efficiency) of non-profit-making organisations, where profit measures are difficult to calculate (particularly in the public sector) (Sueyoshi, 1991). Moreover, DEA can measure the relative efficiency of a group of organisations in their use of multiple inputs to produce multiple outputs, in which the efficient production function is not known or easily specified.

There are many permutations to the DEA approach; however, the fundamental objective is to 'envelope' the data by producing a piecewise linear fit via linear programming techniques. In other words, instead of using regression methodology to fit a smooth relationship, a piecewise linear surface is produced which encompasses the observations (see Evanoff and Israilevich, 1991).

The technique derives a frontier for each organisation in the sample based on the output and input utilisation of all institutions in the sample. DEA does this by comparing several organisations' (denoted p) actual outputs (Q_{jp}) and inputs (X_{ip}). DEA identifies the relatively more efficient best practice subset of organisations and the subset of institutions which are relatively inefficient (and the magnitude of their inefficiencies) compared with the best practice organisations

(Colwell and Davis, 1992). In other words, following Colwell and Davis (1992), we maximise:

$$E_p = \frac{\sum_{j=1}^{m} u_j Q_{jp}}{\sum_{i=1}^{n} v_i X_{ip}} \tag{33}$$

subject to $E_p \leqslant 1$ for all p and weights v_i, $u_j > 0$.

The above model is computed repetitively with each organisation appearing in the objective function in order to derive individual efficiency ratings. Colwell and Davis (1992) also note that each firm will either have a derived efficiency rating either of $E = 1$, which indicates relative efficiency, or $E < 1$, which indicates relative inefficiency. It is noteworthy that $E = 1$ is a best practice unit, which is not necessarily efficient but that is not less efficient compared with other organisations. As a result, DEA provides us with a relative efficiency measure, not an absolute estimate.

A major drawback of DEA, however, is that it assumes no statistical noise and all the error term in the estimation is attributed to inefficiency (Mester, 1993; Sueyoshi, 1991). In addition, DEA estimates give only an upper bound to efficiency measures (see Schmidt, 1986), so that it is difficult to use DEA to compare efficiency among firms. Another major disadvantage, pointed out by Colwell and Davis (1992), is that the DEA frontier is defined on the outlier rather than on the whole sample and is thereby particularly susceptible to extreme observations and measurement error. Moreover, application of DEA to the private sector may not be justifiable because of the presence of freedom to redeploy resources to another industry. Berg and Kim (1991) also indicated that the non-parametric DEA cannot take into account market structure and that this is important given their findings that efficiency scores are not independent of market structure characteristics. Moreover, inadequacies in data or sample size could vitiate DEA results.

Using either the stochastic frontier or DEA approach, the objective is to generate an accurate frontier. However, the two techniques use significantly different approaches to achieve this objective. Because the parametric approach generates a stochastic cost frontier and the DEA approach generates a production frontier one may expect differences in the efficiency projections of either technique.

The parametric technique for generating cost relationships implies information on factor prices and other exogenous variables, knowledge of the proper functional form of the frontier and the one-sided error structure, and an adequate sample size to evaluate reliable statistical inferences. The DEA technique utilises none of this information and as a result fewer data are required, fewer assumptions have to be made and a smaller sample can be utilised (Evanoff and Israilevich, 1991). However, statistical inferences cannot be made using the DEA approach.

Another principal difference is that the parametric approach uses a random error term around the frontier, while the DEA approach does not. Thus, the DEA technique will account for the influence of factors such as regional factor price differences, regulatory differences, luck, bad data and extreme observations as 'inefficiency'. One would expect the DEA approach to produce greater measured levels of inefficiency than the stochastic frontier approach.

CONCLUSIONS

This chapter has outlined the theoretical considerations relating to scale, and efficiency matters in the banking industry. A particular problem relates to output definition, with many authors choosing the intermediation approach and defining different types of assets and off-balance-sheet items as output. More recent studies, such as Berger and Humphrey (1992a) and Pulley and Humphrey (1993), make a stronger case for the inclusion of deposits as an output, given that the processing of deposits business contributes a substantial proportion to many banks' total costs. The main features of the different types of functional form used to estimate cost and revenue efficiencies are outlined, together with a discussion of the stochastic cost frontier and data envelope analysis used to estimate X-inefficiencies in banking markets. Empirical findings of the US and European studies will be discussed in detail in Chapter 6.

6

Scale and scope economies in banking markets, empirical evidence from the United States and Europe

INTRODUCTION

This chapter analyses the methodology and results of US and European cost studies. Many studies investigating economies of scale and scope have been undertaken on banking markets over the last 30 years. The subject addressed in these studies has been concerned with various questions, such as whether or not an increase in bank output could lead to lower average cost, whether costs vary for different institutions of the same size and whether cost reductions brought about through increased output could be higher for specialised or more universal operations. Hopefully the analysis in this chapter should answer these questions. At the least it will bring together a diverse literature and will help focus on the issues relating to costs in European banking.

THE EARLY COST STUDIES IN US BANKING

The earliest studies can be distinguished according to the different definitions of bank output used.

Earning Assets as the Measure of Bank Output

The first major systematic study of banking cost was undertaken by Alhadeff (1954). Alhadeff compared costs of Californian branch and unit banks of different sizes for the years 1938–50. The branch bank series were obtained from the data for four large branch banks in California and the unit bank figures were drawn from data published by the Federal Reserve Bank of San Francisco. Output was defined as the ratio of loans plus investments to total assets. Inputs were deposits on which interest was paid, labour and miscellaneous costs (i.e. overhead and depreciation on building and equipment, legal costs). Moreover, the banks were divided into eight groups according to their size as measured by total deposits. Alhadeff's analysis of scale economies can be summarised in the very simple cost function as follows:

$$C = f(Q) \tag{1}$$

where Q (earning assets) are loans and investments, and C (total costs) includes interest, wage and miscellaneous costs. Scale economies occur if average costs (C/Q) decline as output size increases. Alhadeff did not develop any systematic theory or model in order to estimate economies of scale.

Alhadeff (1954) found that there are economies of scale in banking; increasing returns for small banks, constant returns for the middle range and increasing returns for the largest banks. In other words, average cost declined for small (up to \$5 million of asset size) and large banks (above \$275 million of asset size) but remained constant for medium-sized banks. He also reported that branch banks had higher average costs than unit banks.

Horvitz (1963) generated results which supported most of Alhadeff's findings. Horvitz used data obtained from available Annual Reports of the Federal Deposits Insurance Corporation for the years 1940–60. He analysed the cost structure using earning assets (loans plus investments) as the output measure. Cost was also defined similar to Alhadeff's study. The study concluded that average cost decreased from the smallest banks to the largest in every year and economies of scale were observed for small and large banks and constant returns for medium-sized banks. The study also reported that the difference in the average cost between small and large banks declined from 1940 to 1960. Moreover, Horvitz noted that for any given size and time deposit ratio, the average cost of branch banks was generally higher than that of unit banks. Above all, the results were in basic agreement with Alhadeff's earlier findings.

Total Assets as the Measure of Bank Output

A major criticism of the Alhadeff (1954) and Horvitz (1963) studies was that if one uses earning assets as the measure of bank output then this has the potential deficiency of excluding other assets (such as trust operations) in the total output variable. Therefore, this might tend to exaggerate the average unit costs of large banks. In order to avoid this potential bias, Schweiger and McGee (1961) and Gramley (1962) in their studies used total assets as a measure of bank output.

Schweiger and McGee (1961) focused on the Seventh Federal Reserve District (where Chicago is located) and there was a secondary focus on the Federal Reserve member banks as a whole. Their sample used 6233 Federal Reserve member banks in 1959. They also divided banks into unit and branch banks, but branch banks in that study were more generally defined than in Alhadeff's. Costs were specified broadly to include wages, interest paid, taxes, depreciation costs and spending on furniture and equipment. They estimated equations separately for branch and unit banks. Multiple regression analysis was employed in their study to account for many of the factors that affect costs rather than bank size. The model they used was based on the following cost function:

$$C = f(Q, i, D, E_j, D_j) \tag{2}$$

where C (total cost) is wage costs plus interest costs and taxes, Q is the deposit size class (e.g. nine classes), i is an indicator of whether the bank is a branch or unit bank, D is a weighting factor of the ratio of time deposits to total deposits, E_j are weighting factors of various types of loans to total assets and D_j are demographic weighting factors. The authors found that there were economies of scale for all banks, very considerable for the smallest banks (up to $50 million in deposits), and decreasing but not disappearing as bank size increases. In other words, they observed that the average cost fell as the size of the bank increased, with the reduction being obvious for banks with above $200 million in assets. Consequently, Schweiger and McGee concluded that large banks have a cost advantage over small and medium-sized banks. It was also pointed out that banks with higher proportions of industrial and commercial loans, instalment loans and time deposits had higher average costs. This finding implied that the output mix played an important role in determining bank costs.

Another important early study on banking costs was conducted by Gramley (1962), who also employed total assets as a measure of bank output. He used a sample of 270 small unit banks, over the period 1956–59, obtained from the banks of the Tenth Federal Reserve District (the Plains and southern Rocky Mountain states). The cost variables included wages and salaries, interest on deposits, taxes and recurring depreciation. Bank size was specified as the natural logarithm of total assets. Using multiple regression analysis, with 15 variables to control for output mix, economies of scale were found for all sizes of banks in the sample as well as a negative relationship between size and average cost. Average cost decreased as bank size increased and therefore, larger banks were found to have a cost advantage over small banks. Gramley argued that small banks may not control their costs as carefully as large banks. However, unable to find a pattern in the cost dispersion between the two sizes of banks, he summarised that 'real' economies of scale were responsible for the negative relationship between unit cost and bank size.

Total Revenue as the Measure of Bank Output

A different approach to the measurement of cost was analysed by Greenbaum (1967). He admitted that using an aggregate measure for output assumes that all items included in that aggregate carry the same weight, which cannot be true. In an effort to address this problem, he developed a weighted output index. He chose current operating revenue as the financial statement account on the grounds that this 'most closely related to the social output concept of Gross National Product' (p. 417). He noted that a bank's gross income is a function of market conditions in its location. Data were drawn from the Fifth and Tenth Federal Reserve districts for 413 and 745 banks. Total cost was specified as the dependent variable. Greenbaum found evidence of a U-shaped average cost curve, indicating that average cost declined for small-sized banks, but increased for large banks. The study emphasised that branch bank operating costs were higher than unit bank costs.

Another study undertaken by Haslem (1968) investigated the correlation between measures of bank profitability and deposit size. Haslem used 64 operating ratios computed for 1963 and 1964 for each Federal Reserve member bank, classified into eight deposit size groups from less than $1 million to $100 million in deposits. Haslem found that profitability was significantly affected by management, size and location. The results implied that the most favourable size category (in terms of net return on capital) is neither the largest nor the smallest. Of eight sizes of banks the seventh largest, $50–100 million total deposits, is most favourable to high profitability. At the other extreme the least profitable bank size was that containing the smallest banks ($1 million and under in total deposits).

Powers (1969) used data obtained from the Report of Condition and the Report of Income and Development in the Seventh Federal Reserve District in 1962 to evaluate evidence of economies of scale for banks in the Chicago area. The data were grouped between branch and unit banks, by using location and product mix characteristics. Like Greenbaum, Powers applied a similar regression analysis approach, in that total revenue was used as a measure of bank output, and the cost measure was the same as that used by Greenbaum (1967). Generally, the results showed evidence of U-shaped or constant average costs, with scale economies for the smallest banks. Moreover, the main result of this study was that branch banks had higher costs than unit banks.

Comparing the above studies, the following conclusions can be drawn. First, studies that use assets as the measure of output tended to find relatively high unit costs for small banks. Second, the two studies conducted by Alhadeff and Horvitz which employed earning assets as the measure of output indicated constant unit cost for medium-sized banks ($5–50 million in assets) and lower average cost for larger banks. On the other hand, the two studies conducted by Schweiger–McGee and Gramley which applied total assets as the output measure showed declining average cost for all ranges of output size. It can be seen that even in the earliest studies of cost economies of the US banking market there was conflicting evidence as to whether scale economies existed or not.

POST-1965 — MULTI-PRODUCT COST STUDIES IN US BANKING

The studies discussed in the previous section used simple statistical models resembling ratio-based analyses, to examine economies of scale in the banking industry. Later studies apply more sophisticated econometric methods. Furthermore, the earliest studies, as illustrated above, use only one measure of bank output whereas later studies consider multiple outputs.

The Cobb–Douglas Cost Function Studies in US Banking

Table 6.1 summarises the results of a number of empirical studies in banking for the US market using the Cobb–Douglas cost function. The results for these studies generally show that economies of scale exist for small to medium-sized banks, whereas diseconomies of scale are present for larger banks. These studies also show that branch banks have higher average costs than unit banks. This is because branch banks are producing different product mixes and not necessarily because of technological differences (Benston, 1965b; Bell and Murphy, 1968).

Benston (1965a) was the first to use a Cobb–Douglas cost function to investigate economies of scale in banking. The data used were for small New England banks over the years 1959–61, with most banks being unit or branch banks with less than five branches. The banks ranged from $3.4 to $55 million in total asset size. The bank outputs were defined as demand deposits, time deposits, mortgage loans, instalment loans, business loans and securities. Costs were grouped into direct and indirect costs, with direct costs allocated to an individual output, and indirect costs allocated to output as a whole. Direct costs consist of wages and miscellaneous costs (e.g supplies, collection expenses and credit reports), whereas the indirect costs included administrative expenses, business promotion expenses and occupancy expenses. Moreover, interest costs were excluded from costs (i.e. both direct and indirect costs).

Benston excluded the interest costs because he argued that they were closely related to the dollar value of deposits. The outputs were measured in terms of number of accounts. Benston argued that the reason for using the number of accounts to measure output was to avoid the confusion between the cost efficiency in the production of large accounts and the cost efficiency of operations. In addition, he indicated that services are primarily related to the number of accounts, therefore operating costs are more closely related to number of accounts rather than the dollar value of accounts. The estimating cost function can be shown as

$$\ln C = f[\ln N_i, \ln A_i, b_j, m_j, d_j, w_i n_j, (N_i/N), p_i, TA] \tag{3}$$

Table 6.1 Cobb–Douglas cost function studies in US banking

Authors	Country and data	Output	Other control variable	Findings
Benston (1965a)	USA. Data obtained from the FCA programme of the Federal Reserve Bank of Boston for the period 1959–61. The size of banks ranged from $3.4m. to $55m. in total assets	Bank outputs are defined as demand deposits, time deposits, mortgage loans, instalment loans, business loans and securities which are measured by the number of accounts	Cobb–Douglas cost function was used. Average account sizes, branching and merger dummies, prices and total assets	Significant economies of scale exist for demand deposits and mortgage loans. Time deposits and instalment loans show significant diseconomies of scale. Branch banks have higher operating costs than unit banks
Benston (1965b)	USA. Data sample as in Benston (1965a) above	The same as Benston's (1965a). Separate cost curves estimated for unit and branch banks	The same as Benston's (1965a)	Economies of scale exist for branch banks
Bell and Murphy (1968)	USA. Data derived from the FCA programme of the Federal Reserve Banks of New York, Philadelphia and Boston for 283 banks. The banks range from $2.8m. to $801m. in total assets	The same as Benston's (1965a)		Economies of scale exist for demand deposits and real estate loans. Slightly diseconomies of scale exist for time deposits and instalment loans. Branch banks have higher operating cost than unit banks
Schweitzer (1972)	USA. Data derived from the banks in the 9th Federal Reserve District for 1964	Lending output index: measured as total loan revenues plus revenue from other sources	Dummy variables: location, bank holding company and Federal Reserve membership	There is a U-shaped cost curve. Economies of scale exist for banks with total assets of less than $3.5m.

Study	Data	Variables/Approach	Findings
Murphy (1972)	USA. FCA data for the year 1968 on 967 banks	Same approach as Bell and Murphy's (1968)	Banks with assets between $3.5m. and $25m. show constant returns to scale and above $25m. appear to have diseconomies of scale
Kalish and Gilbert (1973)	USA. FCA data for 898 banks in 1968	Similar approach to Schweitzer's (1972)	Banks are characterised by constant returns to scale The cost curve is U-shaped. Unit banks have the lowest operating cost followed in turn by affiliated banks and branch banks
Daniel, Longbrake and Murphy (1973)	USA. Cross-section of 967 banks from FCA programme in 1968	Number of demand deposits accounts	Larger banks improve operating efficiency by using computer technology
		Similar variables used as Bell and Murphy's (1968). Average size variable, annual wage rate, rental rate, number of branches	
Longbrake and Haslem (1975)	USA. FCA data for 967 banks in 1968	Same approach as Daniel, Longbrake and Murphy's (1973)	In general, unit banks have the lowest average operating cost. The number of branches operated by branch banks have a small effect on average operating costs per dollar of demand deposits
Mullineaux (1975)	USA. FCA data for 1970 from the Federal Reserve Bank of Boston, New York and Philadelphia	Similar approach as Benston's (1965) and Bell–Murphy's (1968)	Dummy variables for branching
			The larger economies of scale are found for unit banks rather than branch banks

where C_i is the allocated cost, N_i is the number of accounts, A_i is the average account size, b_j are the branching dummies, m_j are the merger dummies, d_j are the demographic variables, $w_i n_j$ is the activity measure, N_i/N is the ratio of accounts, p_i is the output price and TA is total assets.

The results indicated that economies of scale were present, but small, for all banking services. Moreover, Benston concluded that size was not an important factor in determining efficient operations. Banks with three or fewer branches were found to have cost benefits. After three branches, costs increased and outweighted the benefits of larger size.

Following on from his earlier study, Benston (1965b) concentrated on the issue of the relative cost efficiency of branch and unit banks. He mentioned that there were two differences in operating costs between branch and unit banks. First, branch banks could be more costly to operate than unit banks of equal size. Second, branch banks may be able to grow larger than unit banks and take advantage of economies of scale that might come from large-scale operations. He used the same regression model as in his previous study. He reported that the positive branching dummy figures indicated economies of scale with additional costs for branch bank operations. However, he concluded that branch banks had large additional occupancy expenses, so that it was more expensive to operate branch banks rather than unit banks.

The next major study of economies of scale in US banking markets also used a Cobb–Douglas cost function, and was undertaken by Bell and Murphy (1968). The main differences between Benston and Bell and Murphy were that the latter use a larger sample of banks, a more comprehensive technique and provide much more detailed results. Bell and Murphy used data from the Functional Cost Analysis (FCA) programme of the Federal Reserve banks of New York, Philadelphia and Boston for 283 banks. The variables employed by Bell and Murphy were similar to those used by Benston. Costs were computed using salaries and fringe benefits for all employees plus capital goods and materials costs. Interest costs were excluded from total cost as in the Benston study. All outputs except for securities were measured as the number of accounts. Dummy variables were employed to distinguish between branch and unit banking.

Bell and Murphy found economies of scale for most bank services such as demand deposits and business and mortgage loans. On the other hand, branching operations were more costly than unit banking operations. In addition, at the firm level, economies of scale were not found in most services, and they found that the marginal additional cost of branching was $5.04 for each account. Moreover, they also reported that a $1 increase in marginal direct cost of processing a demand deposit account increased service charges by around 32 cents. In other words, service charges responded to cost changes but in an inelastic fashion.

Schweitzer (1972) examined a large sample of relatively small banks in the Ninth (Minneapolis) Federal Reserve District for the year of 1964 from Call and Income data. He focused on holding companies in his study because there were no branch banks in his sample. Bank output was defined as lending output, exactly following Greenbaum's earlier definition. He employed two dummy variables for holding company status, two dummy variables for location and a dummy variable for Federal Reserve membership. Schweitzer calculated cost as total operating expenses less service and exchange charges on deposit accounts, which includes interest cost. Using duality theory, Schweitzer computed a Cobb–Douglas cost function in lending output and dummy variables as follows:

$$\ln C = f(\ln Q, \ln ld_j, \ln hcd_k, \ln frd) \qquad (4)$$

where C is cost, Q is the lending output, ld_j are the location dummy variables, hcd_k are the holding company dummies, and frd is the Federal Reserve membership dummy variable. Economies of scale were calculated from the coefficient on the output variable in the regression.

Schweitzer concluded that there was a U-shaped average cost curve. That is, economies of scale exist but were exhausted at low output levels. The optimum bank size was less than $50 million in loans. Banks with assets between $3.5 and $25 million were grouped by constant returns to scale. Accordingly, banks with assets above $25 million appeared to have diseconomies of scale. He also indicated a significant negative relationship between organisational form and costs. In other words, affiliated banks were found to have lower costs. Thus, the form of organisation affected the cost function.

Murphy (1972) updated previous studies by using FCA data for the year 1968 for 967 banks. He found that the coefficients for outputs were not significantly different from unity in general using Cobb–Douglas regression analysis. He pointed out that banking was characterised by constant returns to scale, a conclusion which differed from his previous work with Bell.

Kalish and Gilbert (1973) examined how size and organisational form affect bank efficiency using 1968 FCA data for 898 US banks. Their study stated that the cost curve was U-shaped, confirming Schweitzer's (1972) results. Moreover, unit banks had the lowest operating cost followed in turn by affiliated banks and branch banks. It was found that at lower output levels, banks affiliated with holding companies had greater cost efficiency. At higher output levels, the reverse was true (i.e. banks affiliated with a holding company had higher average costs at higher levels of output).

Daniel, Longbrake and Murphy (1973), using data provided by a cross-section of 967 banks from the Federal Reserve's FCA programme in 1968, focused on the effects of technology on bank economies of scale for demand deposits. The sample consisted of mainly small or medium-sized banks. In this study, they applied a cost function similar to that of Bell and Murphy:

$$\ln C = f[\ln N_i, \ln p, \ln r, w_i n_j, (N_i/N), B] \qquad (5)$$

where C_i is the operating cost which excluded interest cost, N_i is the number of demand deposit accounts, A_i is the average size variable, p is the average annual wage rate, r is rental rate for capital, $w_i n_j$ is the activity measure, N_i/N is the ratio of regular chequeing accounts to total chequeing accounts, B is the number of offices. They found that it was more efficient for banks with fewer than 10 600 accounts to use conventional accounting systems, whereas the operating efficiency of larger banks was improved by using computer technology.

Further research undertaken by Longbrake and Haslem (1975) investigated the effects of bank size and organisational form on the cost of producing demand deposit services, using data on 967 banks from the FCA for 1968. In general, they found unit banks had the lowest average costs, but this finding was reversed as the number of accounts per office and average deposit size increased, with the lowest average overall performance for large banks. Among their findings it was shown that the number of offices operated by a branch bank had a small effect on average operating costs per dollar of demand deposits. In addition, the average cost declined for all banks except for unit banks that were not affiliated with holding companies.

Mullineaux (1975) used FCA data for 1970 from the Federal Reserve districts of Boston, New York and Philadelphia to estimate Bell and Murphy style equations for unit and branch banks. The model estimated was as follows:

$$\ln C = f[\ln N_i, \ln A_i, b_j, hc_j, d_j, w_i n_j, (N_i/N)p_i, TA] \tag{6}$$

where C_i is the operating cost, N_i is the number of accounts, A_i is the average account size variable, b_j are the branching dummies, hc_j are the holding companies dummies, d_j are the demographic variables, $w_i n_j$ is the activity measure, N_i/N is the larger measure ratio of accounts, P_i is the output price and TA are total assets. The demographic variables included a wage index and a concentration index. Mullineaux found that there were economies of scale for unit banks, but that economies were small for the branch banks. Mullineaux explained the estimated higher costs of branch banks. In the high interest rate periods of the 1960s, much of the observed increase in banking was no doubt related to the interest prohibitions on demand deposits and restriction on interest paid on time and savings deposits.

In general, the Cobb–Douglas studies indicate that there are economies of scale for most of the individual services offered by banks. There are various limitations, however, to the above studies. First, this analysis has been undertaken primarily on small banks, mainly institutions with less than $1 billion in deposits. Second, these studies employed the Cobb–Douglas functional form which does not allow for a U-shaped cost curve. Third, the cost function is heavily restricted and therefore does not allow us to examine evidence of economies of scope. The major conclusion that can be drawn from the Cobb–Douglas cost function studies of the 1960s was that economies of scale appeared to be present in US banking, since most of the studies report a decreasing average cost curve over a relatively large range of bank outputs. The studies in the 1970s, however, show a different pattern, indicating that in general scale economies exist but are only very small.

The Translog Cost Function Studies in US Banking

In this section we survey US banking cost studies which employed the translog cost function methodology in the 1980s. These studies can be divided into two broad groupings according to the definition of bank output used.

Production Approach

The first study to use the translog cost function methodology to estimate scale economies was undertaken by Benston, Hanweck and Humphrey (1982b). They used a measure of output, a Divisia index, specified as the weighted average of the number of accounts of outputs. Five outputs were aggregated in this index: demand deposits, time and savings deposits, real estate loans, instalment loans and business loans. The weights depended on the number of accounts of each type of output by their proportionate share in total operating cost. The model was estimated using data drawn from the Federal Reserve's FCA programme from 1975 to 1978. Furthermore, homogeneity variables for holding company affiliation, state branching status and average account size were included in the model.

Their findings indicate that there was evidence of the existence of U-shaped cost curves. They found that unit banks with above $50 million in deposits recorded diseconomies of scale, while banks in branching states experienced small economies of scale. This study concluded that the optimum size of a bank was relatively small, between $10 and $25 million in deposits, and they also showed that holding company affiliation had no effect on operating costs.

Benston et al. (1983) used five different banking outputs: demand deposits, time and savings deposits, real estate loans, commercial loans and instalment loans, in their translog estimation of bank costs. Data for 852 banks were drawn from the Federal Reserve's FCA programme for 1978. Total costs corresponded to the sum of all operating expenses, excluding interest payments. The cost function estimated in this study can be summarised as follows:

$$\ln C = f[\ln q_i, \ln p_i, (\ln p_i \ln p_j), (\ln q_i \ln q_r), (\ln q_i \ln p_j),$$

$$\ln A_i, (\ln A_i \ln q_i), \ln B, (\ln B \ln q_i), H, (h \ln B)] \qquad (7)$$

where q_i are the outputs (demand deposits, time and savings deposits, real estate loans, instalment loans and commercial loans), p_i are input prices (labour and capital), A_i is a weighted average of deposits or loan sizes, B is the number of branches and H is a binary variable for holding company status.

The authors found evidence of economies of scale at the branch level for all deposit size classes, although these were not statistically significant for the largest banks. In addition, for unit banks, economies of scale were reported for banks up to $75–100 million in deposit size whereas diseconomies of scale appeared at all unit banks with more than $200 million in deposits.

Benston et al. also attempted to estimate economies of scope; however, because of limitations of the translog methodology, they were not able to obtain evidence of economies of scope. Consequently, inter-product cost complementarities were tested and the results indicated that for unit banks there was some evidence of pairwise cost complementarities.

Clark (1984) estimated scale economies in the US commercial banking industry by using a Box–Cox transformation of the translog function. The data employed in estimation of the cost function were obtained from the Report of Income and the Report of Condition for 1205 unit banks published by the Board of Governors of the Federal Reserve System, for 1972–77. The total cost of the respective banks was defined as the average of total operating expenditures over the sample period. Bank output was measured as earning assets. Clark concluded that economies of scale existed for relatively small-sized banks. The estimates of output elasticity of cost also seemed to be rather insensitive to the choice of a measure of bank output.

The following two studies were undertaken by Gilligan, Smirlock and Marshall (1984) and Gilligan and Smirlock (1984) who focused on the multi-product nature of the banking firm. Gilligan, Smirlock and Marshall estimated bank cost functions that took into account the multi-product nature of the banking firm. Bank outputs were defined as the number of deposit accounts and loans accounts serviced. Moreover, the average dollar amount of deposits and loans, input prices of labour and capital were included in their model. Thus, because of the nature of the production approach which was taken, operating costs were employed by the authors to examine the existence of economies of scale and scope. Gilligan, Smirlock and Marshall (1984) used data from the Federal Reserve's FCA programme for the year 1978 which included 714 banks with less than $1 billion in asset size. They found that bank output was characterised by scope economies. They also concluded that the cost benefits of expansion were achieved for small banks with less than $25 million deposits but diseconomies beyond $100 million deposits. Moreover, the authors attempted to determine a numerical value for scope economies, and their calculation suggested that there was a saving of 17% for unit banks and 29% for branch banks that produce deposits and loans jointly as opposed to separately. (It should be pointed out that no standard errors for these scope economy findings were provided and so the statistical significance of these results should be treated with caution.)

Gilligan and Smirlock (1984) examined economies of scale and scope by using data from Call Reports of Income and Condition by the Federal Reserve Bank of Kansas City for more than 2700 unit state banks for the years from 1973 to 1978.

Bank output was defined using two different measures in terms of either liabilities or assets: (i) dollar amount of demand deposits and time deposits; (ii) dollar amount of loans and securities. They found that there were slight economies of scale for banks with less than $10 million deposits and diseconomies above $50 million deposits, applying both output approaches.

One potential difficulty of Gilligan and Smirlock's study was that they assumed that input prices were constant. In other words, input prices do not affect the marginal cost of outputs differently when the level of price changes. Given this drawback, the input price variables were not included in the translog model.

Using a different approach, Lawrence and Shay (1986) analysed the effects of computer technology upon economies of scale and scope as well as the elasticities of substitution between inputs (labour, capital and computers), applying a translog cost function to an extensive database taken from the FCA programme from 1979 to 1982. They used four outputs: the dollar value of deposits, loans, investments and non-balance-sheet items. They utilise three input prices: an interest rate, a wage rate and computer rental rate. They also used the control variables of average loan size, average deposit size and the number of branches. Total cost was defined as operating cost plus interest expenses. The functional form they estimated can be summarised as follows:

$$\ln C = f[\ln q_i, \ln p_i, (\ln p_i \ln p_j), (\ln q_i \ln q_r),$$

$$(\ln q_i, \ln p_j), \ln B, ALOANS, ADEPS] \tag{8}$$

where C is total costs (operating cost plus interest expenses), q_i are the outputs (deposits, loans, investments and fee-based banking activities), p_i are the input prices (interest rate, wage rates and computer rates), B is the number of branches, $ALOANS$ is the logarithm of average loans size, and $ADEPS$ is the logarithm of average deposit size.

The findings indicated that the samples for 1979–82 showed constant returns to scale, but when the analysis was undertaken by quartile (according to deposits size) there were significant economies of scale. Lawrence and Shay (1986) also found that branch banks had major and significant scale economies at all size levels, for all years 1979–82, whereas only the smallest unit banks have significant economies of scale in general. Furthermore, significant scope economies were found between deposits and loans as well as deposits and investments; however, significant diseconomies of scope were reported between investments and loans.

Kolari and Zardkoohi (1987) focused on the issue of scale and scope economies for a sample of banks' data drawn from the FCA programme of the Federal Reserve over the period 1979–83 using three different models which represent three different stages of bank production and a new definition of economies of scope. Model I defined output as the dollar value of demand and time deposits. Model II specified output as the dollar value of loans and securities, and Model III specified output as the dollar value of loans and total deposits.

One of the main conclusions of their statistical analyses was that cost curves were U-shaped. In other words, significant economies of scale were indicated for US banks with up to $50 million in deposit size, whereas diseconomies appeared beyond the level of $50–100 million in deposit size, except in 1983.

Based on their measurement of the degree of economies of scope, Kolari and Zardkoohi (1987) found evidence of scope economies, yet their results showed that large banks did not appear to have a cost advantage compared to small banks in terms of joint production. The study also indicated (p. 123) that unit banks had somewhat greater scope economies than branch banks in the US market and

> These finding are not sufficient to conclude that small banks are at no disadvantage relative to large banks, because it is possible that large banks can reap relatively greater scope benefits than small banks can from the joint production of multiple bank services.

Kolari and Zardkoohi (1987) also pointed out that banks had a competitive advantage over financial service institutions that produce only either deposit services or loans services. In general, their results indicated that banks can reduce the cost of expansion by 30–50% by increasing outputs jointly rather than separately. Moreover, large banks do not have a cost advantage over small banks with respect to expanding outputs at the same time.

Kolari and Zardkoohi also examined economies of scale and scope (in all models) for unit banks and branch banks for 1970, 1980 and 1982, respectively. Their results implied that unit banks had cost curves that were flat and branch banks had U-shaped or upward-sloping cost curves in general. Models I and III indicated either economies or diseconomies, Model II implied that there were scale economies up to about $200 million in deposit size. In general, branch banks showed U-shaped average cost curves, with minimum costs occurring in the range of $50–200 million in deposits.

Their tests on different groups of US banks (farm banks, city banks, wholesale banks, retail banks) reported the following. Farm banks (which have high proportions of agricultural loans) consistently showed flat cost curves for all models. The other groups showed U-shaped cost curves, although in some years the curves were either L-shaped or upward-sloping. However, the scope findings indicated that joint production of banking services can reduce costs considerably, in comparison to separate production, therefore showing the extent to which large banks can find ways to improve their scale efficiency in the future. They concluded that in the USA, 'The banking industry could become more prone to dominance by large banks' (Kolari and Zardkoohi, p. 146).

Overall, the results of the translog studies suggest that there are U-shaped average cost curves in the US banking market. These studies conclude that economies of scale exist but at relatively low levels of output, somewhere between $25 and $200 million in deposit size, and there is little consensus as to the optimal size of the banking firm. These studies exclude the concept of global scope economies and only focus on cost complementarities, where they find evidence of product complementarity. There are, however, important limitations to the use of these results for public policy prescriptions since the FCA data used in the estimates ignore large banks and concentrate on smaller institutions (Hunter, Timme and Yang, 1990).

Intermediation Approach

Studies Using the Functional Cost Analysis (FCA) Database and Other Samples of Small US Banks Murray and White (1983) examined the production technology facing credit unions in Canada (although clearly not a US banking study we classify it in this section because of its relative importance as a translog intermediation approach evaluation of scale and scope economies). Using the data generated from a survey of Canadian credit unions in 1977, the study tested for economies of scale, economies of scope, and other production characteristics in a multi-product context. Following Sealey and Lindley (1977), outputs were defined to be the dollar value of mortgage loans, other loans and investments in excess of reserve requirements. Input prices were identified as wages for labour, capital, the price for fixed capital, and interest paid on demand deposits and time deposits. Moreover, incremental information on wage rates, rental processes, hours worked and organisational structure was obtained through a separate questionnaire. There were also three control variables, namely the number of branches, risk and growth. The Murray and White formulation can be expressed as follows:

$$\ln C = f[\ln q_i, \ln p_i, (\ln p_i \ln p_j), (\ln q_i \ln q_r),$$

$$(\ln q_i \ln p_j), \ln B, RISK, GROWTH] \tag{9}$$

where C is total costs which were calculated for all labour and real capital expenses, plus the interest and dividends paid to depositors and shareholders, q_i are the outputs (mortgage and other loans and investments), p_i are input prices (for interest on demand and time deposits, labour and capital) and B is the number of branches; $RISK$ — the dollar value of doubtful accounts divided by dollar value of total assets to proxy for risky loans — and $GROWTH$ — the logarithm of the dollar value of total assets in 1977 divided by 1976 values to eliminate the effects of aberrant disequilibrium costs — are included as control variables.

The study found that economies of scale existed in most of the credit unions studied. The results imply that credit unions in Canada experienced significant increasing returns to scale as they expanded their level of output. The authors reported that there was also strong evidence of cost complementarity or jointness in production between mortgage and other lending activities. Moreover, the findings indicated that large, multi-product credit unions were more cost efficient than small, single-product credit unions.

Berger, Hanweck and Humphrey (1987) formulated two new multi-product economy measures, expansion path scale economies and expansion path subadditivity. They attempted to re-examine the ambiguities of scope economies in some of the previous studies for depository financial institutions. The study defined bank output in the same way as in Benston et al. (1983) and this analysis used both the production and intermediation approaches. A translog cost function was fitted to the data from the 1983 FCA of the Federal Reserve Banks' System for 413 branching state banks and for 214 unit state banks (separately). The study introduced new measures in evaluating product mix and scope economies and it was not based on pairwise cost complementarities. Expansion path subadditivity was used to measure whether a representative bank of a specific size class produced a combination of output but in smaller size. The results of this test showed that two banks produce a given bundle of output more cost effectively than one bank at the levels of $10 million up to $1 billion in deposits.

The results indicated that there was evidence of scale economies but in general, these results were substantially different for branch and unit state banks in the USA. Branch banks showed slight scale economies at the branch level and slight diseconomies of scale at the level of the banking firm, whereas unit state banks showed large diseconomies of scale for large banks. These diseconomies for large unit state banks, combined with data indicating substantially higher costs than similarly sized branch banks in the USA, suggested that these banks were not competitively viable.

In measuring scope economies, the authors modified the translog cost function by substituting levels of output for logarithms of output. To estimate such a function for specialty firms, the study used the following procedure. Firstly, the number of accounts and average size of the accounts that was produced were set to zero. Secondly, the direct cost of the product that was not produced was set to zero. Thirdly, the total level of output was held constant by setting the number of branches for each new firm at the same level as the non-specialised firms.

Moreover, scope economies were evaluated for two cases. In the first, the deposit function was separated from the loan function; and in the second, each product was assigned to a specialty firm. The study concluded that there were diseconomies of scope in banking; that is, output mix was determined for reasons other than cost considerations, including risk diversification, customer convenience and joint demand of products.

Gropper (1991) examined the direction and magnitude of the possible shifts in the structure of banks' costs, using data from the period 1979–86 from the FCA programme of the Federal Reserve System. The study focused particularly on economies of scale for smaller and medium-sized banks. The study found that economies of scale existed beyond small levels of output for the years prior to 1982 and also significant scale economies were present in later years for branch banks and unit state banks. The study also pointed out that the degree of scale economies increased over the 1979–86 period.

In general, studies in the 1980s used new econometric techniques, that is, the translog methodology, in examining scale and scope economies. The banking industry in the USA was generally specified by a U-shaped average cost curve. As we have seen, the empirical studies based on the translog methodology so far, were concerned with banks smaller than $1 billion in total deposits. Therefore, these studies are not especially useful for estimating the effects on operating costs of banks with total deposits over $1 billion. The implications from these results are that small US banks are inefficient because they operate under increasing returns to scale, and inefficiencies could exist for banks over $100–200 million in deposits. These findings would appear to be in conflict with recent merger activity in the USA (see Moynihan, 1991). Like the translog production approach, the intermediation studies also indicate evidence of economies of scale for relatively small banks. Overall, the conclusion is that evidence of economies of scale exist for US banks with less than $50 million in deposit size. Until very recently, cost studies on the US banking market have excluded large institutions. Rhoades (1985d) pointed out that larger banks are most active in merger activity and most vocal about expanded product and geographic expansion powers. The following more recent studies focus on large US banks with deposit size of over $1 billion.

Studies Using Data Samples on Large US Banks   Hunter and Timme (1986) examined the nature of technical change in the banking industry, and investigated its influence on bank scale economies. They analysed data obtained for 91 large US bank holding companies located in 20 different states over the period 1972–82 for a total of 1001 observations. Bank outputs were defined as the dollar volume of all loans, securities and deposits. The empirical results implied that technical change produces significant cost reductions for banks. Hunter and Timme reported significant economies of scale when total cost was specified as just operating cost, whereas when interest expenses were included in total cost they found constant returns to scale. They concluded that the inclusion of interest expenses, derived from increased competition in an increasingly deregulated and inflationary market, had offset the scale and technical change cost benefits.

Shaffer and David (1986) analysed data from June 1984 obtained from the Call and Income Reports for the 100 largest US banks with asset size over $1 billion. The authors used a hedonic translog cost function to correct for heterogeneity across banks and also attempted to quantify the benefits of diversification. Bank output was defined only by the asset side of the balance sheet and the dollar value of assets was used to measure bank output. Deposits were taken as inputs; however, the price of deposits was not included as an explanatory variable in the model in order to capture any relationship between risk and diversification. Shaffer and David (1986, p. 5) stated that:

> Theoretically, larger banks should be able to attain lower risk through diversification, all else being equal. This benefit of diversification should manifest itself as a lower cost of uninsured deposits, all else equal. If total expenses are defined to include

interest expenses, then this scale-related benefit would be reflected in the cost variable. However, for this effect to be measured, it is essential that we do not include the price of funds as an additional regressor. Otherwise, the interest savings of a more diversified bank would be 'explained away' by the price variable.

Dummy variables were employed to account for unit and branch banking. The study concluded that scale economies existed for US banks up to $37 billion in asset size.

Shaffer and David (1986) and Hunter and Timme's (1986) methodologies, however, are subject to criticism because they used a vector as a single composite commodity. This forced the proportions of the various outputs that result in the composite to be fixed, so that only constant changes in outputs could be considered. The relative marginal cost of any two outputs was imposed to be independent of input prices (i.e. the cost function is separable in output). Although both studies indicated economies of scale for large banks, this result may have come from aggregation bias. Kim (1986) has implied that there existed increasing returns to scale at the branch level and constant returns to scale at the firm level for large US banks when no such aggregation was forced. When aggregation was imposed, the estimated economies of scale showed increasing returns to scale at the banking firm level. Hence Kim (1986) concluded that aggregation bias was significant (i.e. aggregation bias resulted in specification errors).

Hunter, Timme and Yang (1990) investigated the subadditivity of costs for a sample of the 311 largest commercial banks in the USA, using a multi-product translog cost function. Firstly, the study analysed the production and product mix economies of large banks (average asset sizes $4 billion). Secondly, the study examined an extension of the grid approach to examining cost subadditivity developed by Evans and Heckman (1984). The grid approach imposes product mix constraints that are derived directly from the product mixes observed between the sample banks. Thirdly, the study also evaluated the traditional ray scale economies as well as the expansion path scale economies and expansion path subadditivity of costs — which were introduced by Berger, Hanweck and Humphrey (1987). The authors' results suggested that the cost functions of large multi-product banks were not subadditive, and hence, there were not measurable cost complementarities in multi-product production among large banks. However, Hunter, Timme and Yang (1990) found opposing results which suggested that large banks would not be better off if they broke up production into groups of specialist banks. That is, they found no strong evidence that costs were subadditive.

Noulas, Ray and Miller (1990) examined scale economies for large US banks with assets in excess of $1 billion. They estimated a translog variable cost function using four outputs, four variable inputs and a quasi-fixed input, which was applied to evaluate economies of scale. The study found that banks with assets between $1 and $3 billion exhibit scale economies; diseconomies set in between $3 and $6 billion and continued through larger bank class sizes.

Continuing the trend of examining scale and scope economies for large US banks, Noulas, Miller and Ray (1993) focused on economies and diseconomies of scope for US banks with assets in excess of $1 billion by using ordinary and hybrid translog cost functions. The major conclusions of their study were that the ordinary translog cost function provided unreliable measures of scope effects and subsequently the results could not be regarded as robust; scope estimates changed in size and magnitude considerably, depending on whether one used the ordinary or hybrid translog methodology. They found that economies of scope did not appear to exist. This study also concluded that existing empirical work on scope effects derived from the translog cost function could be limited because of estimation error.

In general, the results from the studies that have focused on large US banks differ from the bulk of the literature which has focused on small US banks. While the majority of studies, which use data from small US banks, show that economies of scale do not appear beyond $100 million in deposit size, the larger US bank studies find that scale economies appear for much larger institutions. For example, Shaffer and David (1986) find scale economies up to $37 billion in asset size and Noulas, Miller and Ray (1990) indicate that banks with assets between $1 and $3 billion exhibit scale economies. The evidence clearly suggests that scale advantages exist well beyond the $100–200 million in the deposit size range. These findings appear to indicate that economies of scale resulting from the smaller bank studies cannot be applied to larger banks. In contrast to the scale economy results for large banks, none of these studies finds evidence of scope economies. The most important conclusions from the studies using data for larger banks is that potential gains from altering scale via internal growth or merger activity can be substantial.

Humphrey's Approach: Cost Dispersion   A study undertaken by Humphrey (1987) marked a new dimension to examining scale economies by investigating cost dispersion among banks of a similar size. Humphrey indicated that variations in cost among banks came from two sources: scale or cost economies across different sized banks and cost differences across similar sized banks. Humphrey concentrated on the second type of variation given that the first item had already been extensively studied. Publicly available balance sheet and cost data on 13 959 banks in the USA over three years, 1980, 1982 and 1984, were drawn from the consolidated Report of Condition and Report of Income and Dividends. Humphrey divided his bank data into 13 size classes and also grouped banks into quartiles according to their average costs. Table 6.2 reveals the average costs by size class and cost quartile for both branch and unit bank in the US market. The study found that estimated cost economies were dominated by differences in average cost levels. Especially, Humphrey found that the difference in average costs between banks with the highest cost and banks with the lowest costs was two to four times greater than the observed variation in average

Table 6.2 Average cost by size class and cost quartile for branch and unit banks, 1984

Size classes ($)	Average cost quartiles ($)				
	1	2	3	4	All Banks ($)
Branch banks					
1. 1m.−10m.	0.085	0.099	0.108	0.126	0.105
2. 10m.−25m.	0.089	0.098	0.105	0.124	0.104
3. 25m.−50m.	0.088	0.097	0.102	0.115	0.100
4. 50m.−75m.	0.089	0.096	0.101	0.114	0.100
5. 75m.−100m.	0.089	0.097	0.101	0.114	0.100
6. 100m.−200m.	0.089	0.097	0.101	0.118	0.101
7. 200m.−300m.	0.089	0.097	0.101	0.113	0.100
8. 300m.−500m.	0.089	0.097	0.103	0.118	0.102
9. 500m.−1bn	0.088	0.098	0.103	0.117	0.102
10. 1bn−2bn	0.089	0.099	0.104	0.117	0.102
11. 2bn−5bn	0.089	0.098	0.103	0.124	0.104
12. 5bn−10bn	0.088	0.094	0.098	0.114	0.099
13. >10bn	0.090	0.096	0.099	0.117	0.102
All banks	0.088	0.097	0.103	0.118	0.102
Unit banks					
1. 1m.−10m.	0.085	0.101	0.110	0.130	0.106
2. 10m.−25m.	0.089	0.099	0.106	0.120	0.103
3. 25m.−50m.	0.088	0.096	0.101	0.112	0.100
4. 50m.−75m.	0.088	0.095	0.100	0.108	0.098
5. 75m.−100m.	0.088	0.095	0.099	0.107	0.097
6. 100m.−200m.	0.088	0.095	0.099	0.107	0.097
7. 200m.−300m.	0.086	0.093	0.099	0.107	0.096
8. 300m.−500m.	0.086	0.093	0.097	0.106	0.096
9. 500m.−1bn	0.088	0.094	0.098	0.108	0.097
10. 1bn−2bn	0.090	0.096	0.101	0.109	0.100
11. 2bn−5bn	0.087	0.091	0.096	0.102	0.095
12. 5bn−10bn	0.094	0.096	0.099	0.110	0.100
13. >10bn	0.082	0.092	0.100	0.104	0.097
All banks	0.088	0.097	0.103	0.116	0.101

Source: Adapted from Humphrey (1987, pp. 28−29).

cost across bank size classes. The results suggested that banks did not lie on the same cost curves over time and that, at any point in time, only a few cases were on the same curve across size classes. The study, therefore, showed considerable cost dispersions across similar sized banks. Dispersion was greatest for the smallest classes of banks and fell as banking groups became larger. The important result was that banks of similar size had substantially different average costs per dollar of total assets. Given these results, the analysis concluded that 'the existence of bank scale economies (or diseconomies) should have little competitive impact relative to those competitive effects which already exist as a result of large differences in cost levels' (Humphrey, 1987, p. 24).

Humphrey (1987) also examined asset cost elasticities for each of the 13 size groups for the years 1980, 1982 and 1984. To measure the elasticities, Humphrey estimated the following simple quadratic translog equation:

$$\ln TC = f[\ln TA, (\ln TA \ln TA)] \tag{10}$$

where $\ln TC$ shows the logarithm of total cost and $\ln TA$ is the logarithm of total assets. On the basis of 1984 data, the study indicated cost economies in banking, however, only for higher-cost and/or smaller banks. Thus, the analysis concluded that these cost economies did not confer competitive advantages for large banks over small institutions.

STUDIES OF SCALE AND SCOPE IN EUROPEAN BANKING MARKETS

Compared with the US literature, the much smaller number of cost studies on European banking appear to reveal greater evidence of scale and, to a lesser extent, scope economies for larger banks. This literature will now be discussed. Firstly we analyse cost studies which focus on the larger European banking markets, and the following section covers those studies that have investigated smaller European banking markets and some recent cross-border European cost studies.

Cost Studies for Large European Banking Markets

The earliest study on economies of scale in the European banking markets was by Levy-Garboua and Renard (1977) who examined the French banking market. Using a sample of 94 banks for 1974, their methodology combined the production and intermediation approach and their results suggested evidence of increasing returns to scale. These results for French banking were confirmed in two later studies undertaken by Dietsch (1988, 1993). Dietsch (1988) adopted the inter-mediation approach for a cross-sectional analysis of 243 banks in 1986. Using the translog methodology this study concluded that, as far as ray economies of scale were concerned, the elasticity of total costs with respect to bank output was close to unity (0.97). This study seemed to indicate that overall scale economies were rather limited, however further analysis of costs associated with individual bank outputs suggested that there was significant potential scale economies to be had (i.e. the partial elasticities of cost with respect to credits and deposits were equal to 0.56 and 0.23, respectively). Martin and Sassenou (1992) used a CES-quadratic function to model a two-output cost function for French banks for 1987. Their main finding suggests that small banks benefit from large economies of scale and scope. Bigger banks incur relatively large diseconomies of scale depending on their output scale and their degree of specialisation.

Dietsch (1993) extended his previous analysis and examined both economies of scale and scope in the French banking markets. Using a sample of 343 banks for 1987, he found strong evidence of economies of scale in the banking industry across all output ranges, whereas economies of scope were not observed at a high level for all combinations of outputs (i.e. the cost complementarity coefficient for loans and investments was 0.093). Dietsch (1993, p. 17) stated that 'For the French banking industry, our results tend to demonstrate that universal banking gives an advantage compared to specialisation and that competition between banks in the future must be analysed on the ground of the imperfect competition theory.'

As far as we are aware, there is little evidence on scale and scope economies in the German and Swiss banking markets. Lang and Welzel (1994) use the standard translog cost function methodology to estimate cost economies for the German cooperative bank sector. Using a sample of over 700 banks they find evidence of scope economies especially for the largest banks. Sheldon and Haegler (1993) and Sheldon (1994), using an efficiency approach, find that Swiss banks with diversified product mixes are more inefficient than specialised banks.

Cossutta et al. (1988), Baldini and Landi (1990) and Conigliani et al. (1991) have analysed the cost structure in the Italian banking industry. Generally, these recent studies suggest that there are economies of scale in this banking system. Cossutta et al. conclude that, at the plant level, economies of scale exist throughout all size ranges and the smallest banks are characterised by constant returns to scale. However, at the firm level, increasing returns to scale were reported only for big and major banks, while other groups showed constant returns to scale. Moreover, Cossutta et al. uncovered evidence of scope economies only for larger banks. Baldini and Landi (1990) using a sample of 294 banks for 1987 stated that scale economies at the plant level increase as bank size becomes larger. At the firm level, scale economies become small and they tend to decrease with the increase in banks' asset size, almost disappearing for the largest banks. This result is confirmed in Conigliani et al. (1991) who indicate evidence of scale economies at the plant level and only for the smaller banks at the firm level. These studies do not find scope economies in Italian banking.

The Spanish banking market has been studied by Fanjul and Maravall (1985) who employ a simple Cobb–Douglas functional form, using cross-sectional data for 83 commercial and 54 savings banks in 1979. They find significant cost economies with respect to accounts per branch and deposits per account yet there appear to be constant returns to scale relating to the number of branches. Rodriguez, Alvarez and Gomez (1993) estimate scale and scope economies for 64 Spanish savings banks using a hybrid translog model. The results for 1990 reveal both scale and scope economies for medium-sized savings banks and diseconomies of scale and scope for larger institutions.

Cost economies studies in the UK have focused on the building society sector mainly because of the limited number of domestic commercial banks with similar business profiles. These include studies by Gough (1979), Cooper (1980), Barnes and Dodds (1983), Hardwick (1989, 1990), Drake (1992, 1995), and McKillop and Glass (1994). All these studies use a range of competing methodologies and report conflicting findings.

Gough (1979) and Barnes and Dodds (1983) both estimated linear average cost functions for the periods 1972–76 and 1970–78 respectively. They found no evidence of economies of scale in the industry. Cooper (1980) estimated a Cobb–Douglas cost function on 1977 data and found that scale economies were prevalent for societies with asset size less than £100 million, whereas larger societies were subject to diseconomies. Hardwick (1989) uses a single output translog cost function model to estimate scale economies from the 1985 annual returns of a sample of 97 building societies. The study finds economies of scale for societies with assets under £280 million and diseconomies of scale for those with assets over £1500 million. Using the same data sample and translog methodology Hardwick (1990) uses a two-output model and finds that there are statistically significant scale economies for societies with assets under £5500 million, yet there is no evidence of scope economies. Drake (1992), using the same methodology but a different data sample (76 building societies in 1988), indicates mild economies of scale for societies in the £120–500 million asset size range but finds no evidence of economies of scope.

McKillop and Glass (1994) use a two-output, three-input, hybrid translog cost function to obtain econometric measures of overall and augmented economies of scale, product-specific scale economies and economies of scope. The data are obtained from the 1991 annual returns for a sample of 89 societies. McKillop and Glass (1994) group building societies into three categories — national, regional and local — depending on their consolidated asset size and number of branches. Scale and scope estimates are then calculated for each category of society as well as the whole industry. Overall, this study finds evidence of significant augmented economies of scale for both national and local societies, but only constant returns for those societies that are regionally based. In terms of augmented input-specific economies, there are unit cost savings associated with the increased use of physical capital for national societies but not for regional societies. The authors argue that this finding positively reflects the fact that larger capital bases coupled with branch networks enable national societies to follow more radical changes in the pursuit of efficiency in the use of the capital inputs (compared to the utilisation of labour inputs). The third major finding is that for regional and local societies cost inefficiencies emerge in the production of mortgage and non-mortgage products, while 'national societies do not appear to exhibit either cost efficiencies or inefficiencies over the production of the two output classes' (McKillop and Glass, 1994, p. 1045). This study also finds no evidence of economies of scope or cost complementarity between the provision of mortgage and non-mortgage outputs.

The most recent study on cost economies in the UK building society market has been undertaken by Drake (1995) who extends his earlier (1992) analysis. Drake respecifies the translog multi-product cost function by including an extra parameter which provides the first empirical test for expense-preference behaviour in UK building societies. The results from this study also reveal important differences from the results provided by Drake (1992) which were obtained under the 'usual' assumption of cost minimisation. In particular, there is no evidence of scale economies found when expense-preference behaviour is taken into account. It is also found that the lack of evidence of economies of scope in the building society industry casts doubt upon the efficiency motive behind the recent wave of diversification and conglomeration in the sector.

Overall, the studies which we surveyed for the large European banking markets suggested that substantial economies of scale exist generally for small and medium-sized banks while evidence of economies of scope is more uncertain.

Cost Studies for Smaller European Banking Markets

Kolari and Zardkoohi (1990), using accounting data for cooperative and saving banks in 1983 and 1984, provide empirical evidence on the cost structure of cooperative and savings banks operating in Finland. They use a translog model and their results indicate that cost curves for both cooperative and saving banks tend to be L-shaped at the plant level and U-shaped at the firm level. They find diseconomies of scope in the joint production of advances and bills and conclude that mergers among smaller banks ought to be preferred to mergers among larger ones.

Glass and McKillop (1992) use the data from one of the largest Irish banks, the Bank of Ireland, for the period 1972–90, to estimate a hybrid translog model. They investigate the process of natural and non-natural technical change, overall scale economies, product-specific scale economies and scope economies. Their results show that apart from the subperiod 1975–78, the bank was characterised by overall diseconomies of scale, whereas product-specific scale economies were reported to be decreasing for investments and increasing for loans. Also the estimated cost function showed diseconomies of scope over the production of two outputs. The estimated parameters reflected technical change in the Bank of Ireland, which was both natural and non-natural in character (the average annual overall rate being 4.96%). Additionally, a positive interaction between scale economies and technical change is indicated.

More recently, Fields, Murphy and Tirtiroglu (1993) examined the fundamental cost–production relationships in a developing country, Turkey, which, they argued, could provide 'useful information in understanding the potential effect of globalising financial markets' (p. 112). The study used data for national commercial banks, of which there were 28 usable observations during 1986 and 27 for 1987. The study indicated no significant evidence of scale economies for either 1986 or 1987. The authors reported that the structure of the relationship between cost and output is similar to those of earlier studies based on different time periods, samples, estimation techniques and types of countries.

Cross-Country European Cost Studies

The most recent studies on cost efficiency in European banking have established global cost functions using data from a range of countries. Vennet (1993b) uses a translog cost function approach to investigate a sample of 2600 credit institutions operating in the EU for the year 1991. Vennet concludes that the optimal scale is situated in the $3-10 billion asset range. 'Above this size level breaking up the bank and/or relative specialisation seems to be the optimal strategy from a cost perspective' (p. 34). In addition, this study also finds that scope economies seem to be related to the nature of banks' financial assets. Allen and Rai (1993) have advanced this approach by utilising the hybrid translog approach to test for the existence of scale and scope economies in international banking using a sample of European, US and Japanese banks. Their results for 1988-91 show that significant economies of scale exist, mainly for small banks in all markets and for medium-sized banks in countries with regulations that prohibit universal banking. Efficiency measures, obtained from stochastic cost frontiers, indicate banks operate less efficiently in separated as opposed to universal banking countries.

Overall, the results of cost studies undertaken on large and small European banking markets show that economies of scale exist; however, there is no consensus as to the level of output at which these economies are exhausted. It is also uncertain whether these economies occur at the branch or firm level. The concept of economies of scope has been investigated by very few studies and it is difficult to draw any conclusion from these results. For instance, in the French banking market, economies of scope have been reported for medium-sized banks by Martin and Sassenou (1992), while Dietsch (1993) found no such evidence. The literature on the Italian banking industry has not found any evidence of economies of scope. In comparison, Rodriguez, Alvarez and Gomez (1993) find evidence of scope economies for medium-sized Spanish savings banks and diseconomies of scope for larger institutions. In the UK, Hardwick (1990) and Drake (1992) indicate that there is no evidence of scope economies for building societies. Yet, in the cross-country studies, Vennet (1993b) concludes that scope economies seem to be related to the nature of banks' financial assets.

RECENT APPROACHES TO ESTIMATING EFFICIENCY IN BANKING MARKETS

Earlier in this chapter we outlined the recent theoretical developments related to evaluating efficiency in banking markets. These 'new' approaches use either stochastic or programming techniques to evaluate cost efficiency. In this section, we will briefly review these studies which use stochastic cost frontier and data envelope analysis (DEA) to examine the cost structure of financial institutions. The principal focus in this section is to identify the methodological issues and the main results of this literature. Chapter 8 covers the most recent European empirical studies.

Berger and Humphrey (1991) analysed inefficiencies for all US banks in 1984. Inefficiencies were measured relative to a 'thick frontier' cost function and were found to dominate measured scale and product mix economies. The study revealed that most inefficiencies were operational in nature, involving the overuse of physical inputs, rather than financial, involving overpayment of interest. Moreover, the authors suggested that their results showed that competitive pressures in banking from deregulation would be focused on banks to cut costs substantially, so that banks could merge with more efficient banks, or exit from the market.

Mester (1993) investigated the efficiency of mutual and stock S&Ls using 1991 data on US S&Ls. The study applied the stochastic econometric cost function approach which allows both the cost frontier and error structures to differ between S&Ls of these two ownership forms. The results suggested that, on average, stock S&Ls are less efficient than mutual S&Ls. It also suggested that deregulation of interest rates and increased competition may have had the predicted effect of curtailing agency problems in mutual S&Ls.

Cebenoyan et al. (1993) focused on whether agency-related inefficiency problems exist in the thrift industry, and, thereby, to infer whether the recent structural shift to stock ownership could be expected to yield efficiency gains for the industry. The authors used a multi-product, translog stochastic cost frontier methodology to examine inefficiency scores for 559 S&Ls operating in the Atlanta Federal Home Loan Bank District in 1988. The results of the study were as follows:

1. The mutual and stock S&Ls in the sample had similar cost structures, allowing the pooling of S&L data.

2. S&Ls have a large range of inefficiency scores, with mean 16% implying that the average S&L may produce its output with only 84% of the inputs actually used.

3. Operating efficiency was not significantly correlated to form of ownership.

Sherman and Gold (1985) were the first to apply DEA to banking by conducting an analysis on 14 branches of a US savings bank. The study adopted the production approach for measuring bank output and assessed the efficiency of 17 transactions. The inputs monitored were labour, office space and supply costs. The results showed that 6 of the 14 branches were relatively inefficient. A major limitation of this study, however, was that the very small sample size probably had a negative effect on the discriminatory power of the analysis.

Parkan (1987) employed the DEA technique to 35 branches of a major Canadian chartered bank in Calgary. This study also applied the production approach to measure output. Parkan constrained the number of outputs and inputs to six by applying a weighting scheme to aggregate some of the initially proposed variables and eliminating others. This was because DEA provides a better contrast in comparing branches with respect to their efficiency when the number of branches is significantly larger than the sum of the number of inputs and outputs. The findings revealed that 11 of the 35 branches were found to be relatively inefficient.

Vassiloglou and Giolias (1990) conducted a similar study to Parkan (1987) and found that only 9 out of 20 branches of the Commercial Bank of Greece in 1987 had a maximum efficiency rating. Tulkens (1990) conducted a larger-scale study, applied the DEA and free disposed hull (FDH) techniques (an approach which avoids the DEA assumption of convexity) to 773 branches of a Belgian public bank and 911 branches of a private bank in the same country. Tulkens found that using the DEA approach less than 6% of the branches were efficient; whereas 74.6% of the public bank's branches are on the FDH frontier compared to 57.8% of the private bank's branches.

The above studies have employed DEA techniques to analyse branch networks of single banks; other studies have extended the application across banks. For example, Rangan et al. (1988) sought to break down the inefficiencies of 215 independent US banks into those originating from pure technical inefficiency and scale inefficiency (i.e. operating at non-constant returns to scale). Unlike the single banks' studies, Rangan et al. used the intermediation approach to output measurement, that is, the dollar value of three kinds of loans and two types of deposits, while the inputs employed in the study were labour, capital and purchased funds. The results revealed that the average value of efficiency for the sample was 0.70. This indicated that on average the banks in the sample could have produced the same amount of output by using 70% of the inputs. Thus, in general, the study showed that a significant amount of inefficiency appeared to be present, almost all of which seemed to result from pure technical inefficiencies. These findings could be compared to those of Elyasiani and Mehdian (1990a) who examined technical and scale inefficiencies on a random sample of 144 US banks in 1985, using a deterministic statistical form of frontier analysis. Unlike Rangan et al. (1988), Elyasiani and Mehdian (1990a) found that scale inefficiency was the important factor.

Rangan et al. (1990) extended their earlier work using a sample composed of both unit and branch bank data. The study investigated whether unit or branch banks' organisational forms influenced the efficiency measures. In order to analyse this issue, the sample was grouped into two subsamples of banks — those banks allowed to operate branches and those that are not. The study found that there were no sizeable differences in efficiency between the two types of banks.

One of the recent UK studies undertaken by Field (1990) employed the DEA methodology to a cross-section of 71 British building societies in 1981. The study found that 86% of the sample were inefficient, mainly due to scale inefficiencies. The contrast between US results and Field's result is that the US studies indicate that the technical efficiency measure is positively related to bank size, and thus the dispersion in firms' efficiency seemed to be accounted for by their size. On the other hand, Field (1990) showed that the overall technical efficiency was negatively correlated with firm size. This could be possibly related to cartelised and oligopolistic market conditions among UK building societies in 1981. Moreover, Drake et al. (1992) undertook a study which had contrasting results to those of Field. Applying DEA to building societies after deregulation in 1988, the study found 37% to show overall efficiency — a marked increase — and this overall efficiency was positively correlated to size.

Elyasiani and Mehdian (1990b) applied the non-parametric DEA approach to measure the rate of technological change (RTC) for a sample of 191 large US banks based on 1980 and 1985 data. The findings of the study revealed that the frontier had shifted inward due to technological advancement to the extent that the banks may have produced the same level of output in 1980 with 90% of the inputs they actually used.

More recently, Berg et al. (1993) have examined banking efficiency in the Nordic countries using DEA techniques. Using a sample of 503 Finnish, 150 Norwegian and 126 Swedish banks in 1990, they found that efficiency differences between banks were most important in Finland and Norway and least important in Sweden. Comparing the best practice frontiers of the three banking markets they found the highest share of the banking industry on the frontier was in Sweden and the lowest in Finland. Most of the banks on the Nordic best practice frontier were Swedish. These conclusions, however, are mainly independent of whether the authors assume variable or constant returns to scale along the efficiency frontier.

CONCLUSIONS

This chapter outlines the theoretical underpinnings of the empirical economies of scale and scope studies. Firstly, this chapter provides a definition of economies of scale and scope and then it focuses on the theoretical problems relating to analysing scale and scope in the banking industry. It is shown that banks are defined as multi-product, multi-plant and multi-input firms. Since they engage in the production of various services utilising factors of production as diverse as labour, capital equipment and deposits, empirical studies face various problems when they examine the cost structure of these firms. Such problems relate to the definition of output and bank total cost; the cost concept of multi-product firms; the functional form of the cost functions; the problem of bank output endogeneity and the effects of technological change.

The cost function approach is an efficient way to model the structure of costs and production for a multi-product firm. The approach does not require any arbitrary a priori constraints on the model of the cost function or production function. For a single output firm, the concept of economies of scale exists if output increases and simultaneously total cost increases less proportionately than output. Of course, economies of scale may change over time depending on technological advances. The interpretation of economies of scale becomes complicated for multi-product firms; economies of scope exist if the cost of producing joint outputs is less than the total cost of producing outputs separately. Therefore, the multi-product firm may achieve cost reductions through both economies of scope and economies of scale.

The second part of this chapter has examined the empirical literature on economies of scale and scope in banking markets. In general, one can conclude that statistical studies of scale and scope economies reveal the existence of optimal cost levels, whose presence stands out more sharply the better the quality of the data and methodology employed. The bulk of these studies investigate the cost structure in US banking markets, and they appear to report different results depending on the size of banks used in their data samples. The majority of US empirical studies have used data from small US banks, and these studies tend to conclude that economies of scale do not appear for banks with more than $100 million in deposits. Studies that use data samples of larger US banks find that scale economies appear for these institutions. The results of the cost studies undertaken on European banking markets appear to suggest that economies of scale are evident, although there is no consensus as to the level of output at which these economies are exhausted.

The concept of economies of scope has been analysed by fewer studies from which it is difficult to draw any general conclusions. Overall, the findings on economies of scale and scope in banking markets appear to show stronger empirical evidence for scale over scope economies. There also appears to be potential cost gains which can be generated from altering scale via internal growth or merger activity and this may be significant in the banking industry.

The findings of the above studies suggest various public policy reasons as to why it is useful to undertake more research in the area of European bank cost structures. With the advent of the single European banking market, it is of interest to evaluate evidence of economies of scale and scope so one can evaluate how market structure and bank costs may alter in the new broader markets and in markets linked by common competitors from 1993 onwards. The following chapter aims to present further evidence on cost economies in European banking by reporting the authors' recent findings on economies of scale and scope in the French, German, Italian and Spanish banking markets.

7

A comparative analysis of scope and scale economies in European banking markets

INTRODUCTION

In Chapter 3 we noted that the Commission of the European Communities (1988a) had stressed in its 1992 single market programme that substantial benefits would accrue to those sectors that can benefit from positive supply-side effects. In particular, 'price reductions occasioned by competitive pressures will force firms to look actively for reduction in costs through the elimination of areas of low productivity or by a greater exploitation of scale economies' (European Economy, 1988, p. 162). Despite the importance of economies of scope and scale, however, we have seen from Chapter 6 that only a few studies have investigated cost characteristics in European banking. No studies, as far as we are aware, have provided cross-country comparisons. This chapter aims to redress this imbalance by reporting the results of our recent cost economy studies. We use the hybrid translog cost function methodology to evaluate evidence of scale and scope economies in four large EU banking markets: France, Germany, Italy and Spain. The chapter also addresses the concept of cost subadditivity.

THE METHODOLOGY

This study adopts the intermediation approach to calculate scale and scope economies in the French, German, Italian and Spanish banking markets. The hybrid translog cost function is used to examine economies of scale and scope for banks with multiple inputs and outputs. The model assumes that banks operate in a competitive environment and aim to minimise costs. We define the banks' cost function by a given vector of outputs, $Q = (Q_1, Q_2, \ldots Q_m)$, using a range of variable inputs, $X = (X_1, X_2, \ldots X_m)$, their input prices $P = (P_1, P_2, \ldots P_m)$ and the number of branches (B). The following function describes the best production process of multi-product banks:

$$Q = h(X, B) \tag{1}$$

with profit-maximising behaviour, the corresponding dual cost function of the form

$$TC = f(Q_1, \ldots, Q_m; \; P_1, \ldots, P_n; \; B) \tag{2}$$

However, the cost function must qualify the duality condition developed by Shephard (1953, 1970) and Diewert (1974), that is, the unique correspondence between the production function and the cost function.

The conventional translog cost function developed by Christensen, Jorgenson and Lau (1973), is a second-order Taylor expansion series in output quantities, input prices and control variables. Using this methodology the cost structure of multi-product financial institutions can be modelled with maximum flexibility, given explicit recognition to each of the outputs. The cost function enables us to estimate overall scope and scale economies and allows us to test for additional restrictions such as non-jointness and homotheticity, and for the Cobb–Douglas functional form.

A major criticism of conventional translog cost methodology is that it does not allow us to evaluate scope economies when one of the outputs becomes zero. Therefore, the hybrid translog cost function developed by Caves, Christensen and Tretheway (1980) and Fuss and Waverman (1981) is used to avoid this limitation. In the case of the hybrid translog function form, the logarithms of outputs in the cost function and share equations are replaced with Box–Cox (1964) transformations. The Box–Cox hybrid transformation methodology evaluates a translog functional form where the output levels undergo a nonlinear transformation and as a result the function can be defined at zero output levels. That is,

$$Q^* = \frac{(Q_i^\lambda - 1)}{\lambda} \quad \lambda \neq 0$$

$$= \ln Q_i \quad \lambda = 0 \tag{3}$$

As λ approaches zero, the hybrid functional form approaches the translog cost function. When λ equals one, the cost function becomes semi-log.

We employ the hybrid translog form as a quadratic approximation to banks' cost functions. For the banking industry, two models are estimated. Model I estimates the cost functions at the plant level by holding the number of branches constant. Model II estimates at the firm level by allowing the number of branches to change, where branches are a function of output. Using the Box–Cox transformation, the hybrid translog cost function for Model I in this study can be viewed as follows:

$$\ln TC = \alpha_0 + \sum_{i=1}^{2} \alpha_i Q_i^* + \sum_{i=1}^{3} \beta_i \ln P_i + \lambda_b \ln B$$

$$+ \frac{1}{2} \left[\sum_{i=1}^{2} \sum_{j=1}^{2} \delta_{ij} Q_i^* Q_j^* + \sum_{i=1}^{3} \sum_{j=1}^{3} \gamma_{ij} \ln P_i \ln P_j + \lambda_{bb} \ln B \ln B \right]$$

$$+ \sum_{i=1}^{3} \sum_{j=1}^{2} \rho_{ij} \ln P_i Q_j^* + \sum_{i=1}^{2} \lambda_{bi} \ln B Q_i^* + \sum_{i=1}^{3} \tau_{bi} \ln B \ln P_i + \varepsilon \quad (4)$$

where $\ln TC$ is the natural logarithm of the total costs (operating and financial cost), Q_i^* the output of products with the Box–Cox transformation (i.e. total loans and total securities), $\ln P_i$ the natural logarithm of ith input prices (i.e. wage rate, interest rate and capital price), $\ln B$ the natural logarithm of the number of branches and α, β, δ, γ, p, λ and τ are coefficients to be estimated.

Since the duality theorem requires the cost function to be linearly homogeneous in input prices, the following restrictions have to be imposed on the parameters of the cost function in equation (4):

$$\sum_{i=1}^{3} \beta_i = 1 \qquad \sum_{i=1}^{3} \gamma_{ij} = 0 \quad \text{for all } j$$

$$\sum_{i=1}^{3} \tau_{bi} = 0 \qquad \sum_{i=1}^{3} \rho_{ij} = 0 \quad \text{for all } j \quad (5)$$

Furthermore, the second-order parameters of the cost function in equation (4) must be symmetric, that is,

$$\delta_{ij} = \delta_{ji} \quad \text{for all } i, j$$

$$\gamma_{ij} = \gamma_{ji} \quad \text{for all } i, j \quad (6)$$

The derived demand for an input or cost share of input, X_i, is calculated by partially differentiating the cost function with respect to the input prices, P_i. This follows from duality theory and is referred to as Shephard's lemma (Christensen, Jorgenson and Lau, 1973), so

$$S_i = \frac{\partial \ln TC}{\partial \ln P_i} = \frac{\partial TC}{\partial P_i} \frac{P_i}{TC} = \frac{P_i X_i}{TC} \quad (7)$$

where S_i is the share of the ith input in the total cost. Thus, the cost share equations in the model can be generated by the cost function equation (4) as

$$\sum_{i=1}^{3} S_i = \sum_{i=1}^{2} \beta_i + \sum_{i=1}^{3}\sum_{j=1}^{3} \gamma_{ij} \ln P_j + \sum_{i=1}^{3}\sum_{j=1}^{2} \rho_{ij} Q_j^* + \sum_{i=1}^{3} \tau_i \ln B + \varepsilon_i \quad (8)$$

The cost function (4) is estimated jointly with the input cost share equation (8) using the iterative seemingly unrelated regression (SUR) estimation technique. Since input cost share equations sum to unity, one cost share equation is omitted from the estimated system of equations (see Berndt, Hall and Hausman, 1974) because Zellner's (1962) iterative SUR technique will only be made operational by deleting one of the cost share equations.

THE DATA AND DEFINITION OF VARIABLES

One of the main reasons for the paucity of cost studies on European banking markets relates to data availability problems. In this study we use banks' balance sheet and income statement data, for 1988, obtained from the London-based International Bank Credit Analysis Ltd (IBCA) database. Accounting data were available for 201 French, 196 German and 244 Italian banks. In the case of Spain, the data on 209 banks were taken from Anuario Estadistico De la Banca Privada (1988) and Blanaces y Cuenta De Resultados De Las Cajas De Ahoro (1988). So as to maximise our sample size, we include commercial, savings and foreign banks in our Spanish sample. Relevant information which was not available in the IBCA database, such as the number of bank branches and employees, was obtained from the following sources. For Italy, the number of branches and employees was obtained from the Italian Banks' Association. The data on branch numbers for French banks were gathered from Comptes Annuels des Établissements de Crédit (1988) and for German banks from *The Bankers' Almanac* (1990). In our model specifications for Italy and Spain, the input price of labour is calculated by dividing staff expenses by total number of reported employees, whereas for France and Germany, it is obtained by dividing staff expenses by the total number of branches since we could not obtain full information on the number of employees for individual banks from these sources.

The empirical approach to output definition used in this study is supported theoretically by Sealey and Lindley's (1977) model of production in depository financial institutions. Bank outputs are measured as total loans and securities, in accordance with Kolari and Zardkoohi (1987) and most other European studies. Given the chosen intermediation approach, we use two categories of outputs, three variable inputs and the number of branches as a control variable in our model. Output can be defined as:

Q_1 total loans which include all class of loans
Q_2 total securities

The input prices used are as follows:

P_1 the average annual wage per employee (average price of labour) in the models for Italy and Spain; and the average annual wage per branch in the models for France and Germany

P_2 the average interest cost per dollar of interest-bearing total deposits (average price of deposits or interest rate)

P_3 the average price of capital, which is calculated by summing the capital expenses and dividing by total fixed assets

The dependent variables include total cost (TC) and cost shares (S_i). Total cost comprises both operating costs and financial costs (interest paid on the total deposits). The cost shares are specified as follows: wages, salaries and employee benefits per dollar of total costs (the cost share of labour, S_1); interest paid on the interest-bearing total deposits per dollar of total cost (the cost share of deposits, S_2); and expenses on capital per dollar of total costs, S_3. Finally, the number of branches (B) is included as a control variable to capture the influence on cost changes in the structure of the banking markets.

EMPIRICAL RESULTS

The hybrid translog cost function parameters are estimated using the SUR procedure for the cost function (4) together with the two-input cost share equations (8), while imposing the linear homogeneity (5) and symmetry (6) restrictions. Moreover, Model II is estimated in the same way as Model I, however there are the following additional restrictions, i.e. $\lambda_b = 0$, $\lambda_{bb} = 0$, $\lambda_{bi} = 0$ and $\tau_{bi} = 0$, for all i.

A maximum likelihood procedure was used to estimate the parameters of the system of equations for each country both at the plant level and firm level. Table 7.1 reports the structural tests for homotheticity, Cobb–Douglas functional form and non-jointness. Homotheticity, which implies separability of the cost function in outputs and all other variables, is rejected at the 5% level for all country equations. The rejection of the homotheticity constraint shows that the unspecified transformation function underlying the cost functions is not separable in outputs, input prices and other control variables. Hence, the empirical study of economies of scale using the hybrid procedure should account for the multiple product and inputs nature of banks. Moreover, the test for Cobb–Douglas functional form is decisively rejected in all cases. Finally, the non-jointness hypothesis

Table 7.1 Structural test results

Test performed	Test statistic		Degrees of freedom		Critical value of Chi-Squared (χ^2) test at the 95% level		Decision	
	Model I	Model II	Model I	Model II	Model I	Model II	Model I	Model II
France								
Homotheticity	3250.5	667.65	8	6	15.5	12.6	Rejected	Rejected
Cobb–Douglas	3190.7	1145.1	21	15	32.7	25.0	Rejected	Rejected
Non-jointness	30.876	7.6743	1	1	3.84	3.84	Rejected	Rejected
Germany								
Homotheticity	4614.5	572.68	8	6	15.5	12.6	Rejected	Rejected
Cobb–Douglas	4836.3	1081.5	21	21	32.7	25.0	Rejected	Rejected
Non-jointness	21.770	8.2462	1	1	3.84	3.84	Rejected	Rejected
Italy								
Homotheticity	577.92	879.15	8	6	15.5	12.6	Rejected	Rejected
Cobb–Douglas	1255.0	1150.3	21	15	32.7	25.0	Rejected	Rejected
Non-jointness	9.5656	2.5994	1	1	3.84	3.84	Rejected	Not rejected
Spain								
Homotheticity	643.51	653.57	8	6	15.5	12.6	Rejected	Rejected
Cobb–Douglas	1407.8	1330.0	21	15	32.7	25.0	Rejected	Rejected
Non-jointness	14.753	12.375	1	1	3.84	3.84	Rejected	Rejected

is rejected both at the plant and firm levels for France, Germany, Italy (except at the firm level) and Spain. This suggests that the marginal cost of one output depends on the level of production of the other output in the French, German, Italian (but not at the firm level) and Spanish banking industry.

Overall Economies of Scope

An appropriate local test for the existence of economies of scope is to examine pairwise cost complementarities. Baumol, Panzar and Willig (1988) illustrate that a sufficient, but not essential, condition for overall economies of scope is the presence of cost complementarities between outputs. Cost complementarities exist if the marginal cost of producing one output decreases when the production of other outputs increases. This can be shown by the following expression:

$$\frac{\partial^2 TC}{\partial Q_i \partial Q_j} < 0 \quad 1 < i, j \leqslant 2 \quad \text{for } i \neq j \tag{9}$$

In equation (9), pairwise cost complementarities are expressed at the mean of the data in our model as

$$\delta_{ij} + \alpha_i \alpha_j < 0 \quad \text{for all } i, j \tag{10}$$

Table 7.2 shows the pairwise cost complementarities for countries, France, Germany, Italy and Spain. If the value is negative, then cost complementarities are said to be present implying economies of scope; a positive value indicates diseconomies of scope; a value equal to zero suggests cost independence.

A problem with this calculation, however, is that the test for cost complementarities is a local test at the mean data point. Berger, Hanweck and Humphrey (1987) report that in the case of translog cost functions it is impossible to have cost complementarities at every data point. In other words, at all levels of output, this condition cannot hold.

Table 7.2 Pairwise cost complementarities[a]

	Model I	Model II
France	0.1856*	0.0808*
	(0.03341)	(0.02915)
Germany	0.2627*	0.2639*
	(0.05631)	(0.09191)
Italy	0.1582*	0.0453
	(0.05114)	(0.02807)
Spain	0.0641*	0.0710*
	(0.02914)	(0.02018)

[a]Approximate standard error in parentheses.
*Significant at 0.01 level.
**Significant at 0.05 level.

A more appropriate indicator of economies of scope has been suggested by Willig (1979), who indicates the degree of economies of scope by considering two outputs, Q_1 and Q_2, and their separate cost functions, $TC(Q_1)$ and $TC(Q_2)$. The joint cost of producing the two outputs is expressed by $TC(Q_1, Q_2)$ and the degree of economies of scope is shown as

$$SC = \frac{TC(Q_1, 0) + TC(0, Q_2) - TC(Q_1, Q_2)}{TC(Q_1, Q_2)} \tag{11}$$

$SC > 0$ or $SC < 0$ indicates overall economies or diseconomies of scope respectively.

Using equation (11), we can examine evidence of overall scope economies in the four banking markets at the plant and firm levels and these are reported in Table 7.3. The results are noticeably different both at the plant and firm levels as well as among the countries. In the case of French banks, scope estimates are significantly positive both at the plant and firm levels for the larger banks. This means that joint production of loans and securities are less costly than their production by different institutions. Small French banks, on the other hand, exhibit significant diseconomies of scope at the plant level. The sample of German banks reveals a mixed picture, with evidence of diseconomies of scope for small and medium-sized banks and economies of scope for the larger ones. For Italian banks, the estimates of scope economies are positive and significant only at the plant level. Finally, the findings for Spanish banks indicate that scope coefficients are positive for fairly small bank sizes (less than $1 billion in assets) yet for larger banks they are significantly negative.

Expansion Path Subadditivity

If the mix of outputs of an industry can be produced at a lower cost by a single monopoly firm than by any combination of smaller firms then the industry cost function is subadditive. The industry will be a natural monopoly. Baumol, Panzar and Willig (1988) have shown that a cost function is subadditive for a particular output vector Q when Q can be produced more cheaply by a single firm rather than by any combination of smaller firms. However, there are no straightforward mechanical criteria that permit us to test whether or not a particular function is subadditive. If Q_i illustrates different vectors of the same products as in

$$\sum_{i=1}^{m} Q_i = Q \tag{12}$$

then subadditivity means that

$$TC(Q) < \sum_{i=1}^{m} TC(Q_i) \tag{13}$$

Table 7.3 Overall economies of scope using the hybrid translog cost function[a]

Total asset sizes ($m.)	France		Germany		Italy		Spain	
	Model I	Model II	Model I	Model II	Model I	Model II	Model I	Model II
0–100	−0.3701	1.8243*	−0.8953***	−0.8977	8.3849*	0.4170	0.4594*	0.4601*
	(0.4372)	(0.5195)	(0.6260)	(0.8201)	(0.2852)	(0.4938)	(0.1551)	(0.1585)
100–300	−0.6742	2.2477*	−0.8485	−0.9290	9.0663*	0.8455	0.6085*	0.6443*
	(0.5077)	(0.6265)	(0.7642)	(0.9109)	(0.4502)	(0.9689)	(0.1779)	(0.1426)
300–600	0.8970	2.8848*	−0.8396	−0.9697	21.8734*	1.1869	−0.6208*	0.6985*
	(0.5913)	(0.7476)	(0.8508)	(0.9537)	(0.6810)	(1.4515)	(0.2169)	(0.1673)
600–1000	1.2431***	3.5653*	−0.7669	−0.9851	51.4163*	1.5015	−0.6628*	−0.7926*
	(0.6605)	(0.8333)	(0.9561)	(0.9959)	(0.8285)	(1.8133)	(0.2571)	(0.1947)
1000–3000	3.1460*	3.9012*	−0.7269	−0.8251	70.4244*	1.8550	−0.6657*	−0.8561*
	(0.7525)	(1.0461)	(1.0758)	(1.0362)	(0.9810)	(2.2069)	(0.3050)	(0.2330)
3000–5000	8.1490*	4.4159*	−0.2200	0.2967*	27.0547*	2.4859	−0.5553***	−0.9174*
	(0.8365)	(1.2137)	(1.2347)	(0.1251)	(1.2837)	(2.9473)	(0.3424)	(0.3657)
5000 >	12.8940*	6.5692*	4.9881*	0.3797*	97.9571*	3.6811	−0.6950***	−0.9431*
	(1.1051)	(1.7577)	(1.3806)	(0.1839)	(1.9765)	(4.4636)	(0.4461)	(0.4783)
All	1.1651***	3.6018*	−0.6246	−0.5642	44.1704*	1.3016	−0.6837*	−0.7854*
	(0.6910)	(0.9146)	(1.0771)	(1.0342)	(0.6921)	(1.5318)	(0.2511)	(0.1893)

[a] Approximate standard error in parentheses.
* Significant at 0.01 level.
** Significant at 0.05 level.
*** Significant at 0.10 level.

where each i represents a different firm. For two products and two firms subadditivity can be indicated as follows:

$$TC(Q) < TC(Q_1^A, Q_2^C) + TC(Q_1^A, Q_2^C) \qquad (14)$$

where A and C are two firms, $Q = (Q_1, Q_2)$, and $Q = (Q_1^A + Q_2^C, Q_1^A + Q_2^C)$.

Cost subadditivity is a measure of the relative efficiency of large and small firms and takes account of both scale and scope economies simultaneously. Baumol, Panzar and Willig (1988) note that the difficulty of testing for subadditivity is that the concept is a global and not a local one. To determine the subadditivity of a cost function at the same output vector Q, it is essential to have information about the value of the cost function for every possible output vector smaller than Q. Secondly, information about the cost function throughout the region is sufficient to determine whether the cost function is subadditive at Q. Additionally, the sufficient condition for cost subadditivity to hold is the presence of decreasing average incremental cost and scope economies up to Q, implying subadditivity at Q (decreasing average incremental cost implies that the product line must be monopolised if industry cost is to be minimised).

Berger, Hanweck and Humphrey (1987) propose the concept of expansion path subadditivity, and examine whether a bank of a given size can produce a combination of outputs more effectively than two banks that produce the same combination of outputs but in smaller size. Figure 7.1 describes an output plane for a banking institution with two outputs, Q_1, Q_2 and two sizes of banks, banks A and C which are small and bank B which is large.

Expansion path subadditivity examines whether the large bank at point B is more cost effective than the two smaller banks represented by points A and C. Expansion path subadditivity can be measured as follows:

$$EPSUB \ (Q^B) = \frac{TC(Q^A) + TC(Q^C) - TC(Q^B)}{TC(Q^B)} \qquad (15)$$

where $EPSUB(Q^B)$ shows cost changes resulting from the breaking of large bank B into smaller banks A and C.

The measurement of economies of scope is a special case of the expansion path subadditivity where smaller banking firms specialise at point D and E in Figure 7.1. From this diagram, it can be seen that economies of scope are present when

$$TC(Q_1^B, 0) + TC(0, Q_2^B) - TC(Q^B) > 0 \qquad (16)$$

According to various commentators (such as Noulas, Miller and Ray, 1993; Berger, Hunter and Timme, 1993) expansion path subadditivity is a more appropriate method than traditional scope economy measures for examining the cost structure of banking markets. Although equation (16) is a special case of equation (15), both equations provide us with different information.

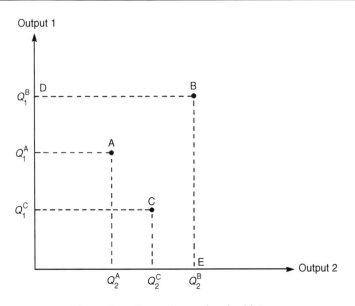

Figure 7.1   Expansion path subadditivity

Equation (15) suggests whether cost effective multi-product firms should be large or small (e.g. point A, C or B). Equation (16) suggests whether the firms should specialise in production (e.g. points D and E).

Table 7.4 shows the expansion path subadditivity results. Negative values indicate that a break-up of large banks into smaller ones brings about lower costs, while positive values suggest the opposite.

In our case, following Berger, Hanweck and Humphrey (1987), we divide the output of the representative bank in each group into two smaller banks. The size of the first bank is calculated by taking the mean value of bank outputs at the previous asset size class. The second bank constitutes the difference between the size of the first bank and the mean value of bank outputs at the present asset size class. Expansion path subadditivity is calculated at both the plant and firm level and the results are reported in Table 7.4. It can be seen that apart from fairly small Spanish banks, the estimated coefficients for expansion path subadditivity are positive, implying that breaking large banks into smaller ones results in higher costs. These results are in line with the findings of Hunter, Timme and Yang (1990) who show that costs are subadditive for the largest US banks and Noulas, Miller and Ray (1993) who found that the break-up of medium-sized US banks (in asset range between \$3 and \$6 billion) resulted in higher costs, thus suggesting a tendency for banks to become large.

Table 7.4 Expansion path subadditivity (%)

Total asset sizes ($m.)	France		Germany		Italy		Spain	
	Model I	Model II	Model I	Model II	Model I	Model II	Model I	Model II
0–100	0.0160	0.0635	0.0200	0.0517	0.4935	0.0656	−0.0408	0.0321
100–300	0.1116	0.4627	0.0529	0.1454	0.6408	0.1197	−0.0295	−0.0282
300–600	0.0805	0.4116	0.0776	0.2333	0.6850	0.1636	0.0641	0.2238
600–1000	0.1313	0.5361	0.0996	0.3201	0.7295	0.1983	0.1373	0.3547
1000–3000	0.1685	0.6574	0.1236	0.4318	0.7535	0.2299	0.1753	0.4604
3000–5000	0.2040	0.7213	0.1549	0.5905	0.7835	0.2828	0.1505	0.5443
5000 >	0.2573	0.5333	0.1322	0.4076	0.7691	0.3450	0.0300	0.6029
All	0.0062	0.0215	0.0264	0.0743	0.3303	0.8255	0.0036	0.0010

Table 7.5 Overall economies of scale using the hybrid translog cost function[a]

Total asset sizes ($m.)	France		Germany		Italy		Spain	
	Model I	Model II	Model I	Model II	Model I	Model II	Model I	Model II
0–100	0.5685* (0.0892)	0.8927 (0.1220)	0.8446 (0.1256)	2.8531* (0.0905)	0.9741 (0.1901)	0.9899 (0.3224)	0.3820* (0.0673)	0.4273* (0.0600)
100–300	0.6094* (0.1050)	0.9776 (0.1511)	0.7048** (0.1407)	3.0548* (0.0819)	0.8162 (0.1985)	0.9980 (0.5051)	0.3225* (0.1663)	0.4089* (0.0742)
300–600	0.5583* (0.1180)	0.9886 (0.1788)	0.7571 (0.1540)	3.1461* (0.0791)	0.7789 (0.2034)	1.0068 (0.6232)	0.3518* (0.2305)	0.4742* (0.0824)
600–1000	0.6393* (0.1266)	1.0288 (0.1975)	0.7327 (0.1672)	3.2885* (0.0799)	0.7300 (0.2172)	1.0056 (0.7034)	0.3513** (0.3096)	0.5304* (0.0928)
1000–3000	0.6992** (0.1470)	1.0721 (0.2305)	0.7207 (0.1808)	3.3058* (0.0878)	0.6306*** (0.2201)	1.0113 (0.7822)	0.3859 (0.3993)	0.6021* (0.1038)
3000–5000	0.7062*** (0.1619)	1.1047 (0.2543)	0.7022 (0.2012)	3.3171* (0.0985)	0.5706*** (0.2409)	1.0132 (0.9093)	0.4481 (0.4750)	0.7318* (0.1206)
5000 >	0.6939 (0.2021)	1.1792 (0.3213)	0.6269*** (0.2155)	3.4478* (0.1061)	0.4520** (0.2680)	1.0194 (1.1230)	0.4345 (0.6126)	0.7387*** (0.1425)
All	0.6323* (0.1350)	1.0416 (0.2104)	0.7052*** (0.1783)	3.2929* (0.0853)	0.7421 (0.2308)	1.0007 (0.6478)	0.3695* (0.3072)	0.5357* (0.0921)

[a] Approximate standard error in parentheses.
*Significantly different from one at 0.01 level.
**Significantly different from one at 0.05 level.
***Significantly different from one at 0.10 level.

Overall Economies of Scale

Following Noulas, Ray and Miller (1990) and Mester (1987a) to estimate overall economies of scale, we calculate the elasticity of cost with respect to output, holding the product mix and non-output variables constant. A measure of overall economies of scale (SE) is given by the following cost elasticity by differentiating the hybrid cost function in equation (4) with respect to output. This gives us

$$SE = \sum_{i=1}^{2} \frac{\partial \ln TC}{\partial Q^*} = \sum_{i=1}^{2} \alpha_i + \sum_{i=1}^{2}\sum_{j=1}^{2} \hat{o}_{ij}Q_j^* + \sum_{i=1}^{3}\sum_{j=1}^{2} p_{ij} \ln P_i + \sum_{i=1}^{2} \lambda_{bi} \ln B \quad (17)$$

If $SE < 1$ then there are increasing returns to scale, implying economies of scale; if $SE = 1$ then constant returns to scale; if $SE > 1$ then decreasing returns to scale, implying diseconomies of scale.

Estimated overall scale economies can be derived for each bank size by evaluating equation (17) to examine how changes in scale affect total cost. We calculate the overall scale economies using the mean data level of output, the number of branches and overall mean levels of input prices for each bank group.

Overall economies of scale and the approximate standard error of the coefficients are reported for the whole sample and for each bank size group in Table 7.5. These results indicate that overall economies of scale exist in the French, German, Italian and Spanish banking markets at the plant level. Moreover, the estimated scale economies are significantly different from one apart from in the cases for: the largest French banks with asset size over $5 billion; small Spanish banks with asset size under $1 billion; German banks with asset size between $100 and $300 million as well as the same country's largest banks with assets over $5 billion. In Italy, the coefficients for all banks' output size ranges vary between zero and one; however, overall scale economies are only statistically significant at the plant level for large banks with asset size over $1 billion. At the firm level overall economies of scale are evident in the Spanish banking market across all output ranges, yet there are significant diseconomies of scale for German banks for all output size groups. The results for French and Italian banks indicate that there are constant returns to scale at the firm level across all output ranges. Overall, these results indicate a prevalence of scale economies at the plant (or branch) level as opposed to the firm level in European banking. Similar evidence of substantial branch-level economies is also found for US banks in a recent study by Murphy (1992).

PRODUCT-SPECIFIC ECONOMIES OF SCALE

Product-specific economies of scale are evaluated by using the average incremental cost (AIC) concept, that calculates how much total cost increases when an output is produced at a specific level rather than not being produced at all. Following Baumol, Panzar and Willig (1988), the measurement of product-specific economies of scale (*PSES*) for product i at output vector Q, is calculated by the ratio of the average incremental cost of the product (AIC_i) to its marginal cost (TC/Q_i) and is given by

$$PSES_i = \frac{AIC_i}{(\partial TC/\partial Q_i)} = \frac{IC_i}{\varepsilon_{TC_{Q_i}} TC} \tag{18}$$

where IC_i is the incremental cost of product i and is defined as equation (19) and $\varepsilon_{TC_{Q_i}}$ is cost elasticity of ith output.

$$IC_i = TC(Q_1, Q_2) - TC(0, Q_2) \tag{19}$$

The product-specific economies of scale are said to exist when the value is greater than one, while values smaller than one imply product-specific diseconomies of scale. In other words, returns to scale of product i at Q are said to be increasing, decreasing or constant as $PSES_i$ are greater than, less than or equal to unity, respectively.

In this study, using the hybrid translog cost function (4), product-specific economies of scale at the expansion point where $Q_i = P_i = B = 1$ are given as follows:

$$PSES_i = \exp(\alpha_0) - \exp\left\{\alpha_0 - \frac{\alpha_i}{\lambda} + \frac{\delta_{ii}}{2\lambda^2}\right\} [\alpha_i \exp(\alpha_0)]^{-1} \tag{20}$$

Table 7.6 provides estimates of product-specific scale economies for both products, total loans and total securities for the French, German, Italian and Spanish banking markets at the plant and firm levels. Apart from Italian banks the coefficients of loans and securities for sample countries both at the plant and firm levels are greater than unity, suggesting increasing returns to scale specific to both products. These results imply that banks in France, Germany and Spain would gain, from a cost standpoint, by increasing their output of loans and securities. Our results are consistent with Glass and McKillop (1992) who find increasing returns to specific loans for Irish banking firms. Moreover, Mester (1987b) found evidence of increasing returns to scale for loans for US S&Ls.

Table 7.6 Product-specific economies of scale

Products	France		Germany		Italy		Spain	
	Model I	Model II	Model I	Model II	Model I	Model II	Model I	Model II
Total loans	1.3633	1.8002	1.3006	1.5666	1.2701	0.8645	2.4113	2.1357
Total securities	3.2431	3.2086	2.6253	2.2572	0.5323	-4.4311	2.3931	2.6112

CONCLUSIONS

This chapter examines the cost structure of four EU banking markets using the hybrid translog cost function methodology. The results indicate noticeable differences across the French, German, Italian and Spanish banking markets, and scope and scale economies appear to be evident in each country over a wide range of bank output levels. Our findings can be summarised as follows:

1. Firm-level economies of scope appear to be evident in French banking at all output ranges, whereas for the other countries our findings are mixed. In Germany banks with asset size greater than $3 billion appear to have firm-level scope economies which are statistically significant. Scope economies are not statistically significant for Italian banks. In Spain we find evidence of significant diseconomies of scope for banks with asset size greater than $600 million. At the plant (or branch) level economies of scope are more prevalent and we find strong economies of scope for large French and German banks as well as for all Italian banks. Plant-level diseconomies of scope are found for the smaller French, German and Spanish banks. From the above we conclude that scope economies are more prevalent at the plant (or branch) level than at the overall firm level.

2. At the firm level scale economies are only found for all sizes of banks in Spain. The French and Italian banking markets exhibit constant returns to scale and the German market reveals diseconomies of scale for all output ranges. In contrast to these firm-level findings economies of scale are more evident at the plant (or branch) level. Plant-level scale economies appear in all output ranges for French banks apart from those with more than $5 billion assets. They occur for Italian banks with asset sizes greater than $1 billion and for German banks with asset sizes ranging between $100 and $300 million and greater than $5 billion. Product-specific economies of scale also appear to be evident in each banking market.

3. Expansion path subadditivity estimates suggest that the break-up of large banks into smaller ones will bring about higher costs, except for small Spanish banks with less than $300 million of assets. These results are in line with the findings of Hunter, Timme and Yang (1990) who show that costs are subadditive for the largest US banks and Noulas, Miller and Ray (1993) who find that the break-up of medium-sized US banks, in asset range between $3 and $6 billion, results in higher costs, suggesting a tendency for banks to become larger.

Overall, these results suggest noticeable differences in cost characteristics across European banking markets and strong evidence of economies of scale and scope at the plant (or branch) level in all but the Spanish market. Cost savings appear to occur mainly through the increased average size of banks' branches rather than through the size of the banking firm. It also appears that scale and scope economies will be important in generating economic gains to EU banking markets under the single market programme. The cost advantages to be had through larger bank size (mainly by increasing the average size of established branches) could also further promote the consolidation trend leading to increased concentration in European banking markets.

8

European banking and the cost implications of mergers

INTRODUCTION

This chapter examines the potential for efficiency gains and cost savings resulting from hypothetical bank mergers both within the French, German, Italian and Spanish banking markets and across their national boundaries. The approach adopted is similar to that of Shaffer (1992, 1993) where bank mergers are simulated and then hypothetical inputs and outputs for the merged institutions are put back into the estimated cost functions and predicted total costs are calculated for the hypothetically merged bank. These costs are then compared with the sum of the original predicted total costs for the individual banks which have been hypothetically merged. If the total costs for the hypothetically merged bank are less than those for the sum of the unmerged original banks then there is a hypothetical cost saving brought about by merger. The within-country merger simulations are based on the hybrid translog cost functions estimated in the previous chapter, whereas for the hypothetical European cross-border bank mergers we estimate a new cost function.

BRIEF OVERVIEW OF THE RECENT MERGER MOVEMENT IN BANKING MARKETS

Over the last three decades, business has become increasingly global. In manufacturing industry, development costs for products such as microchips, new drugs, automobiles and planes are so high that companies must serve worldwide markets to cover fixed costs, while economies of scale in production speed up the need for worldwide operations. Thus, as manufacturing and trade become global, service industry firms have been forced to become bigger, thus stimulating mergers within and across national boundaries.

During the 1980s, European banking and financial services markets have experienced major structural changes, including a significant reduction in the number of independent banking institutions. This change has partly been the result of the increased pace of bank mergers and acquisitions (see Bank of England, 1993; Lafferty Business Research, 1993). For instance, in Europe between 1984 and 1987 the annual averages were 99 deals in the banking sector and 42 in insurance (Lafferty Business Research, 1993). However, in 1988 these figures almost doubled. Roughly half of the European banking deals were between institutions in their own domestic markets, and a quarter each were attributable to intra-Community and other international deals. Within the EU, Table 8.1 shows that there was a considerable increase in both the number of domestic bank mergers and acquisitions of minority holdings during the late 1980s.

Substantial increases in cross-border activity within the EU was one of the most important characteristics of the restructuring process undergone by financial institutions during the late 1980s. Table 8.2 shows that the number of cross-border acquisitions in banking and insurance increased in the years between 1986 and 1990. Banking merger and acquisition activity revealed a gradual increase, whereas in the insurance sector the trend was less consistent.

Many of these mergers have been driven by new kinds of economic pressures and by the lifting of restrictive regulations that had previously isolated banks from

Table 8.1 Domestic banking mergers in the EU 1986−90 (including acquisitions of majority holdings)

Year	No. of mergers
1986−87	22
1987−88	53
1988−89	51
1989−90	65

Source: Lafferty Business Research (1993).

Table 8.2 Cross-border banking mergers and acquisitions in the EU 1986−90

Year	No. of mergers	
	Within EU institutions	EU and non-EU institutions
1986−87	3	10
1987−88	12	13
1988−89	16	16
1989−90	23	25
Total	54	64

Source: Lafferty Business Research (1993).

competition. By far the most important structural change has been the introduction of the EU's single market programme, which has generated both defensive and offensive strategies. Firstly, financial institutions are strengthening defensively their home position in order to meet the competitive challenges arising from other domestic and foreign contenders. Secondly, many institutions have taken advantage of the more liberal environment by expanding offensively into foreign markets. With the advent of the single market in financial services, there has been a tendency for financial institutions to increase their size to match the larger 'European single market'. The onset of financial liberalisation and deregulation coupled with the single market programme in Europe led to an increase in the number of institutions merging either within domestic markets or across borders. Perhaps the most significant structural change affecting European banking has been the trend towards abolition of exchange control regulations. Other important changes have included the removal of legal barriers and administrative regulations, allowing mergers, acquisitions and other alliances to take place, both within domestic markets and across national frontiers. Continuing economic and deregulatory forces have prompted further mergers during the 1990s.

Changes in legislation, regulation and competition in banking as well as general economic conditions have affected the profitability of European banks in recent years and the following forces also appear to have increased the incentive for banks to merge:

1. Banks face new competition from both financial and non-financial firms. Non-bank financial institutions can now offer services and compete with banks' transaction accounts and traditional bank lending markets. Moreover, a number of types of institutions can compete with banks in the production of financial services, such as mutual funds.

2. Banks have lost their monopoly on offering consumer savings accounts. In Europe, interest rates on consumer time and savings accounts have been deregulated. Banks have had to offer interest-bearing accounts to compete with unregulated and booming money-market funds and other investment media. As a result, the growing consumer demand for non-bank investment media (brought about by low nominal interest rates) has increasingly affected banks' profitability.

3. The position of banks as credit-granting intermediaries has been corroded by alternative lower-cost forms of credit extension.

MOTIVES FOR MERGING

There are many reasons why a corporation may wish to merge. This section will only discuss which are the most relevant to banks, because a full discussion of this topic lies outside the scope of this chapter. Gitman (1991) and Brigham

(1991) have stated that the primary goal of a merger is to maximise the owner's wealth as reflected in the acquirer's share price. Moreover, specific motives, which include benefits such as growth or diversification, synergy, economies from increased managerial skill or technology, tax considerations, increased ownership liquidity, and maintaining control, should only be pursued when these are said to be consistent with owner wealth maximisation. Revell (1987, p. 26) lists the following motives for merger:

- to secure unrealised scale and scope economies;
- to carry out the rationalisation of branch networks;
- to enable the demands of large customers to be met;
- to match the size of other banks in international banking;
- to meet foreign bank competition in the domestic market;
- to achieve economies in investment for automation.

Banks that wish to expand may find that a merger can be used to achieve these objectives. Bank expansion may also be less costly through merger than through internal growth or diversification. In addition, a merger may reduce the number of competitors and also help reduce the risk associated with new products. Synergy is said to exist when a whole is greater than the sum of its parts ('2 plus 2 equals 5'). The synergistic benefits from bank merger are generally expected to result from four main sources:

1. operating scale economies, generally from cost reductions when two banks are combined;
2. financial economies, that could include a higher price/earning ratio, a lower cost of debt or a greater debt capacity;
3. differential management efficiency, which indicates that the management of one firm is relatively inefficient, so the profitability of the acquired assets could be improved by merger;
4. increased market power resulting from greater market share of merged institutions.

Humphrey (1985) pointed out that although scale and scope economies do not seem to exist for larger US banks, these institutions may merge for the following reasons:

1. Larger banks, in particular the money-centre institutions, appear to be able to operate (without strong regulatory interference) using greater leverage, i.e. cheaper deposits and debt per dollar of (expensive) equity capital.
2. Larger regional and money-centre banks face somewhat lower costs of purchased funds such as certificate deposits, Federal funds, Eurodollars. They also find it easier to raise large amounts of purchased funds.

3. Larger banks are seemingly better able to diversify their assets and reduce risk. They can offer a broader range of services to customers and play a role in both domestic and international markets.

4. Larger banks have higher levels of executive compensation than their smaller counterparts.

The first three motives (greater leverage, lower cost of purchased funds, and risk and product diversification) should all result in higher profits, and hence represent a logical reason for merging and becoming larger. Of course, this may not apply in the fourth case.

Mergers may bring about improvement in net interest margins, because merged banks may be able to realise economies of scale in holdings of cash (e.g. cash and deposits at other banks) and in securities held as liquid assets. For example, if a smaller organisation is combined with a larger bank, the proportion of short-term securities and other liquid assets might fall since large banks tend to hold lower liquidity ratios than smaller banks. It also may result in external funds being raised at a lower cost. By decreasing holdings of cash and/or securities, management could move funds from non- or low-interest-earning to higher-return assets, i.e. from cash to loans and securities.

A larger or dominant bank may have a more aggressive or sophisticated products and services pricing structure for products and services, which might improve both interest and non-interest income. Furthermore, it is also possible that a merger may give rise to a repricing of some types of loans, deposit accounts and bank services at the acquired bank in an attempt to improve profitability. *Ceteris paribus*, changes in loan and deposit pricing may result in higher net income/assets ratios; and increases in fees (i.e. deposit service charges) may also increase the bank's ratio of non-interest income to assets.

Additionally, mergers may allow the dominant bank to enjoy economies of scope by distributing a range of products through the newly combined network system. This can also improve the ratio of both net interest and non-interest income to assets. On the other hand, a bank merger could potentially reduce non-interest expense/assets by consolidating back office operations and information systems. These economies may result from a reduction in staff numbers, sharing computer hardware and software or/and improving back office productivity. Merging banks could achieve economies of scale in marketing activities, e.g. product development and advertising. Mergers might also create opportunities to eliminate redundant management positions or to close overlapping branch networks.

PREVIOUS STUDIES

Studies of bank mergers can be classified into two broad groups of literature. The first group examine the financial implications of actual mergers by analysing financial ratios and stock prices. For exposition purposes we term these the event-day bank merger studies. The second group use cost function analysis to analyse the cost implications of simulated bank mergers. These we call the cost function studies.

Event-day Bank Merger Studies

The majority of studies which investigate bank mergers tend to be of an event-day nature, where actual mergers are investigated. The studies investigate pre-merger and post-merger financial ratios and stock prices to identify changes in corporate behaviour.

Rhoades (1986) used an extensive US sample of 413 acquired banks and 3600 non-acquired banks, over the years 1968–84, to examine pre- and post-merger performance. The findings provide no indication that the performance of the average acquired firm improved after the merger. His later study (1990) compared a sample of 68 acquired firms and 322 non-acquired large banking organisations (banks with assets exceeding $1 billion) between 1981 and 1987 to determine whether acquired firms tend to be poor performers. The results showed that acquired firms were not necessarily poor performers before acquisition and that their post-acquisition performance did not necessarily differ from that of other firms.

Boyd and Graham (1988) analysed the effects of bank holding company (BHC) expansion into prohibited business areas by simulating mergers between actual BHCs and non-bank firms, using data for 249 publicly traded bank and non-bank financial firms during 1971–84. Their merger simulations indicated that when BHCs combine with securities firms or real estate developers, the volatility of returns increased as did the risk of failure, whereas combinations of BHCs and life insurance companies seemed to reduce both the volatility of returns and the risk of failure.

Spindt and Tarhan (1992) analysed the broader issue of the profitability of bank mergers. The authors focused on US bank mergers which occurred in 1986, comparing bank performance two years before and two years after each merger to a matched pair of banks that did not merge over the five-year period, 1984–88. The results indicate that independent target banks typically underperformed the comparison group in the pre-merger period. Spindt and Tarhan also found that the combined institutions generally increased their ROE (return on equity) after merger.

Cornett and Tehranian (1992) examined the post-acquisition performance of large bank mergers between 1982 and 1987. They found that the merged banks experienced greater improvements in their corporate performance than the US banking industry as a whole. This seemed to be due, at least partly, to the merged banks' greater ability to attract loans and deposits per dollar of equity, as well as to the resultant improved employee productivity and assets growth. This study also found significant correlations between the abnormal announcement-period stock returns and various performance measures, indicating that the market anticipates improved performance of the merged bank when acquisitions are announced.

Linder and Crane (1992) examined changes in non-interest expenses for New England bank mergers during the period 1982–87. They found that there was a significant reduction in non-interest expenses as a proportion of total expenses after merger. Their findings also suggested that cost savings did not result in significant increases in operating profits.

Srinivasan and Wall (1992) analysed the impact on operating efficiency of merging BHCs. The authors examined the ratio of operating expenses to assets of BHCs involved in mergers for the period 1982–86. They found that the operating expense ratios of holding companies involved in any kind of merger started out significantly 'more efficient' than a national composite of banking organisations that did not merge during this period. The median operating cost ratios for the 'merging' holding companies then rose significantly after the merger and ended up closer to the median of the national composite.

Srinivasan (1992) used the same sample as Srinivasan and Wall (1992) to examine merger-related changes in non-interest expenses for US BHCs. The study focused on the ratio of non-interest expenses to the sum of net interest income and non-interest revenue. The study found that the non-interest expense ratio for the acquirer declined significantly after the merger.

Recently, Rhoades (1993) conducted tests to determine whether there was an increase in efficiency, as measured by various expense-to-assets ratios, of merged banks relative to other banks. This study examined the efficiency effects of a sample of 898 horizontal bank mergers and acquisitions in the USA between 1981 and 1986. Rhoades found that horizontal bank mergers did not have a significant effect on efficiency relative to other banks. Moreover, a greater degree of deposit overlap between merging banks had no impact on bank efficiency. The results also suggested that, in general, acquiring banks were more efficient than target banks.

Most of the studies cited above conclude that no major benefits occur from merger on the cost side, although Cornett and Tehranian (1992) and Spindt and Tarhan (1992) find various benefits on the revenue or output side.

Cost and Profit Function Bank Merger Studies

The second group of studies use mainly cost or profit function analyses to investigate the implications of bank mergers. The main US cost function studies have been undertaken by Savage (1991), Shaffer (1992, 1993), Berger and Humphrey (1992b), Murphy (1992) and Rhoades (1993), whereas the only profit function merger analysis has been undertaken by Akhavein, Berger and Humphrey (1994). Fixler and Zieschang (1993) take a different approach and evaluate productivity changes. As far as we are aware the only European cost efficiency bank merger analysis has been undertaken by Revell (1987) and Berg (1992).

Savage (1991) measured the potential cost savings associated with mergers resulting from closures of branches in overlapping markets using a sample of 41 US large banks. The results of his merger simulations between banks with at least 200 branches suggested that, if the two largest banks in the same state closed one-half of their branches in overlapping markets, then the total number of branches in the United States would be reduced by only 2.7%. He concluded that the cost savings that may be achieved by mergers and branch consolidations are relatively small.

Shaffer (1992) estimated a hybrid translog cost function and used the parameters to calculate the cost savings associated with simulated bank mergers. Cost function parameters were estimated for the period 1984–89 for US banks with assets in excess of $1 billion. The data in the analysis represented 57% of all US banking assets as of 1988. Quarterly Call Reports from March 1984 to June 1989 comprised the source of data, providing a total of 4426 observations in a pooled cross-section time-series dataset. The effect on bank costs of the hypothetical mergers was measured by comparing predicted costs of the two banks as unmerged banks with the predicted costs of the merged entity. Shaffer (1992) found that while 45% of the simulated mergers showed a reduction in costs (with 19% revealing savings greater than 10%), the majority of the mergers were predicted to increase cost. This was particularly true for the largest bank mergers (with assets of more than $10 billion); Shaffer's results also indicate that any mergers between large banks should be chosen carefully on the basis of economic fundamentals, not randomly.

Murphy (1992) conducted two merger simulations using an estimated translog cost function for data obtained from the Federal Reserve's Functional Cost Analysis (FCA) programme for the years 1987, 1988 and 1989. He examined the magnitude of savings brought about by acquiring a failed-bank deposit franchise and subsequently closing some of the failed banks' branches. By simulating mergers between operating and failed banks, he showed that the closure of branches, after acquisition, led to a reduction in cost.

Berger and Humphrey (1992b) use the distribution-free frontier method to determine the efficiency effects of actual bank mergers. Their comprehensive study found very small, statistically insignificant, average X-efficiency benefits from mergers among banks with over $1 billion in asset size. They also found that there were no efficiency gains associated with mergers in which the acquirer was more efficient than the acquired bank or in which both banks were represented in the same local market.

Rhoades (1993) follows on a similar theme and investigates whether banks involved in horizontal (within-market) mergers achieve efficiency improvement relative to other firms. The analysis covered 898 US bank mergers from 1981 to 1986. Efficiency is measured by various expense ratios and the study uses OLS and logit analyses to investigate changes in the ratios of merged and other banks from the pre- to post-merger period. Rhoades finds that horizontal bank mergers did not yield efficiency gains. Despite the fact that this study predominantly focused on small bank mergers, the findings are similar to studies based on only large mergers such as Berger and Humphrey (1992).

Shaffer (1993) employs a different approach. Instead of evaluating the efficiency effects of actual mergers, he attempts to examine the potential for efficiency gains and losses. He extends his earlier study using the stochastic 'thick frontier' approach to simulate the potential effects of scale and product mix, branch closure and X-efficiency changes on the impact of mergers on bank costs. After estimating a cost function he simulates over 20 000 random merger pairings among 210 banks with over $1 billion in assets. He finds that scale and product mix effects, as well as some assumed closings of the branches of acquired banks, will have only a negligible effect on total costs (less than 2% on average), whereas X-efficiency gains or losses have the potential for being large. For example, if the banks in the most efficient quartile acquire other banks, the predicted cost savings are as much as 21% if the managerial efficiencies can be transferred to the acquired component of the bank. Of course if the opposite occurs there is potential for 21% efficiency losses.

Fixler and Zieschang (1993) use a non-standard efficiency measure — Tornquist productivity indices — constructed for every bank in their sample. For each bank productivity is measured by a value-weighted output index divided by a value-weighted input index. Overall they find that acquiring banks are about 40–50% more efficient than other banks prior to merging and that they continue to have the same advantage over other banks years after the merger. Berger, Hunter and Timme (1993) note that this finding contrasts with the results of the cost studies of bank mergers and this is possibly because they include revenue effects in their output index as well as costs in their input index. It may well be the case that output or revenue efficiencies are more important than input or cost efficiencies relating to bank mergers.

Akhavein, Berger and Humphrey (1994) develop this idea by examining profit efficiency of large US bank mergers during the 1980s. The study uses Berger's (1993) 'distribution free' frontier methodology on a sample of 57 'megamergers' between 1980 and 1990. Changes in the position of merging banks before and after a merger relative to the efficient frontier, and relative to non-merging banks, indicate a significant 16% increase in average profit efficiency rank. Overall, 'profit efficiency improvements were significantly associated with a somewhat more efficient bank acquiring and restructuring a less efficient institution and related to the relatively poor pre-merger performance of *both* merger partners' (Akhavein, Berger and Humphrey, 1994, p. 27).

Colwell and Davis (1992) have stressed the importance of the efficiency implications of bank mergers, yet there have only been two major studies in this area in the case of European banks. Revell (1987) reviewed historical merger and acquisitions among core banks in various European countries between 1958 and 1981 and concluded that beyond a certain point size was sought for reasons of competitive power. The study also concluded that mergers were far from being a certain way of increasing efficiency. Berg (1992) adopts a more technical approach and uses DEA to compare input efficiencies and evaluates productivity growth for a sample of merging and non-merging Norwegian banks between 1984 and 1990. He finds that mergers have little effect on bank input efficiency and that there are indications that productivity setbacks are experienced when mergers take place.

Other studies such as Molyneux (1991) and Bank of England (1993) have examined cross-border activity in European banking markets but have not examined the cost implications of bank mergers. Using our cost function estimates from previous chapters, we use a similar approach to Shaffer (1992, 1993) to estimate the cost implications of hypothetical bank mergers in European banking markets.

METHODOLOGY AND MERGERS SIMULATION

The following analysis examines hypothetical mergers between banks in four countries: France, Germany, Italy and Spain. We also examine hypothetical mergers across national boundaries. The present study is based on various simplifying assumptions that have also been adopted by Boyd and Graham (1988, 1991) and Shaffer (1992, 1993). It is assumed that the merged bank is simply the sum of two individual banks. Except for input prices, the total assets, loans, securities and branches are consolidated and input prices are taken as the means of those for two individual banks. This approach also assumes that there are no further cost synergies resulting from a restructuring of the product mix and the merged portfolio, and that the hypothetical merger in the model does not shift either bank closer to the production frontier in cases where ex-ante allocative or technical inefficiency existed. Furthermore, the model also assumes that there are no branch closures by the merged bank even if both banks are operating in the same market. Obviously, this assumption may cause us to understate the potential reduction in cost. The assumption of no branch closures is probably reasonable for mergers between banks from different countries; however, mergers between the largest banks within a domestic market would usually be expected to involve substantial consolidation of overlapping branch networks (see Savage, 1991). Mergers within domestic markets might therefore be expected to reduce cost by a greater proportion than cross-border mergers, because of the potential for rationalisation of overlapping branch networks.

The criteria we use for simulating hypothetical mergers is straightforward. For the domestic market mergers, all banks with assets exceeding $1 billion in 1988 are hypothetically merged. For instance, in our sample, the number of banks with asset size over $1 billion are 88, 128, 71 and 84 and the possible number of hypothetical merger cases are 3828, 8128, 2485 and 3486 for France, Germany, Italy and Spain, respectively.

We use the hybrid translog cost functions estimated for France, Germany, Italy and Spain in 1988 to evaluate whether there are cost savings from large bank mergers within those countries. For each hypothetical merger, the sum of predicted costs for the separate unmerged banks (which are calculated by inserting values of regressors from each individual bank into the relevant estimated cost functions) is compared with the predicted costs for the hypothetical merged banks. If the figure for the sum of predicted total costs for the separate banks exceeds the hypothetical post-merger predicted total cost, the model implies that the merger of that given pair, if carried out, would make possible a reduction of total costs.

For the hypothetical European cross-border mergers we focus only on European megabanks. We estimate a European hybrid translog cost function (with exactly the same specifications as those for the individual country estimates) using 1988 data on French, German, Italian and Spanish banks combined. The sample is the 371 banks from these countries which have total assets of more than $1 billion. The hypothetical merger simulations are carried out for banks with assets over $5 billion. The total number of banks amounts to 124, generating 7626 possible hypothetical merged pairings of banks. We identify cost savings resulting from hypothetical mergers in the same way as the country mergers described above.

RESULTS

Results for Individual Countries

Table 8.3 shows that the average merger yielded a 0.912% decrease in the predicted total cost for Spanish banks whereas for France, Germany and Italy, the average merger generated a 2.098, 0.082 and 4.585% increase in the predicted total cost respectively. These findings are consistent with the economies of scale results reported in Chapter 7.

Table 8.4 shows that in Italy, 93.96% of possible pairs (2335 out of 2485), and in France 67.14% of possible pairs (2570 out of 3828) cause an increase in total costs. However, 56% of the possible bank pairings (4552 out of 8128)

Table 8.3 Summary statistics for hypothetical mergers

	France	Germany	Italy	Spain
No. of pairs	3828	8128	2485	3486
Mean	2.098	0.082	4.585	−0.912
Minimum	−16.749	−56.695	−3.835	−30.968
Maximum	22.067	72.957	16.054	32.826

Note: A negative value shows cost reduction while a positive value indicates cost increasing in percentage.

Table 8.4 Distribution of cost-saving and cost-increasing hypothetical mergers

	France		Germany		Italy		Spain	
	No.	%	No.	%	No.	%	No.	%
Cost saving	1258	32.86	4552	56.0	150	6.04	1825	52.37
Cost increase	2570	67.14	3576	44.0	2335	93.96	1661	47.63
Total	3828	100	8128	100	2485	100	3486	100

in Germany and 52.37% of possible bank pairings (1825 out of 3486) in Spain cause a reduction in total cost. These results illustrate the lack of opportunity for cost savings between larger banks in Italy compared with the other three banking systems.

Table 8.5 provides descriptive statistics for all hypothetical bank mergers which yielded cost reductions. The largest cost savings occurred in Germany, followed by Spain, France and Italy. Substantial cost savings appear to be achievable through hypothetical mergers between megabanks in Germany. Although not shown in the table, the 28 German banks in 1988 with assets of more than $10 billion allow 378 possible pairings, all of which would show a decrease in costs ranging from 0.373 to 42.654%. Table 8.6 shows the number of pairs which have hypothetical cost savings exceeding 5, 10 and 25%. In Germany, 57% of cost-saving pairings (2595 out of 4552) cause an improvement of more than 10%, compared with 44.2% and 8.66% (807 and 109 pairs) in Spain and France respectively. No substantial cost savings over 5 or 10% appear to occur through hypothetical big-bank mergers in the Italian banking markets. This indicates that cost savings resulting from hypothetical mergers appear to be relatively larger in the German and Spanish banking markets than in other countries.

Table 8.5 Descriptive statistics on cost-saving hypothetical mergers

	France	Germany	Italy	Spain
No. of pairs	1258	4552	150	1825
Mean	4.227	12.688	1.048	9.300
Minimum	0.005	0.004	0.002	0.007
Maximum	16.749	56.695	3.835	30.968

Table 8.6 Distribution of cost-saving hypothetical mergers

Reduction in costs	France		Germany		Italy		Spain	
	No.	%	No.	%	No.	%	No.	%
> 25%	—	—	387	8.50	—	—	12	0.66
> 10%	109	8.66	2595	57.00	—	—	807	44.22
> 5%	430	34.18	3622	79.57	—	—	1302	71.35

Tables 8.7(a)–(d) show the hypothetical mergers between large banks in the French, German, Italian and Spanish banking markets respectively which create the largest savings. For France (Table 8.7(a)), the largest cost savings are generated by the merger of the central organisation of two very large mutual and cooperative sectors: Crédit Mutuel and Groupe des Banques Populaires. Around 3000 local associations operate within the Crédit Mutuel group. These are organised on a mutual basis, but do not generally specialise by sector. The Banques Populaires also have mutual status although nowadays the activities of these banks are similar to those of commercial banks. The majority of large cost savings are created by hypothetical mergers between these institutions (Crédit Mutuel and Groupe des Banques Populaires) and smaller specialised private or investment banks. These combinations, however, seem unrealistic, given the different ownership characteristics and business mixes of the types of institutions. They do indicate, however, that there are opportunities for substantial cost savings through banks merging, albeit through unusual combinations.

For Germany (Table 8.7(b)), there appear to be substantial cost savings resulting from hypothetical bank mergers. These again appear to be generated by markedly different institutions merging. For example, the largest cost saving, 56.695%, is created by the hypothetical merger

Table 8.7(a)   The largest hypothetical cost savings for French bank mergers

Hypothetical bank merger pairs	Change (%)
Crédit Mutuel/Groupe des Banques Populaires	16.749
Banque Stern[a]/Groupe des Banques Populaires	15.985
Banque Stern/Crédit Mutuel	15.931
Cetelem/Groupe des Banques Populaires	15.168
Cetelem/Crédit Mutuel	15.159
Banque OBC-Odier Bungener/Groupe des Banques Populaires	15.112
Banque OBC-Odier Bungener/Crédit Mutuel	15.103
Banque Dumenil-Leble/Crédit Mutuel	14.538
Banque Dumenil-Leble/Groupe des Banques Populaires	14.533
Banque Française du Commerce Extérieur/Crédit Mutuel	14.109
Banque Française du Commerce Extérieur/Groupe des Banques Populaires	14.100
Union Industrielle de Crédit/Crédit Mutuel	14.060
Union Industrielle de Crédit/Groupe des Banques Populaires	14.046
Banque Stern/Cetelem	13.260
Banque Stern/Banque OBC-Odier Bungener	12.671
Banque OBC-Odier Bungener/Cetelem	12.319
Banque Française du Commerce Extérieur/Banque Stern	12.112
Banque Française du Commerce Extérieur/Cetelem	11.961
Banque Française du Commerce Extérieur/Banque OBC-Odier Bungener	11.393
Credisuez/Cetelem	11.255

[a]On 19 June 1992 merged with Banque Pallas Farance and name changed to Banque Pallas Stern.

Table 8.7(b)   The largest hypothetical cost savings for German bank mergers

Hypothetical bank merger pairs	Change (%)
Südwestdeutsche Genossenschafts-Zentralbank/SchmidtBank	56.695
Genossenschaftliche Zentralbank-Stuttgart/Schmidtbank	52.697
Genossenschaftliche Ze.-Stuttgart/Südwestdeutsche Genossenschafts-Zentralbank	51.324
DG Bank/Südwestdeutsche Genossenschafts-Zentralbank	42.654
DG Bank/Schmidtbank	42.096
Baden-Württemdergischebank/Südwestdeutsche Genossenschafts-Zentralbank	41.928
Baden-Württemdergischebank/Schmidtbank	40.737
Südwestdeutsche Genossenschafts-Zentralbank/Rheinische Hypothekenbank	39.626
Baden-Württemdergischebank/Genossenschaftliche Zentralbank-Stuttgart	39.215
Stadtsparkasse München/Südwestdeutsche Genossenschafts-Zentralbank	38.803
Nassauische Sparkasse/Südwestdeutsche Genossenschafts-Zentralbank	38.548
Sparkasse Krefeld/Südwestdeutsche Genossenschafts-Zentralbank	38.316
Sparkasse Pforzheim/Südwestdeutsche Genossenschafts-Zentralbank	38.171
Rheinische Hypothekenbank/Genossenschaftliche Zentralbank-Stuttgart	37.759
Stadtsparkasse München/Genossenschaftliche Zentralbank-Stuttgart	36.818
Nassauische Sparkasse/Genossenschaftliche Zentralbank-Stuttgart	36.517
Stadtsparkasse Düsseldorf/Südwestdeutsche Genossenschafts-Zentralbank	36.422
Sparkasse Krefeld/Genossenschaftliche Zentralbank-Stuttgart	36.301
Sparkasse Pforzheim/Genossenschaftliche Zentralbank-Stuttgart	35.992
Hamburger Sparkasse/Genossenschaftliche Zentralbank-Stuttgart	35.889
Südwestdeutsche Genossenschafts-Zentralbank/Dresdner Bank	35.763

between Südwestdeutsche Genossenschafts-Zentralbank and SchmidtBank. Südwestdeutsche Genossenschafts-Zentralbank is a regional credit cooperative institution which operates as a clearing house to cooperative banks, enabling them to provide a universal banking service. SchmidtBank is a private commercial bank which provides banking services to wealthy customers. Both institutions have small branch networks and their businesses are primarily specialist. It is unlikely that a merger between the two institutions would result in the cost savings predicted because their production functions are so different. Other large cost savings result from hypothetical mergers between commercial banks and regional cooperative banks, and between savings and mortgage banks. For example, the hypothetical merger between the sixth largest commercial bank, DG Bank, and Südwestdeutsche Genossenschafts-Zentralbank generates a 42.654% reduction in predicted total cost. Moreover, hypothetical mergers between savings banks (e.g. Stadtsparkasse München, Nassauische Sparkasse, Sparkasse Krefeld) and cooperative banks generate substantial cost savings. Savings banks are very important in Germany (rivalling commercial banks) and are mainly municipal or district banks operating in specific geographical areas. Various laws govern the operations of savings banks, which aim to encourage savings and giro transactions, to provide credit for low- and middle-income households and to serve the financial requirements of local communities. Savings banks are also owned primarily by local or regional governments (see Revell, 1987). Other large cost savings results appear for hypothetical mergers between mortgage banks (such as Rheinische Hypothekenbanken) and cooperative banks. In general, the largest cost savings are generated by hypothetical pairings which seem unrealistic in practice, although we will show later that hypothetical mergers between the largest German commercial banks also generate substantial cost savings.

In Italy (Table 8.7(c)), the predicted cost savings are relatively small. The largest saving results from a merger between two savings banks: Cassa di Risparmio di Ravenna and Cassa di Risparmio di Verona Vicenza Belluno. Thereafter the cost savings come from hypothetical mergers between commercial banks and savings banks such as Cassa di Risparmio di Ravenna and Banco di Santo Spirito. On 1 August 1992 the latter merged with Banco di Roma, and the name changed to Banca di Roma whose hypothetical merger generates a 3.642% reduction in predicted total cost. It is noteworthy that the following banks appear in most cost-saving pairings: Cassa di Risparmio di Ravenna, Cassa di Risparmio di Verona Vicenza Belluno and Credito Italiano, perhaps implying that these

Table 8.7(c)   The largest hypothetical cost savings for Italian bank mergers

Hypothetical bank merger pairs	Change (%)
Cassa di Risp di Ravenna/Cassa di Risp di Verona Vicenza Belluno	3.835
Cassa di Risp di Ravenna/Banco di Santo Spirito	3.642
Cassa di Risp di Ravenna/Credito Italiano	3.608
Cassa di Risp di Verona Vicenza Belluno/Credito Italiano	3.278
Banco di Santo Spirito/Cassa di Risp di Verona Vicenza Belluno	3.266
Banco di Santo Spirito/Credito Italiano	3.132
Cassa di Risp di Ravenna/Banca Toscana	2.616
Cassa di Risp di Ravenna/Banca di Credito Piemontese	2.542
Banca Toscana/Cassa di Risp di Verona Vicenza Belluno	2.301
Banca Toscana/Credito Italiano	2.286
Banca di Credito Piemontese/Cassa di Risp di Verona Vicenza Belluno	2.238
Banca di Credito Piemontese/Credito Italiano	2.232
Cassa di Risp di Ravenna/Credito Fondiario e Sez Opere Pubbliche	2.227
Cassa di Risp di Ravenna/Banco di Chiavari e della Riviera Ligure	2.187
Banco di Santo Spirito/Banca Toscana	2.125
Banca di Credito Piemontese/Banco di Santo Spirito	2.063
Cassa di Risp di Ravenna/Cassa di Risp di Reggio Emilia	2.017
Credito Fondiario e Sez Opere Pubbliche/Credito Italiano	2.007
Credito Fondiario e Sez Opere Pubbliche/Cassa di-Verona Vicenza Belluno	1.980
Banco di Chiavari e della Riviera Ligure/Credito Italiano	1.957

Table 8.7(d)   The largest hypothetical cost savings for Spanish bank mergers

Hypothetical bank merger pairs	Change (%)
Banco de Progreso/Caja de A. Y M. de del C.C.O. de Burgos	30.968
Banco de Progreso/Banco de Granada	29.920
Banco de Granada/Caja de A. Y M. de del C.C.O. de Burgos	29.865
Banco de Progreso/Caja de A. Provincial de Gerono	27.234
Caja de A. Y M. de del C.C.O. de Burgos/Caja de A. Provincial de Gerono	26.993
Banco de Progreso/Caja General de A. de Canarias	26.864
Caja de A. Y M. de del C.C.O. de Burgos/Caja General de A. de Canarias	26.603
Banco de Granada/Caja de A. Provincial de Gerono	25.816
Banco del Comercio/Banco de Progreso	25.559
Banco de Granada/Caja General de A. de Canarias	25.438
Banco de Progreso/Banco Natwest Espana	25.364
Banco del Comercio/Caja de A. Y M. de del C.C.O. de Burgos	25.217
Caja de A. Y M. de del C.C.O. de Burgos/Banco Natwest Espana	24.965
Banco de Progreso/Caja de A. Y Monte de Piedad de Extremadura	24.729
Banco de Progreso/Caja de A. de Jerez	24.501
Caja-Y Monte de Piedad de Extremadura/Caja-Y M. de del C.C.O. de Burgos	24.314
Caja de A. de Jerez/Caja de A. Y M. de del C.C.O. de Burgos	24.082
Banco del Comercio/Banco de Granada	24.028
Banca de Castilla/Banco de Progreso	23.846
Caja de A. de Murcia/Banco de Progreso	23.734

institutions are 'good' merger partners. In most cases it also appears that cost savings are generated by large banks merging with the smaller ones.

Finally, in Spain (Table 8.7(d)), it appears that substantial cost savings result from hypothetical mergers between investment banks and savings banks and between pairs of savings banks. The hypothetical merger between the investment bank, Banco de Progreso and the savings bank, Caja de Ahorros y Monte de Del CCO de Burgos, results in the largest saving of 30.968%, but is perhaps unlikely in reality. Mergers between savings banks such as Caja de Ahorros y Monte de Del CCO de Burgos and Caja de Ahorros Provincial de Gerono (26.993% cost saving) are perhaps more likely given their similar ownership, business strategy and production characteristics. Hypothetical mergers between commercial banks and savings banks (e.g. Banco de Granada and Caja de Ahorros y Monte de Del CCO de Burgos) also brought about noticeable cost savings (29.865%).

Tables 8.8 and 8.9 present analogous results for cost-increasing mergers. Descriptive statistics for hypothetical mergers which generated cost increases are shown for France, Germany, Italy and Spain in Table 8.8. For those hypothetical mergers which increased costs, the average increase was much higher in the German market than elsewhere. Furthermore, as Table 8.9 shows, for Germany, 59.84% (2140 out of 3576 pairs) of possible pairings exhibit an increase of

Table 8.8 Descriptive statistics on cost-increasing hypothetical mergers

	France	Germany	Italy	Spain
No. of pairs	2570	3576	2335	1661
Mean	5.195	16.335	4.947	8.327
Minimum	0.004	0.001	0.010	0.002
Maximum	22.087	72.957	16.054	32.826

Table 8.9 Distribution of cost-increasing hypothetical mergers

Increase in costs	France		Germany		Italy		Spain	
	No.	%	No.	%	No.	%	No.	%
> 50%	—	—	106	2.96	—	—	—	—
> 25%	—	—	776	21.70	—	—	18	1.08
> 10%	255	9.92	2140	59.84	161	6.90	567	34.14
> 5%	1163	45.25	2791	78.05	1006	43.08	1066	64.18

more than 10%, compared with 34.14, 9.92 and 6.90% (567, 255 and 161 pairs) in Spain, France and Italy, respectively. Some information, not shown in the tables, is of specific interest. For example, the hypothetical mergers among the 9 largest Spanish banks (with asset size over $10 billion) allow 36 possible pairings, which create cost increases ranging from 4.476 to 23.980%. In Germany, over 50% of cost increases result from mergers between banks with assets of less than $10 billion. As the size of the hypothetically merged bank increases, the percentage of mergers which increase costs becomes smaller. It seems that in Germany, large bank mergers reduce costs whereas small bank mergers increase costs.

Tables 8.10(a)–(d) show the hypothetical mergers between large banks in the French, German, Italian and Spanish banking markets respectively which create the largest cost increases.

In France (Table 8.10(a)), the 10 largest increases resulted from mergers between Electro Banque and other relatively small commercial, investment or cooperative banks. Electro Banque SA, with one branch, is a commercial bank owned by Alcatel Alsthom (98.32%) and is the telecommunications firm's banking company. It is clearly a specialist operation and is unlikely to merge with any of the suitors cited in Table 8.10(a). Below the Electro Banque mergers, the results are more varied and large cost increases appear to result from mergers between commercial banks (e.g. Banque de Bretagne, Banque Harvet) and other types of financial firms such as finance houses (i.e. SOVAC), investment banks (i.e. Banque Sofirec, Banque Internationale de Gestion et de Trésorerie, Crédit Industriel de Normandie) and public credit institutions (e.g. Union Industrielle Crédit). Overall, the results suggest that cost-increasing mergers resulted mainly from hypothetical link-ups between very specialist institutions and banks.

Table 8.10(a)   The largest hypothetical cost increases for French bank mergers

Hypothetical bank merger pairs	Change (%)
Union Française de Banques Locabail/Electro Banque	22.067
Banque de Bretagne/Electro Banque	21.507
Banque Sofirec/Electro Banque	21.445
Banque Régionale de l'Ouest/Electro Banque	20.970
Banque Intérnationale de Gestion et de Trésorerie/Electro Banque	20.938
Crédit Industriel de Normandie/Electro Banque	20.304
Banque du Crédit Mutuel Lorraine/Electro Banque	20.300
Société de Banque Occidentale/Electro Banque	20.214
Société Bordelaise de Crédit Ind. et Comm./Electro Banque	20.004
Union de Banques à Paris/Electro Banque	19.506
Banque Sofirec/Sovac	16.142
Banque de Bretagne/Sovac	16.062
Banque Sudameris/Union Industrielle Crédit	16.019
Banque du B T P/Banque Harvet	16.001
Banque Régionale de l'Ouest/Banque Harvet	15.356
Banque Sudameris/Banque Harvet	15.205
Banque du B T P/Banque Sofirec	14.675
Banque Sofirec/Banque de Bretagne	14.641
Banque de Bretagne/Banque du B T P	14.539
Banque Harvet/Banque Intérnationale de Gestion et de Trésorerie	14.443

For Germany (Table 8.10(b)), it is noticeable that the cost increases are very large. The largest increase, 72.957%, resulted from the merger between Berenberg Bank (an investment bank with two branches) and Deutsche Bank Saar (a commercial bank subsidiary of Deutsche Bank). The top cost-increasing mergers appear to be generated by mergers between specialist banks (private commercial banks, investment banks, mortgage banks) such as Berenberg Bank, Deutsche Bank Saar, Sal Oppenheim, Süddeutsche Bodencreditbank and Deutsche Hypothekenbank. In general, mergers that include mortgage banks (such as Süddeutsche Bodencreditbank, Rheinboden Hypothekenbank, Deutsche Hypothekenbank) create large cost increases, such as the merger between Süddeutsche Bodencreditbank and Deutsche Bank Saar which generated a 68.088% increase in predicted total cost. Overall, these results indicate that cost-increasing mergers resulted from hypothetical link-ups involving specialist institutions.

For Italy (Table 8.10(c)), the largest cost increase is generated by the hypothetical merger between Istituto Bancario San Paolo di Torino (a public commercial bank and the largest Italian bank in our sample in 1988) and Banca Popolare di Cremona (a cooperative bank). Moreover, Istituto Bancario San Paolo di Torino is a partner in 10 out of the 11 hypothetical mergers which create the largest increases in cost. There are cost-increasing hypothetical mergers between cooperative banks (e.g. Banca Popolare di Cremona, Banca Popolare di Ancona, Banca Popolare Udinese, Banca Popolare di Verona) and commercial banks (i.e.

Table 8.10(b) The largest hypothetical cost increases for German bank mergers

Hypothetical bank merger pairs	Change (%)
Berenberg Bank/Deutsche Bank Saar	72.957
Süddeutsche Bodencreditbank/Deutsche Bank Saar	68.088
Berenberg Bank/Süddeutsche Bodencreditbank	67.651
Deutsche Bank Saar/Rheinboden Hypothekenbank	64.669
Berenberg Bank/Rheinboden Hypothekenbank	64.223
BHW Bank/Deutsche Bank Saar	63.982
Sal Oppenheim/Deutsche Bank Saar	63.560
Deutsche Hypothekenbank/Deutsche Bank Saar	59.771
Deutsche Hypothekenbank/Berenberg Bank	59.359
Deutsche Hypothekenbank/Süddeutsche Bodencreditbank	57.817
Rheinboden Hypothekenbank/Deutsche Hypothekenbank	54.657
Hypothekenbank in Hamburg/Süddeutsche Bodencreditbank	52.764
Deutsche Hypothekenbank/Sal Oppenheim	52.717
Deutsche Schiffsbank/Deutsche Bank Saar	52.403
Berenberg Bank/Deutsche Schiffsbank	51.980
Deutsche Bank Saar/Ulmer Volksbank	51.946
Deutsche Schiffsbank/Süddeutsche Bodencreditbank	51.748
Berenberg Bank/Ulmer Volksbank	51.487
Süddeutsche Bodencreditbank/Ulmer Volksbank	51.339
Süddeutsche Bodencreditbank/Württembergischebank Hypothekenbank	50.764

Table 8.10(c) The largest hypothetical cost increases for Italian bank mergers

Hypothetical bank merger pairs	Change (%)
Banca Popolare di Cremona/Istituto Bancario San Paolo di Torino	16.054
Cassa di Risp della Pr. di Teramo/Istituto Bancario San Paolo di Torino	15.788
Cassa di Risp di San Miniato/Istituto Bancario San Paolo di Torino	15.533
Cassa di Risp di Fermo/Istituto Bancario San Paolo di Torino	15.459
Credito Lombardo/Istituto Bancario San Paolo di Torino	15.320
Banco San Paolo di Brescia/Istituto Bancario San Paolo di Torino	14.849
Banca Popolare di Ancona/Istituto Bancario San Paolo di Torino	14.678
Cassa di Risp Della Provincia di Teramo/Banca Emiliana	14.677
Istituto Bancario San Paolo di Torino/Banca Agric. Pop di Ragusa	14.489
Istituto Bancario San Paolo di Torino/Banca Popolare Udinese	14.443
Istituto Bancario San Paolo di Torino/Cassa di Risp di Rimini	14.410
Cassa di Risp di San Miniato/Banca Emiliana	14.355
Cassa di Risp di Fermo/Banca Emiliana	14.179
Banca di Piacenza/Istituto Bancario San Paolo di Torino	14.172
Credito Lombardo/Banca Emiliana	14.041
Cassa di Risp della Provincia di Teramo/Cassa di Risp di San Miniato	14.002
Banca del Monte di Parma/Istituto Bancario San Paolo di Torino	13.864
Cassa di Risp della Provincia di Teramo/Cassa di Risp di Fermo	13.809
Cassa di Risp della Provincia di Teramo/Credito Lombardo	13.688
Banca Emiliana/Banca Popolare di Verona	13.257

Istituto Bancario San Paolo di Torino, Credito Lombardo, Banca Emiliana) as well as between savings banks (for example, Cassa di Risparmio della Provincia di Teramo, Cassa di Risparmio di San Miniato, Cassa di Risparmio di Fermo) and commercial banks. Overall, the results for Italy suggest that mergers are much more likely to result in cost increases than cost savings.

For Spain (Table 8.10(d)), the biggest cost increases are found for mergers between commercial banks and specialist investment banks: e.g. between Banca Catalana and Banco Industriel de Bilbao, the hypothetical merger generated a 32.826% increase in predicted total cost. Other significant pairings are between commercial banks (combinations between Banco de Santander, Bankinter, Banco Pastor, Banca Catalana) or savings banks (combinations between Caja de Ahorros y Monte de Piedad de Madrid). The results suggest that cost-increasing mergers are generated by link-ups between commercial banks which have a strong regional focus. In these cases there are no branch overlaps after the merger, perhaps suggesting that the cost estimates are not generally overstated. Recent big-bank mergers that have occurred in the Spanish market, between Banco Industriel de Bilbao and Banco de Vicaya in 1988 and Banco Central and Banco Hispano Americano in 1992 (Morgan Stanley, 1990, 1993b) have led to increases in cost, despite the merged banks being able to shed substantial branch numbers. However, cost savings may still arise from the long-term restructuring of these organisations. In Spain, mergers between large banks have been supported and encouraged by the government which sees the need for Spanish banks to become

Table 8.10(d)   The largest hypothetical cost increases for Spanish bank mergers

Hypothetical bank merger pairs	Change (%)
Banco Catalana/Banco Industriel de Bilbao	32.826
Banco de Santander/Banco Industriel de Bilbao	32.240
Bankinter/Banco Industriel de Bilbao	32.211
Banco Pastor/Banco Industriel de Bilbao	31.120
Bankinter/Banco Catalana	26.261
Banco de Santander/Banco Catalana	26.240
Banco Pastor/Banco Catalana	25.600
Banco Pastor/Banco de Santander	25.219
Banco Catalana/Caja de A. Y Monte de Piedad de Madrid	24.951
Banco de Pastor/Bankinter	24.580
Banco de Santander/Bankinter	24.545
Bankinter/Caja de A. Y Monte de Piedad de Madrid	24.018
Banco de Santander/Caja de A. Y Monte de Piedad de Madrid	23.984
Banca Catalana/Banco Arabe Espanol	23.652
Banca Catalana/Banco Central	23.532
Banco Pastor/Caja de A. Y Monte de Piedad de Madrid	23.491
Banca Catalana/Banco del Comercio	23.330
Banca Catalana/Banco Atlantico	23.251
Bankinter/Banco Central	22.496
Banco Central/Banco Hispano Americano	22.453

larger if they are to compete in Europe and take up the advantage of the opportunities offered by the EU single market programme (see Lloyd-Williams, Molyneux and Thornton, 1994).

Overall, the results from Tables 8.5–8.10 suggest that mergers between large banks within domestic banking markets can generate substantial cost savings or increases depending on the merger partners. In general, opportunities for cost-saving mergers appear greater in Germany and Spain than in France and Italy. In fact the prospects for cost-saving mergers in Italy, based on our analysis, look relatively thin. In addition, the biggest cost savings and cost increases are generated by hypothetical mergers (in most cases) between quite different banking organisations. Such mergers would be unlikely in practice. Given these findings, the following section aims to evaluate the cost implications of more selective bank mergers.

Predicted Cost of Selected Bank Mergers

The following examines the effects of hypothetical mergers among the 20 largest banks (generally with assets greater than $10 billion) on total cost in France, Germany, Italy and Spain. The results are reported in Tables 8.11(a)–(d) respectively. In general, the results suggest that as in the previous analysis, the cost implications of merger depend very much upon the partner chosen.

In France (Table 8.11(a)), mergers involving large banks such as Banque Paribas, Cie Financière Cic et de l'Union Européenne, Groupe des Banques Populaires, Crédit Mutuel, Banque Française du Commerce Extérieur, and Credisuez generally cause a reduction in predicted total cost when the merger partner is either a similar sized or a larger bank. For example, the greatest cost saving for French banks results from the hypothetical merger between Groupe des Banques Populaires and Crédit Mutuel, which generates a 16.75% fall in total cost. The second largest cost saving results from the hypothetical merger between Crédit Mutuel and Banque Française du Commerce Extérieur. On the other hand, a hypothetical merger between the largest two banks Crédit Agricole and Banque Nationale de Paris results in a 4.36% increase in predicted total cost. It appears that Crédit Agricole, Banque Nationale de Paris, Crédit Lyonnais, Société Générale, Compagnie Bancaire and Crédit Local de France are not good merger partners. This might relate to the state ownership characteristics of Banque Nationale de Paris, Crédit Lyonnais and Société Générale, which may have pursued non-profit-maximising objectives in 1988, when they were still fully nationalised.

De Boissieu (1990) has argued that French banks have been operating in a relatively protected environment, which has relieved them from some pressures to minimise costs, has created certain patterns of expense-preference behaviour, and has caused X-efficiency to emerge and become extensive. As a result, in addition to possible risk avoidance, imperfect competition has led to overstaffing, large

Table 8.11(a)   The effect of hypothetical mergers on predicted cost for specific pairs among the largest top 20 French banks

Name of bank pairs	Change[a] (%)
Crédit Agricole/BNP	4.36
BNP/Crédit Lyonnais	3.84
Crédit Lyonnais/Société Générale	4.22
Société Générale/Banque Paribas	1.83
Banque Paribas/Cie Financière	4.02
Cie Financière/Banque Worms	8.40
Groupe des Banques Populaires/Crédit Mutuel	−16.75
Crédit Mutuel/Banque Française du Commerce	−14.11
Crédit Foncier France/Credisuez	−4.41
Banque Indosuez/Cie Financière	5.93
Banque Française du Commerce/Credisuez	−10.75
Crédit Commercial de France/Crédit du Nord	3.62
Compagnie Bancaire/Crédit Mutuel	−10.41
Crédit Local de France/Sogenal	−1.89
Crédit Industriel ET/Crédit Agricole	5.58
Crédit du Nord/BNP	3.55
Caisse Centrale des Banques/Credisuez	−3.31
Sogenal/Groupe des Banques Populaires	−10.60
Banque Worms/Banque Française du Commerce	−4.18
Credisuez/Sogenal	−6.89

[a]Percentage change in predicted cost due to merger. Negative values indicate cost reductions while positive values indicate an increase in cost.

branch networks, slack in organisational structures and, consequently, inefficient use of resources. All this suggests that there are substantial opportunities to reduce costs through consolidation in the French market. However, for French banks, cost reduction through big-bank merger may be relatively problematic because, as Morgan Stanley (1993a) have pointed out, the prospects for rationalisation of the domestic retail network are severely limited in practice because of legal and other commitments to the powerful French trade unions. French bank expense ratios, which have remained generally in the 70–75% range in recent years for major retail banks, require a significant change in the legal environment or in labour union laws to fall significantly in the foreseeable future.

From Table 8.11(b) it can be seen that hypothetical pairings among the largest German banks create substantial cost savings. The marriages between Deutsche Bank and Dresdner Bank, Dresdner Bank and Commerzbank, Commerzbank and Bayerische Vereinsbank and Hypo-bank and DG Bank resulted in 25.26, 25.47, 22.96 and 25.04% decreases in predicted cost. However, the simulation between Berliner Bank and Deutsche Centralbodencredit-AG, Depfa-Bank and Deutsche Hypothekenbank Frankfurt, and Landwirtschaftliche Rentenbank and Hamburger Sparkasse shows a hypothetical increase in cost of 27.46, 10.74 and 6.79% respectively. It can be observed that Kreditanstalt für Wiederaufbau

Table 8.11(b) The effect of hypothetical mergers on predicted cost for specific pairs among the largest top 20 German banks

Name of bank pairs	Change[a] (%)
Deutsche Bank/Dresdner Bank	−25.26
Dresdner Bank/Commerzbank	−25.47
Commerzbank/Bayerische Vereinsbank	−22.96
Bayerische Vereinsbank/Dresdner Bank	−23.00
Hypo-Bank/DG Bank	−25.04
DG Bank/Deutsche Bank	−30.13
Kreditanstalt für Wiederaufbau/Berliner Bank	5.33
Depfa-Bank/Deutsche Hypothekenbank Frankfurt	10.74
BFG Bank/Kreditanstalt für Wiederaufbau	−14.33
Deutsche Hypothekenbank Frankfurt/Berliner Bank	24.23
DSL Bank/Dresdner Bank	−18.68
Landes Kreditbank Baden Württemberg/Landwir. Ren.	1.73
Deutsche Girozentrale-Kommunalbank/Deutsche Bank	−24.76
Rheinische Hypothekenbank/DG Bank	−32.71
Berliner Bank/Deutsche Centralbodencredit	27.46
BHF Bank/Deutsche Hypothekenbank Frankfurt	8.13
Landwirtschaftliche Rentenbank/Hamburger Sparkasse	6.79
Frankfurter Hypothekenbank/Berliner Bank	9.20
Deutsche Centralbodencredit/Frankfurter Hypothekenbank	11.00
Hamburger Sparkasse/Deutsche Centralbodencredit	25.15

[a]Percentage change in predicted cost due to merger. Negative values indicate cost reductions while positive values indicate an increase in cost.

(which was founded in 1948 to provide long-term export credits and credit for the reconstruction of the economy), Deutsche Hypothekenbank Frankfurt, Berliner Bank, Landwirtschaftliche Rentenbank and Deutsche Centralbodencredit-AG are merger partners which cause large cost increases. On the other hand, substantial savings can be generated by hypothetical mergers between Germany's large commercial banks. Commercial banks such as Deutsche Bank, Dresdner Bank and Commerzbank have always played an important economic role not only as providers of funds to industry, but also as owners of companies and providers of liquidity to the government. These banks are usually regarded as being among the strongest in the world. Morgan Stanley (1988) stated that the German banking system is ready for rationalisation; however, the structure of private, state and regional banks makes restructuring very difficult. Our results, which indicate substantial cost savings through megamergers, suggest strong economic reasons for consolidation within this sector.

In Italy (Table 8.11(c)), hypothetical cost savings are often achievable when Monte Dei Paschi di Siena, Credito Italiano, Cariplo, Banco di Santo Spirito and Cassa di Risparmio di Verona Vicenza Belluno are merger partners. Specifically, the pairs Cassa di Risparmio di Verona Vicenza Belluno and Credito Italiano, Credito Italiano and Banco di Santo Spirito, Monte Dei Paschi di Siena and

Table 8.11(c)   The effect of hypothetical mergers on predicted cost for specific pairs among the largest top 20 Italian banks

Name of bank pairs	Change[a] (%)
Istituto Bancario San Paolo di Torino/BNL	10.19
BNL/Monte dei Paschi di Siena	2.13
Monte dei Paschi di Siena/Credito Italiano	−1.45
Banca Commerciale Italiana/Cassa di Ris. di Verona	−1.01
Banco di Napoli/Istituto Bancario San Paolo	10.40
Credito Italiano/Banco di Santo Spirito	−3.13
Banco di Roma/Monte dei Paschi di Siena	2.13
Cariplo/Banca di Napoli	3.30
Banco di Sicilia/Banca Commerciale Italiana	3.25
Banca Popolare di Novara/Banco di Santo Spirito	−0.67
Istituto Mobil. Itali/Cassa di Ris. di Verona	−1.52
Banca Nazionale dell'Agrico./Credito Italiano	−1.51
Creditop/Istituto Bancario San Paolo di Torino	10.14
Banco Ambrosiano Veneto/Banco di Santo Spirito	−0.57
Banco di Santo Spirito/Cassa di Ris. di Verona	−3.27
Banca Popolare di Milano/BNL	3.42
Cassa di Risparmio di Verona/Credito Italiano	−3.28
Banca Toscana/Banca di Roma	3.91
Credito Romagnolo/Banco di Sicilia	6.56
Mediobanca/Credito Italiano	−1.37

[a]Percentage change in predicted cost due to merger. Negative values indicate cost reductions while positive values indicate an increase in cost.

Credito Italiano result in small cost reductions. The vast majority of hypothetical mergers, however, show an increase in predicted costs. For example, the largest banks such as Istituto Bancario San Paolo di Torino, Banca Nazionale del Lavoro, Banca Commerciale Italiana, Banca di Napoli, Banca di Roma and Banca di Sicilia are not cost efficient, and pairings among this group raise costs, e.g. Istituto Bancario San Paolo di Torino and Banca Nazionale del Lavoro (10.19%), Banca Nazionale del Lavoro and Monte Dei Paschi di Siena (2.13%), Banca di Napoli and Istituto Bancario San Paolo di Torino (10.40%), Banca Commerciale Italiana and Banca di Sicilia (3.25%), Banca Popolare di Milano and Banca Nazionale del Lavoro (3.42%).

The reason why we find few cost reductions relating to hypothetical mergers is perhaps related to the way in which the Italian market has been regulated. In 1988, Italy was probably the most regulated of the major banking markets in the EU. Banks were restricted to certain types of lending (either short term or medium term) and there was strict control on branch openings. Nearly all the Italian banks in our sample are under state ownership (of one form or another) and strict liquidity and capital controls were in place at this time. Since the late 1980s, many of these restrictions have changed as a result of moves towards deregulation under the EU single market programme. There was (and still is) a general perception that the Italian banking industry was over-banked but under-branched, with 1000 banks and only 13 000 branches.

Moreover, Italian banking was still split between short- and long-term institutions. Commercial banks usually lend short term, offering loans of up to 18 months' duration. They offer some medium- and long-term products, but only through clearly defined divisions or sections. There have, however, been moves for commercial banks to link up with long-term institutions; for example in 1992, Istituto Bancario San Paolo di Torino, the largest commercial bank in Italy, acquired 90% of Creditop, a long-term lending institution.

Bank merger in Italy is also fraught with some important structural obstacles in that ownership is by control. Capital in such cases is provided by endowment funds rather than shares. The Amato law passed in 1989 allows Italian banks to change their ownership structure so that organisations can effectively become incorporated with share capital. In this way it is possible for similar, complementary or neighbouring institutions to merge. This is the first step towards rationalisation, which seems a likely prospect for the small to medium-sized banks. Even large institutions are likely to be squeezed in an increasingly competitive market, especially in the context of the 1992 single market programme, although the above analysis suggests that few big-bank mergers will result in opportunities for substantial cost savings.

It is also noteworthy that our hypothetical merger simulations are conducted at the firm level. Since Italian banking markets are over-banked and overstaffed, with constant returns to scale at the firm level, it is not surprising that the vast majority of hypothetical simulated merger pairings show increases in predicted total costs.

Recently Morgan Stanley (1993a) have suggested that, over the last few years, rationalisation and restructuring have been disappointing in the Italian banking market. The 1989 Amato law facilitated mergers from a fiscal perspective; however, few banks have taken advantage of the opportunity. While the current political uncertainties continue and privatisation is still being pursued, Morgan Stanley (1993a) argue that one is unlikely to see any significant large mergers taking place. This again appears to support our findings for 1988.

Finally, in Spain (Table 8.11(d)), Caja de Pensiones para la Vejez y de Ahorros de Cataluna y Baleares, Banco Hispano Americano (which merged with Banco Central in 1992), Banco Exterior de Espana (now part of Argentaria), Banco Popular Espanol, Caja de Ahorros de Galicia-la Coruna and Banco Urquijo appear to be good merger partners for mergers with smaller banks with the exception of the simulation between two savings banks, Caja de Barcelona and Caja de Pensiones para la Vejez y de Ahorros de Cataluna y Baleares, where costs increased by 3.15%. Our results suggest that there are no cost savings from mergers between the top 20 largest Spanish banks. The large Spanish banks are generally overstaffed and have lower standards of technology than their European counterparts (Morgan Stanley, 1989). It seems that they are not

Table 8.11(d)   The effect of hypothetical mergers on predicted cost for specific pairs among the largest top 20 Spanish banks

Name of bank pairs	Change[a] (%)
Banco Bilbao Vizcaya/Banco Central	19.03
Banco Central/Banco Espanol de Credito	15.61
Banco Espanol de Credito/Caja de Cataluna-Baleares	15.67
Caja de Cataluna-Baleares/Banco Central	8.30
Banco Hispano Americano/Banco de Santander	18.48
Banco de Santander/Bankinter	25.22
Banco Exterior de Espana/Banca Catalana	19.14
Caja de Monte de Piedad de Madrid/Caja de Valencia	16.79
Banco Popular Espanol/Caja de Barcelona	4.35
Caja de Barcelona/Caja de Cataluna-Baleares	−3.15
Bankinter/Banca Catalana	26.26
Banco de Sabadell/Caja de Cataluna-Baleares	4.65
Banca Catalana/Banco de Santander	26.24
Caja de Ahorros de Cataluna/Banco Urquijo	12.50
Banco Atlantico/Banco Pastor	21.48
Caja de Zaragoza Iber Caja/Caja de Galicia-Coruna	12.86
Banco Pastor/Banco de Sabadell	19.94
Caja de Ahode Valencia/Banco Hispano Americano	11.67
Caja de Galicia-Coruna/Caja de Cataluna-Baleares	0.97
Banco Urquijo/Banco Atlantico	14.89

[a]Percentage change in predicted cost due to merger. Negative values indicate cost reductions while positive values indicate an increase in cost.

as capable of controlling their operating costs as the smaller Spanish banks. For example, a 19.03% increase in cost results from the hypothetical merger between Banco Bilbao Vizcaya and Banco Central, and a 26.24% increase from the merger between Bankinter and Banca Catalana. Two recent mergers between large Spanish banks also indicate the difficulties associated with reducing costs. The first in 1988 was between two large regional commercial banks, Banco de Bilbao and Banco de Vizcaya, which created the largest banking group in Spain with 14% of total banking assets. The merger brought about substantial reductions in overlapping branches and staff numbers and cost increased by 9% on a group level. Staff costs increased by 8% and other costs advanced by 11%. Operating costs as a percentage of operating income increased by 1.5 to 49.4% (Morgan Stanley, 1990). The second case was the 1992 merger between Banco Central and Banco Hispano Americano into Banco Central Hispano. The merged bank had 3500 branches and employed 30 000 people in its principal banking entity. The first stage of the rationalisation programme envisaged the closure of over 500 branches in its mainstream operations by the end of 1993. Around 200 branches had been closed or merged by the end of 1992 and over 300 disappeared by 1993. A further 100 branches were scheduled for closure in 1994. Staff numbers fell by nearly 3000. However, despite these costs, operating costs still increased by 4.5% in 1992 (Morgan Stanley, 1993a). Given the lack of cost incentives for the top 20 banks to merge, perhaps strategic motives will play a more important role in encouraging consolidation in the Spanish banking industry, especially given the government's desire to encourage big-bank mergers. If we consider the findings from the previous section it seems that there are greater opportunities for cost-saving mergers between medium and smaller-sized banks rather than mergers between the top 20 institutions in Spain.

The results for the hypothetical mergers between the 20 largest banks in each country show that substantial cost savings can be generated from mergers between Germany's top commercial banks. In Italy, the analyses indicate that most of hypothetical mergers imply an increase in costs. Evidence from Spain and France is less clear-cut. Substantial cost savings in Spain appear to occur for hypothetical mergers between medium and smaller banks rather than mergers between top 20 organisations. Finally, in France cost savings seem to result from hypothetical mergers between either the largest specialist institutions or medium-sized banks.

The results of Hypothetical Bank Mergers across Borders in Europe

The 1980s was a decade of cross-border mergers in the banking industry (Bollenbacher, 1992). The main objectives for instituting cross-border mergers are to expand the institution's market-place, to gain new customers, to increase the geographical coverage, and obviously to do more business. The EU's Cecchini Report (1988) emphasised the potential for substantial gains related to economies of scale in linking as result of the EU's single market programme after 1992. Two important supply-side benefits may follow from the single market process. Firstly, savings resulting from rationalisation and economies of scale may lower production costs. Secondly, improvements in productivity may result from a reallocation of resources (human, financial and technological) or industrial restructuring through rationalisation or mergers.

Cross-border mergers are distinctly different from domestic mergers. The primary purpose of a cross-border merger is to expand into new markets, whereas the main purpose of a domestic merger is to increase market share and capacity. Cross-border mergers between sizeable commercial banks are likely to add branches to the bank's network, while the domestic merger is often aimed at closing overlapping branches in the same market. While cross-border mergers are designed to increase the customer base, domestic mergers often seek to reduce the workforce.

In the USA, a number of studies (Shaffer, 1992; LaWare, 1991; Cornett and De, 1991; Holder, 1993; Dunham and Syron, 1984; Phillis and Pavel, 1986) have predicted that interstate bank mergers are less likely to generate cost synergies than intrastate mergers, on the grounds that no overlapping branch network exists across states. Srinivasan and Wall (1992) also find that opportunities for cost reductions are greater when the merger partner operates in the same deposit market.

Table 8.12   Summary statistics for hypothetical cross-border mergers[a]

Descriptive statistics	Overall	Cost savings	Cost increasing
No. of pairs	7626	2159	5467
Mean	7.06	5.39	11.97
Minimum	−27.38	0.007	0.013
Maximum	74.91	27.38	74.91

[a]Percentage change in predicted cost due to merger. A negative value shows a cost reduction while a positive value indicates an increase in cost.

Table 8.13   Distribution of hypothetical cross-border mergers

Change in cost	Cost saving		Cost increasing	
	No.	%	No.	%
>50%	—	—	41	0.75
>25%	2	0.092	721	13.99
>10%	322	14.91	2406	44.00
>5%	932	43.17	3830	70.06

Tables 8.12 and 8.13 provide the summary results of simulation of the cost effects of hypothetical cross-border European bank mergers. The average hypothetical merger yields a 7.06% increase in predicted total cost, compared with the sum of total costs of the unmerged banks. These results appear to be consistent with our economies of scale results for cross-border European bank mergers in which constant returns to scale were found for all sizes of large banks. Our results show that 28.31% of the possible pairings (2159 out of 7626) cause a reduction in cost, with 14.91% of these (322 pairs) showing an improvement of more than 10%. However, it can be seen that in a large majority of the mergers (5467 pairs or 71.69%) costs are predicted to increase, with 44.0% of these cases (2406 out of 5467 pairs) producing increases in costs exceeding 10%.

The results suggest that reductions in cost are often possible with hypothetical mergers between Italian and German banks. This could be related to the structure of both banking systems, which in general are both over-banked and in the Italian case under-branched. It also suggests that mergers between traditionally strongly capital-based and lower-cost northern universal banks and relatively labour-intensive and higher-cost southern banks generate the greatest cross-border cost savings. Table 8.14 shows the largest hypothetical cost savings among European banks with assets of more than $5 billion. The highest cost saving (27.38%) would have occurred by hypothetically merging the Italian savings bank, Cassa di Risparmio di Verona Vicenza Belluno, with a German mortgage bank, Allgemeine Hypothekenbank. In fact the top five cost-saving cross-border mergers all involved the Allgemeine Hypothekenbank, suggesting that this is a good cross-border merger partner. In general, the majority of pairs with cost reductions of

Table 8.14   The largest cost savings for hypothetical cross-border mergers

Name of bank pairs	Change (%)
Cassa di Risparmio di Verona Vicenza Belluno/Allgemeine Hypothekenbank	27.38
Mediobanca/Allgemeine Hypothekenbank	25.37
Allgemeine Hypothekenbank/Banco di Santo Spirito	24.53
Banca Toscana/Allgemeine Hypothekenbank	24.47
Allgemeine Hypothekenbank/Banca Populare di Milano	23.25
Bayerische Landesanstalt für Aufbaufinazierung/Banca Toscana	20.75
Banca Toscana/Hypothekenbank in Essen AG	20.21
UFB Locabail/Allgemeine Hypothekenbank	19.68
Sovac/Stadtsparkasse Köln	19.64
Banco Atlantico/Hypothekenbank in Hamburg	18.89
Banco de Sabadell/Westfalische Hypothekenbank	18.23
Mediobanca/Münchener Hypothekenbank	16.03
Bayerische Landesanstalt für Aufbaufinazierung/Credito Romagnolo	15.55
Münchener Hypothekenbank/Banca Toscana	15.00
Münchener Hypothekenbank/Banca Nazionale dell'Agricoltura	14.75
Cassa di Risparmio di Verona Vicenza Belluno/Hypothekenbank in Essen	14.66
UFB Locabail/Credito Romagnolo	14.08
Credito Romagnola/Banque Sudameris	14.03
Mediobanca/Cie Financière	11.11
Credito Romagnola/Caja de Zaragoza Iber Caja	11.09

Table 8.15   The largest hypothetical cost increases for cross-border European bank mergers

Name of bank pairs	Change (%)
Deutsche Hypothekenbank Frankfurt/Groupe des Banques Populaires	66.39
Deutsche Hypothekenbank Frankfurt/Crédit Mutuel	65.71
Frankfurter Hypothekenbank/Groupe des Banques Populaires	60.21
Frankfurter Hypothekenbank/Crédit Mutuel	59.64
Compagnie Parisienne de Reescompte/Deutsche Hypothekenbank Frankfurt	58.79
Deutsche Hypothekenbank Frankfurt/Banque Française du Commerce	57.63
Cetelem/Industriekreditbank AG	57.51
Cetelem/Frankfurter Hypothekenbank	57.00
Cetelem/Südwestdeutsche Genossenschafts Zentralbank	52.14
Rheinische Hypothekenbank/Crédit Mutuel	49.62
Kreditanstalt für Wiederaufbau/Groupe des Banques Populaires	45.28
Credisuez/Südwestdeutsche Genossenschafts Zentralbank	44.72
Compagnie Parisienne de Reescompte/Baden-Württembergischbank	41.48
Südwestdeutsche Genossenschafts Zentralbank/UFB Locabail	40.14
Banque Comm. pour l'Europe du Nord/Kreditanstalt für Wiederaufbau	39.69
Credisuez/Berliner Bank	38.46
Banque Comm. pour l'Europe du Nord/Baden-Württembergischbank	38.17
Compagnie Parisienne de Reescompte/Rheinische Hypothekenbank	37.68
Caja de Barcelona/Deutsche Hypothekenbank Frankfurt	35.16
Banco de Santander/Crédit Mutuel	35.12

more than 10% resulted from hypothetical mergers between Italian and German banks.

In contrast, Table 8.15 shows that the hypothetical mergers which cause the largest increases in costs are generally between the largest French and German banks. Again these mergers tend to be between specialist banking institutions in considerably different areas of business.

Table 8.16 shows the effect of hypothetical mergers on predicted costs among a sample of cross-border mergers between the largest banks. The pairings are taken from among the top 10 banks (according to total assets) of each country. From Table 8.16, it can be seen that the opportunities for cross-border mergers to increase costs appear to be greater than for such mergers to save costs. For instance, if the largest French and German banks hypothetically merged, total cost would increase by 9.854%. Moreover, if the largest French bank (i.e. Crédit Agricole) and Italian bank (i.e. Istituto Bancario San Paolo di Torino) hypothetically merged, the predicted total cost would only increase by 1.79%, whereas the merger between the largest German bank, Deutsche Bank, and Istituto Bancario San Paolo di Torino would result in a 7.02% increase in total cost. The merger between the largest Spanish bank, Banco Bilbao Vizcaya, and Istituto Bancario San Paolo di Torino would generate a 6.63% increase in cost. Cost savings were no greater than 7% in any hypothetical cross-border merger involving the largest banks. In addition, the potential for substantial cost savings resulting from cross-border mergers between Europe's biggest banks appears to be somewhat limited. These results clearly conflict with the views of the EU's Cecchini study, which placed substantial emphasis on the cost advantages associated with cross-border mergers in the EU.

LIMITATIONS OF THE HYPOTHETICAL MERGER ANALYSIS

In our model the hypothetical merger simulations are based on simple assumptions. Following Shaffer (1993) and Boyd and Graham (1988), for each possible hypothetical pair, the pre-merger bank costs were estimated at the observed input prices for individual banks, while post-merger costs were calculated at the mean input prices for the given pairs. We also assume that the procedure does not change demand-side factors. Furthermore, it is assumed that the merged banks are simply the sum of the two individual unmerged banks. Banks are merged according to their accounting values. Consolidated total assets, loans and securities for the hypothetically merged bank are generated by summing the assets, loans and securities of the two individual banks. In addition, it is assumed that the merged banks do not benefit from further cost synergies that might result from the combination or restructuring of output mix as well as out-of-pocket merger costs, or merger premiums. Given that restructuring opportunities are one of the main perceived advantages of bank merger (i.e. through widespread closures of overlapping branch networks post-merger), our estimates clearly understate the

Table 8.16   The effect of hypothetical mergers between specific pairs of large European banks on predicted costs

Name of bank pairs	Change[a] (%)
Crédit Agricole/Deutsche Bank	9.85
Banque Nationale de Paris/Banca Nazionale del Lavoro	1.44
Crédit Lyonnais/Commerzbank	8.17
Société Générale/Banca di Sicilia	0.34
Banque Paribas/Kreditanstalt für Wiederaufbau	22.50
Cie Financière CIC/Banco Bilbao Vizcaya	6.78
Groupe des Banques Populaires/Dresdner Bank	32.05
Crédit Mutuel/Kreditanstalt für Wiederaufbau	45.17
Crédit Foncier France/Cariplo	3.41
Banque Indosuez/Credito Italiano	−0.30
Deutsche Bank/Istituto San Paolo di Torino	7.02
Dresdner Bank/Banco Central	10.56
Commerzbank/Banca Popolare di Novara	−0.93
Bayerische Vereinsbank/Groupe des Banques Populaires	30.57
Hypo-Bank/Banca Popolare di Novara	−2.88
DG Bank/Credito Italiano	−7.03
Kreditanstalt für Wiederaufbau/Banco de Santander	18.24
Depfa-Bank/Banco di Napoli	−4.30
BFG Bank/Banco Central Hispano Americano	10.20
Deutsche Hypothekenbank Frankfurt/Banca Commerc. Italiana	−2.03
Istituto San Paolo di Torino/Crédit Agricole	1.79
Banca Nazionale del Lavoro/Banco de Santander	−2.12
Monte dei Paschi di Siena/DG Bank	−6.03
Banca Commerciale Italiana/Cie Financière CIC	−6.53
Banco di Napoli/DG Bank	−4.86
Credito Italiano/Deutsche Hypothekenbank Frankfurt	−2.81
Banco di Roma/Depfa-Bank	−2.64
Cariplo/Hypo-Bank	−0.49
Banco di Sicilia/Deutsche Hypothekenbank Frankfurt	−0.57
Banca Popolare di Novara/Depfa-Bank	−6.25
Banco Bilbao Vizcaya/Deutsche Bank	13.98
Banco Central/Banca Nazionale del Lavoro	3.62
Banco Espanol de Credito/BFG Bank	10.90
Caja de Cataluna-Baleares/Cariplo	3.12
Banco Central Hispano Americano/Banco di Napoli	1.95
Banco de Santander/Banca Commerciale Italiana	−3.83
Banco Exterior de Espana/Dresdner Bank	8.59
Caja de Piedad de Madrid/Commerzbank	6.76
Banco Popular Espanol/Société Générale	5.12
Caja de Barcelona/Monte dei Paschi di Siena	−1.31

[a]Percentage change in predicted cost due to merger. Negative values indicate cost reductions while positive values indicate an increase in cost.

cost savings to be had. They do, however, indicate that restructuring is virtually essential, say in the Italian market, if cost savings of any size are to be obtained. This is not the case for the German mergers.

In general some of the merger assumptions could lead to bias in the results. These factors can be grouped as follows:

1. *Random merger partners.* The merger simulations have been carried out hypothetically, ignoring any prior information about pairs. In reality, senior management would select the better merger partners. Bank managers would not pick up partners exhibiting disagreeable financial arithmetic unless improvements were expected.

2. *Big-bank mergers.* The study uses data predominantly for large-size banks. The analysis neglects hypothetical mergers with small banks or other financial institutions.

3. *Merger premiums or cost.* In the analysis, it assumed that there are no premiums or out-of-pocket merger costs. Boyd and Graham (1988) have pointed out that it is difficult to incorporate these within the simulation. Merger premiums may be substantial (e.g. exchanges of shares or cash buy-outs). Although these factors could be detrimental to the attractiveness of potential mergers, their inclusion in the analysis was beyond the scope of this study.

4. *No restructuring post-merger.* Our results therefore perhaps understate cost savings that can be made because they do not simulate, say, branch rationalisation post-merger.

5. *Other limitations.* The analysis uses data for one year only, 1988. The results might not necessarily be the same if data for different years were employed. In addition, standard methodological problems associated with the use of the hybrid translog cost function could affect the results. Furthermore, mergers between large banks could in reality be impractical because of national and European competition law, incompatible ownership characteristics and other factors not taken into consideration in the present analysis.

CONCLUSIONS

This chapter examines the potential for improvements in efficiency and cost savings resulting from bank mergers both within the French, German, Italian and Spanish banking markets and also across their national boundaries. Our findings can be summarised as follows:

1. The evidence for the individual domestic banking markets suggests that mergers between large banks can generate substantial cost savings or increases depending on the merger partners. The results generally indicate

that opportunities for cost-saving mergers seem to be greater in Germany and Spain than in France and Italy. In fact the prospects for cost-saving big-bank mergers in Italy (without substantial restructuring) appear to be very limited. In addition, the biggest cost savings and cost increases result from hypothetical mergers (in most cases) between quite different banking organisations. Such mergers would probably be unlikely in practice.

2. Our selective results for the hypothetical mergers between the 20 largest banks within domestic banking markets imply that substantial cost savings can be generated from mergers between top commercial banks in Germany. For Italy, the analysis shows that the vast majority of hypothetical mergers shows an increase in predicted total costs. The findings from Spain and France are less clear-cut. In Spain, cost savings appear to occur for hypothetical mergers between the largest and smallest banks within the top 20 (i.e. the first, second or third largest banks merging with, say, the eighteenth, nineteenth or twentieth largest). Finally, cost savings in France seem to result from hypothetical mergers between either the largest specialist institutions or second-tier medium-sized banks.

3. The evidence from our analysis of bank mergers across borders in Europe suggests that cost savings for this type of merger seem to be somewhat limited. In general, cost savings appear to be generated by mergers between Italian and German banks, whereas the biggest cost-increasing mergers are brought about by hypothetical mergers between French and German institutions. The cost advantages brought about through hypothetical cross-border mergers do not appear to generate the substantial benefits suggested by the EU in their study of the single market programme.

Overall, these results indicate that mergers between large banks either within domestic banking markets or across national borders can create substantial cost savings or cost increases depending on the merger partners chosen. The empirical evidence strongly supports the view that merger partners should be carefully selected given the substantial variation of cost outcomes.

9

Efficiency in European banking

INTRODUCTION

We saw earlier in Chapter 5 that most studies of bank cost structures have focused on the cost advantages resulting from the scale and scope of production. There are, however, other aspects of efficiency which researchers have just begun to examine, such as technical and allocative efficiency. Productive efficiency implies that firms optimise their behaviour with respect to input and output decisions. Production takes place in an environment where managers attempt to maximise profits by operating in the most efficient manner possible. The competitive model also implies that firms which fail to do so will be driven from the market by more efficient operators. However, when natural entry barriers or regulation reduce the degree of competition, inefficient firms could contrive to prosper.

> While scale and scope economies have been widely studied, relatively little attention has been paid to measuring what appears to be a much more important source of efficiency differences — X-inefficiencies, or deviations from the efficient frontier (Berger, Hunter and Timme, 1993, p. 222).

Put simply, differences in managerial ability to control costs or maximise revenues seem to be larger than the cost effects of the choice of scale and scope of production. In Berger, Hunter and Timme's (1993) review of the literature they find that X-inefficiencies account for around 20% or more of costs in banking, while scale and product mix inefficiencies, 'when accurately estimated', are usually found to account for less than 5% of costs.

Despite the large volume of research on X-inefficiencies in general since its introduction in the 1960s (see Leibenstein, 1966) there has been relatively little banking research until recently. This is not to say that economists have not recognised the importance and potential gains of reducing banking X-inefficiencies (see e.g. Commission of the European Communities, 1988a), but empirical research has been lacking. Although there is a virtual consensus that X-inefficiency differences across banks are large and dominate scale and scope efficiencies, there is no agreement on how to measure X-inefficiencies in banking. Nor is there a consensus on the average level of X-efficiency in the banking industry.

X-efficiency covers all technical and allocative efficiencies of individual firms (as distinct from scale and scope economies). Essentially, this kind of efficiency is measured, or modelled, as kinds of distance measures that reflect a firm's own position in relation to its 'efficient' production frontier.

There are two main frontier techniques that have been used in this literature. Berger, Hunter and Timme (1993) review these and some of their technical aspects. The two main techniques are stochastic frontier analysis and data envelope analysis (DEA) which were briefly discussed in Chapter 5. Two other approaches, the thick frontier approach (TFA) and the distribution-free approach (DFA) are 'hybrids' of the stochastic frontier approach. Berger, Hunter and Timme (1993, p. 228), however, caution that:

> There is no simple rule for determining which of these methods best describes the true nature of the banking data. This would not be a problem if all of the methods arrived at essentially the same conclusion. Unfortunately, this is not the case — in fact, the choice of measurement method appears to strongly affect the level of measured inefficiency.

ESTIMATING BANKING EFFICIENCY

Stochastic Frontier Analysis

Stochastic frontier analysis is increasingly being used to investigate cost inefficiencies in banking markets. In this approach the cost function of the most efficient producers (the efficient cost frontier) is estimated and an institution's deviation from the frontier comprises two components, a random error (v) and an inefficiency (u). The part of the error term which represents deviations from the frontier is assumed to be drawn from a two-side distribution, while the inefficiency is assumed to be drawn from a one-side distribution, because inefficiency increases cost. Bauer (1990) and Greene (1990) note that the half-normal distribution has become the standard choice for the one-sided distribution even though more flexible distributions are available. Berger, Hunter and Timme (1993a), in a detailed review of the bank efficiency literature, confirm this view and suggest that further investigation into the distributional assumptions underlying the stochastic frontier approach needs to be carried out.

The methodology for estimating a stochastic or 'efficient' frontier can be outlined as follows. Following Ferrier and Lovell (1990) inefficiency scores for individual banks can be estimated using the stochastic approach as introduced by Aigner, Lovell and Schmidt (1977), Meeusen and van den Broeck (1977) and Battese and Corra (1977). The single-equation stochastic cost function model can be given as

$$TC = TC(Q_i, P_i) + \varepsilon_i \tag{1}$$

where TC is observed total cost, Q_i is a vector of outputs and P_i is an input price vector.

Following Aigner, Lovell and Schmidt (1977), we assume that the error of the cost function is

$$\varepsilon = u + v \tag{2}$$

where u and v are independently distributed. Typically, u is usually assumed to be distributed as half-normal, that is, a one-sided positive disturbance capturing the effects of inefficiency, and v is assumed to be distributed as two-sided normal with zero mean and variance σ_2^2, capturing the effects of the statistical noise. Furthermore, given the distributional assumptions for the error terms u and v, the density function of the composite error term can be written as

$$g(\varepsilon) = \frac{2}{\sigma} f\left(\frac{\varepsilon}{\sigma}\right) [1 - F(\varepsilon \lambda \sigma^{-1})] \tag{3}$$

where $\sigma = (\sigma_u^2 + \sigma_v^2)^{1/2}$, $\lambda = \sigma_u/\sigma_v$, $f(.)$ and $F(.)$ are the standard normal density and the distribution functions for a standard normal random variable, respectively. The log-likelihood function can be shown as

$$\ln \varphi = \frac{N}{2} \ln \frac{2}{\pi} - N \ln \sigma + \sum_{i=1}^{N} \ln[1 - F(\varepsilon_i \lambda \sigma)^{-1}] - \frac{1}{2\sigma^2} \sum_{i=1}^{N} \varepsilon_i^2 \tag{4}$$

where N is the number of observations. Jondrow et al. (1982) have shown that the ratio of the variability (standard deviation, σ) for u and v can be used to measure a bank's relative inefficiency, where $\lambda = \sigma_u/\sigma_v$, is a measure of the amount of variation stemming from inefficiency relative to noise for the sample. Estimates of this model can be computed by maximising the likelihood function directly (see Olson, Schmidt and Waldman, 1980).

Observation-specific estimates of technical inefficiency, u, can be calculated by using the distribution of the inefficiency term conditional on the estimate of the composed error term, as proposed by Jondrow et al. (1982). The mean of this conditional distribution for the half-normal model is shown as

$$E(u_i|\varepsilon_i) = \frac{\sigma \lambda}{1 + \lambda^2} \left[\frac{f(\varepsilon_i \lambda/\sigma)}{1 - F(\varepsilon_i \lambda/\sigma)} + \left(\frac{\varepsilon_i \lambda}{\sigma}\right) \right] \tag{5}$$

where $F(.)$ and $f(.)$ are the standard normal distribution and the standard normal density function, respectively. $E(u/\varepsilon)$ is an unbiased but inconsistent estimator of u_i, since regardless of N, the variance of the estimator remains non-zero (see Greene, 1993, pp. 80–82). Allen and Rai (1993), Yuengert (1993) and Mester (1993) all use the half-normal specification to test for inefficiency differences between financial institutions mainly in the US market.

Stevenson (1980), however, has analysed the case in which u has a truncated normal distribution with parameters μ_i, which is allowed to differ from zero in either direction, and variance σ_u^2. Greene (1990) has shown that the mean of the conditional distribution for the truncated normal model can be obtained by replacing $\varepsilon_i \lambda / \sigma$ in equation (5) with

$$\mu^* = \frac{\varepsilon_i \lambda}{\sigma} + \frac{\mu}{\sigma \lambda} \tag{6}$$

where μ is the mean of the non-truncated distribution.

Finally, in the case where the inefficiency term is drawn from a normal-exponential and gamma distribution the mean of the conditional distribution is given as follows:

$$E(u_i | \varepsilon_i) = \gamma + \sigma \left[\frac{f(\varepsilon_i \lambda / \sigma)}{F(\varepsilon_i \lambda / \sigma)} \right] \tag{7}$$

where γ equals $\varepsilon - \theta \sigma^2$ (using our notation $\sigma = \sigma_v$ and $\sigma = 1/\sigma_u$).

To calculate the inefficiencies a standard translog cost function (see Noulas, Miller and Ray, 1993; Kaparakis, Miller and Noulas, 1994) incorporating a two-component error structure, is usually estimated using a maximum likelihood procedure. An example of this can be shown as follows:

$$\ln TC = \alpha_0 + \sum_{i=1}^{2} \alpha_i \ln Q_i + \sum_{i=1}^{3} \beta_i \ln P_i + \lambda_{\mathrm{b}} \ln B$$

$$+ \frac{1}{2} \left[\sum_{i=1}^{2} \sum_{j=1}^{2} \delta_{ij} \ln Q_i \ln Q_j + \sum_{i=1}^{3} \sum_{j=1}^{3} \gamma_{ij} \ln P_i \ln P_j + \lambda_{\mathrm{bb}} \ln B \ln B \right]$$

$$+ \sum_{i=1}^{3} \sum_{j=1}^{2} \rho_{ij} \ln P_i \ln Q_j + \sum_{i=1}^{2} \lambda_{\mathrm{b}i} \ln B \ln Q_i + \sum_{i=1}^{3} \tau_{\mathrm{b}i} \ln B \ln P_i + \varepsilon \tag{8}$$

where TC is total cost, comprising operating cost and financial cost (interest paid on deposits), Q_1 are total loans, Q_2 are total securities, P_1 the average annual wage expenses per branch, P_2 the average interest cost per dollar of interest-bearing deposits, P_3 the average price of capital, calculated as the ratio of total capital expenses to total fixed assets, B the number of branches, ε the stochastic error term and α, β, σ, λ, δ, ν and τ are coefficients to be estimated.

Data Envelope Analysis (DEA)

DEA models technical and allocative inefficiencies as deterministic deviations (i.e. as relative 'efficiency scores') from a bank's 'best practice' frontier. This is derived deterministically from the specific dataset and prespecified input and output measures used. This approach, then, implicitly assumes that there are no random fluctuations from the respective production frontier estimates. In effect, all deviations from the estimated frontier comprise inefficiency under DEA measures. Despite the apparent economic and econometric limitations of this kind of assumption, recent research has suggested that the kind of mathematical programming procedure used by DEA for efficient frontier estimation is comparatively robust: see, for example, Seiford and Thrall (1990, p. 28). See also Chapter 5.

EUROPEAN RESEARCH

Although European research on scale and scope efficiencies, X-efficiency and related policy aspects (like the alleged gains from mergers) has not matched the volume of respective US research, this has begun to change in recent years. Given the recognised, key importance of the European financial sectors in achieving the overall economic gains sought by deregulation and 'free market solutions' in resource allocation within European economic systems, the need for good research is pressing. Fortunately, there is now a strong and growing movement towards greater empirical research into European bank efficiency and related policy aspects.

One of the early students of banking (and wider financial sector) efficiency was Revell, and the Institute of European Finance at Bangor has since its inception established a track record in studying what might be called the 'industrial economics of banking'. Revell (1987, 1989) surveyed the empirical research on banking efficiency in the context of the movement towards bigger banks in Europe. Although both of these studies were concerned with Spain, Revell explored the extensive US literature and considered its relevance to the European banking sector. Revell (1987, p. 280) stated that:

> One general conclusion of the argument of this report is that economies of size in banking are difficult to define and measure. They exist in certain respects and in certain parts of a bank's operations, but they are not so important as the arguments used in favour of the suggested mergers seem to assume. The striking fact about the reasons advanced in favour of mergers among large banks is that they have barely changed during the past 70 years.

Revell also suggested (1987, p. 281) that mergers are generally far from being a 'quick, sure way of increasing efficiency'. Since this seems to be a widespread banking experience in a scenario of expanding balance sheets, these 'adjustment' and managerial costs are likely to be exacerbated in the present climate of much slower growth, a de-emphasis on 'growth for growth's sake', and increasing securitisation.

Revell's general policy view is that whenever economies of scale can be proved to exist, the authorities (he was exploring the Spanish case) should encourage more sharing of facilities and the consortium approach between banks.

Efficiency in the German Banking Market

Altunbas, Evans and Molyneux (1994) use an approach similar to Kaparakis, Miller and Noulas (1994) to evaluate inefficiencies for the German banking market. The existing literature evaluating universal banking systems gives little empirical attention to the efficiency of banks operating under these systems (see e.g. Benston, 1994; John, John and Saunders, 1994; Steinherr and Huveneers, 1994; Saunders, 1994; Saunders and Walter, 1994). Sheldon and Haegler (1993) and Sheldon (1994) have investigated the Swiss market and they found that banks with diversified product mixes are more inefficient than specialised banks. In the Altunbas, Evans and Molyneux (1994) paper a stochastic cost frontier analysis is undertaken to calculate technical inefficiencies for banks in the German market.

The study uses balance sheet and income statement data from 1988 for a sample of 196 German banks, obtained from the London-based International Bank Credit Analysis Ltd (IBCA) database. Data on the number of branches was obtained from *The Bankers' Almanac* (1989). Overall, the sample represented around 65% of the German banking industry in asset terms. Kempf (1985), Gardener and Molyneux (1990) and the Deutsche Bundesbank (1989) provide the authors with a bank classification model. Bank types and organisation forms are cross-checked in *The Bankers' Almanac* (1989) which provided information on banks' ownership characteristics. Five categories of banks are identified, having four ownership types: private (or joint-stock) commercial banks; public (local-government owned) savings banks; mutual cooperative banks; central organisations and mortgage banks both of which have mixed ownership.

Table 9.1 reports the maximum likelihood parameter estimates of the stochastic cost frontier for German banks and Table 9.2 shows the inefficiency scores. The mean inefficiency score for all banks at 24% suggests that German banks could produce the same output with 76% of the current inputs if they were operating efficiently. These inefficiency scores are broadly in line with US studies. For example, Evanoff and Israilevich (1991) surveyed the productive efficiency results for 10 US studies and found inefficiency levels ranging between 13 and 51%. Cebenoyan et al. (1993), Berger, Hancock and Humphrey (1993) and Bauer et al. (1993) find mean inefficiency levels in commercial and savings banks in the ranges 21–52, 10–40 and 15–17% respectively. Kaparakis, Miller and Noulas (1994), using a sample of 5548 US banks, estimate mean inefficiencies of 9.8% and find that banks generally become less efficient with increasing size.

Both the mean and median inefficiency scores suggest that the mixed ownership specialist banks — the mortgage banks and central organisations — are less efficient than the other groups of German banks. In fact the statistics for the private commercial banks compared with the public savings and mutual cooperative banks appear to be similar. Further statistical testing indicated that inefficiency scores for public savings banks and mutual cooperative banks were not significantly different. Inefficiency levels for private commercial banks, on the other hand, appear to be significantly different from

Table 9.1 Maximum likelihood parameter estimates of the translog stochastic cost frontier

Parameter	Estimate	Parameter	Estimate
α_0	5.66 (5.011)	γ_{33}	0.01 (0.0418)
α_1	0.51* (0.0798)	ρ_{11}	0.01 (0.0195)
α_2	0.38* (0.0581)	ρ_{12}	−0.08* (0.0254)
β_1	0.78* (0.1704)	ρ_{21}	0.04* (0.0138)
β_2	0.27 (0.1999)	λ_b	0.44* (0.0568)
δ_{11}	0.09* (0.0257)	λ_{bb}	−0.06 (0.0674)
δ_{12}	−0.05** (0.0171)	λ_{b1}	0.04 (0.0224)
δ_{22}	0.13* (0.0273)	λ_{b2}	−0.08** (0.0302)
γ_{22}	−0.06* (0.0257)	σ_u/σ_v	1.22 (0.7061)
γ_{13}	0.06 (0.0323)	$\sqrt{(\sigma_u^2 + \sigma_v^2)}$	0.49** (0.2310)

Standard errors of estimated parameters are shown beneath in parentheses.
*Significantly different from zero at 0.01 level.
**Significantly different from zero at 0.05 level.
Note: In estimating the model, we exclude three variables, that is, the interactive variable between the average deposit price and total loans and the interactive variables between input prices and the number of branches due to high multicollinearity among the explanatory variables.

Table 9.2 Technical inefficiencies according to bank types and ownership status

Ownership	Mean	Median	Standard deviation	Minimum	Maximum
Private commercial	0.300	0.267	0.130	0.059	0.628
Mortgage	0.470	0.435	0.248	0.112	0.935
Public savings	0.269	0.241	0.192	0.059	0.884
Mutual cooperative	0.238	0.220	0.075	0.163	0.364
Central organisations	0.480	0.436	0.293	0.155	0.703
All banks	0.240	0.191	0.134	0.059	0.935

the aforementioned banks even though mean and median technical inefficiencies for all three groups are around the 25% level. These three categories of banks, despite having different ownership characteristics, are universal in nature. The mortgage banks and central organisations, with mixed ownership characteristics and yielding inefficiency scores which are not significantly different, appear to be more specialist in their operations. Our results tentatively suggest that specialist banks operating in the German universal banking market are significantly less efficient than their broader-based bank counterparts. In addition, different ownership characteristics — whether private, publicly owned or mutual — do not appear to have a large effect on the absolute level of bank inefficiencies in the German market.

Efficiency in the Italian Banking Market

Altunbas, Molyneux and Di Salvo (1994) estimate levels of technical inefficiency in the Italian credit cooperative banking sector between 1990 and 1992. They find that inefficiency levels for this sector appear to be quite low compared with other studies. The mean inefficiency score for 1990 was 13.1% which indicates that in this year Italian credit cooperative banks could produce the same output with 86.9% of the inputs if they were operating efficiently. Mean inefficiency levels appear to be greater in 1991 and 1992. Table 9.3 provides a description of the inefficiency scores for the cooperative bank sector between 1990 and 1992. Table 9.4 gives a breakdown according to regional location. The analysis of bank inefficiency across geographical regions suggests that credit cooperative banks operating in the north-east central region of Italy (comprising Veneto and Emilia) are significantly less efficient than those operating in the north-west and north-east border regions. The authors also find that in two of the years under study the north-east central banks are also significantly less efficient than those operating in the south. The reason they find these relationships is perhaps related to size differences in banks across regional samples and this is an area which deserves fuller investigation. Regional differences in the level of technical inefficiency in the credit cooperative bank sector, however, do not appear to be large, with extreme median values ranging between 9.4 and 13.3% in 1990, 12.3 and 15.8% in 1991 and 13.8 and 17.6% in 1992.

A more recent study by Gobbi (1995) investigates changes in productivity in the Italian banking market between 1984 and 1992 using the DEA approach. Using a sample of 75 banks Gobbi (1995) finds that total global productivity of Italian banks fell between 1990 and 1992 compared with the periods 1984–86 and 1987 and 1989. This was perhaps to be expected given the branch expansion programme undertaken by many banks after restrictions were removed on branching.

Table 9.3   Descriptive statistics of inefficiency scores

Years	No.	Mean	Median	Standard deviation	Minimum	Maximum
1990	516	0.131	0.116	0.1125	0.015	2.118
1991	452	0.159	0.132	0.1481	0.020	1.711
1992	483	0.176	0.151	0.1578	0.022	1.447

Table 9.4   Inefficiency levels of banks according to regional location

Location	No.	Mean	Median	Standard deviation	Minimum	Maximum
1990						
North-west	88	0.104	0.094	0.055	0.015	0.264
North-east border	199	0.135	0.111	0.159	0.024	2.118
North-east central	101	0.149	0.133	0.083	0.030	0.653
Central	39	0.137	0.129	0.061	0.029	0.284
South	89	0.129	0.120	0.063	0.033	0.280
1991						
North-west	96	0.150	0.123	0.145	0.023	1.164
North-east border	180	0.158	0.127	0.167	0.020	1.715
North-east central	96	0.170	0.155	0.114	0.031	0.990
Central	35	0.151	0.158	0.062	0.036	0.295
South	45	0.172	0.124	0.183	0.021	0.900
1992						
North-west	93	0.182	0.146	0.180	0.025	1.213
North-east border	177	0.150	0.138	0.116	0.022	1.322
North-east central	89	0.184	0.165	0.087	0.028	0.537
Central	37	0.199	0.176	0.165	0.042	1.068
South	87	0.205	0.140	0.236	0.022	1.447

Resti (1995) uses both linear programming and stochastic cost frontier analysis to examine cost efficiency for a sample of 270 Italian banks over the period 1988–92. He finds that the two estimation procedures generally provide similar efficiency results. Overall, Resti finds that northern-based Italian banks are more efficient than their southern counterparts and that there is a positive relationship between productive efficiency and banks' asset quality. The efficiency of Italian banks, which generally ranges between 70 and 80%, did not, however, increase over the period 1988–92.

Efficiency in the UK Banking Market

The earliest studies of efficiency in the UK banking market were undertaken by Field (1990) and Drake and Weyman-Jones (1992a). Field (1990) employed DEA methodology to a cross-section of 71 British building societies in 1981. The study found that 86% of the sample were inefficient, mainly due to scale inefficiencies. Field (1990) showed that the overall technical efficiency was negatively correlated with firm size. This finding could possibly have been related to the cartelised and oligopolistic market conditions among UK building societies in 1981. Moreover, Drake and Weyman-Jones (1992a) undertook a study which had contrasting results to those of Field. Applying DEA to building societies after deregulation in 1988, the study found 37% of the industry to be efficient and this overall efficiency was positively correlated to size.

Drake and Weyman-Jones (1992b) extend their analysis further by comparing the efficiency of the UK building society sector using both DEA and stochastic cost frontier techniques. The results of the non-parametric DEA analysis showed that only around 4% of the sample were overall efficient and this suggested that UK building societies, on average, could have produced the same level of overall output with around 12.5% less inputs. Some societies, however, appear to be operating at efficiency levels below 60%. Drake and Weyman-Jones (1992b) break down overall efficiency into two components — technical efficiency and allocative efficiency. Their results clearly indicate that the majority of the overall inefficiency is accounted for by the latter with a mean efficiency index of 0.92 and a minimum value of 0.59. This finding suggests that the bulk of the inefficiency observed for UK building societies is attributable to the choosing of the array combination of inputs rather than to the inefficient usage of these inputs.

Finally, although the stochastic cost frontier analysis suggested that productive inefficiency was fairly minimal, compared with DEA, the two alternative approaches provided 'remarkably consistent efficiency rankings in the context of UK building societies' (Drake and Weyman-Jones, 1992b, p. 17).

Drake and Howcroft (1995) use DEA to investigate the relative efficiency of UK clearing bank branches. They use a sample of 190 branches drawn from one of the largest UK clearing banks. Out of the sample of branches some 107 (56.32%) are found to be relatively efficient. The mean efficiency rating for the sample of branches is 0.92, although there appears to be considerable diversity across branches in terms of efficiency levels as evidenced by a relatively large standard deviation and the minimum observed efficiency score of 0.505. In addition to calculating indices of technical efficiency for all the branches, this measure was decomposed into scale efficiency and pure technical efficiency. Approximately 48% of branches in the sample exhibited pure technical inefficiency whereas only 40% exhibited scale inefficiency. When analysed in terms of size groupings, the efficiency results suggested that plant size was a significant influence on efficiency, especially technical and scale efficiency. The size distribution of the branches exhibiting increasing and decreasing returns to scale were strongly suggestive of an asymmetric U-shaped average cost curve.

From their novel analysis Drake and Howcroft (1995) suggest that for their sample, the optimum branch size was in the total lending range of £3–5.25 million and an optimum average staffing level of around nine. They also conclude (p. 10):

> The finding of a significant negative relationship between all three measures of efficiency and branch cost income ratios suggests that DEA can provide bank management with a powerful tool for improving efficiency, lowering cost income ratios and improving profitability.

Altunbas, Maude and Molyneux (1995) use a one-output (total earning assets), three-input, stochastic cost frontier approach to calculate inefficiency scores for the UK market in 1993. The model assumes an exponential distribution for the efficiency term in the estimation (although the results appear to be robust to alternative distributional assumptions). Their results are shown in Table 9.5.

Overall the results show that the UK bank and building society sector is remarkably efficient, that is, the bulk of institutions lie close to the best practice frontier. For all institutions, the mean inefficiency score at 6.33% means that the same level of output could be produced with 93.67% of the current inputs if they were operating efficiently. A further breakdown of the descriptive statistics comparing the 9 major banks and 83 building societies reveals that on average the banks are more efficient than their building society counterparts. This is shown in Table 9.6.

Table 9.6 shows that the inefficiency scores for banks are exceptionally low, with the maximum (or worst efficiency) at only 7.3%. This compares with the building society sector that has an outlier — the Alliance and Leicester Building Society — at 60.8%, by far the least efficient financial institution in our sample. Tables 9.7(a) and (b) provide a listing of all the banks and building societies in our sample with the relevant inefficiency scores.

Table 9.5 UK bank and building society inefficiency scores, 1993

Size category	Number	Mean	Median	Standard deviation	Minimum	Maximum
Banks and building societies over £4bn in assets	22	0.0831	0.0395	0.1252	0.0183	0.6080
Building societies between £1 and £4bn	12	0.0602	0.0488	0.0388	0.0146	0.1323
Building societies between £200m. and £1bn	18	0.0505	0.0468	0.0256	0.0148	0.0946
Building societies between £50m. and £200m.	23	0.0517	0.0398	0.0325	0.0157	0.1602
Building societies under £50m.	17	0.0692	0.0493	0.0611	0.0191	0.2467
All institutions	92	0.0633	0.0432	0.0707	0.0146	0.6080

Table 9.6 Banks versus building societies. Efficiency score comparison, 1993

	Number	Mean	Median	Standard deviation	Minimum	Maximum
Banks	9	0.0389	0.0289	0.0221	0.0183	0.0733
Building societies	83	0.0659	0.0461	0.0737	0.0146	0.6080

Table 9.7(a) Banks and building society inefficiency scores, ranked according to asset size

Row	Name of banks	Total assets	Inefficiency
1	BARCLAYS (C.)	1 63 000	0.0733
2	NATIONAL WESTMINSTER BANK (C.)	1 52 000	0.0725
3	ABBEY NATIONAL PLC (C.)	79 900	0.0183
4	MIDLAND (C.)	75 400	0.0289
5	LLOYDS BANK (C.)	71 600	0.0532
6	Halifax	67 200	0.1853
7	ROYAL BANK OF SCOTLAND GROUP	36 000	0.0200
8	Nationwide	35 000	0.0840
9	STANDARD CHARTERED (C.)	31 900	0.0369
10	BANK OF SCOTLAND (C.)	30 700	0.0193
11	TSB GROUP (C.)	25 400	0.0276
12	Woolwich	25 200	0.0912
13	Alliance & Leicester	21 100	0.6080
14	Leeds Permanent	19 500	0.0368
15	Cheltenham & Gloucester	17 700	0.0306
16	Bradford & Bingley	13 900	0.0715
17	Britannia	12 900	0.0413
18	National & Provincial	12 700	0.0377
19	Bristol & West	8 140	0.1657
20	Northern Rock	7 280	0.0327
21	Yorkshire	5 350	0.0307
22	Birmingham Midshires	4 330	0.0619
23	Portman	3 060	0.0780
24	Coventry	2 970	0.0409
25	Skipton	2 910	0.1323
26	Leeds & Holbeck	2 450	0.0190
27	Chelsea	2 210	0.0435
28	Derbyshire	1 650	0.0461
29	North of England	1 510	0.0595
30	Norwich & Peterborough	1 380	0.1281
31	Cheshire	1 370	0.0146
32	West Bromwich	1 240	0.0828
33	Principality	1 200	0.0516
34	Newcastle	1 190	0.0255
35	Staffordshire	955	0.0148
36	Nottingham	819	0.0381
37	Dunfermline	812	0.0261
38	Lambeth	524	0.0946
39	Stroud & Swindon	524	0.0714
40	Cumberland	508	0.0540
41	Scarborough	398	0.0848
42	National Counties	362	0.0583
43	Furness	337	0.0740
44	Leek United	334	0.0346
45	Cambridge	323	0.0897
46	Progressive	320	0.0263

continued overleaf

Table 9.7(a)   (*continued*)

Row	Name of banks	Total assets	Inefficiency
47	Darlington	268	0.0621
48	Marsden	255	0.0661
49	Hinckley & Rugby	249	0.0228
50	Kent Reliance	229	0.0278
51	Newbury	218	0.0396
52	Saffron Walden Herts & Essex	216	0.0230
53	Market Harborough	194	0.0320
54	Melton Mowbray	187	0.0670
55	Universal	185	0.0398
56	Barnsley	179	0.1602
57	Hanley Economic	167	0.0732
58	Ipswich	165	0.0587
59	Greenwich	145	0.0189
60	Monmouthshire	139	0.0221
61	Mercantile	130	0.0376
62	Teachers'	120	0.0662
63	Vernon	115	0.0321
64	Mansfield	105	0.0835
65	Scottish	105	0.0758
66	Loughborough	98	0.0421
67	City & Metropolitan	94	0.0263
68	Tipton & Coseley	90	0.0342
69	Manchester	87	0.0871
70	Chesham	80	0.0270
71	Dudley	73	0.0582
72	Holmesdale	57	0.0157
73	Chorley & District	54	0.0382
74	Buckinghamshire	53	0.0202
75	Earl Shilton	52	0.0734
76	Bath Investment Building Society	49	0.1426
77	Tynemouth	48	0.0493
78	Penrith	46	0.0222
79	Stafford Railway	45	0.0381
80	Harpenden	40	0.0748
81	Nottingham Imperial	38	0.0191
82	West Cumbria	36	0.0830
83	Beverley	35	0.0320
84	Shepshed	31	0.0553
85	Swansea	30	0.0428
86	Gainsborough	27	0.0342
87	Catholic	23	0.0752
88	Ilkeston Permanent	16	0.2467
89	Clay Cross Benefit	16	0.1618
90	The Standard	15	0.0214
91	Ecology	13	0.0508
92	Londonderry Provident	7	0.0278

Table 9.7(b) Bank and building society inefficiency scores ranked according to inefficiency score

Row	Name of banks	Total assets	Inefficiency
1	Alliance & Leicester	21 100	0.6080
2	Ilkeston Permanent	16	0.2467
3	Halifax	67 200	0.1853
4	Bristol & West	8 140	0.1657
5	Clay Cross Benefit	16	0.1618
6	Barnsley	179	0.1602
7	Bath Investment Building Society	49	0.1426
8	Skipton	2 910	0.1323
9	Norwich & Peterborough	1 380	0.1281
10	Lambeth	524	0.0946
11	Woolwich	25 200	0.0912
12	Cambridge	323	0.0897
13	Manchester	87	0.0871
14	Scarborough	398	0.0848
15	Nationwide	35 000	0.0840
16	Mansfield	105	0.0835
17	West Cumbria	36	0.0830
18	West Bromwich	1 240	0.0828
19	Portman	3 060	0.0780
20	Scottish	105	0.0758
21	Catholic	23	0.0752
22	Harpenden	40	0.0748
23	Furness	337	0.0740
24	Earl Shilton	52	0.0734
25	BARCLAYS (C.)	163 000	0.0733
26	Hanley Economic	167	0.0732
27	NATIONAL WESTMINSTER BANK (C.)	152 000	0.0725
28	Bradford & Bingley	13 900	0.0715
29	Stroud & Swindon	524	0.0714
30	Melton Mowbray	187	0.0670
31	Teachers'	120	0.0662
32	Marsden	255	0.0661
33	Darlington	268	0.0621
34	Birmingham Midshires	4 330	0.0619
35	North of England	1 510	0.0595
36	Ipswich	165	0.0587
37	National Counties	362	0.0583
38	Dudley	73	0.0582
39	Shepshed	31	0.0553
40	Cumberland	508	0.0540
41	LLOYDS BANK (C.)	71 600	0.0532
42	Principality	1 200	0.0516
43	Ecology	13	0.0508
44	Tynemouth	48	0.0493
45	Derbyshire	1 650	0.0461
46	Chelsea	2 210	0.0435

continued overleaf

Table 9.7(b)   (*continued*)

Row	Name of banks	Total assets	Inefficiency
47	Swansea	30	0.0428
48	Loughborough	98	0.0421
49	Britannia	12 900	0.0413
50	Coventry	2 970	0.0409
51	Universal	185	0.0398
52	Newbury	218	0.0396
53	Chorley & District	54	0.0382
54	Nottingham	819	0.0381
55	Stafford Railway	45	0.0381
56	National & Provincial	12 700	0.0377
57	Mercantile	130	0.0376
58	STANDARD CHARTERED (C.)	31 900	0.0369
59	Leeds Permanent	19 500	0.0368
60	Leek United	334	0.0346
61	Tipton & Coseley	90	0.0342
62	Gainsborough	27	0.0342
63	Northern Rock	7 280	0.0327
64	Vernon	115	0.0321
65	Market Harborough	194	0.0320
66	Beverley	35	0.0320
67	Yorkshire	5 350	0.0307
68	Cheltenham & Gloucester	17 700	0.0306
69	MIDLAND (C.)	75 400	0.0289
70	Kent Reliance	229	0.0278
71	Londonderry Provident	7	0.0278
72	TSB GROUP (C.)	25 400	0.0276
73	Chesham	80	0.0270
74	Progressive	320	0.0263
75	City & Metropolitan	94	0.0263
76	Dunfermline	812	0.0261
77	Newcastle	1 190	0.0255
78	Saffron Walden Herts & Essex	216	0.0230
79	Hinckley & Rugby	249	0.0228
80	Penrith	46	0.0222
81	Monmouthshire	139	0.0221
82	The Standard	15	0.0214
83	Buckinghamshire	53	0.0202
84	ROYAL BANK OF SCOTLAND GROUP	36 000	0.0200
85	BANK OF SCOTLAND (C.)	30 700	0.0193
86	Nottingham Imperial	38	0.0191
87	Leeds & Holbeck	2 450	0.0190
88	Greenwich	145	0.0189
89	ABBEY NATIONAL PLC (C.)	79 900	0.0183
90	Holmesdale	57	0.0157
91	Staffordshire	955	0.0148
92	Cheshire	1 370	0.0146

One can tentatively suggest that given the above findings there are perhaps limited opportunities for substantial efficiency gains through structural reorganisation of the UK retail banking market.

Efficiency in the Turkish Banking Market

A recent paper by Altunbas, Molyneux and Murphy (1995) uses a similar approach to the aforementioned studies to investigate the relative inefficiency of public and private banks operating in Turkey between 1991 and 1993. The study also addresses the question of privatisation in the Turkish banking market. Table 9.8 shows the inefficiency scores for each category of bank. In 1993 the mean inefficiency score for all banks at 49.2% suggests that Turkish banks could produce the same output with 50.8% of the current inputs if they were operating efficiently. These inefficiency scores are substantially larger than the findings in earlier studies.

Both the mean and median inefficiency scores suggest that the Turkish public commercial banks are less efficient than their private counterparts. Foreign bank subsidiaries and branches also appear to be highly inefficient for the period under study. Descriptive statistics for the public development and investment banks, on the other hand, suggest that these are the most efficient institutions operating in the Turkish market.

After further tests, however, the authors find that the results indicate no strong statistical evidence of inefficiency differences between public and private banks, over the three years under study. They argue that the lack of any clear distinction between inefficiencies of public and private banks can perhaps be explored by examining inefficiency scores for each bank.

In general they come to two main conclusions. First, the efficiency of public and private banks seems to differ according to the heterogeneous nature of bank types within individual groupings. They note that there may be some types of public banks operating in particular business areas and subject to various forms of ownership and competition that may be highly efficient. Alternatively, there may be other types of public banks that are not. Put simply, the private versus public bank dichotomy may be too simplistic for investigating efficiency differences between Turkish banks because these banks are too heterogeneous. As a consequence, characteristics other than ownership type appear to be more important in determining bank efficiency levels in the Turkish market.

Secondly, the inefficiency scores for individual banks suggest that there may be some public banks which are 'good' candidates for privatisation if efficiency gains are sought, whereas others are not. They conclude that the discipline of the market 'may well encourage Etibank and Sümerbank to improve their efficiency but it is hard to see how privatisation of some of the country's most efficient public banks, such as Ziraat, Vakif and Iller Bank can be justified on efficiency

Table 9.8   Inefficiency levels of banks according to banking groups

Type of banks	No.	Mean	Median	Standard deviation	Minimum	Maximum
1991						
Public — commercial	7	0.570	0.437	0.496	0.084	1.487
Private — commercial	26	0.413	0.192	0.435	0.043	1.321
Foreign — subsidiaries	9	0.512	0.549	0.372	0.036	0.976
Foreign bank branches	12	0.665	0.743	0.416	0.121	1.511
Public — development and investment banks	2	0.133	0.133	0.055	0.094	0.172
Private — development and investment banks	7	0.213	0.100	0.236	0.041	0.649
All banks	63	0.462	0.300	0.418	0.036	1.511
1992						
Public — commercial	6	0.406	0.225	0.358	0.118	1.013
Private — commercial	31	0.297	0.233	0.251	0.097	1.233
Foreign — subsidiaries	9	0.402	0.339	0.337	0.140	1.253
Foreign bank branches	11	0.326	0.280	0.189	0.096	0.717
Public — development and investment banks	3	0.225	0.222	0.077	0.150	0.303
Private — development and investment banks	8	0.288	0.302	0.144	0.107	0.449
All banks	68	0.321	0.245	0.248	0.096	1.253
1993						
Public — commercial	6	0.839	0.376	1.022	0.090	2.700
Private — commercial	32	0.426	0.289	0.355	0.047	1.228
Foreign — subsidiaries	9	0.516	0.553	0.420	0.085	1.298
Foreign bank branches	11	0.440	0.200	0.420	0.072	1.140
Public — development and investment banks	3	0.307	0.383	0.148	0.136	0.401
Private — development and investment banks	9	0.601	0.450	0.562	0.065	1.849
All banks	70	0.492	0.352	0.478	0.047	2.700

grounds' (see also Oral and Yolalan, 1990 for an account of Turkish branch efficiency).

Efficiency in the Scandinavian Banking Market

Other important research on efficiency in banking continues to be undertaken in Scandinavian banking markets. In particular the work by Berg, Forsund and Jansen (1991, 1992), Berg et al. (1993) and Berg, Forsund and Bukh (1995) stands out as a major contribution to the literature. The earlier studies focused on the Norwegian market whereas the latter papers consider a range of Scandinavian banking markets. For example, Berg et al. (1993) use DEA to measure the X-inefficiency of banks in three Nordic countries (Finland, Norway and Sweden).

An innovative technique (a form of Malmquist productivity index) was used to model the banking frontier technologies. Overall they found that Swedish banks tended to be more efficient than their Nordic counterparts.

In their most recent study, Berg, Forsund and Bukh (1995) apply DEA to the banking industries of Denmark, Finland, Norway and Sweden. Productivity differences between banks from different countries were measured using Malmquist indices and these were decomposed into one term describing different distances from the national best practice frontiers and another describing the difference between these national frontiers. The authors found that the largest Danish and Swedish banks were among the most efficient units in their pooled Nordic sample, whereas only one large Finnish bank and one large Norwegian bank were more than 90% efficient. Berg, Forsund and Bukh (1995) conclude that the Danish and Swedish banks are in the best position to expand in a common Nordic banking market.

Bank Efficiency in Spain and Portugal

A substantial amount of research on Spanish banking productivity has been undertaken by economists at the University of Valencia (see e.g. Doménech, 1991, 1992; Doménech and Pérez, 1992a, b; Doménech, Pérez and Quesada, 1993; Pastor and Pérez, 1994; Pastor, Pérez and Quesada, 1994; Pérez and Quesada, 1994). The main focus of this work has been to investigate productivity in the banking market, evaluating improvement in cost efficiency by measuring total factor productivity. Pérez and Pastor have found that banking productivity in Spain increased substantially between 1986 and 1992 and that savings banks were relatively more productive than their commercial bank counterparts. Savings bank total factor productivity increased from 0.623 in 1986 to 1.046 in 1992, compared with 0.461 to 0.757 for commercial banks over the period.

Pérez and Quesada (1994) provide details of changes in productivity for the main savings and commercial banks between 1986 and 1992 which also emphasise that the productivity gains experienced by large Spanish banks have been very intensive, 'the likely result of strategies aimed at improving their competitive position' (p. 7). The same study shows measures of relative technical efficiency for both commercial and savings banks operating in Spain in 1992. The authors use DEA to calculate these results. Figure 9.1 reports these findings and indicates that a group of commercial banks representing up to 40% of the sector operates with an efficiency 20% or lower below the most efficient level. Furthermore, within 10% of the most efficient level are 60% of the savings bank sector but only 20% of the commercial banks.

Pastor, Pérez and Quesada (1994) undertook an international comparison of banking efficiency. Measuring productive change using Malmquist indices and employing DEA, Spanish banking efficiency was compared with seven other

Technical efficiency score

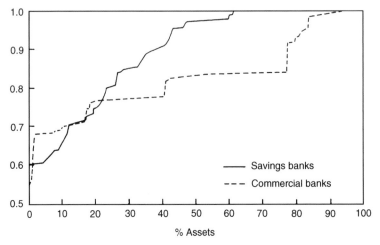

% Assets

Figure 9.1 Efficiency distribution according to share in total assets, 1992 (Note: number of savings banks = 53, number of commercial banks = 54. Source: CECA and CSB)

countries (the USA and six other European countries). They found that Spain and the USA seemed to have the highest banking efficiency.

A number of recent papers by Griffell-Tatjé and Lovell (1994a, b, 1995a, c) investigate the use of the Malmquist (1953) productivity index to evaluate productivity in the Spanish savings banks sector. Griffell-Tatjé and Lovell (1994b) demonstrate that the Malmquist productivity index captures the contributions of technical efficiency change and technical change to productivity change, but fails to capture the contribution of scale economies to productivity change and so the measure is systematically biased in the presence of increasing or decreasing returns to scale. The authors develop what they call a 'generalised Malmquist productivity index' that includes the contribution of scale economies. Using a linear programming application to productivity change in Spanish savings banks over the period 1986–91, they find that the conventional Malmquist index understates productivity change in small banks experiencing economies of scale and overstates productivity change in large banks experiencing diseconomies of scale. (The (1995a) paper theoretically confirms this finding.) Griffell-Tatjé and Lovell (1995b, c) use DEA techniques combined with the above index approach to investigate productive efficiency and total factor productivity in Spanish saving banks in the same period. They find that neither branching nor mergers provide an adequate explanation for the size or nature of the productivity decline observed over the period. They also conclude that DEA can serve as an 'extremely useful tool in the measurement and the analysis of productivity change' (Griffell-Tatjé, 1995b, p. 15).

Soares de Pinho (1994) uses the stochastic cost frontier approach to estimate relative efficiency of Portuguese banks between 1987 and 1991. A two-input two-output (including deposits) cost frontier is estimated on a pooled sample of 140 observations. The author finds that the inefficiency results are sensitive to model specification especially in relation to different definitions of the cost of capital. Overall Soares de Pinho (1994):

> ... finds an average productive efficiency value of 0.826 ranging from 0.471 to 0.963. The interpretation for this is that, on average, Portuguese banks use 17% more real resources than are actually needed for the production of their output bundles.

So as to evaluate the determinants of these inefficiency scores, the author undertakes regression analysis and finds that market share has little effect on relative efficiency, yet 'older banks show, on average, higher efficiency scores, which may be associated with the fact that most of their fixed assets are already fully depreciated and they may also benefit from cheaper rents on their premises'. The author also finds that Portuguese nationalised banks are less efficient than private ones and that over the period of study average industry efficiency grew about 1% each year.

Irish Bank Efficiency

Lucey (1995b) examines the interaction between profits and efficiency using a sample of 17 Irish banks for the years 1988–91. In contrast to many previous techniques used for assessing economic models of efficiency, the method adopted allows for a finer decomposition of profit loss which can be attributed to allocative or technical inefficiency and these can be derived both for inputs and outputs. Following on from the work of Berger, Hancock and Humphrey (1993), the study estimates a multi-input-output profit function using a systems multivariate nonlinear least squares approach. Profit-level inefficiencies are then broken down into five categories:

1. *Input allocative inefficiency* — bad input plans, based on mispriced inputs.
2. *Output allocative inefficiency* — bad production plans, based on misperceptions of final products prices.
3. *Input–output allocative inefficiency* — a combination of the above.
4. *Input technical inefficiency* — incorrect input mix.
5. *Output technical inefficiency* — incorrect output mix.

The results are shown in Table 9.9.

Table 9.9 shows that total losses due to inefficiencies amounted to just over 20% of the average realised profits. The preponderant part of the loss is due to technical inefficiency rather than allocative inefficiency. This implies that for the

Table 9.9 Decomposition of profit inefficiency in Irish banking

		% of average profits	% of total inefficiency
Total inefficiency	3.55	20.76	100.00
Allocative inefficiency	0.62	3.63	17.46
Input allocative inefficiency	0.03	0.18	0.85
Output allocative inefficiency	0.59	3.45	16.62
Technical inefficiency	2.93	17.13	82.54
Input technical inefficiency	0.71	4.15	20.00
Output technical inefficiency	2.22	12.98	62.54

period under study Irish banks were not necessarily formulating poor plans, but seemed to be poor at implementing them. The major inefficiencies appear to arise on the output side rather than on the input side, thus the mix of outputs appears to be a more crucial decision as compared to the mix of inputs.

OVERVIEW OF THE EFFICIENCY STUDIES

US researchers using stochastic frontier methodology have generally found average banking inefficiency to be around 20–25% of costs. DEA researchers, on the other hand, have produced results ranging from less than 10% to over 50%. The handful of stochastic frontier European cost studies seem to find inefficiency levels more in line with the US DEA studies. However, this may relate to the wide variety of banking firms operating in various European markets. Note that when similar institutions are investigated, such as the UK building societies and the Italian cooperative banks, inefficiency levels are low. Berger, Hunter and Timme (1993, p. 228) suggest that a difficulty associated with these techniques is that they often produce different rankings even with the same dataset (and even where there is close correlation between the techniques on average efficiency levels). Even where the same technique is used, results can be sensitive to the specification and measurement of input and output variables, and what variables are classed as fixed and variable.

Berger, Hancock and Humphrey (1993) use a distribution-free stochastic estimator to explore banking efficiency derived from the profit function. One interesting finding is that larger banks are on average substantially more X-efficient than smaller ones. It is suggested that this finding might offset some of the scale diseconomies found for larger banks in cost studies. This research also suggests that larger banks may be able to achieve high-value output bundles. This research redefined scope economies as 'optimal scope economies' that are output-efficient as well as input-efficient: most inefficiencies were found to result from deficit output revenues (rather than excessive input costs). They find that optimal scope economies obtain for most, but not all, firms.

Berger, Hunter and Timme (1993, p. 231) make several suggestions for future research on banking X-efficiency. They suggest more research comparing these techniques is needed in order to facilitate comparisons of results. This may, for example, produce pre-testing procedures in order to decide the best technique to use for a particular dataset. The recent work by Berger, Hancock and Humphrey (1993), Akhavein, Berger and Humphrey (1994) and Lucey (1995b) suggests that more research is needed on output inefficiencies: these look to be as large, if not larger, than input inefficiencies.

CONCLUDING REMARKS: WHERE DO WE GO FROM HERE?

It is clear that there is a great deal of exciting, complex and useful econometric work emerging from all of this research. Overall, the econometric work to date suggests fairly limited scale economies from bank growth alone, although in certain areas (like technology development) size seems to be more important. We have shown from the analysis presented in Chapters 6 and 7 that there may be significant scale economies from a plant-level perspective. Other studies in US banking indicate stronger product or line of business economies. In this general respect the recent work by McAllister and McManus (1993) and Akhavein, Berger and Humphrey (1994) is very interesting. The former *inter alia* bring in financial risk, which appears to be a key element in the calculus of overall scale efficiency in modern banking. The latter draw attention to the profit function and output efficiency in computing X-efficiency and scope economies. The Humphrey (1987) work on cost dispersion is also very important since it signals *inter alia* the question of X-inefficiencies. It may also be a reminder that other determining factors may be important (and missing) in contemporary empirical work on bank efficiency.

One of the main messages from this chapter is that a great deal more work is needed on X-efficiency research in banking. One major aim here from a modelling perspective must be to tackle the problem of the sensitivity of bank rankings (their relative 'efficiency scores') using different frontier techniques, and different banking input and output definitions and measures. There is an urgent need for good comparative research in this area, and the development of suitable pre-testing (exploratory) procedures to decide which is the best technique to use, given an objective (measurement purpose) and a specific kind of dataset. This kind of research seems to be important simply because X-efficiency gains appear to be so much higher than scale and scope efficiencies in banking.

One supposes that the practical, strategic and policy implication of all this research is that contemporary econometric research does not necessarily support the view that size alone produces greater banking 'efficiency'. There do appear to be some scale and scope economies obtainable from size, but these seem to be limited and soon exhausted beyond a fairly small asset size. However, branch- and product-level scale efficiencies look more promising. There also appears to be significant scale economies in large-scale technology investment in banking. Generally speaking, though, managerial efficiency, the concept of X-efficiency, appears to be a much more important strategic and policy consideration. There is only a small number of European studies which study whether X-inefficiencies are higher for smaller banks compared with the bigger ones or for specialist banks compared with universal ones. More work is clearly needed in these key areas.

It is also not clear that the empirical evidence to date supports the view that deregulation by itself produces productivity gains in banking. US experience seems to be that deregulation has generally raised banking costs, but not measured output. Although consumers may have benefited, banks have not. This kind of result might be, of course, the result of methodological and empirical measurement difficulties. Strategic and managerial factors, which are clearly important in the real world, stimulate a related concern that 'partial quantitative models' may sometimes be too limited a reflection of reality. In all of this research we need to think carefully about the kinds of costs, revenues and associated variables actually targeted by management in their decision-making. We need to get closer to the actual variables that drive key management decisions. With fast-developing banking markets and banking's almost revolutionary capacity for change, this seems to be an essential requirement.

References

Abraham, J.P. and F. Lierman (1991) 'European banking strategies in the nineties: a supply side approach', *IEF Research Papers*, No. 91/8.

Adar, Z., T. Agmon and Y.E. Orgler (1975) 'Output mix and jointness in production in the banking firm', *Journal of Money, Credit and Banking*, **7**, (May), 235–243.

Aigner, D., C. Lovell and P. Schmidt (1977) 'Formulation and estimation of stochastic frontier production models', *Journal of Econometrics*, **6**, 21–37.

Akhavein, Jalal D., A.N. Berger and D.B. Humphrey (1994) 'Profit efficiency effects of megamergers in banking', Paper presented at the Nordic Banking Research Seminar, 12–14 February 1995 at Venastal, Norway.

Alhadeff, D.A. (1954) *Monopoly and Competition in Banking* (Berkeley: University of California Press).

Alhadeff, D.A. and C.P. Alhadeff (1975) 'Bank entry and bank concentration', *Antitrust Bulletin*, **20** (Fall), 471–483.

Aliber, Robert Z. (1975) 'International banking: growth and regulation', *Columbia Journal of World Business*, **10**(4), 9–15.

Allen, L. and A. Rai (1993) 'Global financial intermediation: universal versus specialised banking', Paper presented at the 20th Annual Meeting of the European Finance Association, Copenhagen Business School, 26–28 August, Published in Section II-D of the *Proceedings*, pp. 1–33.

Altunbas, Y., L. Evans and P. Molyneux (1994) 'Universal banks, ownership and efficiency. A stochastic frontier analysis of the German banking market', University of Durham Economics Department Working Paper (preliminary version/unpublished in 1994).

Altunbas, Y. and P. Molyneux (1994a) 'The concentration–performance relationship in European banking — a note', *Institute of European Finance Research Papers in Banking and Finance*, RP 94/12, pp. 1–12.

Altunbas, Y. and P. Molyneux (1994b) 'Sensitivity of stochastic frontier estimation to distributional assumptions: the case of the German banks',

Institution of European Finance Discussion Paper (preliminary version, unpublished in 1994).

Altunbas, Y., P. Molyneux and R. DiSalvo (1994) 'Inefficiency in the Italian credit cooperative bank sector — a stochastic frontier analysis', Institute of European Finance Discussion Paper (preliminary version, unpublished in 1994).

Altunbas, Y., P. Molyneux and N.B. Murphy (1995) 'Privatisation, efficiency and public ownership in Turkey — an analysis of the banking industry 1991–1993', Institute of European Finance Discussion Paper (preliminary version, unpublished in 1994).

Altunbas, Y., D. Maude and P. Molyneux (1995) 'Efficiency and mergers in the UK (retail) banking market', Institute of European Finance Working Paper, pp. 1–40 (forthcoming).

Andersen, Arthur (1993) *European Banking and Capital Markets — a Strategic Forecast*, Research Report (London: The Economist Intelligence Unit).

Anuario Estadistico de la Banca Privada (1988) Consejo Superior Bancario (Madrid: CSB).

Arrelli, M. and S. Micossi (1992) 'Saving and investment in the world economy and Italy's place', *Review of Economic Conditions in Italy, Banco Di Roma*, No. 1, Jan–April.

Arrow, K.J. (1971) *Essays in the Theory of Risk-Bearing* (Amsterdam: North-Holland).

Arrow, K.J., H.B. Chenery, B. Minhas and R.M. Solow (1961) 'Capital–labour substitution and economic efficiency', *Review of Economics and Statistics*, **43**, 225–250.

Artis, M.J. (1968) 'The Monopolies Commission Report', *Bankers' Magazine*, **CCVI**, September.

Aspinwall, R.C. (1970) 'Market structure and commercial bank mortgage interest rates', *Southern Economic Journal*, **36** (April), 376–384.

Baer, Herbert and Larry, R. Mote (1985) 'The effects of nationwide banking and concentration: the evidence from abroad', *Federal Reserve Bank of Chicago Economic Perspectives*, **9**(1) (January/February), 3–16.

Bailey, E.E. and A.F. Friedlaender (1982) 'Market structure and multiproduct industries', *Journal of Economic Literature*, Sept. 20, 1024–1048.

Bain, J.S. (1956) *Barriers to New Competition* (Cambridge, Mass.: Harvard University Press).

Baldini, D. and A. Landi (1990) 'Economie di scala e complementarieta' di costo nell'industria bancaria italiana', *L'Industria*, No. 1, 25–45.

Baldwin, R. (1989) 'The growth effects of 1992', *Economic Policy*, No. 9 (October), 248–281.

Baltensperger, E. (1980) 'Alternative approaches to the theory of the banking firm', *Journal of Monetary Economics*, **6**, 1–37.

Baltensperger, E. and J. Dermine (1990) 'European banking: prudential and regulatory issues', in J. Dermine (ed.), *European Banking in the 1990s* (London: Blackwell), pp. 17–36.

Banco de Espana (1993) 'Changes in the Spanish banking systems workings in the period 1989–1992', *Banco de Espana Economic Bulletin*, July, 41–51.

Bank of England (1992) 'The Maastricht agreement on Economic and Monetary Union', *Bank of England Quarterly Bulletin*, **32**(1), February, 64–69.

Bank of England (1993) 'Cross-border alliances in banking and financial services in the single market', *Quarterly Bulletin*, **33**(3), August.

Bank of England (1994) 'Economic and Monetary Union in Europe', Bank of England Fact Sheet, May 1994.

Bank of Italy (1994) 'Ordinary general meeting of shareholders', *Abridged Report for the year 1993*.

The Banker (1988) 'Top 500', **138**(749), July, 56–151.

Banque de France (1992) *Annual Report 1992*, Paris.

Barnes, P. and C. Dodds (1983) 'The structure and performance of the UK building society industry 1970–78', *Journal of Business, Finance and Accounting*, **10**, 37–56.

Barnett, W.A. and Y.W. Lee (1985) 'The global properties of the miniflex Laurent, generalised Leontief and translog flexible functional forms', *Econometrica*, **53**, November, 1421–1437.

Battese, G.E. and G.S. Corra (1977) 'Estimation of a production frontier model: with application to the pastoral zone of Eastern Australia', *Australian Journal of Agricultural Economics*, **21**(3), December, 169–179.

Bauer, P. (1990) 'Recent developments in the econometric estimations of frontiers', *Journal of Econometrics*, **46**, 39–56.

Bauer, P.W., A.N. Berger and D.B. Humphrey (1993) 'Efficiency and productivity growth in U.S. banking', in M.O. Fried, C.A.K. Lovell and S.S. Schmidt (eds), *The Measurement of Productive Efficiency: Techniques and Applications* (Oxford: Oxford University Press).

Baumol, W.J. (1977) 'On the proper test for natural monopoly in a multi-product industry', *American Economic Review*, **67**, December, 809–822.

Baumol, W.J., J.C. Panzar and R.D. Willig (1988) *Contestable Markets and the Theory of Industry Structure*, revised edition (New York: Harcourt Brace Jovanovich).

Beckers, D. and C. Hammond (1987) 'A tractable likelihood function for the normal-gamma stochastic frontier model', *Economics Letters*, **24**, 33–38.

Beighley, H.P. and A.S. McCall (1975) 'Market power and structure and commercial bank installment lending', *Journal of Money, Credit and Banking*, **7**, November, 449–467.

Bell, F.W. and N.B. Murphy (1967) 'Economies of scale in commercial banking', Federal Reserve Bank of Boston, August.

Bell, F.W. and N.B. Murphy (1968) 'Economies of scale and division of labour in commercial banking', *Southern Economic Journal*, October, 131–139.

Bell, F.W. and N.B. Murphy (1969) 'Impact of market structure on the price of a commercial bank service', *Review of Economics and Statistics*, **51**, May, 210–213.

Benston, G.J. (1965a) 'Economies of scale and marginal costs in banking operations', *National Banking Review*, **2**(4), June, 507–549.

Benston, G.J. (1965b) 'Branch banking and economies of scale', *Journal of Finance*, May, 312–331.

Benston, G.J. (1972) 'Economies of scale of financial institutions', *Journal of Money, Credit and Banking*, **4**, May, 312–341.

Benston, G.J. (1994) 'Universal banking', *Journal of Economic Perspectives*, **8**(3), Summer, 121–143.

Benston, G.J., A.N. Berger, G. Hanweck and D. Humphrey (1983) 'Economy of scale and scope', *Proceedings of the Conference on Bank Structure and Competition*, Chicago, Federal Reserve Bank of Chicago.

Benston, G.J., G.A. Hanweck and D.B. Humphrey (1982a) 'Scale economies in banking: a restructuring and reassessment', *Journal of Money, Credit and Banking*, **14**, 435–456.

Benston, G.J., G.A. Hanweck and D.B. Humphrey (1982b) 'Operating costs in commercial banking', *Federal Reserve Bank of Atlanta Economic Review*, 6–21.

Berg, S. Atle (1992) 'Mergers, efficiency and productivity growth in banking: the Norwegian experience', *Norges Bank Arberds Notat*, Oslo, June 12.

Berg, S. Atle, Finn R. Forsund and Eilev S. Jansen (1991) 'Technical efficiency of Norwegian banks: the non-parametric approach to efficiency measurement', *Journal of Productivity Analysis*, **2**(2), 127–142.

Berg, S. Atle, Finn R. Forsund and Eilev S. Jansen (1992) 'Malmquist indices of productivity growth during the deregulation of Norwegian banking (1980–1989)', *Scandinavian Journal of Economics*, **94**, S212–S228.

Berg, S.A., F.R. Forsund, L. Hjalmarsson and M. Suominen (1993) 'Banking efficiency in the Nordic countries', *Journal of Banking and Finance*, **17**(2–3), April, 371–388.

Berg, Sigjborn Atle, Finn R. Forsund and Nikolay Per Bukh (1995) 'Banking efficiency in the Nordic countries: a few-country Malmquist index analysis' (mimeo).

Berg, S.A. and M. Kim (1991) 'Oligopolistic interdependence and banking efficiency: an empirical evaluation', *Norges Bank Research Paper*, No. 1991/5.

Berger, A.N. (1993) 'Distribution-free estimates of efficiency in the US banking industry and tests of the standards distributional assumptions', *Journal of Productivity Analysis*, **4**, September, 261–292.

Berger, A.N. (1995) 'The profit–structure relationship in banking — tests of market-power and efficient-structure hypothesis', *Journal of Money, Credit and Banking*, **27**(2), 404–431.

Berger, A.N., D. Hancock and D.B. Humphrey (1993) 'Banking efficiency derived from the profit function', *Journal of Banking and Finance*, **17**, April, 317–347.

Berger, Allen N. and Timothy H. Hannan (1989) 'The price–concentration relationship in banking', *The Review of Economics and Statistics*, **71**, 291–299.

Berger, A.N. and T.H. Hannan (1992) 'The price–concentration relationship in banking — a reply', *Review of Economics and Statistics*, **74**, February, 376–379.

Berger, A.N. and T. Hannan (1993) *Using Efficiency Measures to Distinguish among Alternative Explanations of the Structure–Performance Relationship in Banking*, Federal Reserve Board Working Paper (Washington: Federal Reserve).

Berger, A.N., G.A. Hanweck and D.B Humphrey (1987) 'Competitive viability in banking: scale, scope and product mix economies', *Journal of Monetary Economics*, **20**, 501–520.

Berger, A. and D.B. Humphrey (1991) 'The dominance of inefficiencies over scale and product mix economies in banking', *Journal of Monetary Economics*, **28**(1), 117–148.

Berger, A.N. and D.B. Humphrey (1992a) 'Measurement and efficiency issues in commercial banking', in Z. Grilliches (ed.), *Output Measurement in the Service Sectors*, National Bureau of Economic Research (Chicago: University of Chicago Press), pp. 245–279.

Berger, A.N. and D.B. Humphrey (1992b) 'Megamergers in banking and the use of cost efficiency as an antitrust defense', *Antitrust Bulletin*, **37**, Fall, 541–600.

Berger, Allen, N., William C. Hunter and Stephen G. Timme (1993) 'The efficiency of financial institutions: a review and preview of research past, present and future', *Journal of Banking and Finance*, **17**, 221–249.

Berle, Adolf A. (1949) 'Banking under the antitrust laws', *Columbia Law Review*, **49**, May.

Berndt, E.R., B.E. Hall and J.A. Hausman (1974) 'Estimation and inference in nonlinear structural models', *Annals of Economic and Social Measurement*, **3**(4), 653–665.

Binswanger, H.P. (1974) 'A cost function approach to the measurement of elasticities of factor demand and elasticities of substitution', *American Journal of Agricultural Economics*, **56**, 377–386.

BIS (Bank for International Settlements) (1994) *63rd Annual Report* (Basle: BIS).

Bisigano, J. (1992) 'Banking in the European Community: structure, competition and public policy', in G. Kaufman, *Banking Structures in Major Countries* (London: Kluwer Academic Publishers).

Bollenbacher, G.M. (1992) *Bank Strategies for the 90s: How to Survive and Thrive in the Global Banking Shake-Out* (Dublin: Lafferty Publications Ltd).

Bourke, P. (1989) 'Concentration and other determinants of bank profitability in Europe, North America and Australia', *Journal of Banking and Finance*, **13**, 65–79 *Statistics*, **64**, 635–645.

Box, G. and D. Cox (1964) 'An analysis of transformation', *Journal of Royal Statistical Society*, Series B, 211–264.

Boyd, J.H. and S.L. Graham (1988) 'The profitability and risk effects of allowing bank holding companies to merge with other financial firms: a simulation study', *Federal Reserve Bank of Minneapolis Quarterly Review*, **No. 2**, Spring, 3–20.

Boyd, J.H. and S.L. Graham (1991) 'Investigating the banking consolidation trend', *Federal Reserve Bank of Minneapolis Quarterly Review*, Spring, 3–15.

Bresnahan, T. (1989) 'Empirical studies of industries with market power', in R. Schmalensee and R. Willig (eds), *Handbook of Industrial Organisation* (Amsterdam: Elsevier), pp. 1011–1058.

Bresnahan, T. and P. Reiss (1990) 'Entry in monopoly markets', *Review of Economic Studies*, **57**, 531–553.

Brigham, E.F. (1991) *Financial Management: Theory and Practice* (New York: Harper-Collins).

Britton, L.C., T.A.R. Clark and D.F. Bell (1992) 'Modify or extend? The application of the structure conduct performance approach to service industries', *The Service Industries Journal*, **12**, January, 34–43.

Brown, Donald M. (1985) 'The relationship between concentration and profitability in the banking industry', Unpublished manuscript presented at the Midwest Finance Association Conference.

Brozen, Y. (1982) *Concentration, Mergers and Public Policy* (New York: Macmillan).

Brucker, E. (1970) 'A microeconomic approach to banking competition', *Journal of Finance*, 25, December, 1133–1141.

Buigues, P. and A. Jacquemin (1988) '1992: Quelles strategies pour le enterprises Europeannes', *Revue Française de Gestrou*, June–August.

Bull. EC. (1991) *Bulletin of the European Community*, Office for Official Publication of the European Communities, **24**(6).

Bull. EC. (1992) *Bulletin of the European Community*, Office for Official Publication of the European Communities, **25**(6).

Bull. EC. (1993a) *Bulletin of the European Community*, Office for Official Publication of the European Communities, **26**(1/2).

Bull. EC. (1993b) *Bulletin of the European Community*, Office for Official Publication of the European Communities, **26**(5).

Bull. EC. (1993c) *Bulletin of the European Community*, Office for Official Publication of the European Communities, **26**(6).

Burgess, D.F. (1974) 'Production theory and the derived demand for imports', *Journal of International Economics*, **3**, 105–121.

Calem, Paul S. and Gerald A. Carlino (1989) 'The concentration/conduct relationship in bank deposit markets', *Federal Reserve Bank of Philadelphia Working Paper*, No. 89–26, October, pp. 1–24.

Canals, J. (1993) *Competitive Strategies in European Banking* (Oxford: Clarendon Press).

Caves, D.W., L.R. Christensen and M.W. Tretheway (1980) 'Flexible cost functions for multiproduct firms', *Review of Economics and Statistics*, August, 477–481.

Caves, R. and D.R. Barton (1990) *Efficiency in US Manufacturing Industries* (Cambridge, Mass: MIT Press).

Cebenoyan, A.S., E.S. Cooperman, C.A. Register and S.C. Hudgins (1993) 'The relative efficiency of stock versus mutual S&Ls: a stochastic cost frontier approach', *Journal of Financial Services Research*, 7, 151–170.

Cecchini, P. (1988) *The European Challenge in 1992: The Benefits of a Single Market* (Aldershot: Gower).

Centre for Business Strategy (1989) *1992: Myths and Realities* (London: London Business School).

Cesarini, F. (1992) 'Recent trends in corporate banking and in bank–customer relationships in the Italian financial system', in J. Revell (ed.), *Changes in Corporate Banking*, IEF Research Monographs in Banking and Finance M 92/3 (Bangor: IEF), pp. 15–33.

Chamberlin, E.H. (1933) *The Theory of Monopolistic Competition* (Cambridge, Mass.: Harvard University Press).

Chandler, Lester V. (1938) 'Monopolistic elements in commercial banking', *Journal of Political Economy*, 46(1), February, 1–22.

Charnes, A., W.W. Cooper and E. Rhodes (1978) 'Measuring the efficiency of decision making units', *European Journal of Operational Research*, 6, 429–444.

Charnes, A., W.W. Cooper, D.B. Sun and Z.M. Huang (1990) 'Polyhedral cone-ratio DEA models with an illustrative application to large commercial banks', *Journal of Econometrics*, 46, 73–91.

Christensen, L.R. and W. Greene (1976) 'Economies of scale in U.S. power generation', *Journal of Political Economy*, 84, 655–676.

Christensen, L.R., D.E. Jorgenson and L.J. Lau (1971) 'Conjugate duality and transcendental logarithmic production function', *Econometrica*, 39(4), July, 255–256.

Christensen, L.R., D.E. Jorgenson and L.J. Lau (1973) 'Transcendental logarithmic production frontiers', *Review of Economics and Statistics*, 55, 28–45.

Clark, J.A. (1984) 'Estimation of economy of scale in banking using a generalized functional form', *Journal of Money, Credit and Banking*, 16, February, 53–68.

Clark, J.A. (1986a) 'Market structure, risk and profitability: the quiet life hypothesis revisted', *Quarterly Review of Economics and Business*, 26(1), Spring, 45–56.

Clark, J.A. (1986b) 'Single-equation, multiple-regression methodology, is it an appropriate methodology for the estimation of the structure performance relationship in banking?' *Journal of Monetary Economics*, 18, 295–312.

Clark, J.A. (1988) 'Economies of scale and scope at depository financial institutions: a review of the literature', *Federal Reserve Bank of Kansas City Economic Review*, **73**, September/October, 16–33.

Clarotti, P. (1984) 'Progress and future developments of establishment and services in the EC in relation to banking', *Journal of Common Market Studies*, **22**, 199–226.

Cobb, C.W. and P.H. Douglas (1928) 'A theory of production', *American Economic Review, Papers and Proceedings*, **18**(1), Supplement, March, 139–165.

Coffrey, P. and J.R. Presley (1971) *European Monetary Integration* (London: Macmillan).

Colwell, R.J. and E.P. Davis (1992) *Output, Productivity and Externalities — the Case of Banking*, Bank of England Discussion Paper No. 3.

Commission of the European Communities (1985) *Completing the Internal Market*, White Paper from the Commission to the European Council, Document (Luxembourg: Office for Official Publications of the European Communities).

Commission of the European Communities (1987) *Treaties Establishing the European Communities* (abridged edition), Office for Official Publications of the European Communities (Brussels: EU).

Commission of the European Communities (1988a) *European Economy: The Economics of 1992*, No. 35, March (Brussels: EU).

Commission of the European Communities (1988b) *The 'Cost of Non-Europe' In Financial Services* (Brussels: Commission of the European Communities), p. 494.

Commission of the European Communities (1991) 'Removal of tax obstacles to the cross-frontier activities of companies', *Bulletin of the European Communities*, Supplement 4/91.

Commission of the European Communities (1992a) *The Maastricht Agreement*, Briefing Note, ISEC/B25/92, 29 September.

Commission of European Communities (1992b) *XXIst Report on Competition Policy 1991*, Office for Official Publications of the European Communities (Brussels: EU).

Commission of the European Communities (1993) 'Growth, competitiveness, employment: the challenge and ways forward into the 21st century', *Bulletin of the European Communities*, Supplement 6/93.

Comptes Annuels des Establissements de Crédit (1988) 'Commission Bancaire', **1**.

Conigliani, C., R. De Bonis, G. Motta, G. Parigi (1991) 'Economie di scala e di diversificazione nel sistema bancario', *Banca d'Italia*, Temi di discussione 150.

Conti, V. and M. Maccarinelli (1993) 'Deregulation and profitability in different OECD banking systems', *IEF Research Papers*, No. 93/18.

Cooper, J.C.B. (1980) 'Economies of scale in the UK building society industry', *Investment Analysis*, **55**, 31–36.

Cornett, M.M. and S. De (1991) 'Common stock in corporate takeover bids: evidence from interstate bank mergers', *Journal of Banking and Finance*, **15**, 273–295.

Cornett, M.M. and H. Tehranian (1992) 'Changes in corporate performance associated with bank acquisition', *Journal of Financial Economics*, **31**, 211–234.

Cossutta, D., M.L. Di Battista, C. Giannini and G. Urga (1988) 'Processo produttivo e struttura dei costi nell'industria bancaria italiana', in *Banca e Mercato* a cura di F. Cesarini. M. Grillo, M. Monti, M. Onado (Bologna: eds. Il Mulino).

Curry, Timothy J. and John T. Rose (1984) 'Bank structure and mortgage rates — a comment', *Journal of Economics and Business*, **36**, 283–287.

Daniel, D.L., W.A. Longbrake and N.B. Murphy (1973) 'The effect of technology on bank economies of scale for demand deposits', *Journal of Finance*, **28**, March, 131–145.

Daskin, Allan J. and John D. Wolken (1989) 'An empirical investigation of the critical Herfindahl index in banking', *Journal of Economics and Business*, **41**, 95–105.

Dassesse, M. (1993) 'Tax obstacles to the free provision of financial services: the new frontier', *Journal of International Banking and Financial Law*, January, 12–16.

De Boissieu, C. (1990) 'The French banking sector in the light of European financial integration', in J. Dermine, *European Banking in the 1990's* (Oxford: Blackwell), pp. 183–226.

De Pecunia (1992a) 'Preparation of business for a single European currency', Association for the Monetary Union of Europe, Special Issue, June.

De Pecunia (1992b) 'The Maastricht Treaty: analysis and comments', **4**(1), 1–108.

Dean, A., M. Durand, J. Fullon and P. Hoeller (1990) 'Savings trends and behaviour in OECD countries', *OECD Economic Studies*, No. 14, Spring 1990.

Demsetz, H. (1973) 'Industry structure, market rivalry and public policy', *Journal of Law and Economics*, **16**, April, 1–9.

Demsetz, H. (1982) 'Barriers to entry', *American Economic Review*, **72**, 47–57.

Deutsche Bundesbank (1989) *Monthly Report of the Deutsche Bundesbank*, **41**(3), Table 13, 32–33.

Deutsche Bundesbank (1993) 'Households' asset situation in Germany', *Monthly Report*, October.

Dietsch, M. (1988) 'Économies d'échelle et économies d'envergure dans les banques de dépôts françaises', mimeo, Institut d'Études Politiques de Strasbourg.

Dietsch, M. (1993) 'Economies of scale and scope in French commercial banking industry', *Journal of Productivity Analysis*, No. 1.

Diewert, W.E. (1971) 'An application of the Shephard duality theorem: a generalised Leontief production function', *Journal of Political Economy*, **79**, 481–507.

Diewert, W.E. (1973) 'Functional forms for profit and transformation functions', *Journal of Economic Theory*, **7**, 284–316.

Diewert, W.E. (1974) 'Application of duality theory', in M.D. Intriligator and D.A. Kendrick (eds), *Frontiers of Quantitative Economics*, Vol. II (Amsterdam: North-Holland).

Diewert, W.E. (1982) 'Duality approaches to microeconomic theory', Chapter 12 in K.J. Arrow and M.D. Intriligator (eds), *Handbook of Mathematical Economics*, Vol. II (Amsterdam: North-Holland), pp. 535–599.

Diewert, W.E. (1992) 'The measurement of productivity', *Bulletin of Economic Research*, **44**(3), 163–198.

Dixon, R. (1991) *Banking in Europe — The Single Market* (London: Routledge).

Doménech, R. (1991) 'Eficiencia y costes en la empresa bancaria. Teoría y aplicaciones al caso español', Doctoral Dissertation, University of Valencia.

Doménech, R. (1992) 'Medidas no paramétricas de eficiencia en el sector bancario español', *Revista Español de Economía*, **9**, pp. 1–15.

Doménech, R. and Pérez, F. (1992a) 'Production and productivity: theory and applications to the Spanish case', *Research Papers in Banking and Finance*, Bangor, **92**(3), 1–30.

Doménech, R. and Pérez, F. (1992b) 'The productivity of the Spanish banking system in the 80's, international comparisons', *BNL Quarterly Review*, **181**, June, 147–70.

Doménech, R., Pérez, F. and Quesada, J. (1993) 'Especialización productiva y resultados de las cajas de ahorro españolas (1986–1991)', *Perspectivas del Sistema Financiero*, **43**.

Dornbush, R. (1991) 'Problems of European monetary integration', in A. Giovannini and C. Mayer (eds), *European Financial Integration* (London: Cambridge University Press), pp. 305–328.

Drake, L. (1992) 'Economies of scale and scope in UK building societies: an application of the translog multiproduct cost function', *Applied Financial Economics*, **2**, 211–219.

Drake, L. (1995) 'Testing for expense preference behaviour in UK building societies', *The Service Industries Journal*, **15**(1), 50–65.

Drake, L. and B. Howcroft (1995) 'A study of the relative efficiency of UK bank branches', *Journal of Banking and Finance* (forthcoming).

Drake, L. and T.G. Weyman-Jones (1992a) 'Technical and scale efficiency in UK building societies', *Applied Financial Economics*, **2**, 1–9.

Drake, L. and T.G. Weyman-Jones (1992b) *Productive and Allocative Inefficiencies in UK Building Societies: A Comparison of Non-Parametric and Stochastic Frontier Techniques*, Loughborough University of Technology Economic Research Paper, No. 92/2 (forthcoming Manchester School).

Dunham C. and R.F. Syron (1984) 'Interstate banking: the drive to consolidate', *New England Economic Review*, Federal Reserve Bank of Boston, May/June, 11-28.

Economist (1994) 'Argentaria after Banesto', May 28, **331** (7865), 115.

Edwards, F.R. (1964) 'Concentration in banking and its effects on business loan rates', *Review of Economics and Statistics*, **46**(3), August, 294-300.

Edwards, F.R. (1965) 'The banking competition controversy', *The National Banking Review*, **3**, September, 1-34.

Edwards, F.R. (1973) 'Advertising and competition in banking', *Antitrust Bulletin*, **18**(1), Spring, 23-32.

Edwards, F.R. (1977) 'Managerial objectives in regulated industries: expense-preference behaviour in banking', *Journal of Political Economy*, **85**, February, 147-162.

Edwards, F.R. and A.A. Heggestad (1973) 'Uncertainty, market structure and performance: the Galbraith Caves hypothesis and managerial motives in banking', *Quarterly Journal of Economics*, **87**, August, 455-473.

Elysiani, E. and S. Mehdian (1990a) 'Efficiency in the commercial banking industry, a production frontier approach', *Applied Economics*, **22**, 539-551.

Elysiani, E. and S. Mehdian (1990b) 'A non-parametric approach to measurement of efficiency and technological change: the case of large US banks', *Journal of Financial Services Research*, **4**, 157-168.

Emery, J.T. (1971) 'Risk, return and the morphology of commercial banking', *Journal of Financial and Quantitative Analysis*, **6**, March, 763-776.

European Banker (1994) 'Mediobanca involvement in privatisation criticised', Lafferty Group Publication, No. 102, May, 1.

European Documentation (1989) *The European Financial Common Market*, Office for Official Publications of the European Communities, Periodical 4.

European Economy (1988) *Creation of a European Financial Area*, Commission of the European Communities, No. 36, May (Brussels: EU).

European Economy (1990) *One Market, one Money — an Evaluation of the Potential Benefits and Cost of Forming an Economic and Monetary Union*, Commission of the European Communities, No. 44, October (Brussels: EU).

European Economy (1993) *Annual Economic Report for 1993*, Commission of the European Communities, No. 54 (Brussels: EU).

European Economy (1994) *Annual Economic Report for 1994*, Commission of the European Communities, No. 56 (Brussels: EU).

Evanoff, D.D. and Fortier, D.L. (1988) 'Reevaluation of the structure-conduct-performance paradigm in banking', *Journal of Financial Services Research*, **1**(3), June, 277-294.

Evanoff, D.D. and P.R. Israilevich (1991) 'Productive efficiency in banking', *Federal Reserve Bank of Chicago, Economic Perspectives*, **15**(4), July/August, 11-32.

Evans, D. and J. Heckman (1984) 'A test for subadditivity of the cost function with an application to the Bell System', *American Economic Review*, **74**, 615–623.

Fanjul, O. and F. Maravall (1985) 'La eficiencia del sistema bancario espanol', Alianza University, Madrid.

Fare, R., S. Grosskopf and C.A. Lovell (1985) *The Measurement of Efficiency of Production* (Boston: Kluwer-Nijhoff).

Farrell, J. and C. Shapiro (1990) 'Horizontal mergers: an equilibrium analysis', *American Economic Review*, **80**, 107–126.

Farrell, M.J. (1957) 'The measurement of productive efficiency', *Journal of Royal Statistical Society*, **120**, Sec. A, 253–281.

Ferrier, G.D. and C.A.K. Lovell (1990) 'Measuring cost efficiency in banking; econometric and linear programming evidence', *Journal of Econometrics*, **46**, 229–245.

Field, K. (1990) 'Production efficiency of British building societies', *Applied Economics*, **22**, 415–425.

Fields, J.A., N.B. Murphy and D. Tirtiroglu (1993) 'An international comparison of scale economies in banking: evidence from Turkey', *Journal of Financial Services Research*, **7**, 111–125.

Financial Industry Monitor (1993) 'New proposals on listing particulars', Lafferty Group Publication, No. 82, February.

Fixler, D.J. and K.D. Zieschang (1993) 'An index number approach to measuring bank efficiency: an application to mergers', *Journal of Banking and Finance*, **17**, 437–450.

Fleschig, T.G. (1965) 'The effect of concentration on bank loan rates', *Journal of Finance*, **20**(2), May, 298–311.

Forestieri, G. and M. Onado (1989) 'Il sistema bancario italiano di fronte alle transformazioni strutturali', section I in G. Forestieri and M. Onado (eds), *Il Sistema Bancario Italiano e l'Integrazione dei Mercati: un Confronto delle Strutture e degli Ordinamenti dei Principali Paesi* (Milan: Universita Bocconi and E. Giuffre Editori).

Forsund, F., C.A. Lovell and P. Schmidt (1980) 'A survey of frontier production functions and of their relationship to efficiency measurement', *Journal of Econometrics*, **13**, supplement, 5–25.

Fraser, D.R. and J.B. Alvis (1975) 'The structure–performance relationship in banking, a dichotomous analysis', *Review of Business and Economic Research*, **2**, Fall, 35–57.

Fraser, D.R., W.J. Phillips and P.S. Rose (1974) 'A canonical analysis of bank performance', *Journal of Financial and Quantitative Analysis*, **9**, March, 287–296.

Fraser, D. and P.S. Rose (1971) 'More on banking structure and performance: the evidence from Texas', *Journal of Financial and Quantitative Analysis*, **6**, January, 601–611.

Fraser, D. and P.S. Rose (1972) 'Banking structure and performance in isolated markets: the implications for public policy', *Antitrust Bulletin*, **17**, Fall, 927–947.

Fraser, D.R. and P.S. Rose (1976) 'Static and dynamic measures of market structure and performance of commercial banks', *Journal of Economics and Business*, **28**, Winter, 79–87.

Frazer, P. and D. Vittas (1984) *The Retail Banking Revolution* (London: Lafferty Publications).

Fuss, R.A. and D. McFadden (1980) *Production Economics: A Dual Approach to Theory and Application* (Amsterdam: North-Holland).

Fuss, R.A. and L. Waverman (1981) *The Regulation of Telecommunications in Canada*, Report to Economic Council of Canada, February.

Gardener, E.P.M. (1990) 'Financial conglomeration: a new challenge for banking', in E.P.M. Gardener (ed.), *The Future of Financial Systems and Services* (London: Macmillan), pp. 258–282.

Gardener, E.P.M. (1992) *Capital adequacy after 1992: The Banking Challenge*, Institute of European Finance Working Paper, No. 92/11.

Gardener, E.P.M. (1994) 'Banking strategies in the European Union: financial services firms after the Cecchini Report', Paper presented at conference on 'Spanish financial system, 1994: the challenges of competitiveness', Fundación fondo para la Investigación Económica y Social/University of Grenada, September, 1994 and forthcoming (1995) in *Perspectives del Sistema Financiero*, pp. 1–34.

Gardener, E.P.M. and P. Molyneux (1990) *Changes in Western European Banking* (London: Allen Unwin).

Gardener, E.P.M. and J.L. Teppett (1990) *The Impact of 1992 on the Financial Services Sectors of EFTA Countries*, European Free Trade Association Occasional Papers, No. 33A.

Gardener, E.P.M. and J.L. Teppett (1991) *Final Report — The Economic Impact of 1992 on the EFTA Financial Services Sectors — A Select Replication Exercise Using the Price Waterhouse/Cecchini Methodology*, confidential study sponsored by EFTA.

Gardener, Edward P.M. and Jonathan L. Teppett (1995) 'A select replication of the Cecchini microeconomic methodology on the EFTA financial services sectors: a note and critique', forthcoming in *Services Industry Journal*, **15**(1), January.

Geroski, P.A. (1988) 'Competition and innovation', *Research in the Cost of Non-Europe Basic Findings*, Vol. 2 (Luxembourg: EU), pp. 339–388.

Geroski, P.A. (1991) *Market Dynamic and Entry* (Oxford: Blackwell).

Gilbert, R. Alton (1984) 'Bank market structure and competition — a survey', *Journal of Money, Credit and Banking*, **16**(4), November, part 2, 617–645.

Gilbert, R. (1989) 'Mobility barriers and the value of incumbency', in R. Schmalensee and R.D. Willig (eds), *Handbook of Industrial Organisation* (Oxford: North-Holland), pp. 475–535.

Gilligan, T. and M. Smirlock (1984) 'An empirical study of joint production and scale economies in commercial banking', *Journal of Banking and Finance*, **8**, March, 67–77.

Gilligan, T., M. Simirlock and W. Marshall (1984) 'Scale and scope economies in the multi-product banking firm', *Journal of Monetary Economics*, **13**, 393–405.

Gitman, L.J. (1991) *Principles of Managerial Finance*, sixth edition (New York: Harper-Collins).

Glass, J.C. and D.C. McKillop (1992) 'An empirical analysis of scale and scope economies and technical change in an Irish multiproduct banking firm', *Journal of Banking and Finance*, **16**, 423–437.

Glassman, Cynthia and Stephen A. Rhoades (1980) 'Owner vs manager control effects on bank performance', *Review of Economics and Statistics*, **62**, May, 263–270.

Gobbi, Giorgio (1995) 'L'efficienza e la produttinta delle banche Italiana nell'ultimo decenio', paper presented at the conference on Deregulation and Efficiency in Banking, IRCEL, Rome, 23/24 February (forthcoming as Bank of Italy Working Paper).

Goldberg, L. and A. Rai (1994) 'The structure–performance relationship for European banking', *Journal of Banking and Finance*, forthcoming.

Gough, T.J. (1979) 'Building society mergers and the size efficiency relationship', *Applied Economics*, **11**, 185–194.

Graddy, D.B. and R. Kyle (1979) 'The simultaneity of bank decision making, market structure and bank performance', *Journal of Finance*, **34**, March, 1–18.

Gramley, L.E. (1962) *A Study of Scale Economies in Banking* (Kansas City: Federal Reserve Bank of Kansas City).

Greenbaum, S.I. (1967) 'A study of bank cost', *National Banking Review*, June, 415–434.

Greene, W.M. (1990) 'A gamma-distributed stochastic frontier model', *Journal of Econometrics*, **46**, 141–163.

Greene, W.M. (1993) 'The econometric approach to efficiency analysis', in H.O. Fried, C.A. Lovell and P. Schmidt (eds), *The Measurement of Productive Efficiency: Techniques and Applications* (Oxford: Oxford University Press).

Griffell-Tatjé, E. and C.A.K. Lovell (1994a) *A New Decomposition of the Malmquist Productivity Index*, College of Business Administration Working Paper, No. 94–392E, the University of Georgia.

Griffell-Tatjé, E. and C.A.K. Lovell (1994b) *A Generalised Malmquist Productivity Index*, College of Business Administration Working Paper, No. 94–410E, the University of Georgia.

Griffell-Tatjé, E. and C.A.K. Lovell (1995a) 'A note on the Malmquist productivity index', *Economics Letters*, **47**, 169–175.

Griffell-Tatjé, E. and C.A.K. Lovell (1995b) 'A DEA based analysis of productivity change and intertemporal managerial performance', *Annals of Operations Research in honour of A. Charnes*, forthcoming.

Griffell-Tatjé, E. and C.A.K. Lovell (1995c) 'Deregulation and productivity decline: the case of Spanish savings banks', *European Economic Review*, forthcoming.

Griliches, Z. (1992) *Measurement Issues in the Service Sectors* (NBER: University of Chicago Press).

Grilli, V. (1989a) *Financial Markets and 1992*, Brooking Papers on Economic Activity, No. 2.

Grilli, V. (1989b) 'Europe 1992: issues and prospects for the financial markets', *Economic Policy*, No. 9, October, 388–421.

Gropper, D.M. (1991) 'An empirical investigation of changes in scale economies for the commercial banking firm, 1976–1986', *Journal of Money, Credit and Banking*, November, 718–727.

Gual, J. and D. Neven (1993) 'Banking', in *Social Europe — Market Services and European Integration*, European Economy, Report and Studies, No. 3.

Guilkey, D. and C.A.K. Lovell. (1980) 'On the flexibility of the translog approximation', *International Economic Review*, **21**, 137–147.

Guilkey, D., C.A.K. Lovell and R.C. Sickles (1983) 'A comparison of the performance of three flexible functional forms', *International Economic Review*, **24**(3), 591–616.

Guiso, L., T. Jappelli and D. Terlizzese (1992) *Why is Italy's Saving Rate so High?* Bank of Italy Discussion Paper, No. 167, April.

Hannan, Timothy H. (1979a) 'Expense-preference behaviour in banking — a re-examination', *Journal of Political Economy*, **87**, August, 891–895.

Hannan, Timothy H. (1979b) 'Limit pricing and the banking industry', *Journal of Money, Credit and Banking*, **11**, November, 438–446.

Hannan, Timothy (1984) 'Bank profitability and the threat of entry', *Journal of Bank Research*, Summer, 157–163.

Hannan, T.H. (1991a) 'Bank commercial loan markets and the role of market structure: evidence from surveys of commercial lending', *Journal of Banking and Finance*, **15**(1), 133–150.

Hannan, Timothy H. (1991b) 'Foundation of the structure–conduct–performance paradigm in banking', *Journal of Money, Credit and Banking*, **23**(1), February, 68–83.

Hannan, T.H. and J.N. Liang (1993) 'Inferring market power from time-series data — the case of the banking firm', *International Journal of Industrial Organisation*, **11**, 205–218.

Hannan, T.H. and F. Mavinga (1980) 'Expense preference and managerial control: the case of the banking firm', *Bell Journal of Economics*, **11**, August, 671–682.

Hanweck, G.A. and S.A. Rhoades (1984) 'Dominant firms, deep pockets and local market competition in banking', *Journal of Economics and Business*, **36**, 391–402.

Hardwick, P. (1989) 'Economies of scale in building societies', *Applied Economics*, **21**, 1291–1304.

Hardwick, P. (1990) 'Multi-product cost attributes: a study of UK building societies', *Oxford Economic Papers*, **42**, 446–461.

Harvey, J.M. (1979) 'Chain banking and market structure in rural banking markets', in *Bank Structure and Competition, Proceedings of a Conference at the Federal Reserve Bank of Chicago*, pp. 212–223.

Haslem, J.A. (1968) 'A statistical analysis of the relative profitability of commercial banks', *Journal of Finance*, **23**, March, 167–176.

Hay, D.A. and D.J. Morris (1991) *Industrial Economics and Organisation — Theory and Evidence*, revised edition (New York: Oxford University Press).

Hayashi, F., T. Ito and J. Slemrad (1988) 'Housing finance imperfections, taxation and private saving: a comparative simulation analysis of the United States and Japan', *Journal of the Japanese and International Economics*, **2**, 215–258.

Heathfield, D.F. and S. Wibe (1987) *An Introduction to Cost and Production Functions* (London: Macmillan).

Heggestad, A.A. (1977) 'Market structure, risk and profitability in commercial banking', *Journal of Finance*, **32**, September, 1207–1216.

Heggestad, A.A. (1979) 'A survey of studies on banking competition and performance', Chapter 9 in F.R. Edwards (ed.), *Issues in Financial Regulation* (New York: McGraw-Hill Book Company), pp. 449–490.

Heggestad, A.A. and J.J. Mingo (1976) 'Prices, nonprices and concentration in commercial banking', *Journal of Money, Credit and Banking*, **8**, February, 107–117.

Heggestad, A.A. and J.J. Mingo (1977) 'The competitive condition of US banking markets and the impact of structural reform', *Journal of Finance*, **32**(6), June, 649–661.

Heggestad, A.A. and S.A. Rhoades (1976) 'Concentration and firm stability in commercial banking', *Review of Economics and Statistics*, **58**, November, 443–452.

Heggestad, A.A. and S.A. Rhoades (1978) 'Multi-market interdependence and local market competition in banking', *Review of Economics and Statistics*, **60**, November, 523–532.

Heggestad, A.A. (1984) 'Comment on bank market structure and competition: a survey', *Journal of Money, Credit and Banking*, **16**(4), November, pp. 645–650.

Hicks, J.R. (1935) 'Annual survey of economic theory: the theory of monopoly', *Econometrica*, **3**, 1–20.

Holder, C.L. (1993) 'Competitive considerations in bank mergers and acquisitions: economic theory, legal foundations, and the Fed', *Economic Review, Federal Reserve Bank of Atlanta*, January/February, 23–36.

Holland, R. (1964) 'Research on banking structure and competition', *Federal Reserve Bulletin*, **50**, November, 1393–1399.

Holmes, P. (1992) 'The political economy of the European integration process', in D. Dyker (ed.), *The European Economy* (London: Longman), pp. 51–70.

Honohan, Patrick and R.P. Kinsella (1982) 'Comparing bank concentration across countries', *Journal of Banking and Finance*, **6**, 255–262.

Horvitz, P.M. (1963) 'Economies of scale in banking', in P. Horvitz et al., *Private Financial Institutions* (Englewood Cliffs, N.J.: Prentice-Hall), pp. 1–55.

Humphrey, D.B. (1985) 'Cost and scale economies in bank intermediation', in R. Aspinwall and R. Eisenbeis (eds), *Handbook for Banking Strategy* (New York: John Wiley), pp. 745–783.

Humphrey, D.B. (1987) 'Cost dispersion and the measurement of economies in banking', *Economic Review, Federal Reserve Bank of Richmond*, May/June, 24–38.

Humphrey, D.B. (1990) 'Why do estimates of bank scale economies differ?', *Economic Review, Federal Reserve Bank of Richmond*, September/October, 38–50.

Hunter, W.C. and S.G. Timme (1986) 'Technical change, organizational form and the structure of bank production', *Journal of Money, Credit and Banking*, **18**(2), 152–166.

Hunter, W.C., S.G. Timme and W.K. Yang (1990) 'An examination of cost subadditivity and multiproduct production in large U.S. banks', *Journal of Money, Credit and Banking*, **22**(4), 504–525.

Hutchison, M.M. (1992) *Budget Policy and the Decline of National Saving Revisited*, Bank for International Settlements Economic Papers, No. 33, March.

IBRO (Inter Bank Research Organisation) (1976) *Banking Comparisons* (London: IBRO).

IMF (International Monetary Fund) (1991) *World Economic Outlook, May 1991* (Washington: IMF).

IMI (Istituto Mobiliare Italiano) (1994) *Prospectus, Subject to Competition*, Istituto Mobiliare Italiano, 1 February.

Italianer, A., C. Ohly, H. Reichenbach and M. Vanheukelen (1992) 'Thirty economic questions on E.M.U.', *De Pecunia*, **IV**(2), September, 21–57.

Jackson, W.E. (1992) 'The price–concentration relationship in banking: a comment', *Review of Economics and Statistics*, **74**, February, 373–376.

Jacobs, D.P. (1971) *Business Loan Costs and Bank Market Structure*, National Bureau of Economic Research Occasional Paper, No. 115 (Cambridge, Mass.: NBER).

John, K., I.A. John and A. Saunders (1994) 'Universal banking and firm risk-taking', *Journal of Banking and Finance*, **18**(2), March, 307–324.

Jondrow, J., C.A. Lovell, I.S. Materov and P. Schmidt (1982) 'On estimation of technical inefficiency in the stochastic frontier production model', *Journal of Econometrics*, **19**, July, 233–238.

Jorgenson, D.W. (1986) 'Econometric methods for modelling producer behaviour', Chapter 31 in Z. Griliches and M.D. Intriligator (eds), *Handbook of Econometrics*, Vol. 3 (Amsterdam: North-Holland), pp. 1841–1915.

Kalish, L. and R.A. Gilbert (1973) 'An analysis of efficiency of scale and organisation form in commercial banking', *Journal of Industrial Economics*, **21**, July, 293–307.

Kaparakis, E.I., S.M. Miller and A.G. Noulas (1994) 'Short-run cost inefficiencies of commercial banks', *Journal of Money, Credit and Banking*, **26**(4), November, 875–893.

Katz, S.E. (1992) 'The Second Banking Directive and the general good clause: a major exception to the freedom to provide services?', *Centre for European Policy Studies, Research Report*, No. 9, September (Belgium: CEPS), pp. 1–58.

Kaufman, B. (1991) *Micro Economics of Savings*, EC Commission Economic Papers, No. 89, December (Brussels: EU).

Kaufman, G.C. (1966) 'Bank market structure and performance: the evidence from Iowa', *Southern Economic Journal*, **32**(4), April, 429–439.

Kempf, U. (1985) *German Bond Markets* (London: Euromoney Publications).

Kim, H.Y. (1986) 'Economies of scale and scope in multiproduct financial institutions: further evidence from credit unions', *Journal of Banking and Finance*, **18**, 220–226.

Kim, M. (1985) 'Scale of economies in banking: a methodological note', *Journal of Money, Credit and Banking*, **17**, 96–102.

Kindleberger, C.P. (1984) *A Financial History of Western Europe* (London: Allen & Unwin).

King, B.F. (1979) 'Entry, exit and change in banking market concentration', *Federal Reserve Bank of Atlanta Economic Review*, March/April, 50–52.

Kinsella, R.P. (1990) 'The measurement of bank output', *Journal of the Institute of Bankers in Ireland*, **82**, part 3, July 1990, 173–183.

Klein, M.A. and N.B. Murphy (1971) 'The pricing of bank deposits, a theoretical and empirical analysis', *Journal of Financial and Quantitative Analysis*, **6**, March, 747–761.

Kolari, J. and A. Zardkoohi (1987) *Bank Cost, Structure and Performance* (Lexington, Mass.: Lexington Books).

Kolari, J. and A. Zardkoohi (1990) 'Economies of scale and scope in thrift institutions: the case of Finnish cooperative and saving banks', *Scandinavian Journal of Economics*, **92**(3), 437–451.

Koutsoyiannis, A. (1979) *Modern Microeconomics*, second edition (London: Macmillan).

Kumbhakar, S.C. (1991) 'The measurement and decomposition of cost-inefficiency: the translog cost system', *Oxford Economic Papers*, **43**, 667–683.

Kwast, M.L. and J.T. Rose (1982) 'Pricing, operating efficiency and profitability among large commercial banks', *Journal of Banking and Finance*, **6**, June, 233–254.

Lafferty Business Research (1993) *Financial Revolution in Europe II: The Revaluation Deepens and Widens* (Dublin: Lafferty Publications Ltd).

Lang, G. and P. Welzel (1994) *Efficiency and Technical Progress in Banking, Empirical Results for a Panel of German Cooperative Banks*, Institut für Volkswirtschaft der Universität Augsburg, WP no. 117, August.

Lau, L.J. (1974) 'Application of duality theory: comments', in M.D. Intriligator and D.A. Kendrick (eds), *Frontiers of Quantitative Economics*, Vol. II (Amsterdam: North-Holland), pp. 176–199.

Lau, L.J. (1986) 'Functional forms in econometric model building', Chapter 26 in Z. Griliches and M.D. Intriligator (eds), *Handbook of Econometrics*, Vol. 3, (Amsterdam: North-Holland), pp. 1515–1552.

LaWare, J.P. (1991) 'Testimony before the Committee on Banking', Finance and Urban Affairs of the US House of Representatives, 24 September, reprinted in *Federal Reserve Bulletin*, **77**(v), 932–948.

Lawrence, C. and R. Shay (1986) 'Technology and financial intermediation in a multiproduct banking firm: an econometric study of I.S.S. banks, 1979–1982', in C. Lawrence and R. Shay (eds), *Technological Innovation, Regulation and the Monetary Economy* (Cambridge, Mass.: Ballinger).

Leibenstein, H. (1966) 'Allocative efficiency vs "X-efficiency"', *American Economic Review*, **56**, 392–415.

Levy-Garboua, L. and F. Renard (1977) 'Une étude statistique de la rentabilité des banques en France en 1974', *Cahiers Économiques et Monétaires*, **5**.

Linder, J.C. and D.B. Crane (1992) 'Bank mergers: integration and profitability', *Journal of Financial Services Research*, **7**, 35–55.

Litan, R.E. (1987) *What should Banks do?* (Washington, DC: Brookings Institution).

Llewellyn, D.T. (1992) 'Banking and financial services', in D. Swann (ed.), *The Single European Market and Beyond* (London: Routledge), pp. 106–145.

Lloyd-Williams, M., P. Molyneux and J. Thornton (1994) 'Market structure and performance in Spanish banking', *Journal of Banking and Finance*, **18**, 433–443.

Lohneysen, E., A. Baptista and A. Walton (1990) 'Emerging roles in European retail banking', *McKinsey Quarterly*, No. 4, Winter, 142–150.

Longbrake, W.A. and J.A. Haslem (1975) 'Productive efficiency in commercial banking', *Journal of Money, Credit and Banking*, **7**, August, 317–330.

Lucey, B. (1995a) 'Investigating profit–efficiency relationships in Irish credit institutions', Trinity College, Dublin, Ireland (mimeo).

Lucey, B. (1995b), 'Profits, efficiency and Irish banks', *Journal of the Statistical and Social Inquiry Society of Ireland*', **24** (forthcoming).

McAllister, P.H. and D.A. McManus (1993) 'Resolving the scale efficiency puzzle in banking', *Journal of Banking and Finance*, **17**, 389–405.

McCall, Alan S. and Manfred O. Peterson (1980) 'A critical level of commercial bank concentration: an application of switching regressions', *Journal of Banking and Finance*, **4**, December, 353–369.

McDonald, F. (1992) 'The single European market', in F. McDonald and S. Deurden (eds), *European Economic Integration* (London: Longman), pp. 16–38.

McKillop, Donal G. and Colin J. Glass (1994) 'A cost model of building societies as producers of mortgages and other financial products', *Journal of Business, Finance and Accounting*, **21**(7), October, 1031–1046.

Malmquist, S. (1953) 'Index numbers and indifference surfaces', *Trubajos de Estadistica*, **4**, 209–242.

Marlow, M.L. (1982) 'Bank structure and mortgage rates: implications for interstate banking', *Journal of Economics and Business*, **34**, Spring, 135–142.

Martin, F. and M. Sassenou (1992) 'Cost structure in French banking: a re-examination based on a regular CES-quadratic form', *Caisse des Dépôts de Consignation*, May, Paris.

Masera, R. (1992) 'The universal bank and credit group: solicitations from the market and prudential regulation', *Review of Economic Condition in Italy*, No. 3, September–December, 341–374.

Mayes, D. (1990) 'The path to monetary union: prospects and problems', *De Pecunia*, **II**(2–3), 237–261.

Meeusen, W. and J. van den Broeck (1977) 'Efficiency estimation from Cobb–Douglas production functions with composed error', *International Economic Review*, **18**, 435–444.

Mester, L.J. (1987a) 'Efficient production of financial services: scale and scope', *Business Review, Federal Reserve Bank of Philadelphia*, January/February, 15–25.

Mester, L.J. (1987b) 'A multiproduct cost study of savings and loans', *Journal of Finance*, **42**, 423–445.

Mester, L.J. (1990) 'Traditional and nontraditional banking: an information-theoretic approach', Paper presented at Conference on Bank Structure and Competition sponsored by Federal Reserve Bank of Chicago, May.

Mester, L.J. (1993) 'Efficiency in the savings and loan industry', *Journal of Banking and Finance*, **17**(2–3), April, 267–287.

Metais, J. (1990) 'Towards a restructuring of the international financial services industry: some preliminary empirical and theoretical insights', in E.P.M. Gardener (ed.), *The Future of Financial Systems and Services* (London: Macmillan), pp. 170–192.

Meyer, P.A. (1967), 'Price discrimination, regional loan rates and the structure of the banking industry', *Journal of Finance*, **22**, March, 37–48.

Mingo, J.J. (1976) 'Managerial motives, market structure and performance of holding company banks', *Economic Inquiry*, **14**, September, 411–424.

Molyneux, P. (1989) '1992 and its impact on local and regional banking markets', *Regional Studies*, **23**, 523–533.

Molyneux, P. (1991) 'European links', *Banking World*, September, 25–27.

Molyneux, P. (1993) 'Europe's single banking market and the role of state autonomy', Paper presented at the ESRC Research Seminar on 'State Autonomy in the EC', Nuffield College, Oxford, 10–11 December.

Molyneux, P. and W. Forbes (1995) 'Market structure and performance in European banking', *Applied Economics*, **27**, 155–159.

Molyneux, P., D.M. Lloyd-Williams and J. Thornton (1994a) 'European banking — an analysis of competitive conditions', in J. Revell (ed.), *Changing Face of European Banks and Securities Market* (London: Macmillan), pp. 3–25.

Molyneux, P., D.M. Lloyd-Williams and J. Thornton (1994b) 'Competitive conditions in European banking', *Journal of Banking and Finance*, **18**(3), 445–459.

Molyneux, P. and J.L. Teppett (1993) 'Structure–conduct–performance in EFTA banking markets', *Bank-en-Financiewezen*, **3**, 133–137.

Molyneux, P. and J. Thornton (1992) 'Determinants of European bank profitability: a note', *Journal of Banking and Finance*, **16**(6), December, 1173–1178.

Mooslechner, P. and Y. Schnitzer (1992) *Structure–Performance in Banking: a First Application to a Banking Market European Style*, Austrian Institute of Economic Research, Working Paper, July.

Morgan Stanley (1988) 'The bank of Europe', *European Banking Commentary*, February.

Morgan Stanley (1989) 'Spanish banking still the most profitable in Europe', *European Financial Commentary*, No. 20, 20–22.

Morgan Stanley (1990) 'Spain: the image and the reality', *European Banking Commentary*, July.

Morgan Stanley (1992) 'Italy: the last bastion of banking regulation in Europe', *European Banking Commentary*, February.

Morgan Stanley (1993a) 'Over banking and over branching', *European Banking Strategy*, 29 April.

Morgan Stanley (1993b) 'European banks and the single market', *European Financial Briefings*, No. 32, 24 February.

Morgan Stanley (1994a) 'New fundamentals for the bank to the year 2000', *European Banking Strategy*, 30 March.

Morgan Stanley (1994b) *Crédit Lyonnais: recovery still pending'*, *European Financial Briefing*, No. 51, 2 August.

Morgan Stanley (1994c) 'Italy: Emerging implications of privatisation', *European Banking Commentary*, 23 March.

Moynihan, J.P. (1991) 'Banking in the 90's — where will the profits come from?', *Proceedings of the Conference on Bank Structure and Competition*, Federal Reserve Bank of Chicago, p. 27.

Mullineaux, D.J. (1975) 'Economies of scale of financial institutions', *Journal of Monetary Economics*, **1**, April, 233–240.

Murphy, N.B. (1972) 'Cost of banking activities: interaction between risk and operating cost: a comment', *Journal of Money, Credit and Banking*, **4**, August, 614–15.

Murphy, N.B. (1992) 'Acquisitions of failed-bank deposits: in market vs. out of market cost effects', *FDIC Banking Review*, **5**(2), Fall/Winter, 24–33.

Murray, J.D. and R.W. White (1983) 'Economies of scope in multi-product financial institutions: a study of British Columbia credit unions', *Journal of Finance*, **38**, 887–901.

Nadiri, M.I. (1982) 'Producers theory', Chapter 10 in K.J. Arrow and M.D. Intriligator (eds), *Handbook of Mathematical Economics*, Vol. II (Amsterdam: North-Holland), pp. 431–490.

Nerlove, M. (1963) 'Returns to scale in electricity supply', in C. Christ (ed.), *Measurement in Economics: Studies in Mathematical Economics and Econometrics in Memory of Yehuda Grunfeld* (Stanford: Stanford University Press), pp. 167–198.

Neven, D.J. (1990) 'Structural adjustment in European retail banking: some views from industrial organisation', in J. Dermine (ed.), *European Banking in the 1990s* (Oxford: Blackwell), pp. 153–178.

Noulas, A.G., S.M. Miller and S.C. Ray (1993) 'Regularity conditions and scope estimates: the case of large-sized U.S. banks', *Journal of Financial Services Research*, September, 235–248.

Noulas, A.G., S.C. Ray and S.M. Miller (1990) 'Returns to scale and input substitution for large U.S. banks', *Journal of Money, Credit and Banking*, **22**(1), 94–108.

OECD (1992a) *Banks Under Stress* (Paris: OECD).

OECD (1992b) *Economies of Scale and Scope in the Financial Services Industry: a Review of Recent Literature* (Paris: OECD).

OECD (1993) *Economic Outlook*, No. 54, December (Paris: OECD).

OECD (1994) *Economic Outlook*, No. 55, June (Paris: OECD).

Office of Fair Trading (1994) *Barriers to Entry and Exit in UK Competition Policy*, Office for Fair Trading Research Paper, No. 2.

Olson, R.E., P. Schmidt and D.M. Waldman (1980) 'A Monte Carlo study of estimators of stochastic production frontiers', *Journal of Econometrics*, **13**, 67–82.

Oral, M. and Yolalan, R. (1990) 'An empirical study on measuring operating efficiency and profitability of banks branches', *European Journal of Operation Research*, **46**(3), 282–294.

Osborne, Dale K. and Jeanne Wendel (1981) 'A note on concentration and checking account prices', *Journal of Finance*, **36**, March, 181–186.

Palmer, J. (1989) *1992 and Beyond*, Commission of the European Communities (Luxembourg: EU).

Panzar, J.C. and R.D. Willig (1975) *Economies of Scale and Economies of Scope in Multi-output Production, Bell Laboratories Economic Discussion Paper*, No. 33.

Panzar, J.D. and R.D. Willig (1977a) 'Free entry and the sustainability of natural monopoly', *Bell Journal of Economics*, **8**, Spring, 1–22.

Panzar, J.C. and R.D. Willig (1977b) 'Economies of scale in multi-output production', *Quarterly Journal of Economics*, **91**, August, 481–494.

Panzar, J.C. and R.D. Willig (1981) 'Economies of scope', *American Economic Review*, **71**(2), May, 268–272.

Parkan, C. (1987) 'Measuring the efficiency of service operations: an application to bank branches', *Engineering Costs and Production Economics*, **12**, 237–242.

Parker, D. (1994) 'The last post for privatisation? Prospects for privatisation of the postal services', *Public Money and Management*, **14**(3), July–September, 17–25.

Pastor, G. (1993) *Spain: Converging with the European Community*, IMF Occasional Paper, No. 101, February.

Pastor, J.M. and F. Pérez (1994) 'La productividad del Sistema bancario español (1986–1992)', *Papeles de Economía*, forthcoming.

Pastor, J.M., F. Pérez and J. Quesada (1994a) 'Efficiency analysis in banking firms: an international comparison', University of Valencia and IVIE Discussion Paper (preliminary version, unpublished in 1994).

Pastor, J.M., F. Pérez and J. Quesada (1994b) 'Indicadores de eficiencia en banca', *Ekomiaz*, forthcoming.

Pelkmans, J. (1992) 'EC92 as a challenge to economic analysis', in S. Borner and H. Grubel (eds), *The European Community after 1992: Perspectives from the Outside* (London: Macmillan).

Penketh, K. (1992) 'The Customs Union', in F. McDonald and S. Dearden (eds), *European Economic Integration* (London: Longman), pp. 1–15.

Pérez, F. and J. Quesada (1994) 'Efficiency and banking strategies in Spain', SUERF Colloquium, 19–21 May, Dublin, on 'The Competitiveness of Financial Institutions and Centres in Europe'.

Phillips, Almarin (1964) 'Competition, confusion and commercial banking', *Journal of Finance*, March, 32–45.

Phillips, Almarin (1967), 'Evidence on concentration in banking markets and interest rates', *Federal Reserve Bulletin*, **53**(6), 916–926.

Phillis, D. and C. Pavel (1986) 'Interstate banking game plans: implications for the Midwest', *Economic Perspectives, Federal Reserve Bank of Chicago*, **10**, 23–39.

Powers, J. (1969) 'Branch versus unit banking: bank output and cost economies', *Southern Economic Journal*, **36**, October, 153–164.

Praet, P. (1992) 'The free provision of financial services in the perspective of a single currency', *De Pecunia*, **IV**(2), September, 107–117.

Pratten, C.F. (1971) *Economies of Scale in Manufacturing Industry*, DAE Occasional Paper, 28 (Cambridge).

Price Waterhouse (1988) 'The cost of non-Europe in financial services', in *Research on the Cost of Non-Europe: Basic Findings*, Vol. 9 (Brussels: EU).

Pulley, L. and Humphrey, D. (1993) 'The role of fixed costs and cost complementarities in determining scope economies and the cost of narrow banking proposals', *Journal of Business*, **66**(3), 437–462.

Quelch, J.A. and J. Hibbard (1991) 'CIGNA world wide', in J.A. Quelch, R.D. Buzzell and E.R. Salama (eds), *The Marketing Challenge of Europe: 1992* (Reading: Addison-Wesley).

Rangan, N., R. Grabowski, H. Aly and C. Pasurka (1988) 'The technical efficiency of US banks', *Economic Letters*, **28**, 169–175.

Resti, Andrea (1995) 'Linear programming and econometric methods for banks. Efficiency evaluation: an empirical comparison based on a panel of Italian banks', Paper presented at the 22nd European Finance Conference, Milan, Italy, 26–28 August.

Retail Banker International (1994) 'Moving towards a virtual bank', 15 April, 10.

Revell, Jack (1983) *Banking and Electronic Fund Transfers* (Paris: OECD).

Revell, Jack (1987) *Mergers and the Role of Large Banks*, Institute of European Finance Research Monographs in Banking and Finance, No. 2; (Bangor: IEF).

Revell, Jack (1989) *The Future of Savings Banks: A Study of Spain and the Rest of Europe*, Institute of European Finance Research Monographs in Banking and Finance, No. 8 (Bangor: IEF).

Revell, Jack (1991) *Changes in West European Public Banks and their Implications for Spain*, Institute of European Finance Research Monographs in Banking and Finance, No. 9 (Bangor: IEF).

Revell, Jack (1992) 'Mergers and acquisition in banking', in A. Steinherr (ed.), *The New European Financial Marketplace* (London: Longman), pp. 79–91.

Revell, Jack (ed.) (1994a) *The Changing Face of European Banks and Securities Markets* (London: Macmillan).

Revell, Jack (1994b) 'Institutional investors and fund managers', *Revue de la Banque/Bank en Financiewezen*, **2**, 55–68.

Rhoades, S.A. (1977), *Structure–performance Studies in Banking. A Summary and Evaluation*, US Federal Reserve Board Staff Economic Papers, No. 92.

Rhoades, S.A. (1979) 'Nonbank thrift institutions as determinants of performance in banking markets', *Journal of Economics and Business*, **32**, Fall, 66–72.

Rhoades, S.A. (1980) 'Monopoly and expense preference behaviour: an empirical investigation of a behaviourist hypothesis', *Southern Economic Journal*, **47**, October, 419–432.

Rhoades, S.A. (1981) 'Does market structure matter in commercial banking', *Antitrust Bulletin*, **26**, Spring, 155–181.

Rhoades, S.A. (1982a) 'Welfare loss, redistribution effect, and restriction of output due to monopoly', *Journal of Monetary Economics*, **9**(3), 375–387.

Rhoades, S.A. (1982b) 'The relative size of banks and industrial firms in the United States and other countries — a note', *Journal of Banking and Finance*, **6**, 579-585.

Rhoades, S.A. (1983) 'Concentration of world banking and the role of US banks among the 100 largest, 1956-80', *Journal of Banking and Finance*, **7**, 427-437.

Rhoades, S.A. (1985a) 'Market share as a source of market power: implications and some evidence', *Journal of Economics and Business*, **37**(4), 343-363.

Rhoades, S.A. (1985c) 'Market performance and the nature of a competitive fringe', *Journal of Economics and Business*, **37**, 141-157.

Rhoades, S.A. (1985d) *Mergers and Acquisitions by Commercial Banks, 1960-83*, Board of Governors of the Federal Reserve System, January, No. 142.

Rhoades, S.A. (1986) *The Operating Performance of Acquired Firms in Banking before and after Acquisition*, Staff Study No. 149 (Federal Reserve Board).

Rhoades, S.A. (1990) *Billion Dollar Bank Acquisitions: a Note on the Performance Effects*, Working Paper (Board of Governors of the Federal Reserve System).

Rhoades, S.A. (1993) 'The efficiency effects of horizontal bank mergers', *Journal of Banking and Finance*, **17**(2-3), April 411-422.

Rhoades, S.A. and R.D. Rutz (1979) *Impact of Bank Holding Companies on Competition and Performance in Banking Markets*, Staff Economic Studies No. 107 (Washington DC: Board of Governors of the Federal Reserve System).

Rhoades, S.A. and Roger D. Rutz (1982) 'Market power and firm size, a test of the 'quiet life' hypothesis', *Journal of Monetary Economics*, **9**, January, 73-85.

Rhoades, S.A. and D.T. Savage (1981) 'The relative performance of bank holding companies and branch banking systems', *Journal of Economics and Business*, **33**, Winter, 132-141.

Robinson, E.A.G. (1958) *The Structure of Competitive Industry*, revised edition (Chicago: University of Chicago Press).

Rodriguez, J.R.O., A.A. Alvarez and P.P. Gomez (1993) 'Scale and scope economies in banking: A study of savings banks in Spain', Universidad De La Laguna, Tenerife, Spain.

Rose, J.T. (1976) 'Industry concentration and political leverage: an empirical test', (Washington DC: Board of Governors of the Federal Reserve System) (unpublished).

Rose, P.S. (1987) *The Changing Structure of American Banking* (New York: Columbia University Press).

Rose, P.S. and Donald R. Fraser (1976) 'The relationships between stability and change in market structure: an analysis of bank prices', *Journal of Industrial Economics*, **24**, June, 251-266.

Rose, P.S. and W.L. Scott (1979) 'The performance of banks acquired by holding companies', *Review of Business and Economic Research*, **14**, Spring, 18-37.

Rossi, N. and I. Visco (1992) *Private Saving and Government Deficit in Italy*, Bank of Italy Discussion Paper, No. 178, October.

Rowley, C.K. (1973) *Antitrust and Economic Efficiency* (New York: Macmillan).

Ruthenberg, D. (1991) 'Structure-performance and economies of scale in banking, in an emerging unified European Market by 1992, Bank of Israel, July, mimeo.

Rybczynski, R.M. (1984) 'The UK financial system in transition', *National Westminster Bank Quarterly Review*, November, 26–42.

Rybczynski, T.M. (1988) 'Financial systems and industrial restructuring', *National Westminster Bank Quarterly Review*, November, 3–13.

Salomon Brothers (1990) *Multinational Money Centre Banking: the Evaluation of a Single European Banking Market* (London: Salomon Brothers).

Salomon Brothers (1993) 'Cost management in global banking: the lessons of the low cost providers', *International Equity Research*, October (London: Salomon Brothers).

Saunders, A. (1994) 'Banking and commerce: an overview of the public policy issues', *Journal of Banking and Finance*, **18**(2), March, 231–254.

Saunders, A. and I. Walter (1994) *Universal Banking in the United States: What Could We Gain? What Could We Lose?* (New York: Oxford University Press).

Savage, D.T. (1991) *Mergers, Branch Closing, and Cost Savings*, Working Paper (Board of Governors of the Federal Reserve System).

Savage, D.T. (1982) 'Developments in banking structure', *Federal Reserve Bulletin*, 787–785.

Savage, D.T. and S.A. Rhoades (1979) 'The effect of branch banking on pricing, profits and efficiency of unit banks', in *Bank Structure and Competition, Proceedings of a Conference at the Federal Reserve Bank of Chicago*, pp. 187–196.

Sawyer, M.C. (1985) *The Economics of Industries and Firms*, second edition (London: Croom Helm).

Scherer, F.M. (1980), *Industrial Market Structure and Economic Performance*, second edition (Chicago: Rand McNally).

Schmidt, P. (1986) 'Frontier production functions', *Econometric Reviews*, **4**, 289–328.

Schneider-Lenne, E.R. (1993) 'The Germany case', *Annals of Public and Cooperative Economics*, **64**(1), 63–71.

Schweiger, I. and J.S. McGee (1961) 'Chicago banking', *Journal of Business*, **34**(3), 203–366.

Schweitzer, S.A. (1972) 'Economics of scale and holding company affiliation in banking', *Southern Economic Journal*, **39**, October, 258–266.

Sealey, C. and J.T. Lindley (1977) 'Inputs, outputs and a theory of production and cost at depository financial institution', *Journal of Finance*, **32**, 1251–1266.

Seiford, L.M. and R.M. Thrall (1990) 'Recent developments in DEA: the mathematical programming approach to frontier analysis', *Journal of Econometrics*, **46**, 7–38.

Servais, D. (1988) *The Single Financial Market*, Commission of the European Communities (Brussels: EU).

Shaffer, S. (1992) *Can Mergers Reduce Bank Costs?* Federal Reserve Bank of Philadelphia, Working Paper No. 91–17/R.

Shaffer, S. (1993) 'Can mergers improve bank efficiency?', *Journal of Banking and Finance*, **17**(2–3), April, 423–436.

Shaffer, S. and E. David (1986) *Economies of Superscale and Interstate Expansion*', Federal Reserve of New York, Research Paper, November.

Shaw, E.R. (1990) *Changes in Organisational Structure in Banking*, IEF Research Papers, No. 90/21.

Shaw, E.R. and J. Whitley (1994) *Regulations at the Crossroads*, IEF Research Paper, No. 94/4.

Sheldon G. (1994) 'Economies, inefficiency and technical progress in Swiss banking', Paper presented at the Société Universitaire Européene de Recherches Financières (SUERF) Colloquim on the Competitiveness of Financial Institutions and Centres in Europe, 19–21 May, Dublin.

Sheldon, G. and U. Haegler (1993) 'Economies of scale and scope and inefficiency in Swiss banking', in N. Blattner, H. Genberg and A. Swoboda (eds), *Banking in Switzerland* (New York: Weidelberg), pp. 103–134.

Shephard, R.W. (1953) *Cost and Production Functions* (Princeton, NJ: Princeton University Press).

Shephard, R.W. (1970) *The Theory of Cost and Production Functions* (Princeton, NJ: Princeton University Press).

Shepherd, W.G. (1985) *The Economics of Industrial Organisation*, second edition (New York: Prentice-Hall).

Sherman I. and F. Gold (1985) 'Bank branch operating efficiency: evaluation with data envelopment analysis', *Journal of Banking and Finance*, **9**, June, 297–316.

Short, Brock K. (1979) 'The relation between commercial bank profit rates and banking concentration in Canada, Western Europe and Japan', *Journal of Banking and Finance*, No. 3, 209–219.

Smirlock, M. (1985) 'Evidence on the (non)relationship — between concentration and profitability in banking', *Journal of Money, Credit and Banking*, **17**(2), February, 69–83.

Smirlock, M. and W. Marshall (1983) 'Monopoly power and expense-preference behaviour: theory and evidence to the contrary', *Bell Journal of Economics*, **14**, Spring, 166–178.

Smith, Lewis P.F. and Quinn, Gerard (1983) 'The development of concentration, competition and competitiveness in European banking', *Evolution of Concentration and Competition Series*, IV/588/83 — EN (Brussels: Commission of the European Community).

Smith, Tynon (1964) 'Competition, confusion and commercial banking', *Federal Reserve Bulletin*, **52**, 488–498.

Soares de Pinho, P. (1994) 'Economies of scale and scope and productive efficiency in Portuguese banking: a stochastic cost frontier approach', Ph.D. Thesis, City University Business School, London, UK.

Spagnolo, L.U. (1993) 'European economic convergence and the international monetary system', *De Pecunia*, **V**(1), 93–113.

Spellman, L.J. (1981) 'Commercial banks and the profits of savings and loan markets', *Journal of Bank Research*, **12**, Spring, 32–36.

Spindt, P.A. and V. Tarhan (1992) *Are There Synergies in Bank Mergers?* Working Paper, Tulane University, New Orleans, La.

Srinivasan, A. (1992) 'Are there cost savings from bank mergers?', *Economic Review, Federal Reserve Bank of Atlanta*, March/April, 17–18.

Srinivasan, A. and L.D. Wall (1992) 'Cost savings associated with bank mergers', *Working Paper 92-2, Federal Reserve Bank of Atlanta*, **Vol. 32**, 1251–1266.

Steinherr, A. (1992) *The New European Financial Marketplace* (London: Longman).

Steinherr A. and C. Huveneers (1992) 'Universal banking in the integrated European marketplace', in A. Steinherr (ed.), *The New European Financial Marketplace* (London: Longman), pp. 49–67.

Steinherr, A. and C. Huveneers (1994) 'On the performance of differently regulated financial institutions: some empirical evidence', *Journal of Banking and Finance*, **18**(2), March, 271–306.

Stevenson, R.E. (1980) 'Likelihood functions for generalised stochastic frontier estimation', *Journal of Econometrics*, **13**, 57–66.

Stolz, Richard, W. (1976) 'Local banking markets, structure and conduct in rural areas', *Bank Structure and Competition, Proceedings of a Conference at the Federal Reserve Bank of Chicago*, pp. 134–148.

Sueyoshi, T. (1991) 'Estimation of stochastic frontier cost function using data envelopment analysis: an application to the AT&T divestiture', *Journal of Operational Research Society*, **42**(6), 463–477.

Taylor, C.T. (1968) 'Average interest charges, the loan mix and measures of competition: Sixth Federal Reserve District experience', *Journal of Finance*, **23**, December, 793–804.

The Bankers' Almanac (1989) Vols 1 and 2, 144th Year of Publication (London: Reed Information).

Thornton, John (1991a) 'Concentration in world banking and the role of Japanese banks', *Economia Aziendale*, **10**(3), 263–272.

Thornton, John (1991b) *The Relative Size of Banks and Industrial Firms in Japan, the United States and the European Community*, Research Papers in Banking and Finance, RP 91/4, (Bangor: Institute of European Finance).

Tirole, J. (1988) *The Theory of Industrial Organisation* (Cambridge, Mass.: MIT Press).

Tolley, P. (1977) *Recent Trends in Local Banking Market Structures*, US Federal Reserve Board Staff Economic Studies, No. 89, May.

Tschoegl, Adrian E. (1982) 'Concentration among international banks, a note', *Journal of Banking and Finance*, **6**, 567–578.

Tulkens, H. (1990) *'Non-parametric Efficiency Analyses in Four Service Activities: Retail Banking, Municipalities, Courts and Urban Transit*, Centre for Operations Research and Econometrics, Université Catholique de Louvain, Discussion Paper No. 9050.

Turner, C. (1994) 'The single market beyond 1992: the EC's plans to reinforce the effectiveness of the international market', *European Access*, No. 1, February, 8–10.

Uzawa, H. (1962) 'Production functions with constant elasticities of substitution', *Review of Economic Studies*, October, 291–299.

Varian, H.R. *Intermediate Economics: A Modern Approach*, second edition, (New York: Norton).

Vassiloglou, M. and D. Giolias (1990) 'A study of the relative efficiency of bank branches: an application of data envelopment analysis', *Journal of Operational Research Society*, **41**, 591–597.

Venables, A. and A. Smith (1986) 'Trade and industrial policy under imperfect competition', *Economic Policy*, October, 622–672.

Vennet, R.V. (1993a) *Concentration, Efficiency and Entry Barriers as Determinants of EC Bank Profitability*, Working Paper, University of Ghent, Belgium, July.

Vennet, R. V. (1993b) 'Cost characteristics of credit institutions in the EC', Paper presented at the 20th Annual Meeting of the European Finance Association, Copenhagen Business School, 26–28 August, Published in Section II-D of the *Proceedings*, pp. 1–38.

Vennet, R.V. (1995) 'The effect of mergers and acquisitions on the efficiency and profitability of EC credit institutions', Paper presented at the 22nd Annual Meeting of the European Finance Association, Milan, Italy, 26–28 August.

Vernon, J.R. (1971) 'Separation of ownership and control and profit rates, the evidence from banking: comment', *Journal of Financial and Quantitative Analysis*, **6**, January, 615–625.

Vesala, J. (1993) *Retail Banking in European Financial Integration*, No. 77, (Helsinki: Bank of Finland).

Vives, X. (1991) 'Banking competition and European integration', in A. Giovannini and C. Mayer (eds), *European Financial Integration* (Cambridge: Cambridge University Press), pp. 9–31.

Wall, L. (1985) 'Why are some banks more profitable than others?', *Journal of Bank Research*, Winter, 240–256.

Ware, R.F. (1972) 'Banking structure and performance: some evidence from Ohio', *Federal Reserve Bank of Cleveland Economic Review*, March, 3–14.

Weiss, S.J. (1969) 'Commercial bank price competition: the case of free checking accounts', *New England Economic Review*, September–October, 3–32.

White, L.J. (1976) 'Price regulation and quality rivalry in a profit maximising model: the case of branch banking', *Journal of Money, Credit and Banking*, **8**(1), February, 97–106.

Whitehead, D.D. (1977) *Holding Company Power and Market Performance: a New Index of Market Concentration*, Federal Reserve Bank of Atlanta Working Paper, December.

Whitehead, D.D. (1978) *An Empirical Test of the Linked Oligopoly Theory: an Analysis of Florida Holding Companies*, Federal Reserve Bank of Atlanta Working Paper, June.

Williamson, O.R. (1968) 'Economies as an antitrust defense', *American Economic Review*, **58**, March(1), 18–36.

Williamson, O.R. (1975) *Markets and Hierarchies: Analysis and Antitrust Implications* (New York: Free Press).

Willig, R. (1979) 'Multiproduct technology and market structure', *American Economic Review*, **69**, 346–351.

Yeats, A.J. (1974) 'Further evidence on the structure–performance relation in banking', *Journal of Economics and Business*, **26**, Winter, 95–100.

Yuengert, A.M. (1993) 'The measurement of efficiency in life insurance: estimates of a mixed normal-gamma error model', *Journal of Banking and Finance*, **17**, 483–496.

Zellner, A. (1962) 'An efficient method of estimating seemingly unrelated regression and tests for aggregation bias', *Journal of the American Statistical Association*, **57**, 348–368.

APPENDIX I REVIEW OF THE US SCP LITERATURE

Authors	Sample	Measure of bank performance	R^2 or $\bar{R}^2$	Measure of market structure	Coefficient on the measure of market structure are significant[a]
Schweiger and McGee (1961)	11 large cities for 1960	Automobile loan rates; instalment loan rates	No econo-metric tests	N	Not available
Edwards (1964)	Data from 1955 and 1957 business loan surveys, 49 SMSAs	Interest rate on business loan	0.36–0.64	CR3	Yes for 1955 data No for 1957 data
Fleschsig (1965)	64 banks in 19 cities, 1960 data Data from 1955 business loan survey, 49 SMSAs	Interest rate on business loans	0.16–0.48	CR3	No
		Interest rate on business loans	0.37–0.51	CR3	No

Comments: Influence of market concentration on interest rates charged on business loans is insignificant when regional variables are included

Edwards (1965)	36 SMSAs, 1962 data	$IT \div TS$ $IL \div TL$ $NI \div TA$	0.20–0.48 0.42–0.70 0.07–0.25	CR2	Yes Yes Yes
Kaufman (1966)	99 counties in Iowa, 1959 and 1960 data	$IL \div TL$ $IT \div TS$ $NT \div TA$	0.200–0.268 0.323–0.409 0.066–0.090	CR1 N	Yes Yes Yes, with CR1 as market structure measure

continued overleaf

APPENDIX I *(continued)*

Authors	Sample	Measure of bank performance	R^2 or $\bar{R}^2$	Measure of market structure	Coefficient on the measure of market structure are significant[a]
Meyer (1967)	Data from 1955 and 1957 business loan survey, SMSAs in unit and limited branch banking states	Interest rates on business loans	0.69–0.73	CR3	Yes for 1955 data / No for 1957 data
Phillips (1967)	Survey of bank rates on short-term business loans in 19 SMSAs	Interest rates on business loans	0.51–0.64	CR3	Yes
Taylor (1968)	1315 banks for 1962	IL ÷ TL Portfolio selection	—	N	No
Weiss (1969)	25 SMSAs for 1968	Offering of no service charge on chequeing accounts	—	N / CR3 / H	Higher concentration related to the absence of free chequeing
Bell and Murphy (1969)	14 market areas in the First Federal Reserve District	Estimated service charge on demand deposits	0.22–0.29	CR3	Yes

Comments: This paper does not present a valid test of the structure–performance hypothesis. Service charge rates for each market do not reflect rates charged in the market, but estimated service charges based on an equation estimated for a sample of banks and economic variables for each market area, which are inserted into the equation for estimating bank service charges

Authors	Sample	Measure of bank performance	R^2 or $\bar{R}^2$	Measure of market structure	Coefficient
Aspinwall (1970)	31 SMSAs, 1965 data	Interest rate on residential mortgages	0.562 / 0.647	CR3 / N	Yes
Brucker (1970)	175 state economic areas, 1967 data for insured banks	Elasticity of loan demand	0.57	CR3	Yes

Study	Data	Performance measure	Value	Concentration	Result
Emery (1971)	980 banks 1967 to 1968	Profitability as measured by deviations from the capital market line	—	N CR1	No effect apart from on deposit mix
Fraser and Rose (1971)	78 Texas cities, 1966 and 1967 data	$IL \div TL$ $IT \div TS$ $SC \div DD$ $NI \div C$	0.41–0.54 0.03–0.14 0.21–0.30 0.07–0.15	CR1	No for 1966 Yes for 1967 No No No
Vernon (1971)	85 large member banks, data for 1961–66	$NI \div C$	0.21	CR3	Yes

Comments: Significant coefficients on CR3 are negative, the opposite of the sign indicated by the structure–performance hypothesis. The article presents only t-statistics, no regression coefficients

Klein and Murphy (1971)	1968 FCA data for banks in 164 SMSAs	Interest rate on time deposits. Service charge revenue divided by: 1. No of DD accounts 2. No of debits to DD accounts	0.24 0.24 0.33	Concentration of time deposits or DD at the largest, 2nd largest and 3rd largest banks in each SMSA	No for all concentration measures

Comments: Average of return on assets is included as an independent variable. Coefficients on concentrations may be insignificant because this performance measure is included as an independent variable

Jacobs (1971)	National survey of interest rates on business loans of 8500 customers at 160 banks in 107 SMSAs	Interest rate on business loans	0.18–0.25	CR3	Yes

continued overleaf

APPENDIX I (continued)

Authors	Sample	Measure of bank performance	R^2 or $\bar{R}^2$	Measure of market structure	Coefficient on the measure of market structure are significant[a]
Fraser and Rose (1972)	71 one-bank towns, 67 two-bank towns, and 16 three-bank towns not in SMSAs, data for 1965 and 1966	IL ÷ TL ITD ÷ TD SC ÷ DD NI ÷ TA NI ÷ C	0.060–0.112 0.023–0.082 0.299–0.320 0.044–0.070 0.074–0.444	N	No No No No
Ware (1972)	Data for 1969 and 1970 for 57 counties in Ohio outside SMSAs	SC ÷ DD NI ÷ C IL ÷ TL IT ÷ TS	0.49–0.51 0.26–0.45 0.42–0.43 0.49–0.61	CR2	No No No No
Edwards and Heggestad (1973)	66 of 100 largest banks, 1954 to 1966	Uncertainty avoidance (variance of profits divided by average profits)	—	CR3	Increased uncertainty avoidance with concentration
Edwards (1973)	36 large banks in 23 SMSAs, 1965 data	NI ÷ C	0.05	CR3	No
Fraser, Phillips and Rose (1974)	1206 Texas banks	Index of performance including many balance sheet items	—	CR1 N	No No
Yeats (1974)	Tennessee and Louisiana counties for 1970	IL ÷ TL IT ÷ TD NI ÷ TA Portfolio selection	0.14–0.35	H Change in H Market share stability	Small effects of concentration but important effect for changes in concentration
Alhadeff and Alhadeff (1975)	Sample of counties 1948 to 1966	Various concentration measures	—	—	New entry significantly reduces national and local concentration

Study	Data	Performance measure	Value	Market structure measure	Lerner index	Elasticity of loan demand
Beighley and McCall (1975)	1968 data for 184 banks in 7 SMSAs	Lerner index	0.42–0.43	Gini coefficient	No	No
		Elasticity of loan demand	0.25	CR3	Yes	No
				N	No	
Comments: Observations from only seven market areas						
Fraser and Alvis (1975)	74 unit banks in 74 market areas in several unit banking states	NI ÷ TA	na	Dummy variable for markets with relatively high CR1	No for all performance variables	
		NI ÷ C	na			
		IL ÷ TL	na			
		SC ÷ DD	na			
		IT ÷ TS	na			
Heggestad and Mingo (1976)	332 banks in 69 SMSAs, survey data for 1973	The following measures are based on a survey:				
		1. Interest rate on passbook savings	0.04	H and I/H	No	
		2. Interest rate on one-year $1000 CD	0.09		No	
		3. Service charge on standardised accounts.	0.11		No	
		4. Charge for returned cheque	0.13		No	
		5. Interest rate on new car loans	0.13		Yes	
Comments: For many banks, interest rates on passbook saving accounts and $1000 CDs were at Regulation Q ceiling rates. For these dependent variables, they should have used Tobit analysis (see Hannan, 1979b)						
Fraser and Rose (1976)	90 Texas counties 1973 data	IL ÷ TL	0.21–0.24	H	No	
		IT ÷ TS	0.26–0.28		No	
		SC ÷ DD	0.40–0.42		No	
		NI ÷ TA	0.42		Yes	

continued overleaf

APPENDIX I (*continued*)

Authors	Sample	Measure of bank performance	R^2 or $\bar{R}^2$	Measure of market structure	Coefficient on the measure of market structure are significant[a]	
					IL–H	SC–DD
Mingo (1976)	384 banks in 9 unit banking states	NI ÷ TA	0.006	H	No	
Rose and Fraser (1976)	704 unit banks in 90 county market areas in Texas, 1970 data	IL ÷ TL SC ÷ DD IT ÷ TS	0.39 0.42 0.35–0.37	N	No	No
				CR1	No	Yes
				CR2	No	No
				CR3	No	Yes
				Entropy	No	Yes
				H	Yes	Yes
				Hall–Tideman index	Yes	Yes
				Relative entropy	No	No
				Gini coefficient	No	No
Heggestad and Rhoades (1976)	228 SMSAs for 1966 to 1972	Market share stability	—	CR3	No	
Stolz (1976)	333 banking offices in 75 rural counties for 1975	Interest rate on household and farm loans SC – DD Non-price competition variables	—	H	Concentration affects most nonprice variables	
Rose (1976)	90 Senational votes	United States Senators vote on the Helm's Amendment to the Financial Institutions Act of 1975	—	CR3	No	

White (1976)	40 SMSAs in statewide branching states	Service quality measured by the number of branch offices	—	H	A decrease of 0.1% in H is associated with a 14.4% rise in the number of bank branches in each SMSA
Edwards (1977)	44 SMSAs in 1962, 1964 and 1966	Labour expenses	—	Separation of monopoly and competitive markets	Yes. Evidence of expense-preference behaviour and a critical level of concentration
Heggestad and Mingo (1977)	236 banks in 52 SMSAs survey data for 1973	Interest rate on new car loan	0.170	H times a dummy variable for areas with low H	Yes
		Monthly service charge on demand deposits (based on a survey of banks)	0.194		Yes
Heggestad (1977)	218 banks in 60 SMSAs, data for 1960–70	NI ÷ TA	0.08	CR3	Yes
Whitehead (1977)	130 banking markets in the Sixth District, 1974 data	IL ÷ TL IT ÷ TS NI ÷ C	0.39–0.45 0.37–0.45 0.39–0.43	N CR3 H	IL–TS: No IT–TS: Yes NI–C: No
Whitehead (1978)	47 banking markets in Florida, 1974 data	IL ÷ TL IT ÷ TS NI ÷ C	0.160–0.262 0.095–0.129 −0.025–0.066	CR3	Yes No No

Comments: Coefficients on CR3 are negative and significant with IL–TL as the dependent variable, contradicting the structure performance hypotheses

continued overleaf

APPENDIX I (continued)

Authors	Sample	Measure of bank performance	R^2 or $\bar{R}^2$	Measure of market structure	Coefficient on the measure of market structure are significant[a]
Heggestad and Rhoades (1978)	187 SMSAs, 1960 to 1972	Market share stability	—	CR3	Yes. Higher concentration leads to a significant reduction in rivalry
Hannan and Mavinga (1980)	366 Pennsylvanian banks for 1970	Bank wage and salary expenses / Bank furniture and equipment expenses / Bank net occupancy expenses	0.76–0.92	Binary variable, one if CR3 exceeds 63% zero otherwise	Yes in all cases
Graddy and Kyle (1979)	463 banks in unit and limited branch banking states, 1974 data	SC ÷ DD / IT ÷ TS / IL ÷ TL	0.34 / 0.25 / 0.37	H	No / No / No

Market structure measure

Authors	Sample	Measure of bank performance	R^2 or $\bar{R}^2$	Performance measure	CR1	N
Harvey (1979)	426 banks in 120 rural counties in 7 states, 1976 and 1977 data	IL ÷ TL / Interest payments on / TD ÷ TD / NI ÷ C	0.26–0.49 / 0.24–0.27 / 0.29–0.42	IL – TL / Interest on TD – TD / NI – C	No / Yes / Yes	Yes / Yes / Yes
Savage and Rhoades (1979)	6619 unit banks, 1977 data	NI ÷ TA / IL ÷ TL / SC ÷ DD / IT ÷ TS	0.160 / 0.131 / 0.096 / 0.210	CR3	Yes / Yes / Yes	Yes / Yes / Yes

Comments: SC–DD are lower in areas with higher CR3 the opposite sign from the structure–performance hypothesis

Study	Sample	Dependent variable	Value	Concentration measure	Significant relationship
Rhoades (1979)	184 SMSAs, data for 1970 and 1972	NI ÷ TA IL ÷ TL SC ÷ DD IT ÷ TS	0.05–0.06 0.21–0.25 0.19–0.22 0.08–0.50	CR3	No Yes Yes No
Rhoades and Rutz (1979)	184 SMSAs, 1970 and 1972 data	IL ÷ TL SC ÷ DD NI ÷ TA	0.22 0.19 0.05	CR3	Yes Yes No
Rose and Scott (1979)	600 banks, 1972 data	IL ÷ TL IT ÷ TS	0.087 0.034	N CR1	IL–TL Yes IT–TS No
Hannan (1979a)	367 banks in 49 local banking markets in Pennsylvania	Wage and salary expenditure Number of bank employees	0.91–0.93	Dummy variable when CR3 is greater than 63%	Yes for both performance measures

Comments: This study finds evidence of expense-preference behaviour in local banking markets

Study	Sample	Dependent variable	Value	Concentration measure	Significant relationship
Hannan (1979b)	About 400 banks in Pennsylvania market areas, 1970 data	Interest rate paid on passbook savings accounts	Used Tobit maximum likelihood analysis	CR3 H N	Yes No Yes
McCall and Peterson (1980)	155 banking markets in 14 unit or county wide branching states 98 of the 155 markets are county markets 270 banks in total for 1968	Lerner index	All markets 0.25–0.80 SMSA markets 0.82–0.85 County markets 0.13–0.92	1/H Number equivalent	Yes in 12 equations

Comments: This study tests for a critical level of concentration. The impact of changes in concentration is greater in concentrated than in unconcentrated markets

continued overleaf

APPENDIX I (*continued*)

Authors	Sample	Measure of bank performance	R^2 or $\bar{R}^2$	Measure of market structure	Coefficient on the measure of market structure are significant[a]
Glassman and Rhoades (1980)	Largest bank in 1406 BHCs, 1975 and 1976 data	NI ÷ TA	0.12–0.13	CR3	Yes
Rhoades (1980)	524 commercial banks for 1976 participating in the Federal Reserves Functional Cost Analysis programme	Expenses / total assets for various expense items Total assets / various groups of employees (25 measures in all)	0.00–0.15 (for 25 equations)	CR3	Yes in only 5 equations

Comments: Expenses are found to be lower in high concentration markets than in low concentration markets, thus rejecting expense-preference behaviour theory

Authors	Sample	Measure of bank performance	R^2 or $\bar{R}^2$	Measure of market structure	Coefficient on the measure of market structure are significant[a]
Osborne and Wendel (1981)	154 Texas banks in 23 towns	SC ÷ DD Service charge rates on DD based on a survey	0.30 0.12	H	No
Rhoades (1981)	3534 banks in 167 SMSAs, data for 1966, 1968, 1969, 1972, 1973, 1974, 1975	IL ÷ TL SC ÷ DD IT ÷ TS NI ÷ TA NI ÷ C	0.14–0.32 0.08–0.23 0.12–0.24 0.05–0.18 0.10–0.29	CR3	Yes in 4 years Yes in 3 years Yes in 4 years No in all years Yes in 2 years

Comments: IT − TS is higher in areas with higher CR3 (when significant), the opposite sign from the structure–performance hypothesis

Authors	Sample	Measure of bank performance	R^2 or $\bar{R}^2$	Measure of market structure	Coefficient on the measure of market structure are significant[a]
Rhoades and Savage (1981)	120 branch banks, 40 BHCs with no branches, and 109 BHCs with branches, 1975 data	NI ÷ TA	0.05	CR3 of deposits in the state in which a bank is located	No

Study	Sample	Dependent variable	Value	Concentration measure	Variable	Significant
Spellman (1981)	106 SMSAs, 1972 data	Profits of S&Ls	0.83–0.90	No. of banks in SMSA / No. of S&Ls in SMSAs		Yes / Yes
Rhoades and Rutz (1982)	6500 unit banks between 1969 and 1978	1. NI ÷ TA 2. Coefficient of variation of NI ÷ TA (Overall risk measure) 3. Equity/assets ratio (balance sheet risk measure) 4. Loan/asset ratio 5. Net loan asset/total loans	0.003–0.06	CR3	1. NI – TA 2. Coefficient of variation NI – TA 3. Equity/asset 4. Loan/asset 5. Net loan losses/total loans	1. Yes 2. Yes 3. Yes 4. Yes 5. No
Rhoades (1982a)	6500 unit banks, data for 1969–78	NI ÷ TA	0.0034	CR3		Yes
Marlow (1982)	62 409 mortgage loans in 444 SMSAs, 1975 data	Interest rate on residential mortgage loans	0.25–0.31	N CR3 CR5		Yes Yes Yes
Kwast and Rose (1982)	Sample of 80 member banks in SMSAs with total deposits over $500 million, data for 1970–77	NI ÷ TA	0.42–0.580	H		Yes

Comments: This paper tests for evidence of the so-called 'quiet life' hypothesis. The results generally indicate that banks with significant market power tend to lower their level of risk

continued overleaf

APPENDIX I (*continued*)

Authors	Sample	Measure of bank performance	R^2 or $\bar{R}^2$	Measure of market structure	Coefficient on the measure of market structure are significant[a]
Smirlock and Marshall (1983)	38 SMSAs for 1978 and 1979, 190 banks in 1979 and 138 banks for 1978	Number of bank employees	0.18–0.86	CR3 Market share of banks (MS)	CR3 — Yes in 1 out of 24 equations MS — Yes in 1 out of 14 equations

Comments: This study finds no strong evidence of expense-preference behaviour of banks

Authors	Sample	Measure of bank performance	R^2 or $\bar{R}^2$	Measure of market structure	Coefficient on the measure of market structure are significant[a]
Hannan (1984)	412 banks operating in the state of Pennsylvania in 1971	Passbook savings rate Total weekly banking hours	0.04–0.05	H	Passbook saving rate Yes; Weekly banking hours No

Comments: (The equations using passbook savings rate as a performance measure are estimated using Tobit Maximum log likelihoods range between 402.6 and 410.4)

Authors	Sample	Measure of bank performance	R^2 or $\bar{R}^2$	Measure of market structure	Coefficient on the measure of market structure are significant[a]
Curry and Rose (1984)	34 SMSAs in 1972 52 SMSAs in 1978	1. Portfolio composition (7 measures) 2. Bank capital (3 measures) 3. Operating efficiency (4 measures) 4. Prices of bank services (3 measures) 5. Bank profitability (3 measures)	Not reported	H	Not given

Comments: This paper tests for the relationship between bank holding company presence and banking market performance: the results suggest that outside bank holding company presence leads to increased bank lending, particularly in the real estate and consumer loan areas

Study	Sample	Profitability measure	Value	Market structure measure	Significant measure	Support for SCP
Wall (1985)	Homogeneous sample of independent SMSA banks	NI ÷ TA NI ÷ C	—	CR3 H	No No	
Smirlock (1985)	2700 unit state banks operating in the 7 state area under the jurisdiction of the Federal Reserve Bank of Kansas City	NI ÷ equity NI ÷ C NI ÷ TA	0.05–0.06	CR3 Market share of banks (MS)	CR3 CR3 MS	Yes when MS not included as an explanatory variable No when MS included as an explanatory variable (or significant and opposite) Yes

Comments: This study finds support for the efficiency hypothesis in banking markets

Study	Sample	Profitability measure	Value	Market structure measure	Significant measure	Support for SCP
Clark (1986a)	1857 banks located in 152 SMSAs in unit or limited branching states, 1973 to 1982	NI ÷ equity standard deviation of NI ÷ equity	0.02–0.05	H Market share of banks (MS)	No No	
Clark (1986b)	1857 banks located in 152 SMSAs in unit or limited branching states, 1973 to 1982	NI ÷ equity standard deviation of NI ÷ equity	Uses 2-stage least squares procedure. (F-test between 1.8 and 65.1)	H Market share of banks (MS)	H MS	Yes No

Comments: In these two studies Clark uses the same data to estimate the SCP relationship. Clark (1986b) is an extension of (1986a) where it is shown how a 2-stage least squares estimation procedure generates different results from OLS. Using 2SLS Clark (1986b) finds evidence supporting the traditional SCP hypothesis on profitability and risk aversion, and also rejects the efficiency hypothesis

continued overleaf

APPENDIX I (continued)

Authors	Sample	Measure of bank performance	R^2 or $\bar{R}^2$	Measure of market structure	Coefficient on the measure of market structure are significant[a]
Evanoff and Fortier (1988)	6300 unit banks located in the 30 states of the USA which permit either unit banking only or statewide branching, for 1984	NI ÷ TA	0.03–0.08	CR3 Market share of largest firm (MS1) Market share of second largest firm (MS2) Market share of third largest firm (MS3)	Yes but only in two equations when MS is not included No or wrong sign when MS variable is included Yes for the MS of the largest firm when sequential MS of 3 largest firms included

Comments: This study finds support for the efficiency hypothesis

Authors	Sample	Measure of bank performance	R^2 or $\bar{R}^2$	Measure of market structure	Coefficient on the measure of market structure are significant[a]
Berger and Hannan (1989)	470 banks in 195 local banking markets observed quarterly over a two and a half year period, Sept 1983 to Dec 1985	Money-market deposit account (MMDA) rate Super-NOW rate 3, 6, 12 + 30-month CD rate	0.33–0.88	CR3 H	Yes in 8 out of 10 equations

Comments: In this study the authors state that 'an alternative form of the efficient structure hypothesis that is consistent with the price concentration results is ruled out as a dominant explanation of the results'

Authors	Sample	Measure of bank performance	R^2 or $\bar{R}^2$	Measure of market structure	Coefficient on the measure of market structure are significant[a]
Daskin and Wolken (1989)	441 banking markets, of which 63 are SMSAs	Lerner index	Maximum Likelihood Estimation Log likelihood 1034 to 1049	H Loan H Deposit	Yes when H loan and H deposits below critical levels. No when above critical levels

Comments: This paper tests for a critical level of concentration in banking markets. The estimated range of critical levels are H loan 0.36–0.38 and H deposits 0.306–0.308

Study	Data	Dependent variable	Values	Measure	Result
Calem and Carlino (1989)	466 commercial banks and Federal savings banks insured by the FDIC in 1985. Sample covers 145 SMSAs	Money market deposit accounts (MMDA's) rate; 3 and 6-month CD rates	0.10–0.26	CR3	MMDAs Yes; 6-month CD Yes; 3-month CD Yes

Comments: A 10% increase in concentration creates a fall in MMDA rate by 5.0 basis points the figure for 6-month CD rate is a fall by 3.4 basis points

Study	Data	Dependent variable	Values	Measure	Result
Hannan (1991a)	Loan survey data from the Federal Reserves Study of the Terms of Bank Lending to Business. Data on 8250 loans originated by 260 banks in August 1984, November 1985 and November 1986	Commercial loan rates for: 1. Floating rate unsecured loans 2. Floating rate secured loans 3. Fixed rate unsecured loans 4. Fixed rate secured loans For loans greater and less than $100 000	August 1984 0.05–0.21; November 1985 0.07–0.38; November 1986 0.06–0.39	H	August 1984 Yes for 1 out of 8 equations; November 1985 Yes for 5 out of 8 equations (1 finding a negative relationship); November 1986 Yes for 5 out of 8 equations

Comments: This study, the author notes, finds strong support for the traditional SCP paradigm

---

[a] Regression coefficients on measures of market structure are listed as statistically significant if their t-statistics (in absolute value) are at least as large as 1.95.

÷ = division sign.
NI = net income.
TA = initial asset.
C = capital.
IL = interest and fees on loans.
TL = total loans.

continued overleaf

APPENDIX 1 (*continued*)

IT	=	interest payment on time and savings deposits.
HD	=	interest payments on time deposits.
TS	=	time and savings deposits.
ID	=	time deposits.
SC	=	revenue from service charges on demand deposits.
DD	=	demand deposits.
CR1	=	one-firm concentration ratio.
CR2	=	two-firm concentration ratio.
CR3	=	three-firm concentration ratio.
H	=	Herfindahl index.
N	=	number of loans in the market.

Source: Gilbert (1984, pp. 619–625) and authors' own updates.

APPENDIX II

Table A1 Maximum likelihood parameter estimates for French banks

Parameter	Coefficient	Standard error	T-ratio	Prob > |T|
α_0	−3.37160	0.23570	−14.303	0.00000
α_1	0.73030	0.06681	10.930	0.00000
α_2	0.30700	0.05325	5.766	0.00000
β_1	−0.46620	0.05742	−8.119	0.00000
β_2	0.41000	0.06320	6.489	0.00000
β_3	1.05620	0.07016	15.054	0.00000
δ_{11}	−0.03650	0.01154	−3.165	0.00155
δ_{12}	−0.03860	0.00806	−4.787	0.00000
δ_{22}	0.02410	0.00846	−2.848	0.00440
γ_{11}	0.00060	0.00576	0.104	0.90000
γ_{12}	−0.04460	0.00859	−5.192	0.00000
γ_{22}	0.00600	0.00742	0.807	0.41939
γ_{13}	0.04400	0.00371	11.852	0.00000
γ_{23}	0.03860	0.00579	6.667	0.00000
γ_{33}	−0.08260	0.00801	−10.306	0.00000
ρ_{11}	0.10379	0.01383	7.505	0.00000
ρ_{12}	0.03036	0.01068	2.842	0.00448
ρ_{31}	−0.11010	0.01123	−9.804	0.00000
ρ_{21}	0.00630	0.00954	0.664	0.50691
ρ_{22}	0.04260	0.01086	3.918	0.00009
ρ_{32}	−0.07300	0.00940	−7.766	0.00000
λ_b	−0.17698	0.01546	−11.449	0.00000
λ_{bb}	−0.03946	0.01723	−2.29	0.02199
λ_{b1}	0.07364	0.01604	4.591	0.00000
λ_{b2}	0.05355	0.01245	4.303	0.00002
τ_{b1}	−0.19640	0.01863	−10.544	0.00000
τ_{b2}	0.00590	0.02103	0.280	0.77917
τ_{b3}	0.19050	0.01597	11.928	0.00000

Table A2 Maximum likelihood parameter estimates for French banks

Parameter	Coefficient	Standard error	T-ratio	Prob > |T|
α_0	−1.2626	0.30230	−4.177	0.00003
α_1	0.47663	0.08226	5.794	0.00000
α_2	0.26735	0.07188	3.719	0.00020
β_1	−0.13030	0.08219	−1.585	0.11287
β_2	0.40110	0.08154	4.919	0.00000
β_3	0.72920	0.08477	8.602	0.00000
δ_{11}	0.05371	0.01542	3.484	0.00049
δ_{12}	−0.04667	0.00943	−4.948	0.00000
δ_{22}	0.07719	0.01348	5.726	0.00000
γ_{11}	−0.05430	0.01005	−5.403	0.00000
γ_{12}	−0.00880	0.01327	−0.664	0.50691
γ_{22}	0.03030	0.00719	4.217	0.00002
γ_{13}	0.06310	0.00428	14.732	0.00000
γ_{23}	−0.02150	0.01155	−1.861	0.06000
γ_{33}	−0.04160	0.01448	−2.874	0.00405
ρ_{11}	0.00780	0.01593	0.488	0.62587
ρ_{12}	0.03710	0.01521	2.438	0.01478
ρ_{31}	−0.01390	0.01384	−1.004	0.32500
ρ_{21}	0.00610	0.01240	0.494	0.62130
ρ_{22}	−0.02340	0.01276	−1.835	0.06658
ρ_{32}	−0.01370	0.01320	−1.037	0.32100

Table A3 Maximum likelihood parameter estimates for German banks

Parameter	Coefficient	Standard error	T-ratio	Prob $> |T|$
α_0	−3.92900	0.34550	−11.374	0.00000
α_1	0.76843	0.08467	9.076	0.00000
α_2	0.38071	0.08622	4.415	0.00001
β_1	−0.41170	0.06766	−6.084	0.00000
β_2	0.52580	0.07663	6.861	0.00000
β_3	0.88590	0.08622	10.275	0.00000
δ_{11}	−0.04968	0.01147	−4.329	0.00001
δ_{12}	−0.02982	0.00905	−3.294	0.00099
δ_{22}	0.00741	0.01437	−5.155	0.00000
γ_{11}	0.12970	0.01013	12.803	0.00000
γ_{12}	0.15980	0.01180	13.542	0.00000
γ_{22}	−0.02820	0.00514	−5.476	0.00000
γ_{13}	0.03010	0.00284	10.609	0.00000
γ_{23}	0.18800	0.01199	15.679	0.00000
γ_{33}	−0.21810	0.01323	−16.487	0.00000
ρ_{11}	0.11094	0.01122	9.889	0.00000
ρ_{12}	0.01750	0.01253	1.392	0.16380
ρ_{31}	−0.09390	0.01282	−7.324	0.00000
ρ_{21}	−0.01730	0.00603	−2.873	0.00407
ρ_{22}	0.04990	0.01263	3.950	0.00008
ρ_{32}	−0.06740	0.01409	−4.783	0.00000
λ_b	−0.15088	0.01402	−10.765	0.00000
λ_{bb}	0.01599	0.00738	2.166	0.03030
λ_{b1}	0.01179	0.00421	2.798	0.00514
λ_{b2}	0.10461	0.00946	11.056	0.00000
τ_{b1}	−0.21037	0.01471	−14.301	0.00000
τ_{b2}	0.05258	0.01224	4.294	0.00002
τ_{b3}	0.15780	0.01647	9.581	0.00000

Table A4   Maximum likelihood parameter estimates for German banks

Parameter	Coefficient	Standard error	T-ratio	Prob > |T|
α_0	−2.81800	0.53820	−5.236	0.00000
α_1	0.63278	0.10090	6.271	0.00000
α_2	0.43918	0.16730	2.625	0.00867
β_1	−0.29120	0.11410	−2.551	0.01073
β_2	0.57580	0.14030	4.105	0.00004
β_3	0.71540	0.12995	5.505	0.00000
δ_{11}	0.06357	0.00695	0.915	0.36020
δ_{12}	−0.01398	0.004634	−3.018	0.00255
δ_{22}	0.08142	0.02180	3.735	0.00019
γ_{11}	0.06270	0.00276	22.717	0.00000
γ_{12}	−0.09720	0.00546	−17.802	0.00000
γ_{22}	0.18270	0.02122	8.611	0.00000
γ_{13}	0.03450	0.002917	11.829	0.00000
γ_{23}	−0.08550	0.00561	−15.240	0.00000
γ_{33}	0.05100	0.01343	3.797	0.00015
ρ_{11}	0.02440	0.02588	0.941	0.34663
ρ_{12}	0.09200	0.03069	2.998	0.00272
ρ_{31}	0.01270	0.02191	0.579	0.53200
ρ_{21}	−0.03706	0.01239	−2.991	0.00278
ρ_{22}	−0.05570	0.01971	−2.826	0.00472
ρ_{32}	−0.03630	0.02194	−1.654	0.10500

Table A5 Maximum likelihood parameter estimates for Italian banks

Parameter	Coefficient	Standard error	T-ratio	Prob > $|T|$
α_0	3.39980	0.37610	9.04	0.00000
α_1	0.78734	0.13770	5.719	0.00000
α_2	0.34874	0.11080	3.148	0.00164
β_1	1.36720	0.08831	15.482	0.00000
β_2	−0.60160	0.03519	−17.096	0.00000
β_3	0.23440	0.07702	3.043	0.01500
δ_{11}	−0.10806	0.04283	−2.523	0.01163
δ_{12}	−0.11639	0.03010	−3.866	0.00011
δ_{22}	0.09880	0.02327	4.245	0.00002
γ_{11}	0.17270	0.01165	14.824	0.00000
γ_{12}	−0.23070	0.00844	−27.334	0.00000
γ_{22}	0.27630	0.00932	29.634	0.00000
γ_{13}	0.05800	0.00562	10.32	0.00000
γ_{23}	−0.04560	0.00678	−6.725	0.00000
γ_{33}	−0.01240	0.00318	−3.913	0.00009
ρ_{11}	−0.14655	0.02995	−4.893	0.00000
ρ_{12}	0.01370	0.02879	0.477	0.63334
ρ_{31}	0.12055	0.02411	5.000	0.00000
ρ_{21}	0.02600	0.01144	2.277	0.02277
ρ_{22}	−0.00172	0.01010	−0.170	0.86498
ρ_{32}	−0.01200	0.02108	−0.569	0.54300
λ_b	−0.00092	0.00677	−0.136	0.89182
λ_{bb}	−0.08962	0.03115	−2.877	0.00402
λ_{b1}	0.21260	0.03287	6.468	0.00000
λ_{b2}	−0.00245	0.02862	−0.085	0.93190
τ_{b1}	0.10007	0.03083	3.245	0.00117
τ_{b2}	0.11348	0.02467	4.600	0.00000
τ_{b3}	−0.21355	0.02544	−8.394	0.00000

Table A6 Maximum likelihood parameter estimates for Italian banks

Parameter	Coefficient	Standard error	T-ratio	Prob > $|T|$
α_0	−2.97000	0.29950	−9.915	0.00000
α_1	0.64872	0.11670	5.558	0.00000
α_2	0.22576	0.10200	2.214	0.02684
β_1	−1.08280	0.09374	−11.551	0.00000
β_2	0.20990	0.05188	4.045	0.00005
β_3	1.87290	0.07487	25.015	0.00000
δ_{11}	0.10839	0.04114	2.635	0.00842
δ_{12}	−0.10120	0.03197	−3.165	0.00155
δ_{22}	0.10422	0.02745	3.797	0.00015
γ_{11}	−0.00590	0.01049	−0.562	0.54500
γ_{12}	−0.09200	0.00678	−13.569	0.00000
γ_{22}	0.03470	0.00898	3.865	0.00011
γ_{13}	0.09760	0.00484	20.154	0.00000
γ_{23}	0.05700	0.00827	6.892	0.00000
γ_{33}	−0.15460	0.00546	−28.299	0.00000
ρ_{11}	−0.00044	0.01619	−0.027	0.97825
ρ_{12}	0.00051	0.01485	0.035	0.97244
ρ_{31}	0.02884	0.01717	1.679	0.09000
ρ_{21}	−0.02840	0.01623	−1.751	0.08001
ρ_{22}	−0.00208	0.01532	−0.136	0.89206
ρ_{32}	0.00157	0.01544	0.101	0.91000

Table A7 Maximum likelihood parameter estimates for Spanish banks

Parameter	Coefficient	Standard error	T-ratio	Prob > $|T|$
α_0	2.18710	0.19260	11.358	0.00000
α_1	0.30415	0.04835	6.290	0.00000
α_2	0.25167	0.06930	3.632	0.00028
β_1	−0.35800	0.08330	−4.297	0.00002
β_2	0.56740	0.09841	5.766	0.00000
β_3	0.79060	0.06597	11.984	0.00000
δ_{11}	−0.00057	0.00167	−0.339	0.73481
δ_{12}	−0.01244	0.00266	−4.679	0.00000
δ_{22}	0.00796	0.00538	1.479	0.13907
γ_{11}	−0.23266	0.03309	−7.031	0.00000
γ_{12}	−0.01224	0.03071	−0.398	0.70520
γ_{22}	−0.00140	0.01308	−0.104	0.91727
γ_{13}	0.24486	0.01492	16.417	0.00000
γ_{23}	0.01360	0.03048	0.446	0.67520
γ_{33}	−0.25846	0.03278	−7.884	0.00000
ρ_{11}	0.03497	0.01936	1.807	0.07084
ρ_{12}	0.06411	0.02735	2.344	0.01906
ρ_{31}	0.01280	0.01005	1.274	0.20500
ρ_{21}	−0.04785	0.01729	−2.768	0.00565
ρ_{22}	−0.00498	0.02490	−0.200	0.84164
ρ_{32}	−0.06910	0.01782	−3.877	0.00050
λ_b	−0.04309	0.04367	−0.987	0.32382
λ_{bb}	−0.01580	0.02208	−0.715	0.47435
λ_{b1}	0.014199	0.00920	1.543	0.12288
λ_{b2}	0.009267	0.01416	0.654	0.51288
τ_{b1}	−0.12732	0.03914	−3.253	0.00114
τ_{b2}	0.11336	0.04171	2.718	0.00657
τ_{b3}	0.01390	0.02746	0.506	0.61496

Table A8　Maximum likelihood parameter estimates for Spanish banks

Parameter	Coefficient	Standard error	T-ratio	Prob > $|T|$
α_0	2.7298	0.2033	13.424	0.00000
α_1	0.3791	0.04521	8.386	0.00000
α_2	0.20037	0.06621	3.026	0.00248
β_1	−0.37080	0.08444	−4.391	0.00001
β_2	0.53420	0.09147	5.840	0.00000
β_3	0.83660	0.08154	10.259	0.00000
δ_{11}	−0.00189	0.00196	−0.962	0.33592
δ_{12}	−0.00498	0.00225	−2.214	0.02681
δ_{22}	0.00548	0.00640	0.856	0.39177
γ_{11}	−0.19640	0.03659	−5.367	0.00000
γ_{12}	−0.07960	0.03029	−2.627	0.00956
γ_{22}	0.04905	0.00844	5.814	0.00000
γ_{13}	0.27604	0.01636	16.875	0.00000
γ_{23}	0.03060	0.03226	0.948	0.35010
γ_{33}	−0.30663	0.03263	−9.398	0.00000
ρ_{11}	0.07800	0.01921	4.060	0.00005
ρ_{12}	0.05150	0.02488	2.070	0.03849
ρ_{31}	0.01400	0.01111	1.260	0.21600
ρ_{21}	−0.09200	0.01597	−5.761	0.00000
ρ_{22}	−0.00790	0.02137	−0.370	0.71110
ρ_{32}	−0.04360	0.01798	−0.242	0.80200

Table A9 Estimated lambda and the test for linearity and log-linearity for hybrid translog cost function[a]

Country and products	Estimated lambda (λ)	Linearity ($\lambda = 1$)	Log-linear ($\lambda = 0$)	Decision[b]	
				$\lambda = 1$	$\lambda = 0$
France					
Total loans	0.1557* (0.0323)	431.08	251.23	Reject	Reject
Total securities	0.1217* (0.0389)	348.37	144.51	Reject	Reject
Germany					
Total loans	0.1283* (0.0397)	488.83	64.894	Reject	Reject
Total securities	0.1646* (0.0435)	321.48	14.650	Reject	Reject
Italy					
Total loans	0.0951* (0.0347)	36.065	7.085	Reject	Reject
Total securities	0.1558* (0.0309)	692.28	26.045	Reject	Reject
Spain					
Total loans	0.2309* (0.0273)	175.50	77.944	Reject	Reject
Total securities	0.2557* (0.0296)	889.85	74.237	Reject	Reject

[a] Approximate standard error in parentheses.
[b] The critical value of γ^2, $0.05 = 3.84$
*Significant at 0.01 level.

Table A10   Bank groups and their total assets

Total asset Sizes ($m.)	Number of French banks	Number of German banks	Number of Italian banks	Number of Spanish banks
0–100	17	4	32	20
100–300	33	16	56	26
300–600	40	25	48	39
600–1000	23	23	37	40
1000–3000	38	60	43	55
3000–5000	13	20	7	11
5000>	37	48	21	18
All	201	196	244	209

Table A11   The comparison of descriptive statistics for France

Variable ($m.)	Mean	Standard errors	Minimum	Maximum
Q_1	3 993.6	14 962.0	3.00	144 600
Q_2	1 149.5	3 362.5	1.00	23 620
P_1	2.00	95.30	0.18	1 020.3
P_2	0.0707	0.0494	0.0112	0.4103
P_3	1.9436	1.7447	0.0038	11.50
B	83.00	470.41	1.000	5 780.0
TC	668.50	2 501.1	2.60	21 420
S_1	0.1838	0.1279	0.0007	0.9837
S_2	0.6734	0.2416	0.0392	1.2972
S_3	0.1571	0.1559	0.0047	1.3064
TA	8 185.3	29 090.0	33.00	242 000

Table A12   The comparison of descriptive statistics for Germany

Variable ($m.)	Mean	Standard errors	Minimum	Maximum
Q_1	4 657.5	13 157.0	5.00	107 237
Q_2	640.3	1 406.6	2.00	11 136
P_1	3.306	10.287	0.124	73.200
P_2	0.0480	0.0221	0.00796	0.1603
P_3	1.5838	2.4369	0.0110	23.00
B	52.47	190.08	1.000	1 900.0
TC	439.30	1 272.4	3.90	11 463
S_1	0.2006	0.1171	0.0097	0.9334
S_2	0.6571	0.1963	0.0159	1.4566
S_3	0.1423	0.1031	0.0044	0.4974
TA	7 291.4	19 713.0	22.00	167 133

Table A13 The comparison of descriptive statistics for Italy

Variable ($m.)	Mean	Standard errors	Minimum	Maximum
Q_1	1 414.4	4 884.4	7.40	37 660
Q_2	385.52	1 089.5	0.10	10 390
P_1	0.0495	0.0065	0.025	0.0865
P_2	0.0748	0.0249	0.0437	0.2338
P_3	0.9602	0.5256	0.2222	4.500
B	46.06	97.181	1.000	577.00
TC	289.21	973.84	1.80	8492.0
S_1	0.2429	0.0480	0.0800	0.3739
S_2	0.5770	0.0735	0.3807	0.8400
S_3	0.1800	0.0477	0.0733	0.3459
TA	3 102.5	10 385	19.40	76 339

Table A14 The comparison of descriptive statistics for Spain

Variable ($m.)	Mean	Standard errors	Minimum	Maximum
Q_1	985.90	2 328.7	0.100	20 281
Q_2	278.78	866.38	0.020	9 547.8
P_1	0.0412	0.0487	0.0138	0.6389
P_2	0.2293	0.3846	0.0100	3.5256
P_3	0.6662	1.5324	0.0070	17.737
B	138.9	320.61	1.000	2 447.0
TC	181.07	416.83	0.500	3 637.1
S_1	0.1836	0.1036	0.0029	0.9725
S_2	0.7003	0.1449	0.0110	0.9860
S_3	0.0760	0.0413	0.0027	0.2318
TA	2 174.0	5 200.0	6.000	45 951

Index

All terms in the index relate to banking and the European Union unless otherwise stated.